NIGHTMARE IN ATHENS

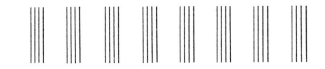

NIGHTMARE IN ATHENS

by

Margaret Papandreou

PRENTICE-HALL, INC., Englewood Cliffs, N. J.

Nightmare in Athens by Margaret Papandreou
© 1970 by Margaret Papandreou
Copyright under International and Pan American
Copyright Conventions
Library of Congress Catalog Card Number: 79-113929
Printed in the United States of America · T
ISBN 0-13-622423-7
Prentice-Hall International, Inc., London
Prentice-Hall of Australia, Pty. Ltd., Sydney
Prentice-Hall of Canada, Ltd., Toronto
Prentice-Hall of India Private Ltd., New Delhi
Prentice-Hall of Japan, Inc., Tokyo

Dedicated to
ANDREAS

More black marks for the junta in Greece . . .

The 34 defendants, who included professors, magistrates, lawyers, students and a retired army general, told of beatings, starvation and psychological pressures . . .

The New York Times, April 19, 1970

U. S. reported ready to send Greek junta new jets, other arms . . .

The United States has decided to resume shipments of heavy arms equipment and weapons to Greece after a three year suspension, informed sources said last night. It was expected that sophisticated jet aircraft would be high on the priority list of new weapons for the Greek military government . . .

Toronto Daily Star, May 11, 1970

THE ABOVE two news items represent clearly the two truths about the situation in Greece today. The United States pours in more and more arms to the junta government while the Greek people continue to resist their oppressors—the brutal military mafia which took control of their country on April 21, 1967.

I was there then. And I was there as the American wife of one of the principal targets of the coup—Andreas Papandreou.

The story that follows is a personal experience. It is my interpretation as an observer and participant in the events which led to the coup of the long dark night when the dictators struck Greece, of the attempt to survive morally and physically under a modern dictatorship.

I have not softened nor hidden my anguish at American involvement in the death of liberty and democracy in Greece. The reader will trace the slow deflation of my illusionary balloon—my naive, if you wish, middlewestern school-girlish set of ideals about what America is and what she stands for. For this, I have no doubt, I will be called anti-American, or names more loaded with emotional and political connotations, but I find no satisfaction and there is no spiteful joy in watching the United States by its actions abroad suffer deep, self-inflicted wounds. My anguish and criticism come out of a love for America, not the opposite.

Perhaps the other significant personal development shows the metamorphosis—under a totalitarian regime—of an essentially non-violent individual—myself—to one participating in plans which had as an aim the violent overthrow of the government. Frustration and despair led to hatred, and finally, a desire to participate, no matter what the method, to this end. I do not say this with shame, but with pride, for the fight I associated myself with, subsequently my husband's fight, was clearly a fight for freedom and human dignity, and in tune with the wishes of the majority of the people. I make it clear, however, that this was the result of *the closing of all political means of opposition or dissent*—leaving only one road available to fight the tyrants of Greece.

In my fight for Andreas' release from prison, I had the help of many friends, particularly the academic community of America. There were many others, too numerous to mention. Some of them appear in this book. To all of them I express my heartfelt appreciation.

Most of all, I want to thank the Greeks who stood by me under extremely difficult and ugly conditions. Although often I despaired and castigated them, I can only look back on what they did and call it magnificent. And I want to express my great admiration for a people who continue now to struggle for freedom, human dignity, and national independence, who have carried on a vast resistance, both passive and active, not completely recognized nor understood by the foreign press, and who are determined not to allow democracy to be snuffed out in the land which gave it birth.

This book is dedicated to my husband Andreas, whose principles and ideals I believe in and love. In a deeper sense, it is dedicated to the Greek people, whose determination and fighting spirit have already made them the moral victors and whose victory in fact cannot be long in coming.

Margaret C. Papandreou

June, 1970

Contents

The free man willing to pay and struggle and die
    for the freedom for himself and others
Knowing how far to subject himself to discipline
    and obedience for the sake of an ordered society
    free from tyrants, exploiters and legalized frauds—
This free man is a rare bird and when you meet
    him take a good look at him and try
    to figure him out because
Some day when the United States of the Earth
    gets going and runs smooth and pretty there
    will be more of him than we have now.

Carl Sandburg
from *The People, Yes*

PART ONE

Before the Crisis

CHAPTER ONE

The Night of the Coup

A SHOT shattered the night. It was hardly a normal sound for the quiet wooded suburb of Athens where we lived. But, then, nothing had been normal for a long time now. I jerked upright in bed and heard footsteps rapidly tapping up the marble stairs leading to the second floor. It was the night guard, Manoli, who shouted, "Mr. Minister, Mr. Minister, men with guns are at the door! What shall I do?" He was pounding on our bedroom door. Andreas and I ripped off the sheet and leaped from bed like rockets from a launching pad. I threw on my pink quilted housecoat. Andreas pulled on his shorts, then his white shirt, wrinkled from its evening wear. We were trapped, and we knew it.

On my side of the bed was a buzzer wired to Petros' house a block away. One long buzz was a signal to him to open his walkie-talkie and get instructions from us in case of an emergency. We had rehearsed it to perfection. I reached down and gave a long, hard buzz, then reached to the shelf under my night table for the walkie-talkie. It wasn't there. By then, Georgie, my fourteen-year-old son, had awakened and was in the bedroom with us.

"For God's sake, George," I shouted, "where is the walkie-talkie?" My natural thought was that the children had removed it. This turned out to be true. George ran to his room, but as the banging and shouting at the downstairs entrance increased, we abandoned the hope of reaching Petros.

Andreas got his automatic, and I heard the ominous click as he cocked it. I gave a frantic last three buzzes, which signified "Help!" and the two of us started up the stairway to the third-floor study.

Going upstairs was instinctive. We wanted to get as far away as we could from the men smashing glass in their attempt to break in. Also, there was a telephone upstairs. I was unaware of George following me, so great was my concern with Andreas and how he could escape from the mob downstairs.

I reached the phone and with trembling fingers, dialed Kastri, the house of my father-in-law, recently the Prime Minister of Greece. The phone was answered by the chauffeur who slept at the house. I shouted in Greek, "Yanni, Yanni, for God's sake send help. They are breaking in the downstairs door!" He responded in a voice that sounded noncommittal and unperturbed. "Send us help. Right away!" I repeated.

Then I turned to Andreas. "Oh, Andreas, he doesn't understand me. Tell him, tell him!"

Andreas took the phone and repeated my plea for help. "Send everything you've got. And fast!"

Another phone call. To Petros. He had heard the buzzer and was dressing. Andreas talked to him. "Do what you can," I heard him say. "Our friends. The President." (This was what his father, George Papandreou, was called.) "Georgios, Kostas, Spyros, and the others. Move fast!"

Petros said something to Andreas, and I heard Andreas say he didn't know who it was, that it could be an assassination gang. When he hung up he told me "Petros says if it's the military, I should give myself up. I shouldn't fight. I will be killed."

We stood for a moment, white-lipped, staring at each other.

We did not want to believe that the dreaded moment had arrived. For almost two years we had lived with threats—assassination, jail, military take-over. For almost two years, despite the dangers, Andreas had led a brilliant political crusade against the forces of power he believed were strangling the life and development of the nation, restricting the freedom of the people, and corrupting democracy. He had clashed with the Palace, the army, the economic elite, and the American Embassy, but he was the hope of the Greek people, and he had refused to compromise in his fight against the establishment. His beliefs were progressive, those of an enlightened democrat. The establishment portrayed him as a communist, or at the least, a communist sympathizer. Now the establishment had decided to use more than smears and threats to stop Andreas.

We heard the shouts of men who had swarmed into the downstairs hall. They would soon find us. I had not even noticed the faces of my two youngest sons, Nick and Andriko, whose beds were in the study during the visit of my parents from the United States.

"I'm going down, Andreas," I said. I felt that if I could ward them off for a while, Andreas might have time to escape. A frantic hope, but what else remained under the circumstances?

My mouth was as dry as parched wood, but out of a need born of desperation, my mind remained clear. Barefoot, I moved with lightning speed down the steps. On the second flight, between the second and main floors, I confronted the intruders. This was a momentary triumph because I did not want them to know anyone had been on the third floor. For all intents and purposes I had just awakened from sleep in my bedroom. At that moment the telephone rang, and I heard the bell interrupted as the cord was torn from the wall.

"We want Andreas!" screamed a short man in a helmet and battle gear, pointing a pistol at me. At the same time, he and two others started pushing me back up the stairway. They brutally pushed at me—elbows and hands in my stomach, on my breasts, on my shoulders. I had to turn around in order not to fall and be trampled by the nervous, screaming gang.

"Andreas is not here!" I shouted.

They paid no attention.

3

When we got to the second floor, they turned first to Georgie's room, just to the left of the stairway. The door was ajar and a quick look revealed that no one was there. The next door was the bedroom where my mother and father were staying. As the men kicked open the door, both my mother and father were coming out, in nightclothes, my father looking as if he wanted to tear the whole contingent apart. He shouted, "What the hell are you doing here?" and made a move toward the gun and bayonet being pointed at him.

I yelled, "They are my mother and father. He doesn't speak Greek. Leave them alone! They are Americans!" I tried to throw the fear of God in them. Americans! Masters and supporters of the Greek army. At the time I did not know whether it was a coup, or a paramilitary group with the purpose of getting Andreas.

"Dad," I said, "don't try anything. They will shoot all of us." My father, a marine in World War I, is fearless. Twice commander of the American Legion, THB Post 187 of Elmhurst, Illinois, he believed that Americans could do no wrong, that fighting communism was the sole aim of American foreign policy, and that anyone who defied the orders of the American government should be put in jail. Yet these were American guns being pointed at us, and he knew that none of us was communist. Later I learned that he had been the first to go downstairs as the soldiers were trying to break into the house. As they shouted to open the door, he shouted back, "I don't have a key," then closed the door between the outer hall and the kitchen nook, and went upstairs to help my mother get up. Fortunately, he had no gun in his room. I think he would have used it.

By then the men were scrabbling through the bedrooms like hounds sighting a kill. They went in our room, searched, and returned. They went into my daughter's room where Sophia and Andreas' mother were huddled, trembling, in their beds. They overturned Sophia's cot, and after she was rolled onto the floor, she scurried under my mother-in-law's bed in utter terror. Finally, the captain in charge sent two soldiers upstairs. I screamed, "Don't touch the children!"

While waiting for the soldiers to return, I kept saying, "Andreas is not here. He is in Kastri! Why don't you listen to me?"

The soldiers came down. Without Andreas. I was puzzled. Had he found a way to escape? The only side hidden from view from the inside of the house was a sheer, straight wall of three floors from the upstairs terrace. Surely the house was surrounded in any case. When I left him, he was opening the doors of the study that led to the terrace. What had happened to him? Where was he?

I felt a glimmer of hope. By now we were gathered in the second-floor hallway, four men guarding us with guns and bayonets. I said to one pointing his weapon at me, "Why do you do this? We have no guns. Don't you see? Why do you keep us at gunpoint?"

He recognized an accent in Greek, or perhaps he knew I was American. He was twenty years old at the most, tall and lanky, with dull gray eyes and a look of contempt.

"Because we like to, ma'am," he said in heavily accented English.

4

The captain disappeared into our bedroom again, then suddenly reappeared and pointed to me. "We'll take her!"

Good. Andreas might, just might, have a chance to escape if they all left, taking me as a "hostage." At that moment, several soldiers came upstairs dragging Manoli, our night guard, with them. Blood trickled from the corner of his mouth.

"One moment he says Andreas is not here, and then he says he is here," one soldier reported in a loud voice to the captain.

"All right," said the captain. He turned to me, spitting out his words: "What do you say to that?"

"If you would just shut up and stop your shouting, I will tell you where Andreas is," I answered.

For a moment they looked as if they believed me, as if in terror I had finally decided to reveal Andreas' hiding place.

I repeated, "He went to Kastri. He is with—"

"We'll search again!" interrupted the leader of the gang, and they began by ripping open a plastic wardrobe standing in the hallway. Then they noticed a locked closet. It was one used by my mother-in-law, who, suspicious of household help, always kept her closet door locked.

"Break it open," one hoarse voice screamed. The hysteria was mounting higher and higher.

"No," said my mother-in-law, to my surprise. "I have a key." This struck me as incongruous at the moment, but they seemed to hesitate as she reached in the drawer of the yellow dresser behind me in the hall. I was anxious to give Andreas time to get away, and I preferred that they break open the door. As she reached for the keys, I put my hand around hers and pretended to help her search. I squeezed her hand tightly and prevented her from pulling out the keys, which were hidden under a pair of Sophia's panties.

"We can't find the keys." I said.

With that information, one of the younger men took his bayonet and started prying the closet door open. Within a few minutes the lock was broken, and he then slashed his bayonet through the clothing hanging there. Had Andreas been hiding in the closet, he would have been cut to pieces.

For some unknown reason, another soldier started yanking open the drawers of the dresser where the keys had been hidden. Sophia, who managed to find her voice, said sarcastically, "You think you're going to find my daddy in there?"

By now other men in battle dress had come upstairs. The captain, in a "special forces" outfit with black beret, gave orders. "You two take that bedroom, you two there, you two there. Come with me," he yelled to four others, and they started up to the third floor.

This, then, was the moment.

I followed them.

As I reached the top of the stairway, I saw that the captain was kicking open the shuttered doors leading out to the veranda. I rushed to get out with them. Huddled in the corner of the veranda was my son George. As it turned out, he had gone onto the veranda with his father and was the only means

5

Andreas had of being boosted to the study-room roof, since the wall was at least fourteen feet high. After boosting his father up, he was unable to get up himself, and had tried to climb down to the second-story veranda, just off our own bedroom. According to George, the moment he put his leg over the railing, two soldiers burst out of our bedroom French doors to search the small balcony, and he drew back in order not to be seen. He then tried to rejoin me downstairs by returning through the study, but the two boys in bed, seeing him pop his head into the study, motioned him to get back, probably thinking he was in danger, or just not thinking anything. His aim was not to expose his father. When neither form of exit seemed possible, he went to a corner of the veranda, squatted, and waited. He later told me that until the soldiers arrived, he was terrified. When they arrived, he lost his fear.

When they discovered George, one put a gun to his head and yelled, "Tell us where your father is or we will kill you!"

George answered, "I don't know."

But right above, lying on his stomach, gun in hand, was his father, trying to decide whether to fight (and get killed) or to wait or to give himself up.

When he heard his son threatened, his decision was made. I wanted to find a way of telling him to stay where he was; I thought there was still a chance we might all escape unharmed. But my tongue was glued to the roof of my mouth, and I was afraid that if I shouted something in English, I would create suspicion rather than give help.

Andreas stood up, his hands raised slightly, and said, "Don't shoot. I'm coming down." He was a white apparition on a black, black night. He looked ten feet tall, a giant from outer space, who had landed on the roof and now towered over the earthlings below. The image was frightening and powerful, and I was afraid of the effect on the nervous gang of military. I thought they would shoot him.

The captain became hysterical at the sight of the risen figure. "Get him, get him!" he screeched to one soldier, and the fellow made a desperate, clawing attempt to scale the sheer wall. At the same time, the captain shouted to Andreas, "Jump, or I'll shoot!"

I was sure now he would shoot.

"Jump, Andreas!" I shouted, too. "Jump!"

Andreas threw his gun down, and it hit to my left and clattered across the tile veranda. Then he jumped, and fell in front of me, virtually in my arms. His knee was badly cut, from falling on a piece of jagged glass from an outdoor lamp. I put my hands out to help him, but other hands jerked him to his feet and with vicious jabs pushed him toward the terrace door. As they staggered and stumbled down the stairway, he told them, "Let me put on my clothes." They followed him into our bedroom. I pushed my way in against a barrier of arms, and stood there helpless as I saw the blood gushing from his knee. "You bastards!" I shouted, but no one heard. He pulled on his trousers, but before he had a chance to put his shoes on, they started shouldering him toward the door of the bedroom. I got his shoes and socks, and tailed after the capture contingent, by now numbering up to fifteen, trying to reach Andreas. I finally handed the shoes and socks to a soldier, who took them.

As he was being shoved to the door, I heard him ask the captain, "Where are you taking me?" and the captain responded, his face dark red and his voice rasping in his throat, "We have accounts to settle with you, Mr. Andreas," and they disappeared through the door.

For some reason, when I reached the door myself, having been elbowed aside by the soldiers, the door was locked. I don't know whether the last soldier reached in and pulled the night lock, or whether I tried opening it, and not succeeding right away, assumed it was locked. All I can remember is standing at the iron grill, my bare feet being cut by bits of glass, and holding on to two bars like a man in jail, saying in a pleading voice to the rear soldiers turning down into the street, "Please, let me speak to my husband. I want to speak to my husband. I want to say something to him." Two soldiers looked back, and later, remembering their faces, I was certain they were sympathetic to my plea. They, as so many of the rest of us, were caught in an iron web which we knew nothing about, and could do nothing about.

I wanted to speak to my husband. I wanted to tell him that I loved him, that everything would be all right, that I would fight for him. But at the same time, I had a sudden image of his bullet-torn body, dumped in the field down at the corner of the block, beyond my help, or anybody's. The captain's remark that "we have accounts to settle with you" echoed and reechoed through my reeling brain as confirmation of my worst fears.

I started to scream, out of control, "They will kill him! They will kill him! Don't you understand?"

My mother grabbed me tightly, her arms a vise around my body as I fought to run out the back door, to cry and shout, to awaken the world.

"No, no, Margaret," she said. "They won't kill him."

I was angry with her. Didn't she understand? Didn't she know what and who these people were? Didn't she realize that Andreas was hated by the Palace, by the Right, by the secret services, and that for months they had been trying to find ways to kill him?

Then I saw the faces of my children. They were gray with terror, and their eyes stared at me with animal fright.

I merely said, "Oh, my God, my God," and crumpled down in a hallway chair.

Nicky said, "They won't kill him, Mommy, they won't kill him."

I answered, "Don't talk to me."

In a few minutes I was up and running to the front door. I shouted through the iron bars, "Help, help! They've taken Andreas!" There was no answer. The neighborhood was completely silent. Not a door opened, nor a window. No light was turned on in response to my shouting. It was a ghost town. It was a yawning abyss. It was the loneliest moment of my life.

I told my father and George to run to Petros' house and to bring him to me so that we could see if there was anything that could be done. But what? If there was a dictatorship, what to do to fight it? And if it was a special security battalion assigned to capture Andreas, then his life would be snuffed out within hours.

Just then I saw a police car driving slowly by. I raced to the door, and this time managed to open it. I ran to the gate. "They've taken Andreas," I told them. "Can't you do something?" The policemen looked at me sadly.

"They've also taken Arnaoutis," one replied.

"They've done what?" I asked, astounded. Arnaoutis was King Constantinos' closest adviser and friend, his personal secretary. He, too, had been dragged from his house.

Now I was truly confused. What did Arnaoutis have to do with Andreas, with the trumped-up charges of treasonable participation in ASPIDA,* and how could they, the establishment, pick up a King's man? The arrest of Andreas must have been backed by the King, I reasoned, and yet . . .

I asked Antigone, my maid, to run around the corner and see if she could get Takis, a political friend of Andreas', to come with his car. I was determined to go to Kastri and tell my father-in-law the grisly story. I was unable to cope with anything more than the brutal arrest of Andreas. The Arnaoutis information was a piece that didn't fit into the puzzle, so I ignored it. My thoughts were so focused on Andreas that I couldn't possibly imagine that a giant manhunt might be going on all over Greece, and that others were experiencing this terror.

Takis came, with his driver, and I climbed into the back seat. I asked him to take me to Kastri. The streets were ominously deserted. We met no car on the entire twenty-minute trip. At some point I thought I heard tanks rumbling along a nearby highway. Whether Takis felt this was a wild-goose chase or not, I do not know. He said very little, except that things like this happened in Greece, and that he had lived through quite a few. This was some consolation. Takis, at least, was still alive. I leaned forward on the edge of the seat, buried my head in my folded arms on the front seat, and tried not to think of the worst. I held myself tight to keep from crying.

An hour had gone by since that shocking moment when I heard the shot pierce the night. It was 3:30 A.M. I had changed into a skirt and sweater and light jacket, removing my pink bathrobe, which was spattered and blotched with blood. My feet were sore; tiny pieces of glass from the front-door pane were embedded in the soles. I remember feeling vaguely pleased with this pain, as if this mark of physical brutality complemented my mental anguish.

We were approaching Kastri now. The only thought I had was that a barricade might have been put up, and I would not be able to get in to see my father-in-law, former Prime Minister of Greece and head of the majority party. Although more conservative than Andreas, he was also a fighter for basic human rights and for the right of the people to participate in decisions affecting their destiny. He had fought almost single-handedly against the fraudulent elections of 1961, winding up his speeches in all corners of Greece with the line "Democracy will win!" How far away and remote that all seemed now. At this moment, however, I was not thinking in political terms. He was Andreas' father and a source of help.

The lights were ablaze when we drew up to the front gate of Villa Galini—"Serenity Villa." One of my father-in-law's night guards, Kostas, was

*ASPIDA, meaning "shield," referred to an army group the establishment charged with conspiring against the state.

standing outside the gate looking red-faced and distraught. I barely noticed him as I bolted from the car and ran up the outdoor steps to the front door. Takis and his driver followed.

The door was slightly ajar, and I pushed in. Standing in the front hallway were Yanni, the chauffeur; Karambelas, my father-in-law's personal and trusted guard of thirty years; and Eleni, the maid. I attacked Yanni, shouting, "Why didn't you send somebody? Why didn't you do something when we called?"

"They came for the President," he said.

Once again, as to the police, I asked in amazement, "They did what?"

"Just after you called, they came and took the President."

The President, Andreas' father, my one source of strength. It came through now with harsh and cruel impact. Dictatorship. That ugly, intolerable word. This, then, was the event we had been dreading, yet expecting; fearing, yet hoping our fears were unjustified. Andreas had said it was inevitable. His father had said at the time King Constantinos made Panayotis Cannellopoulos Prime Minister, just a few weeks before, that "the worm was in the apple." So this was the end of a long and valiant battle for a more democratic Greece, waged first by my father-in-law, then by Andreas. Or was it? Perhaps it was too soon to say.

Eleni's face was streaked with tears. I looked at her helplessly. Near her feet was a suitcase, sitting there impertinently, packed and waiting.

"What's that?" I asked.

"The President's suitcase," she answered.

"What for? Do you know where they have taken him?"

"No," answered Karambelas, "but we will find out and send it to him."

It gave me a funny kind of comfort, as if George Papandreou had suddenly decided to go on a trip and had telephoned his maid to prepare his suitcase and send it on to him.

"Did they hurt him when they came?" I asked. He was seventy-nine years old and had been in bed the day before with a touch of flu and fever. His heart had been weakened by an attack in 1966. I wondered how he would be affected by a screaming, shouting band breaking into the house at 2:30 in the morning and hauling him off. Even while the thought crossed my mind, however, I was sure the "old man," as he was affectionately called by the people, had conducted himself with his usual aplomb.

"They rang the bell," Karambelas told me, "and while soldiers held the rest of us at gunpoint, two went upstairs to waken him. I heard the President ask them to step out into the hallway while he dressed, but they remained inside. After about ten minutes he came down fully clothed, and they walked him out the door."

"They weren't pushing him?"

The answer was no. We stood silently, Karambelas, Yanni, Eleni, Takis, his driver, and I. We were a pitiful-looking group, stunned, frightened, tearful. Karambelas, trying to break the tense stillness in a positive fashion, said that it wasn't the first time, that it had happened before. To my father-in-law, yes. He had been exiled five times and imprisoned five times during his fifty-year

9

political career. This nonchalance was meant to reassure me, and it did, if only briefly.

"What shall I do? Should I pack a suitcase?"

He said I should. Then he asked about Andreas and I told him our experience in a few words, and that Andreas was bleeding when he left. I knew what they were all thinking. The President will probably be safe, although he may be sent into exile, but surely Andreas was in great danger. They didn't say it, but we were all aware that his life was at stake, if it had not already been blotted out by a firing squad.

There was nothing more for me to do at Kastri. Then suddenly, Karambelas remembered something. "Hurry home," he said, "and burn all of Andreas' papers. Or get rid of them somehow."

"But I don't think I have any of Andreas' papers. They are all at his office, or wherever he keeps them."

"Never mind what kind of papers you have, whatever they are, get rid of them."

It was something to do. There were guns in the house for our personal protection. Those I knew I should dispose of. There might be some of Andreas' papers in the file cabinet in the third-floor study, a study that had become mine after Andreas entered politics. And when I remembered what a foul fuss the Greek press had made about a letter of mine the Novas government discovered and published, I decided that anything I had could be used, twisted, and distorted by these military minds.

I asked Karambelas to let me know if he had any word of the President, and he agreed to. His face was grim as I left.

As we passed the iron gate, I saw Kostas, now a guard of a house empty of its moving spirit, inhabited by three desolate people. Tears were rolling down his fat ruddy cheeks.

My home was even more desolate and dreary. My father, George, and Petros had circled around Psyhico trying to decide what to do. Then George remembered that Norbert Anschuetz, chargé d'affaires of the American Embassy, lived at Camellia Street, just five minutes from Guizi Street, where we lived. They found Mrs. Anschuetz at home and awake. Norbert had been reached by the embassy sometime earlier and had left in a hurry. She had been unable to reach him because her line had been cut. She suggested that they come back later in the day in case she heard something. In the meantime, my mother had gotten everyone at home to dress, simply because no one could sleep, and dressing was something to do. On his return home, George took pictures of the mess in the house at the suggestion of my mother, who tried to divert the children's attention from the horror of the experience they had been through.

It was nearly five o'clock in the morning. As I walked in the door, I was startled by the telephone bell. One of the phones yanked from the wall was a plug telephone, and my father had replugged it. The other was useless, its broken wires dangling from the wall. I snatched the receiver.

"This is Aleko, from Piraeus," the voice said. "You remember me? I publish ———," and he gave me the name of a local newspaper. I said yes, but I didn't remember him. "They have taken your husband?" he asked. I said yes.

"They are arresting by the thousands down here," he said in a whispery voice. "I am calling from a kiosk and must move quickly, but I am a friend of Andreas' and want to help." The first volunteer! But his next question threw me.

"What shall we do?" What to do, what to do, I thought, amazed.

"What should you do?" I shouted. "Tell the people to rise!"

A lone appeal to an intangible something—the people, the only force that Andreas commanded. A large portion of the people were ours, but they were ours at the ballot box, in a democratic society in free elections. Could they be asked to bare their breasts to guns and tanks, and to a ruthless use of armed power?

"I will try, Mrs. Margarita," he responded, "but I can't find any of our leaders. They have either been arrested or gone into hiding."

I told him to do what he could. He said he would call back, and then added, "Remember, I am Aleko." I understood then that it was a false name, that he had taken the risk of mentioning his newspaper to identify himself, but that from then on he would be simply "Aleko." It was the beginning of a long list of false names used by friends over the telephone, in written messages, in letters, and eventually by me as we adopted the methods of survival in a police state.

After I hung up, I turned to Petros, Takis, and his driver and beckoned them to follow me up to the study. It was still dark, but dawn would soon break, and I felt the need to hurry under the cover of night. We all agreed that the essential task was to get the guns and papers out, away from the house, where they could be subsequently disposed of. I asked Petros to bring me two empty suitcases from the upstairs storage room. Quickly we dumped in the guns, one from a locked desk drawer, one from behind a stack of books on the bookshelf, and the one still lying on the terrace where Andreas had flung it down. I found bullets in a box with the gun behind the books. More ammunition was kept, I knew, on a top shelf above our bedroom closet. If there was even more, I didn't know where Andreas hid it. Then I started through the file drawers. "Correspondence—Andreas, 1964"—into the suitcase. "Key Posts in Government, 1964"—into the suitcase. "Outdoor Art Festival, 1964"—left in file drawer. "Social"—left in drawer. "Correspondence—Maggie, 1965"—into the suitcase. And on it went. Takis' driver wanted me to dump everything, but I would have needed several more suitcases, and most of the material was truly innocuous. I had health-education material from my Minnesota University days and from my days with the U. S. Public Health Service. There were files on children's books, household equipment, recipes, home furnishings, summer house plans, names of books on Greece. Could these in any way be considered subversive? We moved fast, all of us feeling that a ring of the doorbell was imminent. Within fifteen minutes after we started, Takis and his driver disappeared down the stairs and into the night, lugging two suitcases with guns, ammunition, and files to their temporary hiding place. I felt relieved. Something had been done. Yet so little.

Downstairs my mother shoved a cup of steaming coffee under my nose. I sat down at the hallway table to try to drink it, and to think. My mouth was still dry, and my hands clammy cold. My body was taut, my stomach quivering with the sensation of a sudden elevator drop every time I thought of Andreas. I tried to guess where he was now. How was his leg? When would I hear of him, and how? Had he been further mistreated? And the big question I tried not to ask myself: "Was he alive?"

I talked to Petros. Good, wonderful Petros—for years a faithful and devoted follower of Andreas', a man who knew him as a boy and was always around to help. He had done the only thing he could do after that last frantic telephone call from us. He had started telephoning friends from a list Andreas had prepared for him for such an emergency, and gave them a prearranged message which informed them that something had happened and that they were to mobilize their people. After three such phone calls, almost all lines in Psychico were cut, including his. He looked scared, and he had reason to be, as a known political collaborator with my husband.

Two of the children, Nikos and Andrikos, had at last fallen asleep on the front couch, their heads in the lap of Andreas' mother, who sat staring into the distance, her face ashen white. Antigone, my maid, had collapsed in a corner chair of the hallway, unable to return to her room, unable to work, and unable to talk. The rest of the family was floating aimlessly around, unable to remain still.

I tried the phone every so often in a futile attempt to call out. The responding strange buzz told me the line was cut for outgoing calls. For some odd reason, however, Piraeus and my friend Aleko were able to call in.

"Aleko here. I have to keep on the move. I can't seem to do much."

"Won't anybody do anything?" I asked. "Is there to be nothing?" Where were the hordes of people in Syntagma Square, screaming themselves hoarse at my father-in-law's speeches? Where were the passionate youths who had pounded on our car as we made our way to a local rally? Where were those lines of cars which had followed our group to Patras, Larissa, Corinth? It was a powerful force, I knew. Yet it was unorganized, leaderless, unarmed, and the communication system had been cut.

"If something happens to me, Mrs. Yannopoulos will call you," Aleko said. Another false name.

"All right," I answered wearily.

It was nearly six o'clock and dawn had washed away the darkness. Through the gaping hole where the glass had been broken by the butt of a gun, I saw a figure standing at the low white gate leading from the street to our door. I walked over to peer out. It was a young boy, about nineteen, in workman's clothes. When he saw me, his handsome dark face lit up, and he broke into a grin.

"Why do you look so frightened, Mrs. Margarita?" he asked.

"Don't you know what has happened?" I responded, opening the door and walking out. Although he had used my name, I didn't recognize him as one of the young people so often around Andreas.

"Don't worry. It will be all right. They cannot defeat us. We will help Mr.

Andreas." Petros was behind me, and when I asked if he knew the boy, he answered that he had never seen him.

"Thank you, thank you," I murmured. He looked strong and full of confidence and without fear. He was a new note in a night of horror and pain. He got on his bike which had been propped against a tree, and with the sun shining full on his face gave me an encouraging wave and pedaled off.

Later in the morning, Petros reported to me that a young workman, around nineteen, had been shot to death on Vassilis Sophias highway when he refused orders to halt *on his bicycle.* I cannot say if it was the same young man, but I never saw him again.

Those hours of April 21, 1967, were the beginning of my nightmare in Athens. What follows is the story of how a midwestern American woman got caught in the web of Byzantine politics and intrigue in the land of Greece, and eventually in the steel mesh of an army take-over. This nightmare is a nightmare from which millions of Greeks still cannot awaken, and they live under the conditions of a dictatorship—fear, intimidation, uncertainty, distortion of human relationships—unwilling subjects of a dictatorial trio, who, with their guns, set themselves up as the representatives of the public will.

CHAPTER TWO

The Beginnings

IT all began for me in February 1948, when I met Andreas, an associate professor of economics at the University of Minnesota. I was heading my own small public-relations office called Chant, Inc., in the Wilmar Building on Nicollet Avenue in Minneapolis. He was twenty-nine and I was twenty-four years old.

Our meeting was in the unromantic setting of a dental office, where I was waiting at the end of the day to help a Greek Cypriot dentist with a book he was trying to write. The dentist was inside with his last patient when Andreas walked into the waiting room, picked up a magazine, and sat down to read. I was working on an advertisement for the rotogravure section of the Sunday Minneapolis *Tribune* for an account I had with the Minnesota Business School. The ad was supposed to attract young girls to the school for courses in typing, shorthand, and general business office training. Twenty minutes passed while I struggled to put together a sentence in French as an "exotic" component of the ad. The man across from me looked foreign. At least he looked as if he might know French. Finally, I decided to ask for help, and I said, "Excuse me, do you happen to know French?" His answer was a polite and cordial "yes," and I explained my problem to him. He got up and sat next to me on the settee, and we soon worked out the form of the French sentence I was grappling with. Andreas had dropped by the office to see whether or not Aris, the dentist and a friend of his, could join him for dinner that evening. Aris came out and explained that he and I had planned to have a sandwich together and work afterward, and then suggested that the three of us might have a drink at the Radisson Hotel before the work started. The work never got started that night. After a few cocktails together, it became clear that Aris was not wanted, and Andreas and I went on to dinner and dancing together, and talked into the early hours of the morning.

We talked about the things that two people attracted to each other talk about—each other. I told him how I was brought up in a small suburb of Chicago, the eldest of five daughters in a poor family, how I struggled to put myself through the University of Minnesota's journalism school, doing all kinds of odd jobs—waitress, bus girl, cashier, library cataloger, burr girl on the assembly line for B-29 cylinder heads, riveter at Douglas Aircraft, hospital nurse's aid, mail-order house clerk, etc. I told him about my first job after graduating from the university with the Hennepin County Tuberculosis Association as public-relations assistant, and now my struggles to put together a public-relations firm of my own. He laughed when I told him my deal with Aris—a chapter for a tooth. Aris would repair a tooth and I would ghostwrite a chapter for his autobiography, the story of an immigrant boy who was torn between staying in America and returning to his native land of Cyprus. He had already titled his book "Thrice a Stranger" because, he said, each time he returned to one or the other country, he felt a stranger there, and he had made the trip three times.

Andreas told me he didn't have this problem. He felt nostalgia for Greece, but no desire to return. The Greece Andreas had left was a dictatorial Greece: 1940, Metaxas. He had tried then, as a high-school and then university student, to organize resistance against the regime. He managed for three years to head an active organization, whose main function was to print and distribute illegal newspapers and pamphlets, not an easy task because Andreas was a natural enemy of the dictatorship which had sent his father in political exile to the island of Andros. Finally, one late night in May 1939, Andreas was picked up at his Psyhico home and taken to jail where he was beaten and tortured, sustaining a broken jaw. When he was released, he had but one thought: to leave the country where freedom had been snuffed out and seemed destined never to return. Europe was largely totalitarian, Hitler had started his war to take over the Continent, and America offered the hope for a free life and a chance to pursue an academic career, which he wanted.

On the pretext of having to take a trip to the States to claim a large inheritance left by one of his mother's relatives, and with the help of an American diplomat who had once rented his mother's Psyhico home, he inveigled a three-month visa from the Minister of Interior (the government was eager for foreign exchange to be brought into Greece), and sailed off to New York, one year after his prison experience. Once there, he enrolled in Harvard's graduate school of economics. Five months later Greece was invaded by Mussolini's army. Andreas was not able to return to fight for Greece, so he did the next best thing by volunteering for the United States Navy. As a political refugee, he could not be conscripted. His Harvard experience had been truly "ivy tower," and he told me that it was in the navy that he learned about Americans and the American way of life. In 1946 he became an American citizen. When he was mustered out of the navy, he returned to Harvard and was asked to stay as an instructor of economics and to head the basic principles course. Soon, he said, supervisory sessions with the teaching assistants under him were no longer needed, for they were talented, capable, intellectually powerful young men, who included some of the top economists in the United States today such as Carl Kaysen, Thomas Schelling, James Tobin, James Dusenberry, Richard Ruggles, and Glen Campbell. In the class a few years ahead of him at Harvard, and preceding him at Winthrop House, was a young student named Jack Kennedy. In 1948, when we met, these names were all unfamiliar to me.

While at Harvard Andreas had been offered an associate professorship from

Minnesota, a post that skipped the assistant-professorship level. It was an attractive offer, and he joined the staff of the economics department at the University of Minnesota for the academic year 1947-48.

I was two years out of the university myself, having been graduated in March 1946, and had taken one course in economics, the principles of economics, which I told him I didn't like. He smiled and said he thought perhaps I hadn't had the right teacher, and I agreed that this must have been the case.

Andreas was a warm and fascinating individual. He said "gijantic" for gigantic, and twisted up American colloquialisms in a most astounding fashion, but otherwise his English was rich and eloquent. I was, to put it frankly, mesmerized. Everything would have been quite perfect except for one fact: he was married. I knew this from the beginning; it didn't come as a shock to me. What did shock me was that with all my wariness, good resolutions, and determination to stay away from complicated involvements—for the protection of my own sensitive nature, if nothing else—I was falling in love with him. His wife was not with him, but was finishing medical school in the East. After several months of a warm, rich love affair, and a deeper and deeper involvement, we decided to break up until the problems of his marriage were resolved, one way or the other. I couldn't long stand being in Minneapolis near him and not with him, and one day I locked the door of my public-relations office, packed my bags, and left Minneapolis, the town that had been my home for seven years as a college student and as a neophyte businesswoman.

During my days with the Hennepin County Tuberculosis Association, I had participated in a chest X-ray program conducted by the U. S. Public Health Service. I met many people in the field of health education, a field that interested me because of its community organization aspects. While the program was going on in Minneapolis and St. Paul, the first of its kind in the nation, I had traipsed around with the health educators watching the mobilization of a community on a voluntary basis for a public health program. At the time, my role was to develop the educational materials— pamphlets, brochures, posters—in an attractive way, write short spots for the radio stations, and find ways to get stories in the newspapers to keep the interest alive. But what really intrigued me were the organizational aspects of the program, and I had at that time begged them to take me with one of the teams doing mass X-ray surveys throughout the United States. But there was no slot on the team for a journalism graduate; health educators were required to have their master's degree in public health.

When they left, I opened up my public-relations office; when I left, a year later, I sought out one of the teams, now doing a survey in Cleveland, and told the chief health educator, Mary Jo Kraft, that I was on my way to Washington to pound on Dr. Derryberry's door (he was head of the health education section at U. S. Public Health Service) and convince him that someone of my talents and dedication should be used.

Thus I landed in Washington, D. C., with the blessings of Mary Jo, and the suggestion that Derryberry take me on as a fledgling health educator, with my academic training to be gotten at some later date when funds could be found for that purpose. I was asked if I would agree to go back to a school of public health for my degree, and to put in at least a year of work after that. School was always a delight for me, and the prospect of being paid to study was overwhelmingly delicious. I had no trouble making this pledge.

Before being assigned to the Cleveland, Ohio, survey, I spent three weeks in Washington for orientation. I was enchanted with the Capital, and wandered through its streets after work and on weekends. Part of my walks always included a search for the Greek restaurants in town, where I would eat by myself, ordering the foods Andreas had introduced me to. Several of these places had Greek records on their jukeboxes and I made out the titles of Greek records Andreas had given me—all left with a friend in Minneapolis—and dropped in my nickels. I listened to such songs as "The Girl with Green Eyes and Purple Eyelashes" and "One Night When It Was Raining," most of them sung by Vembo, the husky-voiced singer of liberation songs that were played clandestinely during the German occupation. I would listen enraptured, a long-legged slender American blonde who seemed to know what Greek songs she wanted, puzzling the restaurateurs. It was one of those silly things that sentimentalists do to conjure up the joy of a past period, and instead bring themselves pain and bitter memories.

After a hitch in Cleveland, my second assignment was to the X-ray survey in Salt Lake City, Utah. That was the summer of 1949. In early September, just as I was settling in to enjoy the riot of fall colors in the mountain ranges which wreathed the city, and just as I was getting to know the community leaders in Brigham Young's Mormon territory, I received a wire from the Public Health Service telling me to prepare quickly for graduate school: funds had been found for my education. School was by now the farthest thought from my mind. A letter which followed listed the public health schools approved for health-education training. They were the University of California, North Carolina, Yale, Johns Hopkins, Michigan, and Minnesota. I hurriedly got my college records together and sent them off to California to apply for admission. The answer I received was that I had insufficient science credits and would have to complete several undergraduate courses before being admitted. I got the same answer from Yale and North Carolina. The *last* place I wanted to go was the University of Minnesota, for obvious reasons. Time was passing, however, and the Public Health Service urged me not to postpone, as I had suggested, my entering a university that fall, if at all possible. I wrote to a friend of mine on the staff of the School of Public Health at Minnesota, Professor Ruth E. Grout, told her my problem, and got the answer that I would be accepted, and could take two undergraduate science courses while doing my graduate work.

Feeling stunned and reluctant, I arrived at the University of Minnesota to begin work two days after classes had started.

My greatest concern was to avoid bumping into Andreas on campus and facing the emotional upset I knew this would bring. As time went by and this failed to happen (skirting, as I did, at some distance the building that contained the economics department), I relaxed, began enjoying my studies, and participated in the social activities of the graduate student body. Once, toward Christmas, when I was riding a packed elevator in the Student Union building, the doors opened to a waiting group of faculty men, and I saw Andreas' face among them. He looked and saw mine in the back of the elevator, then the doors closed as someone said, "No room." In a climate where everyone's face was red from cold and breathing was heavy from wintry walking, no one distinguished my condition from the others as we got out on the next floor. The second time I saw him was again in the Student Union, his back to me at a counter where cigarettes were sold, and I walked by fast, my eyes straight forward. From then on, I avoided the Union building as much as possible.

May came, and I was walking across campus one morning, feeling rather smart in my newly purchased yellow trench-style raincoat, enjoying the feel of youth and spring, when I realized that I was off schedule, and at least ten minutes late for my morning seminar. The campus was almost deserted with classes under way, and I rashly decided to take the shortcut which led me directly in front of the economics building. I was so sure that I wouldn't run into Andreas at this time of the day, and so intent on making up time to reach my classroom, that I failed to notice the figure walking toward me until I was too close to turn and disappear down a side path. I knew the walk—a jaunty, long stride with feet slightly turned out. There was no doubt that it was Andreas. I decided to walk by silently, pretending to be engrossed in my own thoughts. I had not been sure he had recognized me that time at the elevator, and if he didn't know I was on campus, I reasoned, he might not recognize me as I passed him.

We passed each other in silence, and I had gotten ten steps farther when I heard my name, "Margaret?" My heart was drumming in my chest, but I turned around with such aplomb that I later truly admired myself for it, put a look of surprise on my face, and said most innocently, "Oh, Andreas, is that you?" He walked back to me and asked how I was, and I explained that I was in a rush, being late for my morning seminar. He asked if he could walk me there, and I answered rather coolly and nonchalantly, "If you like."

In the short period of time it took to get to my class, we covered quite a bit of ground—what I had been doing, what he had been doing, that he was leaving Minnesota to accept a professorship at Northwestern in Evanston, and that he would like very much to explain some things to me. He hinted that his marriage was breaking up, and I remember thinking "I've heard that before." When he left, he had taken my phone number and address.

We went out several times that spring for dinner, and always enjoyed the evening; but I kept my emotions on ice, so as not to affect my decision to marry a fellow graduate student in July. Andreas knew I had a boyfriend—that much I told him—but he didn't know how serious it was. I was whirling off into a state of confusion as old wounds were being opened up; my mind was telling me one thing, my heart another.

Perhaps if Andreas hadn't left for a conference in Maine immediately at the end of the academic year, the course of events would have been different. We agreed to be in touch with each other, he from Northwestern, and I from some unknown destination, since my assignment from the Public Health Service had not yet come through. One night after I returned from a late evening in June, my roommate at the rooming house where I lived told me a long-distance call had come for me from the East. No message was left, and the person didn't call back. That call, which was from Andreas, could have made a difference, too. As it was, the days were passing, my wedding preparations were under way, and on July 14 I dropped the "Miss" and became "Mrs."

By the time Andreas reached Northwestern, I was in Los Angeles on a chest X-ray program, and my husband was registered for classes at the University of Southern California. My marriage was a shock for Andreas, who was indeed separating from his wife, not because of me, but because their marriage hadn't worked out.

In November 1950 the Los Angeles *Examiner* carried a news story on George Papandreou in Greece. Impulsively, I clipped it out and sent it to Andreas in an envelope bearing the printed return address of the South East Health Center, where my office was. I started getting letters from Andreas, addressed to my maiden name, since he didn't know my married name. I read them but left them unanswered.

During the winter I was transferred to Albuquerque, New Mexico, and my husband returned to Minnesota to finish his Ph.D. We were to try a temporary separation, for our marriage, undoubtedly doomed from the start under the circumstances, was not going well. At Easter-vacation time, my husband flew down, and we decided to get out of a situation which had become unbearable for both of us.

On August 30, 1951, Andreas and I got married.

What we had at that time in our relationship has never changed, but has deepened and matured with the years.

After our marriage, we returned to the University of Minnesota, and in 1952 started becoming active in American politics, inspired by the nomination of Adlai Stevenson for Democratic presidential candidate. Andreas became chairman of the Minnesota Stevenson Forum Committee, and we watched dejectedly Stevenson's defeat on election night at the television set of Walter Heller's house, a man who later became head of the Council of Economic Advisers under President Kennedy. We joined the Democratic-Farm-Labor party, and both of us were sent in 1954 as delegates to the Minnesota State convention which nominated Orville Freeman for governor, a race he won. Here I renewed my acquaintance with Hubert Humphrey, for whom I had done some campaigning during college days when he ran for mayor of Minneapolis. Andreas met him for the first time and agreed to have the Stevenson Forum Committee, still functioning, help him in a future senatorial campaign.

When we left Minnesota for the University of California, we left politicking behind, and Andreas became highly involved in university activities, and I highly involved in having my third and fourth children and running a home. Andreas' only brush with politics was to join a board of economic advisers for Pat Brown, governor of California.

Our involvement in Greek affairs came on gradually, but it was for me in its own way a love affair, starting in 1959 when we arrived in Greece with the four children and my mother-in-law, who lived with us, for a Fulbright year to study "economic and cultural obstacles to economic development in Greece." We rented a house built of pinkish rock, a color I was often to gaze on through the years on the mountain of Hymettus at the time of dusk. This house was in Ekali, less than a mile from Kastri where my father-in-law lived. The pull of Greece was upon us. It was, perhaps, especially powerful upon me.

Democracy, that much abused word, did not have firm foundations in Greece. The democratic spirit, however, was deeply ingrained. The majority of the Greek people called themselves democrats, yet they had never experienced anything remotely resembling a Scandinavian, a British, or an American type democracy. They greatly appreciated the benefits of an open, democratic society—freedom of speech, freedom of press, freedom of assembly, privacy of the home, etc.—without understanding their responsibilities. Most of them had been raised in authoritarian homes, under authoritarian governments, with governmental patronage and favoritism the natural consequence of the Turkish occupation where the local pasha determined who was to get what. Therefore even the concept of committee functioning was alien to them, as was decision making by consensus. Their concept of democracy was closer to the notion of anarchy: everyone should be free to do whatever he wanted, with no restrictions. They had been learning, however, and were actually at the beginning of a modern democratic society.

This individualism of the Greek, however, often given as the explanation of his being ungovernable, is not an innate characteristic. It is the result of the fact that he has had to fight for self-preservation in a colonial atmosphere; he has never been master in his own house. He has never had to take the responsibility of governing himself, of working with his fellow citizens for the national interest, for there has always been some sponsor power who determined his fate, and his chief aim was to placate that sponsor power.

The strategic position of Greece in the southern Mediterranean, plus its weakness because of size, has made it a football for the big powers for most of its modern history. Thus the British for many decades created in Greece an economic as well as a political colony. This relationship of mother country and colony contributed to the backwardness of Greece and the atrophy of its own deep-rooted institutions. Foreigners were brought in as kings and grafted onto the system as a means of control within the country by the sponsor power. The Greeks, who are basically republican by conviction, always resented this imposition in their internal affairs. Yet whenever a popular movement that was antagonistic to the monarchy and the supporting complex of Palace, army, and foreign power developed, it was crushed by that alliance of powers.

In 1944 when the Germans left, the popular mood was progressive and leftist. The British, depleted and exhausted by the war, turned their colony over to the Americans, who helped, through the Truman Doctrine, to squelch that mood. The civil war of 1946-49 was the result. Churchill's meeting with

20

Stalin in Teheran in October 1944 had assigned Greece to the western sphere of influence, and the western powers were unopposed in their interference in Greece.

This foreign intrusion into Greece and the need by the mother power to control the internal affairs of the country through the Palace, had the following results: the King, not able to rely on the support of the people for power, relied on the army, and turned it into a praetorian guard for the monarchy. Education remained stagnant, classical, and compulsory through only the first six grades on the thesis that an enlightened public was a dangerous public. The union movement remained under the tutelage and direction of the government, its leaders able to be "elected" only if they had the blessing of the government. The King himself took a great interest in overseeing this movement. A few farmer's cooperatives which developed in Macedonia were organized by politicians for political purposes, not as an indigenous development. Diplomatic posts abroad were the purview of the Palace and diplomacy was little more than public relations for the monarchy. Foreign investors were given special privileges over the Greek business entrepreneur and negotiated through the embassy of the protector power or through the Palace. A small Greek business elite was favored by the Palace and given immense help by the National Bank of Greece. The party of the Right was the King's own political instrument. Other parties consisted of a cluster of deputies around one authority, the leader, and were personal parties, not modern democratic parties. Hierarchy of party leadership was vague, sometimes almost to the point of being nonexistent.

When the Americans first took over from the British in 1947, they seemed to be dedicated to making Greece a viable democracy and giving due consideration to popular forces other than those that were strictly communist. With the intensification of the cold war, Greece began to look more and more to them like a military base, not a nation of people. Nonetheless, they opposed any dictatorial solutions even when Greeks were fighting Greeks and the political world was in chaos.

In 1955 the United States selected Constantine Karamanlis as the Prime Minister, with the agreement of the Palace, and he proved to be an able and effective leader and dependable ally. He ruled well enough to win two elections on his own, although aided by the fact that he faced a splintered and weakened Center opposition.

Greece represented to Andreas the frustration and agony of living in a totalitarian environment, his memories still vivid of the dictatorial Greece he had left, and he was less susceptible to the awesome, hypnotic effect, the spell, that Greece casts on those who visit her. The clear, light air of Attica, spiced with the smell of herbs and mountain flowers, is nature's answer to LSD. One's emotions are sprung from Pandora's box. The "fix" one gets is a heightening of the senses—sight, taste, smell—all emerging from a somnolent state to give new dimensions to daily living. One is transported overnight from the chilling bustle of life in a modern industrial state to the warm, dazzlingly bright sunlight of a magic ancient land.

By spring of 1960 we were in a dialogue—Andreas and I, Andreas and his friends, Andreas and his father. The question was "Should Andreas return to Greece to play a role in Greek public affairs?" Like a soap opera. "Can Helen Trent have romance over the age of forty?" It was a serious question for us, however. The pressures were great, and they included mine. Andreas' position, quite apart from having to give up a good and fruitful career as an economist in the States, was that the forces which existed in Greece would never allow him to play an important role in the destiny of the country. His independence of mind, his progressive ideas, his commitment to full democracy—all of these, he said, would make it necessary for these forces to destroy him. How prophetic he turned out to be! My own position was that he had something special to give Greece: American know-how, knowledge and training in problems of economic development, modern methods. He was unimpressed.

At the end of the summer of 1960, we took the children, George, age eight, Sophia, age six, Nick, age four, and Andriko, age one and a half, and led them up the gangplank of the *Olympia,* Greek Line, and headed to New York and then, we thought, back to California and an academic career. It was at the moment of departure that Andreas had misgivings about his decision. The boat was pulling away from the dock, and a group of friends were waving forlornly to our six faces peering over the rail. The harbor of Piraeus opened up to us as we moved out, leaving sailboats, yachts, and fishing vessels outlined against the coast like colorful lace fringe. Behind were the homes and buildings of Piraeus, sparkling white in the distance as they caught the rays of the setting sun. The *Olympia* gave three loud blasts on its sea horn, and for a moment I expected the scene in front of me to crack and fall into pieces like a piece of fine crystal.

Andreas had thought of one possibility that could bring us back to Greece in a scientific capacity. During the Fulbright year, Andreas had grown to feel that Greece needed a research center. He had in mind as a prototype the Brookings Institution in Washington, D. C., although on a much smaller scale. Together with Carl Kaysen, who was in Greece doing a special study on American economic aid in Greece (he is presently head of the Princeton Institute for Advanced Studies and was special White House adviser to President Kennedy), Andreas had made a proposal to the American Embassy in Athens, and argued that there was a real need for such an organization to do studies crucial to economic development in Greece, and that support from American funds would be a true service to Greece.

The response had been a flat and humiliating "no" by Sam Berger, the chargé d'affaires. According to him, American professors were always coming through with such proposals. The requests were piled knee-deep in his office, etc., etc. Actually, knee-deep was not very high, for Berger was America's counterpart of Greece's Markezinis, both short and thin, and both forever making up for their lack of height with the boom of their voices and an authoritative manner. Neither is very pleasant to deal with.

This was the first "formal" contact we had had with the embassy, although we had been frequently seeing official Americans in a social context. It was disheartening. Sam Berger had been immediately negative and disdainful. It was to be the beginning of a series of disillusionments with the American Embassy in Athens. Before we left Greece, the Greek government, under Karamanlis, had shown an active interest in the project, and, in fact, had pushed for its creation. Andreas had left with the government a report describing how such a research center could be organized, what it could achieve, and how funds might be raised to finance it.

By the time we reached New York, the idea that Andreas himself might be the creator of this center had taken hold, and the need of a native boy to return to do something for his homeland grew strong. The next five months back in America were totally involved with arrangements for making the center a reality. The first and foremost hurdle had been jumped. Ford and Rockefeller foundations promised substantial grants for a five-year period under the auspices of the University of California to support the project. We started then to make arrangements for our trip back to Greece. Among other things, we sold our house in the Berkeley hills, found a new home for our dog, Lady, and persuaded another Greek (also an American professor) and his wife to accompany us on this new venture and become part of the nucleus for the research center.

We had been gone from the university for the year 1959-60, returned for half a year, and were about to leave again. Our friends in California were extremely helpful and assisted us in our packing, the way one packs clothes for someone assigned to a mental institution. On their lips was the unuttered question "How could anyone really want to move to another country?" One professor said slyly, "If you're picking out small countries, there's also Albania." Apart from their friendship to us, and their desire to see Andreas stay on in California, they did not consider it a wise move. They were totally aware that the transition was not going to be easy.

January 15, 1961, found us soaring above the morning mist which shrouded the Golden Gate Bridge, winging our way toward the Near East, fatigued from last-minute activities, and armed with sleeping pills we planned to administer covertly to four active children.

Andreas had also been offered a job as economic counselor to the Bank of Greece to conduct research and direct the Research Studies Division, a role that he felt he could combine in a compatible way with that of setting up and directing the Center of Economic Research. Also, his salary from the Bank of Greece would free Center money for additional scholars from abroad. Later, he would be frequently attacked by hostile elements in Greece and abroad for having accepted a high salary, tax-free. What these accusers failed to add was that all salaries at the bank were tax-free, and his salary was no "special arrangement," but the scale salary for the job of bank counselor. In any case, these turned out to be incompatible roles, and he soon resigned his post at the bank and went on the Center's payroll.

Four months passed. Andreas received his first blast from the rightist press in response to a report he had submitted recommending radical changes in higher education, reforms badly needed in a country trying to raise its standard of living. They suggested that he go home, meaning back to the States. Apart from this, nothing seemed to be happening. The research center was bogged down in red tape, had no work space yet, and did not exist officially on paper. Because the Greek government had contributed money to it, it had to be set up under the auspices of one of the ministries—in this case, the Ministry of Education. This unwieldy, complicated, bureaucratic body was now in the slow process of interpreting the decree setting up the Center, the second decree drawn up after Andreas rejected the first.

On the family front, we were comfortably settled into Andreas' boyhood home in Psyhico, which after the addition of a third-floor study was quite adequate for our needs. We had registered the older children in a Greek public school near our home, George in third grade, Sophia in first. They knew only a few words of Greek, but with a daily diet of lessons and exposure, they made rapid progress. For the two at home, Nick and Andriko, I hired Louiza, a powerful Greek governess, short and square, a disciplinarian, and very committed politically to us. With her, I myself started speaking Greek, and in our long conversations I learned quite a bit about life in Greece from a woman embittered by the fate of the average Greek. She was tough and not always honest, having learned from childhood that all methods are acceptable in a society where survival is every man's major fight. She tangled with the kitchen personnel simply because she had to assert continually her superiority to them. She tangled with the man who drove Andreas' bank car because she refused to be treated as something less than a human being simply because she was a woman. She tangled with my mother-in-law because she felt the children were being spoiled by her. Eventually, I had to let her go.

On the political front, Parliament was beginning to debate the electoral law, and there was talk of elections in the fall of 1961 or the spring of 1962. Since 1946, the first elections after World War II, Greece had gone through many elections, almost all of them won by the Right. Because of the civil war following the occupation, and the efforts of the British to keep Greece out of the hands of the communists, the army and state machinery were put in the hands of royalists and extreme-right elements backed behind-the-scenes by the Army. This "parallel power," as Andreas called it, made it difficult for any party except that representing these interests to obtain government. Coupled with this was the inability of the Center parties to organize into a truly strong alternative or to develop a grass-roots organization. The Left continued to get between 10 and 25 percent of the popular vote, somewhat astounding in view of their defeat in the civil war, and in view of the propaganda and terrorist activities aimed against them. To top it off, huge sums of American aid assisted the governments in power.

The Center parties in 1961 were in their usual state of disunity, and there seemed to be no reason for Papandreou, Sr., to be optimistic about his chances of coming out on top in an election. The electoral system being proposed was called the kindred party system, and I was amazed to hear that the American Embassy supported it. Still a novice in Greek political affairs, and a novice in general on America's foreign policy, I had rather naïvely accepted what I had been told in social gatherings with embassy personnel, specifically that America had ceased interfering in internal matters and was carrying on perfunctory, routine diplomatic activities. I wondered what business it was of the embassy to give its support to any system. Did it also do this in France, in England, in Denmark, in Italy? Surely an electoral system was strictly an internal affair. My education on America's role in the internal affairs of Greece was to be a bitter one.

Winter of 1961 was not a happy winter. The adjustment for both of us was hard. I had no appetite and lost considerable weight. Andreas was spending hours away from the home in an attempt to see people who could move the government machinery and get his organization functioning. We had household help, which relieved me of household duties, but made my house more of a factory than a home—and a source of much friction. With my free time I started formal lessons in Greek, did a lot of reading, and visited museums and historical spots in and around Athens. I had difficulty developing friendships, except among a few Greek women who had spent some time in America and who had developed a value system similar to mine.

Andreas and I didn't ask each other the question, but it was there. Had we made the right decision?

CHAPTER THREE

Maneuvers of the Establishment to Stay in Power

TALK of elections was in the air during the winter of 1961. According to the Constitution, Karamanlis was entitled to another year of government, but it was his privilege, as in most parliamentary systems, to call for earlier elections. Word was out that he was moving toward this decision.

It might be helpful to explain briefly the party system in Greece, and the party configuration of Parliament that winter. There were three hundred seats in the Greek Parliament representing a country of eight million people. The country was divided into fifty-two constituencies, and each party could run candidates in all of them, although a smaller party might forego an area where it had no strength. To complicate matters, each constituency was assigned a certain number of seats, belonging to the entire constituency, not a one-area-one-seat system, and a party could field the number of candidates for seats available in the constituency. Because any one party could not win all seats, its own candidates competed with each other for votes from the party's supporters, as well as against candidates of the other parties. This can best be described, in American terms, as a combination primary and general election at the same time. Hostilities developed among candidates of the same party fighting their fellow candidates that far surpassed the feelings toward the opposition party candidates. It was a huge handicap to party unity.

In addition to this, deputy candidates were chosen in almost all cases by the party leader. He would spend time in consultation with a small group of advisers, with people from the candidate's community, or maybe in private communion with himself. The criteria for choice of a man were vague and varied in each case. Naturally, the leader tried to choose men who were likely to win, but sometimes nothing more than commitment and loyalty to the leader were required. This arbitrary exercise of power gave the leader a tremendous voice in his party's affairs.

Most of these weaknesses of the system worked to the disadvantage of the Center groups. The Left was bound together by a common ideology and an organizational scheme. The Right was not only the King's party, but had established a heirarchy of order and party unity by virtue of years in government. Within the Center there was not only a diversity of views, but a constant battle for leadership and the benefits that went with being a party head.

At the time elections were being considered, the Center was composed of the Papandreou party, the Baltatzis Argricultural party, the Party of Ten (which didn't have a party leader in the traditional sense, but a party spokesman, Novas) and the Progressive party of Markezinis. None of them singly had more than ten seats in Parliament. There were deputies of the Center who called themselves independents. Karamanlis' National Radical Union party (ERE) was the majority party with 171 seats, and the United Democratic Left (EDA) was the opposition party with 75 seats.

With elections coming up, all attention was turned to the electoral law. Each time prior to elections, the government party worked out and submitted an electoral law to Parliament, devising one, naturally, best suited to keeping itself in power. Gerrymandering could be considered a mild impropriety as compared to the intricate maneuvers of a Greek electoral law. This year the maneuver emerged with the title "kindred party system." Explaining this law would be like describing a complicated formula in an advanced algebra class. Political strategists and mathematicians had put their heads together to accomplish some practical goals: the diminution in parliamentary strength of the Left, the achievement of a strong Center opposition, and a victory of the Right. The Communist party had been outlawed in Greece after the civil war, but had representation in the legal party of EDA. When EDA received 24 percent of the popular vote in 1958, the Americans and the Palace got a case of the nervous Nellies and were determined not to allow this to be repeated. It was conceivably the reason for earlier elections—to change the party pattern in Parliament. It should be noted that the law was designed to develop a strong Center—but in *opposition*. The Right was to get its usual support to remain in power.

One provision of the kindred party system was meant to force a welding together of the disparate parties in the Center by penalizing small parties in the election. If a single party did not receive a specified percentage of the total popular vote, it could not benefit by the "second distribution" of parliamentary seats. About fifty seats were involved in this second distribution and would be assigned to parties according to their percentages of the total vote. For example, a party with less than 10 percent of the popular vote was not entitled to participate in this grab bag of parliamentary seats. A small party which wanted to get the maximum of its candidates seated had a better chance by fusing with others into one large party. It was an attempt on the part of the power complex to forge a united opposition party so as to make sure that the left-wing EDA would not emerge again as the opposition party in Parliament.

The kindred party title came about as a result of a scheme to divide parties into "national" and "antinational" parties. All of those falling into the national category were kindred souls and would be given a weighted advantage when distribution of seats occurred after the election, a reward for being on the right side of the fence. The only antinational party according to this concept would have been EDA. But it would have meant a preelection arrangement between ERE and the Center not only to collude against the Left by running together as "relatives" in this national category, but to agree to a majority-minority party arrangement. In other words, it offered the Center the

27

role of opposition in Parliament in place of EDA, but foreclosed any possibility of its winning the election. When ERE saw resistance to this scheme as the law was explained in the corridors and private offices of the Parliament building, it impugned the patriotism of the Center forces for not supporting this anticommunist electoral device, as it was described by its authors.

The American Embassy position was not only anticommunist, which was expected, but continued to be strongly pro-Karamanlis. This favoring of one party to the exclusion of other noncommunist democratic parties added fuel within the Center ranks to the already blazing fire of discontent with the American factor. There was basic goodwill among the Greek people toward the Americans at this time, but they were puzzled, if not yet irate, with the policy of discrimination toward parties practiced by the representatives of the American government in Athens. They wondered why the Americans wouldn't want the goodwill of the entire democratic camp—Right through Center—perhaps 75 to 80 percent of the people, instead of always sticking with the limited forces of the Right.

The trial balloon was up. Behind-the-scenes discussions were thick and heavy. The law had not been brought to the floor for open debate. In the midst of this an event occurred which I mentally entitled "The Midnight Ride of Paul Revere," although it bore no resemblance to that historical moment. It was not American, but "Balkan" in character, similar to the days when princes went galloping around the territory to secret meetings, making secret deals.

It was ten o'clock one winter evening. We were having cocktails prior to dinner at a friend's home in Old Athens near the Acropolis. Five couples made up the party. Andreas was called to the phone, which concerned me at that hour, and I wondered whether something was wrong at home. A voice at the other end said: "Don't express any sign of recognition or repeat who I am when I tell you."

"Go ahead" was my husband's reply.

"This is the secretary to His Royal Highness, Prince Constantinos."

"Yes" was the reply.

"The Prince would like very much to see you and discuss some things with you."

"Fine. That can be arranged."

"Tonight."

"Tonight?"

"Yes, tonight."

"Well, I'm at a dinner party, and this is rather awkward . . ."

"Please come. It is urgent. Make some excuse and drive directly to the Palace where I will be waiting for you."

Andreas made his excuses to the host and hostess. I walked to the door with him and he informed me that he was on his way to the Palace at the request of Prince Constantinos. He told me to say nothing.

When I returned, the group was in heavy discussion, and I sat down to finish my drink and my cigarette, trying to imagine what cloak-and-dagger activity Andreas might be getting into. An old classmate of Andreas' sitting next to me leaned over and said, "Apparently he's been called by higher-ups." He winked. Being a dutiful wife, and not knowing how much this friend knew, I mumbled that being a member of the Papandreou family had its peculiarities—and let it go at that.

We had dinner without Andreas. By midnight I was sipping my second after-dinner cognac, tired of making conversation and wondering why Andreas was so long cooped up in the Palace with the twenty-two-year-old future monarch of Greece.

At half-past midnight he arrived, looking chilled and hungry. The other guests left, and the host and hostess sat with us at the table while Andreas ate, but no one referred at all to his absence. On the way home he told me the story.

He arrived at the Palace near Syntagma Square at 10:30 and was ushered into a very huge and cold anteroom where the King's secretary was waiting. The Athens Palace was not used by the royal family for living quarters, but for social and business occasions and obviously for night rendezvous. This explained the fact that none of the rooms was heated on this crisp winter night. The secretary was medium-height, well-built, good-looking. He was educated and cultured. His name was Makis Arnaoutis. For half an hour the two of them chatted, waiting for the Prince who had called Andreas on urgent business.

The Prince appeared, striding in with the easy grace of an athlete, looking much like a college undergraduate on an American campus. Under his suit he wore a V-neck navy-blue cashmere sweater. His clothes, his style, and his manner were informal and casual and were coupled with a self-assurance that bordered on arrogance, not uncommon in the male species at that age, Prince or not.

The conversation soon got to the heart of things: the electoral system. He asked for Andreas' opinion. Andreas answered that he was too new in Greece to take a stand. He added that he was head of a research center and preferred to remain outside of political issues.

"But your father does not want the kindred party system."

"No. That much I know."

"I wonder if I were to talk to your father if I could have your moral support . . . have you with me, that is."

"Of course, I can be with you. That can be arranged."

"Since I'm the son of my father and you're the son of yours," he smiled, "I thought we could arrange it this way . . ."

"Yes, of course. When shall we plan it for?"

"Tonight."

"Tonight?"

"Would you call him?" asked the Prince.

"I'm not sure he's home, but I'll give it a try . . ."

The Prince pointed to the phone.

"Father? Andreas here. I'm with the Prince."

Long pause on the other end of the phone. "What did you say, my boy?" finally came through.

"I say I'm at the Palace with the Prince, and he wants us to come up and see you."

"Tonight?"

"Yes, now."

Silence. Then, "Bring him up."

This trip from downtown Athens to Kastri is a twenty-five-minute ride, normal driving. With repeated comments on the need for secrecy, the Prince hopped into his Mercedes sports car. Andreas joined him. They sped off down Vassilis Sophias, the main highway, a squad car of bodyguards behind them, sirens wailing. Papandreou is the only politician who lives in Kastri. Within twenty minutes this "secret" cavalcade was roaring into Kastri, its destination an open secret.

Papandreou was waiting in the study. He offered drinks. The Prince took a beer. The Prince stated that he would like to discuss the electoral law with the President, that he would like to describe the merits of the kindred party system. The President replied that he was planning to discuss this issue with the King the following week. Then, said the Prince, you had better discuss it with me now, because I will be regent for the next two weeks. His Majesty is leaving the country tomorrow.

The President hesitated for a moment, then said, "All right, let's talk."

The fire in the corner of the study burned slowly down as the three of them sat in the softly lit room and talked: the President, leader of an opposition party in Parliament, and likely leader of a united Center opposition, sat behind his huge carved oak desk; his son, an economics professor from the University of California, and the twenty-two-year-old Glüksberg-Hohenzollern heir to the Greek throne sat at the side of the desk. The room was lined with books—classics and politics—stacked in carved oak bookcases which extended to within one foot of the exceptionally high ceiling.

Heavy bronze-colored velvet draped the two tall windows of the room. In the daytime one could see through one window, facing the desk, a garden full of rose bushes, my father-in-law's favorite flower, and from the other a forest of pines extending over an acre of land. On the corner of the desk sat a slender, modern-designed glass vase which with the coming of spring would hold a single rose, the pride of that day's bloom. My father-in-law insisted that roses be shown individually, so that each one's beauty get its just acclaim. He was known to carry a rose with him into Parliament on days when he gave a speech. Behind him on the top of a row of cabinets was a picture of Andreas taken about the time I had met him, when he was twenty-nine years old. A large world globe and a few ashtrays were the only other objects on the cabinet. On one of the shelves inside the cabinet was a box of candy, a secret uncovered by the children. There was a quiet intimacy to the room.

The Prince talked at length on the various features of the kindred party system, which he knew well. He stressed that the law was designed for the

30

benefit of all patriotic Greeks, implying that it was the national duty of dedicated politicians to support it.

When the Prince had finished his half-hour dissertation, without interruption from either Andreas or his father, the President spoke. His style was that of tutor to pupil, kind but firm. It was a long lecture delivered with his usual eloquence and clarity, the same attributes that had given him the reputation as Greece's greatest orator.

Back in the car on the return trip, the Prince's only comment was "I guess your father won't accept the kindred party system." Then the discussion turned to cars, cars in general—styling, speed, maneuverability, and the like. The midnight ride was completed.

Later that summer King Paul was interviewed in his summer palace on the island of Corfu by Cyrus Sulzberger of *The New York Times*. The subject was the "future of kings," and the King discussed the role a monarch should play in order to maintain his position as a symbol to the people of "something better than themselves." Sulzberger wrote: "King Paul feels democratic sovereigns should always remain close to their subjects but out of politics; that 'ordinary common sense' is the paramount regal requisite . . . . For him, the cardinal rules for future kings remain: earn popular respect and affection; rely on common-sense judgment; store away knowledge with experience; stay above and apart from politics."

I have often wondered if King Paul felt that the "midnight ride" on the electoral law was in keeping with this advice for future kings.

Within a short time after this incident, and while the discussion on the kindred party system was still hot, Andreas was called by the head of the American CIA in Greece, Laughlin Campbell. Their meeting took place in a neutral home in Kifissia, and the discussion was short, but not sweet. Andreas was asked to arrange a meeting between his father and the CIA in the person of Campbell. Campbell explained that he was not on good terms with Andreas' father because of a past quarrel.

Andreas asked, "Can I tell him what the meeting will be about?"

"Yes. The kindred party system."

There it was again.

"I know my father's views on the kindred party system" was Andreas' answer. "I have just recently been through a training course," he smiled.

"He's against it," replied Campbell, rather curtly.

"He's against it, and for good reasons." Andreas gave briefly the points his father had made to the Prince. He said that it was an undemocratic law and that it committed the Center to accepting second position before the race even got started. As Andreas talked, Campbell's face started to redden. Before Andreas had a chance to finish, Campbell pulled his hefty, tall frame out of the armchair, and in a sudden surge of anger, he shouted, "You tell your father that we get what we want!"

Andreas contained his own anger. "Exactly that?" he asked.

"Exactly that."

"All right," Andreas said, rising to leave. "I will tell him—in your exact words."

He told his father. But his father was unperturbed. Without the agreement of the Center parties that they would ally themselves with ERE as kindred members of a national grouping, the passing of the law in Parliament, which ERE could do because of its majority, made little sense. It would then be obliged to impose the alliance by court action, a ridiculous idea.

Campbell, on this occasion, did not get what "he" wanted, nor did the Palace, nor did ERE—despite pressure and maneuvers. Instead they brought to the floor for debate a variation of the system without the "kindred" aspect. It was a momentary victory for the Center, but the establishment complex did not intend to give up easily.

CHAPTER FOUR

An Island Interlude

ONE morning in late May we got up, swung open the balcony doors, gazed across the backyard pines furry with gold, and concluded that this was a day to take off for the islands. The research center and the political center were having their problems, and our mood was low; but as we headed the Volvo in the direction of the ferryboat to Evea, and the sun climbed in the sky, our spirits climbed, too.

Georgie and Sophia were delighted to be removed temporarily from the rigors of a Greek public school, and Nick was pleased to be included with the older children. Baby Andy remained at home with our governess, Louiza. He too must have yearned for the feeling of freedom, the lightheartedness that overtook us as we pushed on to an unknown destination—somewhere on one of the islands of the Sporades.

We passed patches of gnarled, silver-tinged olive trees, tall stalks of bamboo, and plots of grapevine bushes set one or two feet apart. Best of all, peeping out from everywhere was the bright red face of the poppy, for it was poppy-time in Greece. Cropping up in plain and crevice, this flower dotted the countryside during the spring months. If, with time, the California landscape blossoms in like manner, it will be because of one of our American professor friends who, enchanted with this capricious, glowing flower, tucked seeds into his suitcase and roamed the California countryside tossing them about.

George started singing the Greek national anthem—the one Greek song the children knew thoroughly, singing it daily in class. We all joined in in a rollicking, boisterous way, puncturing the silence of the countryside with the short, rhythmic, staccatolike phrases. Here and there the song shifted into warmer, more sentimental passages. It felt "Greek" to me, representative of the people and the landscape. It was a song dedicated to freedom and liberty.

As we reached the peak of the mountain which forms the backdrop to Oropos, we spotted the ferryboat leaving the shores and heading for Evea. This meant a wait of one hour before its return. With no need to hurry, we wound slowly down the mountainside, staring at the village people, houses, and animals like ordinary tourists. Animals outnumbered people, and the picturesque donkey was our favorite. One economic historian, not claiming to be an authority on donkeys, made the observation that Greek donkeys have the softest, most gentle eyes of any nation's donkeys. I believe this is an example of "air intoxication," part of the magic spell Greece casts over its visitors. Even the donkeys look better!

A true story about Greek donkeys took place many years ago on the island of Spetses. With the increase in tourist trade on that island, the mayor began to feel self-conscious and embarrassed by the habits of the donkeys, who regularly scattered evidence of their presence along the main street of the port town. He issued a decree. The decree stated that from now on all donkeys must wear *pania*, or diapers! General instructions were given on style and construction, and any owner not conforming to this order was subject to a fine.

All red-blooded donkey-owners rebelled, as did the rest of the islanders when they saw the animals in their new attire. "We have done many things for the tourist, and have accepted quite a bit of disruption in our lives" was the general comment, "but this is going too far—diapers on our donkeys!"

The decree stayed in effect long enough to cause the fall of the island government (and for the islanders to take pictures of this effrontery which they showed later to tourists). In the elections which followed, if one is to believe the tales in the tavernas, the mayor who campaigned on this clean-up plank lost.

The tiny village port was lined with small cafés. In front of each, twirls of smoke from an outdoor spit carried the aroma of roast lamb, tantalizing in the early morning hours. We had forgotten the existence of Athens, that the Center decree was waiting a plethora of signatures, including King Paul's, and that Andreas had been told to "go home." We ordered an *ouzo*, a clear powerful fluid with the deceptive taste of smooth anise. We looked longingly at the *kokoretzi*, lamb innards, being turned slowly over hot charcoal with a hand crank by a waiter in a white short-sleeved shirt. We concluded that it was too early in the trip to risk stomach upsets, and chose instead black olives and white goat cheese. The children and I used our Greek enthusiastically, if not correctly, and found what was to be true all along: the people were delighted with our attempts and easily understood what we were trying to communicate. When we would hesitate over a word, they would smile broadly and say, "Poli discoli," meaning "very difficult language," with a pride both in our achievement and in the fact that they spoke a difficult tongue.

The children discovered that when they said their last name was "Papandreou," they were given more attention, and very often candy and gifts. Any political name would have achieved a similar effect, but Papandreou was a particularly old, respected political name and carried with it the glow of greatness. With no television and no outstanding athletic team, politics was the national sport. My superficial observation was that it was a game, played as such by the participants. The supporters reminded me of local fan clubs. Parties were highly personal and the personality of the leader determined the success of a party rather than any set of principles or specific program. The fan clubs formed the cheering sections when the candidate arrived and did the proselytizing in the coffeehouses afterward. The politician himself paid for the cost of the activity—a banquet, a loudspeaker system, handbills—either from his private income or from contributions made by wealthy industrialists, shipowners, or businessmen in Athens. Grass-roots participation, organization, and contribution were nonexistent, except for the Left. Apart from the passionate emotional involvement of the people, visits of political personalities were like traveling road shows.

In a country as poor as Greece, large sums of money could be gotten only from the wealthy segment of the population, and even mass small contributions by political followers would amount to little, and the politician was thus dependent on those groups which were dedicated to maintaining the status quo. This resulted in a concentration of power in the hands of the few. Geographically, Athens was the mecca of this power. Everything was decided there.

"So, your *papou* is Papandreou?" I heard the café owner asking Nicky. "And you, you will be Prime Minister someday, yes?"

By now several of the local storekeepers had gathered at our white wooden table on the sea. One, after proclaiming himself a Papandreouist, had drawn Andreas aside. He displayed snapshots, and talked to him fervently and intensely. Andreas passed the pictures to me, and I understood that a daughter was in the marriage market and Andreas was being asked to act as a broker in Athens for this desirable commodity. I knew about the dowry system in Greece, and I knew that in the villages most marriages were arranged by the parents, but this was the first time I had seen how the market worked. The girl's attributes were described in detail by her earnest father. She was a graduate of a local high school, and therefore an educated girl. She was healthy and strong and a good housekeeper. She had a sunny disposition. She was physically attractive, as attested by the photographs. She was a virgin. And, most important, he could offer as dowry a small apartment in Athens (this was a huge dowry for a village girl). He complained bitterly about a deal that he had made months earlier with a civil servant in Athens, who had insisted that the father also supply furniture for the apartment. On that basis he would agree to marry the daughter. The father retorted that when he died his property in Oropos would be divided between his two daughters and therefore the man had a "second installment" to look forward to. The man was not satisfied, and the deal was dropped.

With promises of letting eligible Athenian men know of the Oropos offer, Andreas shook hands all around, and we moved toward the arriving ferryboat. The shopkeepers patted the children on their heads and sent "greetings to the President."

During these simple discussions I noticed once again, as I had on prior occasions, the tremendous rapport Andreas developed with the common people. He both talked and listened, the latter being an uncommon Greek trait. He spoke in *demotiki* the popular language, not *katharevusa,* a manufactured language used in written documents and by the educated as a mark of distinction. He was taller than most Greeks and one could see his head jutting up in the midst of a circle of men, faces looking up at him with respect, interest, and warmth.

When we drove off the ferryboat on the other side, we continued on a dusty hot road, twisting among ridges where smoky-gray scrub bushes clung to rocks. The road wound up and across the island of Evea to the port of Kimi, where we parked the car in a barnlike garage near the ticket office and purchased tickets for a ship headed for the island of Skyros. The captain of the ship, who came to join us over a glass of wine after lunch, easily persuaded us to extend our tickets and continue to the island of Skiathos, stopping by Skyros on our return trip. He described the golden sand beaches of Skiathos, the lush forests, the crystal-clear air, the excellent fishing, and, most important, the lack of tourists on the island. He warned us, in fact, that accommodations would be primitive but that the natural beauty would make up for it.

At midnight we arrived, sleepy-eyed and yawning, but not so dulled by travel that we couldn't appreciate the sound and sights of an island port—the swinging lanterns on the pier, the shouts of men assisting in the tying of the boat, the spanking of disturbed waters against the sides of the fishing boats anchored nearby, and the smell of fish, oil, and jasmine in the air. We caught then and there, and will have it always, the disease Lawrence Durrell calls "islomania."

We found clean rooms above a restaurant, cots with thin, hard mattresses and rough, nubby cotton sheets. The cost was ten drachmas (thirty-three cents) per bed. The pungent odor of blown-out wicks lingered in the air as we plunged into bed. We slept deeply and comfortably until dawn, when the cackles of roosters and the shouts of fishermen and roving vegetable vendors awakened us.

The restaurant served Turkish coffee mixed with hot milk for breakfast. With it we were given jagged-cut thick pieces of whole-wheat bread, sweet butter, and a thick amber-colored honey which had a mellow flavor. On another plate were large slabs of manouri, a mild sweet white goat cheese.

The beach of the golden sand described to us by the ship captain was two hours away. We hired a *venzini,* a boat propelled by a small gas-power engine, and decided to spend the entire day out. In an old variety store on the main street, we purchased lines, hooks, and squares of cork. The store reminded me of old-time general stores in the Midwest. Huge sacks of grain sat open on the floor in the front of the counter. Small bolts of inexpensive fabric lined the wall shelves. Hanging on hooks were tangles of brightly colored cheap patent-leather belts for ladies. Nails, hammers, pots and pans, paints, and candies were on display.

Along with the boat came a young fisherman and his mate, an older toothless man who nevertheless smiled constantly. They were delighted to earn the money, but more than that, they were excited about the day's activity with new people. Few inhabitants ever left the island—it cost too much—and as yet, tourists were rare. This made us something special. We were treated royally, but not with servility.

The democratic spirit that regards people as individuals and not as members of a higher or lower class is deeply ingrained in the Greek people. And with this spirit it is distressing that they have had to fight so long and hard to try to establish democracy in their country. This constant instability of Greece's system of government can be explained by the doggedness of vested interests to maintain their power and fight change, and by the inability of the fiercely individualistic average Greek to organize and work with his compatriots for a common cause. In addition to this, independent of the will of man, of the desire of the Greeks to attain full democracy, of their love of equality and freedom, Greece does not have a vast continent or a rich land—circumstances that help in the maintenance of democracy. Fate has given her a beauty fit for the gods, but a barren beauty, breathtaking, but harsh on mere mortals. Without the means of production, the country has been beset by economic ills. This misery, coupled with impatience and exploitation by foreign powers, creates the conditions for extreme solutions to the people's problems.

With broad new straw hats covering both our heads and our pale limbs, we headed for the venzini carrying our lunch basket and fishing gear. As we shoved off, the island children on the pier and the fishermen mending their nets with hands and toes, all shouted "Yasoo, kalo taxidhi," meaning "Good-bye and good trip."

We watched breathlessly as the island port magically became a toy town, the houses turning into tiny white boxes clustered on the side of the mountain and the boats into toy fishing vessels rocking in the gleaming blue below. The sharpness of detail and the sense of dimension remained for some time in the clear, bright spotlight of the sun until at last it flattened into one dimension, a stage setting, a backdrop to the drama of life, a postcard, a painting, an exquisite color print in a book on classical landscape. We rounded the corner of the cove where the village lay and saw the shore of the island stretching for miles, a ribbon of beige separating the blue Mediterranean from the deep green hills, wild with brush and trees. Most of the trees were pine, but occasionally a cyprus could be seen, its topmost tip reaching high above the other trees, standing in slender black-green splendor.

For an hour we moved along, a hundred meters from shore, listening to the hypnotic put-put of the engine, not talking, and enjoying the heat of the sun as it soaked into our skins. A light breeze was caused by the movement of the boat. The children trailed their fingers and toes in the soft, tranquil, cool water and watched the bubbles and ripples they made spread out into a larger and larger fan sparkling with reflected colors and white foam. We were approaching an artistically placed tumble of rocks jutting up directly in our path, and fisherman Yanni put the venzini into neutral. His grinning partner, Pericles, drew out a pail containing bait from under his seat, and we knew that fishing time had arrived. This was by no means the best time for fish; no Greek fisherman would dream of fishing in midmorning, but we were not professionals. Pericles told us that rock fish may bite at any time of the day. He told us to look down, and we saw at a depth of fifteen to twenty feet colorful multicolored fish, playfully darting around the rocks, sometimes disappearing under them. Three baited hooks went over the side of the boat, and three eager, excited faces watched the bait, glistening in the water, sink slowly to the bottom. The clarity of the water made it possible to watch the fish approach the hook. The children prematurely jerked their lines up from time to time and the open-mouthed fish would jackknife and dart away.

The haul was immense. Twenty fish, each about six inches long, in less than an hour, enough for three fish apiece for lunch. The fish were not all alike. Various "tribes" evidently lived below, and their costumes were glorious. One light brown fish had a deeper brown design across his back, as if a child had taken a huge crayon, made some crisscross lines, and finished at the head with two dots. They were storybook fish, fit for playing with mermaids and having storybook adventures. Sophia, with her tender little heart, began to feel sorry for them as they flapped around on the bottom of the boat, struggling to breathe, and urged that we send them back to their rocky abode. This was scornfully rejected by the two boys, and by the rest of us who were beginning to feel hungry. Andreas carried on a conversation with the fishermen—about their lives, their dreams, their problems—in a relaxed manner I had not seen for months.

We headed toward the beach of the golden sand with great curiosity. All the sand looked golden to me. But this was different. This sand sparkled, and where the water was shallow, it sparkled through the water, giving the water a golden hue, too. As the waves lapped up on the shore and then receded, they left a tiny line of gold, a fine, wispy, cobwebby reminder of where the water had kissed the sand and drawn back. The beach and the hills behind it were uninhabited. It was a dream beach, soon to go the way of all romantic, beautiful, isolated, quiet spots of the world, for a few years after our visit, through the Greek tourist office a French company built a resort there.

Yanni and Pericles said they would clean the fish and start a fire while we took a swim. Hot and uncomfortable by now, we accepted the suggestion readily and were soon slipping through silky, cool, buoyant water. George donned fins and snorkle and swam some distance to a clump of rocks and the kind of underwater growth that would assure the existence of sea urchins. He dove down several times and came up with five big ones, their bodies showing pink-purple through the black bristles, rich with eggs. This was our hors d'oeuvre. We cut the underbelly open with Yanni's pocket knife and using small seashells scooped the eggs from their nesting places, four or five well-protected sacs in a circle around the outer edge of the belly. The flavor was fishy and salted perfectly by nature. A poor man's caviar.

The fish were fried in Yanni's frying pan in several inches of pure olive oil. From the pan they were placed in a row on a clean, dry, flat rock, and as soon as they cooled, we picked them up in our fingers and pulled white succulent pieces off the backbone until we were left with only a head and skeleton. But every good Greek knows that the head is the sweetest part of the fish—so that went, too. A wooden bowl mysteriously appeared from Yanni's boat and in it went wedges of fresh tomatoes, sliced onions, and chunks of feta cheese, along with the always present olive oil. Village bread and a half-gallon jug of retsina wine, cooled in the sea, completed our meal. Yanni and Pericles watched our pleased faces with pride.

Yanni, tall, dark, moustached, and ruggedly handsome, was unmarried at thirty-five. He must have been the "dream catch" of many an island maiden. Pericles, looking more like a grandfather, was still an active father, with three children and one on the way. His oldest was a fourteen-year-old girl whom he could no longer support in school, and he begged me to find an American family that would take her and give her additional education. He assured me she would work hard for them in every way possible. "At least, if she gets to America, she has a chance to make something of her life," he said. "Here is nothing." I thought about my own daughter and wondered if I could cope with the emotional heartache of sending her at fourteen to another land, probably never to see her again. I looked at this wonderful, toothless, endlessly grinning old man, and marveled.

Siesta time. We found thick carpeting of pine needles in the shade, encircled at the outer edges by dappled sunlight, and the invitation to sleep was too great for even restless Nick to resist. When we awoke, we spied Yanni scrambling up a wide-trunked pine tree, gathering pine cones and tossing them down into springy masses of moss and vine. The children huddled around Yanni when he climbed down, watching with delight while he broke open the cones with his tanned, powerful hands. Using a rock as a tool, he split open the shells of the nuts and offered these tiny, delicate-tasting treasures to the children. Soon they were likewise engaged, and I believe they and Yanni could have spent hours in this languid employment. They babbled away in Greek, discussed the fastest way of getting the shells off the nuts, teased each other (especially Sophia and Yanni), and munched away happily. Andreas sat propped against a tree, tossing pebbles at a nearby big rock, and watched the scene with satisfaction.

This carefree joie de vivre is a quality belonging to children, but the Greeks have lost none of it in growing up. Perhaps that is why they express such open fondness for children; they have a kind of kinship, a secret that they share—that adults are really kids, just bigger.

I was reminded of two examples of this quality. It was the preceding winter during a snowfall, in which the snow was moist, soft, and packable, the temperature just below freezing. Cars steamed to the suburbs ten miles outside of Athens and returned with gleeful occupants sporting their trophy—a snowman, small or large, in a variety of poses, perched on the tip of the radiator, an ornament for the cap. The town took on a carnival air.

On another occasion I saw two grown men, respectable, sober, standing in the rear of the elevator discussing business. The door opened and admitted a woman in an outrageous hat, feather quivering with each movement of her head. The men looked at her, looked at each other, and started a muffled giggling, uncontrolled. For the nine floors of the ride, the giggling continued, and when the door closed after them on the floor, those of us in the elevator could hear the giggles turn into whoops and hollers as they found their reprieve from the restraint imposed by the presence of the woman. Childlike? Yes, in both cases.

In late afternoon we left the beach of the golden sand, our skins tingly, sensitive, and warm—the beginning of a good suntan. In the few more days we remained in Skiathos we added to that suntan, exploring other beaches, other fishing spots, other pine groves. None, however, matched the magic beach of gold.

Yanni and Pericles helped carry our suitcases to the ship for our return trip. Pericles brought his wife and family down to the pier to meet us and wave good-bye. The children were in their best clothes, ill-fitting as cheap clothes always are, but clean and recently pressed. They wore shoes, rarely done by island children except on special occasions. We were being given VIP treatment by Pericles and his family, and I was very touched.

We had no sooner settled on the boat when the children struck up a conversation with one of the few passengers, an old man in his seventies by the name of Panayotis. Eventually he came over and introduced himself to Andreas, and the two were soon in a lively political discussion. It was the first such conversation since we left Athens, and we realized that we were heading home to the real world of problems and issues. Feeling reluctant as yet to leave the land of ozone and pine scent and deep blue waters, we readily agreed to the old man's suggestion, a short stopover on Skyros, Panayotis' home, something we had tentatively planned anyway. There he had raised four boys, one of whom he had just visited on the island of Skiathos. He was proudly carrying a gift from his son which he kept closely to his side in a box, a new Lux lamp. We also learned that he was the island poet.

Although he couldn't read or write, he had published a book of poems by telling them to a friend, who wrote them down. Most of them, he told us, were about the island and its people, and many of the poems told the story of the flu epidemic in 1918, which wiped out half the population and necessitated, as he said, a complete reconstruction of the island society—the widow of Stavros wed the widower of Maria, the widow of Heracles wed the widower of Pagona, etc.

"You will stay with me," he said, "in my home."

"There are five of us," Andreas replied. "It is impossible."

"No, no. Not impossible. We have room, plenty room. My wife will not forgive me if I permit you to remain at the hotel." His eyes sparkled with excitement, and one got a glimpse of the dashing young Zorba he must have been. His hair was silver-gray, thick and wiry, his head leonine. Bushy eyebrows, still almost jet black, jutted out over sea-blue eyes, and one's gaze was distracted from the eyes only by the charm of his wide mouth and healthy teeth.

We accepted his invitation, not convinced that he had room, but concerned lest we offend him. From the port in Skyros, we took a rickety bus on a road skirting mountain cliffs, a breathtaking and harrowing ride to the other side where Panayotis' donkey waited, tied to a tree. We loaded the animal with our suitcases, coats, sweaters, and the two smaller children and began a mile hike across sandy soil on a narrow path. As we continued, we purchased groceries for the house from the garden plots of village cottages, getting acquainted with the villagers along the way. At the tip of the island, the house of Panayotis came into view, white like the others, low and oblong in shape. Behind it was a majestic windmill, long unused, judging from its broken spokes and state of disrepair. Facing us was the terrace. Lavender wisteria climbed the sides of the house and hung partially over the terrace opening. Two doors led off the back of the terrace, one to a bedroom, the other to a kitchen. A small door at the narrow end of the porch and directly opposite the entry opened onto a primitive bathroom.

The woman coming to greet us was Panayotis' second wife, his first having died some years earlier. She was tall, fine featured, and slender. She approached us with graceful movements, and if she was astonished at the arrival of five unexpected guests, her graciousness belied it. After the greetings were over, she turned to her husband, calling him "Mister" and queried him on his trip, then suggested that we come in out of the sun and have a cool drink of *visinada*, a grape concentrate, homemade, to which cold water is added.

That evening we ate a tasty fresh fish soup from a big iron pot, cooked over an open fireplace in the kitchen. The bedroom had been made up. Our bed was a large double bed with an unshapely, thick straw mattress. A single bed cot had been pulled in and made up for two children—one at each end. George had a straw mattress on the floor. When we protested that we were taking their bedroom, they simply smiled and said they had more room over there, pointing vaguely in the direction behind the kitchen.

The children's eyes were puffed and sleepy, their faces flushed from hot soup and a touch of wine, and their bodies tired from the day's activities. Nick's blond hair shone in the candlelight, his usually tense body relaxed, almost limp.

When the children were in bed, Andreas and Panayotis took out the Lux lamp and started fiddling with it. There were instructions in Greek which Andreas read out loud, and when the old man finally got it lit, it started emitting short explosive pops. Cursing, he shut it off.

I was glad. The Lux threw a powerful stark light which changed the intimacy of the room. Instead of seeing the twinkle in Panayotis' eyes, one saw the wrinkles in his face. Instead of seeing the grace of his wife's hands, one saw wear and dryness. They were signs of a life of drudgery and hardship. The candles gave youth and glow, and the far recesses of the terrace faded into darkness and mystery. It was in this setting, drinking home-brewed retsina wine and eating feta cheese made from the milk of their own goat, that we heard the poems of Panayotis. He recited them with ease, unselfconsciously, proudly.

At midnight we turned in. The host and hostess asked us if there was anything else we wanted and expressed the hope that the bed would be comfortable. We said "Kali nichta," closed the door, and were soon in a deep, dreamless slumber on the tip of a Greek island in the Aegean, guarded by an old, broken-down windmill.

In the morning we discovered that Panayotis and his wife had slept on a blanket on the cement floor of the terrace.

CHAPTER FIVE

The Campaign, Greek-Style, 1961

AFTER a lengthy and pedantic debate in Parliament, the government passed (by ERE's 170 votes on June 23, 1961) the "reinforced proportionate system," a system that was more acceptable to the Center parties than the kindred system, but which still gave decided advantages to the government party. Many of the provisions remained the same. Under this system 250 deputies were elected by a strictly proportional vote. The remaining 50 seats were divided among parties receiving 24 percent or more of the popular vote. This cut off the Left and small parties and gave special benefits to the majority party.

Two features of the law the Center fought against were the inclusion of the military in the voting and a rider that stipulated the method under which the elections following 1961 would be conducted. Regarding the first, it was known that there could be no free vote in the military. Always under the control of the Right, soldiers were obliged to vote as they were ordered, and the penalties for not doing so were heavy. As for the rider, naturally the Center wanted to have the right to determine its own electoral law should it be in power.

The Center parties insisted on a "service government" to conduct elections, a not unprecedented request in Greek political life. Service governments were made up of people who were not politicians and functioned only for the purpose of carrying on elections. This did not make them nonpolitical. They were normally rightist governments, chosen by the King, but they created the impression of neutrality and gave a psychological boost to the party not in power.

With no election date set, and the possibility that elections would not be held until the constitutional period of four years was up (1962), the Center parties spent the summer negotiating with each other, trying to find a formula for uniting into one party. Markezinis sent word to Papandreou that he was interested in joining the Democratic Center, Papandreou's party, giving up the leadership of his own Progressive party, but wanted control over the organization of the campaign. Markezinis was Minister of Coordination under Papagos, Prime Minister prior to Karamanlis, and was chief mover for the devaluation of the drachma, which turned out to be a successful monetary policy. It is said that in a heated discussion Markezinis may suddenly jump on top of his chair and continue his argument from there, arms flailing dramatically in the air. He had a passionate and dedicated small following in Athens, particularly among the businessmen who saw him as a financial wizard. I saw him often on the streets of downtown Athens, meticulously dressed, patent-leather pointed shoes, cane on arm, tipping his hat to the businessmen standing in their shop doors. My children have a book called "A Froggie Would A'Courtin' Go," and I was reminded of the cover picture every time I saw Mr. Markezinis.

Sophocles Venizelos, the son of the great Venizelos who governed Greece on and off during the second and third decades of this century, was maneuvering for a union of all Center parties under the direction of a governing council. The leader would be chosen after the Center won the elections. General George Grivas, a royalist known for his guerrilla exploits in helping the Cypriots to gain independence from England, wrote a letter to Papandreou asking him to withdraw from the leadership of the Center in order to facilitate union.

Every small party, every individual, had its own particular solution to the problem of unification. Insidiously the heat of the summer slowed the pulse of the most ardent political operators. Summer was not the time for politics in Greece. The lure of the sea, the islands, cool summer evenings of seashore dancing under the stars, long siestas, tourist-watching, made life pleasant and sweet, and the *mañana* philosophy prevailed.

Just as the deputies and party chiefs were beginning to emerge from summer political hibernation, Karamanlis announced elections for October 29. As stipulated by the Constitution, the announcement was made forty days ahead of the date of elections. The service government, consisting of a new Prime Minister, General Dovas, the chief of the royal military house staff, and Defense Minister Potamianos, the King's honorary general adjutant, as well as other new ministers, was installed on September 19.

The surprise announcement, which caught the Center parties off guard, was a shrewd move on the part of Karamanlis. Under the pressure of a specific election date, the Center parties quickly closed ranks and declared themselves a single party under the leadership of George Papandreou, with Venizelos second in command. The tardiness of this unification was a great campaign gift to ERE, which used it to play on the theme that the Center Union (the new name of the party) was rife with internal problems and difficulties and could not possibly give a stable government. In a country that had had a decade of war and civil strife, the theme of security and stability was a potent one.

The campaign got under way with speeches throughout Greece, and Andreas and I tagged along with the President's caravan like loyal camp followers, watching with elation the growing size and passion of the crowds. September went well. But by the beginning of October reports describing violence in some of the rural regions of Greece were coming in. On October 10 *Athinaiki* printed an editorial, entitled "The Terrorists," which began:

> *A gang is taking over Greece. The agents of this gang beat and violate, threaten and terrorize; they prevent gatherings, they forbid*

the distribution of free electoral materials, and they exercise dramatic pressure under which "free and objective" elections are supposed to take place. During the 18 days which separate us from the 29th of October, a worsening of this terrorism is promised . . . .

About this time Papandreou protested to the Minister of Interior and to the Prime Minister that his deputy candidates were reporting acts of violence in regions where they were campaigning. Officials intimated that the prime target was the far Left. This was supposed to give some respectability to the terrorism. Such activities, once started, draw no line, and the attack upon far leftists was enlarged to include democrats. Papandreou had been hoping to attract this group of left-of-center noncommunist voters during the campaign. He was positive that such terrorist tactics would cause them to refuse to vote, or to vote for ERE in order to appease their tormentors. The service government promised to disarm TEA, the paramilitary rightist force in Greece, saying they would do this a week before elections. This was supposed to insure freedom of elections! It gave verbal promises to Papandreou that it would strengthen its vigilance and look into reports of violence.

No change in the prevailing atmosphere occurred, however, and following reports of fresh outbreaks of terrorism, Papandreou issued a declaration sanctioning the right of his party's candidates to defend themselves and their people by all lawful means against the abuses of authority. In the middle of October he had an interview with King Paul and made a vigorous personal protest against the force and violence being used.

During this period, despite these indications of trouble ahead, we were excited and confident. There were many signs, even to an objective observer, that a bandwagon effect had begun, that the Center Union was "catching on" as a real alternative to the government of the past six years. The big question was: Was there time to translate this effect into a sufficient number of votes by October 29 to assure victory?

My father-in-law's charismatic leadership generated enthusiasm. But this was not a presidential election. He would become Prime Minister only by the election of enough deputies to give him a majority in Parliament. A deputy is voted in from a local district and local issues become paramount. In a country where the state is tied up with all activities—welfare, licensing, visas, admission to the university—the deputy of the party in power has a huge advantage. Patronage practices are excessive. Despite this, the Greek has a national pride, and if he is inspired by the leader of a party, he may choose that ballot at election time. Each party prints its own ballots of a color different from other parties. The voter chooses his ballot from piles laid out on a table in front of the people who act as clerks for the election. All of this is in clear view of the local policemen, party workers, secret service, etc. He can choose one color and go into the voting booth and vote "secretly." Or he can take all ballots, but must drop the unused ones in a basket ready for that purpose. Would voters choose the Papandreou "color"; would they be fearful under the conditions of voting, or would local considerations prevail?

At the beginning of the campaign ERE was confident. Karamanlis was putting on a statesmanlike show, making such statements as "I don't care whether you vote for me or the Center Union, as long as you don't cast a vote for EDA." He was trying to create the image of a national leader, above party politics. His first post-election declaration emphasized this theme: "I contributed to the results of the elections because of my fight against communists, but also by my electoral law for the benefit of the national opposition, risking for its sake, my majority and strength." What Karamanlis said about the electoral law was partially true, but it was because they had not chosen an electoral law more favorable to them that they had to resort to other methods to gain "majority and strength."

By the time we went to the last campaign speech in Patras, in the Peloponnesus, the confidence felt earlier by ERE had vanished. ERE supporters attending my father-in-law's speech were visibly disturbed by the overwhelming reception, the passion, the fervor. The crowd filled the large square of Patras and spilled over into the side streets.

I remember that night, one week before the elections. The President spoke from a balcony of an apartment house. I watched from an adjoining balcony and marveled at his power, the steady richness of his voice, the hypnotic rhythm of his speech. He was the maestro, the people his orchestra. He liked the sense of power he felt over the multitudes, the feeling of being in complete command, and from them he extracted the music he wanted—the rippling, joyous sounds as he struck with his wit, the applause as he made a solid serious point, the roars as he moved to his climax, when he held his right hand high out in front of him, the fingers spread as if he were casting a spell on his listeners, and suddenly rolled his hand into a fist, which came crashing down on the rostrum with brute force to emphasize the passion he felt for what he was saying. Although I had seen him several times by now, this Patras speech—coming as it did at the height of confidence and enthusiasm—was a work of art in the ancient Greek tradition of great oratory. He often said himself, and it was true, that he competed only with his speeches of the past, and all of Greece agreed, friends and foes, that no one could come close to his oratorical powers.

When he walked in from the balcony that night, he was tired but elated, his face flushed a healthy pink from the effort. His shirt and suit coat were wet from perspiration, and he moved immediately to a side room to wash and change his clothes. I knew that a portion of that time would go to combing his iron-gray mane of hair, thinning on the top, but wavy and long in the back. Then he emerged, ready for the accolades and bravos on his speech. He loved flattery; he expected it and accepted it enthusiastically, not with any smugness, but with a grin of boyish pleasure.

No matter how many times I saw this, it was always the same—as if he had just finished his first public performance and the local townspeople were saying, "That kid's got talent!" Sometimes one would catch him searching out the faces of his close friends while others were shaking hands and patting him on the back, his look saying, "You see—I did it!"

CHAPTER SIX

The Birth of the Unyielding Fight

ELECTION eve, October 29, 1961. Gathered at the home of George Papandreou in Kastri, we were a small group—unusually small, it occurred to me, for a national election in which Papandreou was the only significant challenger to the government in power. I thought of America and visualized a national election there: the restless crowd of relatives and party stalwarts, the phone systems, the switchboards, the cameramen, the television equipment. Would the aspiring candidate for the top post in the country closet himself away from the people, or was this peculiarly Greek? Or was it peculiarly my father-in-law?

He was across the room now, listening carefully to reports coming in from areas outside of Athens.

That night, from all appearances, was just another election for Papandreou. How many times had he been through this? Ten? Twenty? His political career stretched back to the days of Eleutherios Venizelos, a name that brings tears even today to the eyes of his compatriots—the tough, freedom-loving inhabitants of Crete. In 1914 Venizelos took the young, twenty-six-year-old Papandreou, fresh from a German university, and made him governor of the island of Lesbos. Two years later, he was made governor of the Aegean. From this beginning, he had by 1961 experienced five exiles and five imprisonments as the political winds shifted willy-nilly in this volatile land. In 1944 he had returned to Greece from Egypt as liberation premier. This was short-lived. When the civil war broke out, he resigned his post and was replaced by a succession of governments. Later he became deputy premier in a coalition government, and played a host of other roles—depending on which Athenian newspaper you read.

It had been a turbulent career, yet no scars remained, neither physically nor, as I came to know him, spiritually. In fact, one would assume by looking at him and by knowing him that the years had strengthened body and spirit. His tall powerful frame was straight, his complexion clear and pink, his movements sure and steady; all belied his age of 72. Ebullient and optimistic, he could wage a fight alone. He had none of the traditional institutions in the country behind him: the royal family, the army, or a "Greek institution"—the American Embassy. Members of his own party were not totally with him, and the majority of the press was against him.

Reports were coming in now from the Peloponnesus. Corinth, Olympia,

Nafplion, Tripolis, Argos. I had a childhood awe of the names of ancient places, but as polling precincts they didn't jibe with images I held. The Spartans should be getting ready for their battle with the Persians and their long overland march to Thermopylae. The Corinthians should be busy at their elaborate temple makings, their carvings, their bargaining at the agora. At the moment I wished they were. The votes showed a preference for the party of the Right, for the six-year-old government of Karamanlis. The President had said earlier that the early returns would establish the trend. I wanted to disbelieve him, to remember how false had been the early trend of Dewey over Truman in 1948.

Was my lay forecasting to be so off? I had predicted a close contest. Returns were showing wide disparity between the two parties. My opinion was similar to that of that noble body of men whom newspapers call political observers. The *Economist* in its confidential bulletin which circulated among foreign embassies had predicted collaboration between the Karamanlis party and the Center Union because according to the opinion of special correspondents it was impossible for the leader of ERE to get a majority, taking into consideration the usual attrition of votes that faced every party in power. *The New York Times* wrote the day after the election that "many observers had predicted a close race between Mr. Karamanlis' party and the Union of Center. . . ."

The forecasters I liked best, however, were the Greeks. Equipment for the game included a flat white package of Greek cigarettes—Papastratos or Aroma or Alpha would do—a stubby little pencil, ability at figures (which all Greeks have, by the way), and an argumentative capacity to prove that the statistics (his own) are correct. Columns were drawn and in them were written the number of seats from each area the party of choice would win in Parliament, explaining why Georgiades would win this time, why Tselos would lose, etc. It was called the numbers game, and it went on for months in every coffeehouse, in every taverna, in every home, in every political discussion. These were partisans, emotional and eloquent in showing that the statistics "prove" their party would come to power.

This night there was no cigarette package hypothesizing. The stark figures were coming in. There were no opportunities for cigarette-box manipulation. An assistant of the President had a huge electoral book in front of him and was making comparisons with the figures of 1958. Iowanna Papadatos was pouring drinks from the small upright desk my father-in-law used as a bar. Athens returns had not yet come in, and we clung to the tiny hope that the trend would be overturned here.

The President looked paler now. Most people had said it was Papandreou's last election, that a man of his age could not expect to maintain strength with the voters for another four years out of office and be considered a strong candidate at the age of seventy-six. Did the President think so, too? I doubt it. His boundless optimism and excitement with life would preclude any thoughts having to do with the "last time," or the "end" of a career. He had expected the race to be close.

We had spoken of it earlier in the day when he stopped by our home in Psyhico after casting his vote.

"Let us toast to good luck!" he said when I offered him a brandy.

He asked, "What is your prediction, Margarita?" as if we hadn't been discussing the issue for weeks now. "Now that it is election day, how do you see things?"

I took a few sips of brandy, relishing the fact that a year and a half in Greece had qualified me for making such a judgment. But then, I was merely appropriating the right of every Greek to have political opinions—and strong ones—on every political issue. I tried in my calculations not to be influenced by the massive crowds I had seen in Salonika, in Patras, in Athens, during the campaign, by the hoarse voices shouting, "Pap-an-dray-o!" "Save Greece!" "You we want!" I tried not to be influenced by my desire to see this man governing Greece.

"It will be 40-40-20," I said. "Forty percent for ERE, 40 percent for you, and 20 percent for EDA. And I consider it possible that you will have an edge on that 40 percent."

"Explain your reasoning," the President asked.

I launched into a rather pedantic analysis: "First of all, Karamanlis has been going down in popular appeal in each election. In 1956 he received 44 percent of the popular vote. In 1958 he received 41 percent of the popular vote. Furthermore, in 1958 there was no united Center opposition, but a smattering of small parties. None of these parties could have received a high percentage of popular votes so that many voters, rather than 'lose' their vote, cast it halfheartedly for Karamanlis or for the Left. Now there is a union of Center parties. So two factors work against him and for you," I said. "One is the attrition of a party in power, the other is the attractiveness of a potential winner in the opposition party."

My father-in-law looked pleased. He was enjoying the prediction and my attempts at analysis. I expected him to make the comment that such an occasion often brought out: "You are becoming a Greek." This was meant as a compliment and generally amused me because he rejected the notion that an American could become excited about political issues, at least not as excited and involved as the Greek. Later I proved how excited an American can get as an observer of American foreign policy in Greece!

"Furthermore," I continued, "it is apparent that Karamanlis feels that the heat is on. At the beginning of the campaign he tried to play a statesmanlike role by saying, 'Vote for me or any other nationalist party, so long as you don't give your vote to the communists.' Halfway through the campaign he stopped this talk. Now he considers you a threat."

I was feeling pleased and happy that afternoon, proud of my "erudite" comments on modern-day Greece. but I didn't realize one thing. All of my predictions were based on one assumption: that elections would be *free*.

Papandreou left our home in Psyhico that warm and pleasant Sunday, full of high hopes and stimulated by the fight. He was an anomaly in the political game. Where most men seemed dedicated to personal power, he was dedicated to principles. Where most men learned to become suspicious of another's motives and expect cutthroat activities, he was naïve to a fault, constantly being surprised by an amoral action. He was definitely a romantic, and sentimental, but he had the passion of an evangelist when it came to fighting for his ideals.

I was not the first to remark on this evangelistlike quality Papandreou displayed. In 1949 Max Eastman wrote in *Plain Talk* the following description of my father-in-law: "I found Papandreou in a modest fifth-floor apartment a few blocks from the American Embassy in Athens. Tall, handsome, large-featured, greyish-haired but vigorous, he had a warmth of glance and manner that suggest the evangelist more than the politician. We were to have 'coffee' together, but our coffee turned into a feast of reason, and when evening came, he invited me to lunch the next day. It was a genuine meeting of minds, and I have never met a mind that seemed more spontaneously humane and liberal."

When election day was over in October 1961, one felt that a cudgel had smashed down on the head of a child. But the defeat was greater than the defeat of one man, of one political party. It was a defeat for democracy.

We sat down to a midnight dinner. Seven remained out of the original small group. Characteristically my father-in-law was buoying up our spirits, but the election results were too stunning to allay our gloom. It appeared that Karamanlis would have 50 percent of the popular vote, Papandreou 35 percent, and the Left 15 percent.

Three things happened which confirmed our suspicion that the results did not reflect the true mood of the country. One was a midnight visit from a man who was politically active in Kavala, an area in northern Greece near the Turkish border. After spending the morning moving around to various voting places, he got in his car and drove the long journey down to Kastri. He arrived in a state of disarray and anguish. He described scenes of beatings and brutality which he had witnessed on the spot. And he described the condition in which many voters appeared at the polls, bruised and battered, proclaiming publicly that they were voting for ERE.

The second event was a telephone call from an Athenian newspaperman. There is no tradition in Greece for the loser of a national election to "concede" his defeat, a much more humane practice than our American one. Since no concession was expected, the newspaperman was obviously calling for another purpose. Andreas went to the phone. After some preliminary discussion, the newspaperman, according to Andreas, shouted, "It stinks! The whole thing stinks! Even the government is scared. Their majority is too large. What does your father have to say? Will he make a statement?"

The President would not make a statement.

The next call was from a member of the American Embassy, whom we knew.

"Sorry about your father," he started out. "How's he taking it?"

"He's not saying" was the reply. "A man knows when he's been taken."

Silence. And then some fishing.

"Well, apparently Karamanlis had more strength than was expected. His development program—"

"Balls!" was Andreas' retort.

"Well, don't let him get excited and do something drastic!"

Such as? we wondered. Challenging the results of the election? The Americans had adopted Karamanlis back in 1955 and have that curious trait, as George Kennan said, of making it appear "reprehensible to voice anything less than unlimited optimism about the fortunes of another government one has adopted as a friend and protégé." Having concluded that Karamanlis was America's best bet, they didn't want to rock the boat, or have it rocked by someone else.

The newspapers carried the results the next day. Headlines in the foreign press were "Mr. Karamanlis' Success Creates Basis for Greater Western Help," "The Demolishing of Communism Characterized as Great Victory for Western World," "The Greeks Voted for Stability and Peace." The percentage of votes for Karamanlis was now edging over 50 percent and the military and civil-service vote, done separately by the electoral law, had not been counted yet. A couple of London papers had some difficulty explaining this "smashing and impressive" victory. The London *Times* tried in this way:

> *The result is a triumph for Karamanlis. His party remains in government after six years, an unprecedented event in postwar years. . . . Those who predicted differently did not count on the idiosyncrasy of the Greek people. They respect the real value of stability and progress. In spite of the large unemployment which exists, and the expansion of Athens at the expense of the rest of the country, the general picture of Greece is good. Despite the bad chapter of Cyprus, the Greek people do not want to return to this chapter. . . . The political life of Greece is an unending adventure.*

From another London paper:

> *The results of the Greek election were received with great surprise by the political British circles. A representative of the foreign office waiting for the final results, said yesterday that the first results proved him wrong entirely, because he expected different results, given the fact that a percentage of "wear and tear" always occurs in the power of the party in government. . . .*

And what about the Athenian newspapers? In 1961 there were thirteen daily papers in Athens, a city with a population of one and a half million people. All the newspapers had strong party affiliations and strong political opinions. Those listing themselves an independent felt they achieved this independence by occasionally writing an editorial urging caution and moderation rather than extremist views. Each political division had its yellow press: the Right, *Acropolis*; the Center, *Athinaiki*; and the Left, *Avghi*. Both Right and Center had newspapers which tried to maintain higher standards of journalism. For the Right, *Kathimerini* and *Mesimvrini*, and for the Center, *Ethnos*, *Vhima*, *Ta Nea*, and *Eleftheria*. None of these papers, as might be guessed from the number, was self-supporting. They were all subsidized in varying degree by the government. Even with opposition newspapers, the government exercised a modicum of control.

The government newspapers announced the results of the election with elation, and one newspaper, *Acropolis*, analyzed the election as follows:

> *A large percentage of Center voters voted for ERE. In some areas it was noted that even some members of the Left voted for ERE.*
>
> *On the other hand, a large number of EDA followers voted for the Center. This explains the fact that in spite of the fact that a large percentage of Center people voted for ERE, the Center maintained its percentage of voters from 1958.*
>
> *In other words, the 10 percent which EDA lost during yesterday's election went to the Center, while a large percent of the old voters of the Center voted for Karamanlis.*

In an editorial it stated how rare a feat was the total victory of Karamanlis: "For the first time in the political history of Greece a political figure is chosen as prime minister for three consecutive years with the order to continue for four more. Even on the international scene very seldom cases like this occur."

The explanations for this stunning victory were particularly difficult to give without referring to Plan Pericles, the army scheme later brought to light for the carrying out of the 1961 elections!

Although Papandreou two days after election had not yet come out with a public statement, rumblings in the government press made it clear that he was going to challenge the results of the election. On October 31 *Acropolis* took it upon itself to point out the role of the Center.

> *The Center Union for its interests and for the sake of the nation must definitely abandon its bankrupt and old party methods and should become a strong, constructive national opposition. It is not going to gain the trust of the Greek people by trying to justify its electoral defeat with continuing noise about "traumocratia"—force and fraud in elections.*

What would the role of the Center Union be? How far had fraud and force gone, and to what extent had it affected the final tally? For two nights and days my father-in-law pondered this question. He spent every moment talking to people from all sections of Greece. He called in his deputies for reports from their areas. He checked and rechecked. What he heard, what was said, what was done, he compiled and eventually published in a book entitled *The Black Book of Elections, 1961.*

On November 1 he came out with the following statement:

> *I charge in the name of the Center Union; I charge before the Greek people and the King that the election results were the product of force and fraud. The public knows that the percentage of votes which gave the mandate to ERE to govern is the product of force*

and fraud. The Service Government of General Dovas, either willingly or unwillingly became completely non-existent, allowing the illegal mechanism of ERE to perform without hindrance. The Center Union would be unworthy of the trust of the Greek people and would betray the flag of democracy under the name in which it fought, if it were to accept without protest the strangulation of the will of the Greek people. If the results of the election of October 29 were to be accepted without protest, democracy would cease to exist in its ancient seat. With complete knowledge of its historical responsibility, the Center Union considers it a duty to proclaim that the government which ERE is going to form is not a legal government of the Greek people, and the Center Union will make its decisions for the present and the future accordingly.

On the same day that Papandreou denounced the results of the election, the returns from the army and civil servants vote came in. *Seventy-eight percent for ERE!*

When it appeared that the Center Union was not going to play the role of constructive and benign opposition, the government got angry. This was reflected in editorials in all of its newspapers attacking Papandreou. Again, quoting from *Acropolis*, the following was written:

Mr. Papandreou gave the last blow yesterday to the Center Union. His statement that the electoral results were a product of violence and fraud created against him a wave of general protest, national wrath and disgust. Mr. Papandreou's target is actually the Greek people. It is they whom he wants to flagellate because they refused again to give him their trust. In his blind attempt, however, to doubt the will of the majority of the people, Mr. Papandreou threw himself into the arms of the Communist Party, becoming an organ of it— and actually without any returns.

Who is the Greek who would not rejoice for all these blessings which were secured by the vote of the people? And who is the Greek who would not want to help his country to exploit its bounty? All of them except the Communists and Mr. Papandreou.

It is a sorry ending to his political career, this antinational stance . . . . if we had elections tomorrow, he wouldn't even be a deputy. The Greek people do not accept political men who because of their rage rip into the side of nationalism. It is a blot on his political history which will always remain.

Papandreou's career had come full circle if one were to take the accusations made against him by much of the liberal foreign press in 1944, and now by the government press in 1961. Now he was considered a "handmaiden of communism." Then when his Government of National Unity moved to Athens from Egypt, and he became the liberation premier, Churchill sent British troops with him to protect his government against insurrection, and he was denounced in the foreign papers as an agent of British imperialism, his government "reactionary" and "monarcho-fascist."

Papandreou was neither of these two things. He believed fervently in democracy, was against totalitarianism from either right or left. But his sympathies were with the West. He showed me a letter which he wrote while in the underground in July 1943, while the Germans still held Athens and all Europe. It was sent to the Greek government-in-exile and the British Headquarters in the Near East.

> Today a new form of antagonism is taking shape. Two world-wide fronts are being formed: Communist Pan Slavism and Anglo-Saxon Liberalism. . . .
>
> Russia, after the present war, will become the strongest offensive power, a menace to Europe. . . . The dissolution of the Comintern was a fraud. . . .
>
> The Greek communists will attempt to seize power after the occupation, not to impose a Soviet Democracy at once, but so that they may form the Coalition Government and dictate its composition. . . . Their final goal will be: internally a Dictatorship of the Greek Communist Party; externally a subjugation of Greece to the U.S.S.R.

This expressed Papandreou's conviction about the situation in Greece in 1943, and it was on the basis of this belief that he developed his strategy on his return to Greece in 1944 as Prime Minister. He has been credited with keeping Greece out of the communist orbit and did so in a climate of liberal world opinion which was often very much against him.

In the United States, for instance, *The Nation* on December 23, 1944, described the situation in an article by Constantine Poulos:

> For from the moment that Papandreou returned to peaceful, orderly, awakened Greece every attempt was made by him, by his rightist ministers, by nationalist, royalist and fascist organizations, and by the Leeper holding company to destroy the power of the Left. Thousands of traitors and quislings were permitted to roam freely around Athens. No collaborators were called to trial or punished by the government. Royalist organizations were secretly armed. Members of the Nazi-organized Security Battalions were spirited out of prison and armed. Wild stories of red terrorism were fed to the local and foreign press. High officials in the various ministries who had faithfully served the Nazi and quisling governments were kept in their posts. . . .

Now, in 1961, the charges on the part of the government press were to vary between claiming Papandreou was a dupe of communism (stupidity) to a collaborationist with the communists (conspiracy). It had become popular and quite effective for the rightist governments since the end of the civil war to tie the label of communism on any troublesome opposition leader. This was to happen again when Andreas entered politics.

It was now Papandreou's turn to wear the label "communist." He had the audacity to challenge the results of the election. Except for a splinter group of Markezinis' Progressives (thirteen deputies), the rest of the party was uniting more firmly under Papandreou's leadership as well as under the force of public reaction and pressure.

What were the people saying after election day, 1961? It was perhaps more what they were *not* saying. The Greek is very astute politically. He has suffered the abuse of authority for hundreds of years. After four centuries of Turkish rule, he won his independence. And in that year, 1829, began the struggle for democracy. It wasn't only independence from foreign powers that the Greek wanted; he wanted his personal independence and freedom to choose his leaders. And he wanted guarantees of civil liberties which would free him from the yoke of totalitarian and authoritarian regimes. With few exceptions, he got instead wars and poverty, corruption and mismanagement, a four-year dictatorship under Metaxas, the Italian invasion, the German occupation, a civil war, and orders from the British first, then the Americans, on how to govern his country. He was to get even more, as fate had it.

What the Greek understood on October 30 when the tabulation of votes was completed was just how far indeed the government's power had gone, and he also knew his future might depend on how loudly and vocally he condemned the government for its actions.

A Cretan who occasionally drove our car for us had found his name scratched from the voting district he had always voted in. It was late in the day when he went to vote, and he was told that he would have to take his protest to a central building in downtown Athens. He found hundreds of people outside the central building waiting to find out what had happened to their voting privileges. Most of these people never found out because the polls closed before the protests could be processed. Then he told me that he still wanted to check on why he had lost his right to vote, but that his wife and father were begging him to forget it. "But," he said, "I lost my right to vote, and I am not a communist. I have medals for having caught two outstanding communists in the Greek mountains of the Peloponnesus when I was a member of the *horofiliki* [village police]!" He then related, without my urging, the details of this capture. His entire point was to prove to me that he had no communist connections, and he did this with anger, but also with fear.

Two days later I asked our governess, Louiza, if she had read that my father-in-law had threatened to take to court three members of the service government for negligence of duty. She looked around warily, warned me to lower my voice, then went and closed the door between the hallway and the kitchen, which as far as I knew contained only our cook, peeling potatoes.

"It's only Tasia," I explained.

"Don't trust anyone" was her retort.

The usually garrulous taxi drivers were silent when questioned about the results of the election. Prior to elections all voiced their opinions readily and vociferously. After that day questions on my part brought silence or something to the effect that it's over with now, what can we do?

In this climate Papandreou began his fight. The challenge, despite its difficulties, attracted him, and I am sure he felt that going down in the twilight of his career fighting for a principle—the right of the people to choose their government through free elections—was superior to no fight at all. We were proud to be witnesses to the birth of the unyielding fight.

CHAPTER SEVEN

American Support for Fixed Elections

ERE'S vote increased from 41 percent of the total vote in 1958 to 50 percent in 1961, its seats from 171 to 176. The Center Union received 34 percent of the total vote cast, giving it 100 seats in Parliament. EDA dropped from the 24 percent it had in 1958 to 14 percent, giving it 24 seats.

While the Center Union was recovering from the loss of the election and trying to stake out its future course, it received its first internal blow. The government had predicted this when its press said, "It must be remembered that the Center Union, built from the party of Papandreou, Agricultural party, Group of Ten, and the Progressive party, *is not going to remain together*"—and thus the blow hurt more. The leader of the Progressive party, Markezinis, declared his departure from the Center Union. He announced: "I did not expect the results of the election. How it happened and its consequences for our country, I will evaluate in time. The Progressive party, conscious of its increased responsibility because its power has increased (from two to eleven seats) through the elections, is going to follow the same road as in the past—responsibility in the new situation." Part of his rush to withdraw from the Center Union was his disagreement with those members who were pushing for abstention or resignation from Parliament.

My father-in-law likened Markezinis' statement of "responsibility" to a man who had just been robbed but didn't cry out "thief, thief," as the burglar made his getaway. Markezinis was going to take the electoral coup with his mouth shut. Although it meant a loss of eleven members, Papandreou was pleased. He had never liked the alliance with Markezinis, the Machiavelli of Greece's political world.

We watched and waited to see how many "soldiers of democracy," as Papandreou called them, would remain with the party. There were many rumors. Baltatzis would quit and take his small Agricultural party with him. Papapolitis was considering withdrawing. Venizelos would split over tactics. Elias Tsirimokos was decidedly against abstention from Parliament.

By November 5, a week after election, two independent members of the Center Union had withdrawn. This left the strength of the party at eighty-seven seats in Parliament. No major groups outside of Markezinis had broken away, but the cement holding the groups together was wet, and time and skill would be needed for it to harden.

On this day Papandreou addressed the Greek people through the newspaper

Eleftheria and told them: "Have courage. Remain loyal and faithful under our honest flag. They were able to perform fraud, but they will not be able to dishonor or conquer us. Maintain your faith. According to your wish we remain united. We have taken a decision to fight to the end for democracy. With the support of all the free and proud Greeks, and with the support of the inspired Greek youth, Democracy shall be re-established in its birthplace."

The government's response to this in *Kathimerini* was that "we hope that after the first days of neurotic behavior which pushes them into acts of desperation and superficiality and the use of strong words, there will be a more positive understanding of reality. . . ."

Five major newspapers in Athens began to support the battle in varying degrees: *Vhima, Ta Nea, Eleftheria, Ethnos,* and *Athinaiki.* The discussion in the newspapers was beginning to turn toward the strategy of the Center Union. What would or should it do vis-à-vis Parliament? Abstain? Resign? Go to the Chamber and fight? There were as many opinions within the party as there were outside. The people were beginning to talk again after their initial silence—how could a Greek *not* talk politics? The President's private view was for resignation from Parliament by all members of the newly formed Center Union. It was the dramatic and powerful thing to do, and would certainly have proved the seriousness and sincerity of the opposition charges. In order to be effective, all members of the Center Union would have to resign, and all were not by any means that ready. The Greek hated to give up present limited power for potential future big power. He is a skillful rationalizer and can find brilliant arguments to justify his action.

It is fair to state that in this case there was also a difference of opinion as to how effective a mass resignation would be. Would it force Karamanlis to new elections—the avowed aim of the Center Union—or would he merely fill the vacated seats with the next in line within the Center Union, the men with the next most votes? And could they be counted on to refuse a parliamentary seat? Karamanlis had the power to do this. Or would he function without a full house? Those who opposed resignation also had another fear: they would lose their public forum. Virtually all political news emanates from the sessions of Parliament. If they were to carry on this struggle for the reestablishment of democracy, they needed to have a platform. In addition a deputy had privileges and a modicum of power, which he would have to forego.

My father-in-law saw quickly that he could not go all the way. Andreas felt this was lack of vision on the part of the deputies, but George Papandreou accepted their reluctance to participate in a big gamble. He chose instead a compromise road, abstaining from Parliament on opening day, the day of the speeches of the King and Prime Minister. His party took their oath of office later "with reservations."

What had been the role of the American Embassy in these political events of Greece? One thing was clear: They had wanted a Karamanlis victory. They wanted a weakened Left, a moderately strong Center, and a victory of the Right. This hope was apparent in their enthusiastic support for the kindred party system. It was apparent in conversations with embassy personnel prior to the elections. It became increasingly apparent after the election when they took the attitude "What's all this fuss about?" They stayed away from all opposition personalities to make sure that no one would have the opportunity to mistake this for support of the opposition position. They made the galling comment that "Greece is not a western-style democracy ... this sort of force and fraud has occurred in Greek elections ... furthermore, we don't believe it accounts for a huge percentage of votes...."

The argument continued, there is a "western-style democracy" and an "eastern-style democracy," and we Americans should be flexible enough to tolerate local differences. This "eastern-style" permits tampering with the freedom to vote, particularly if that tampering is in the right direction. It is often said that the United States cannot impose its style of democracy on other nations. It is unfortunate, perhaps, that this is the one thing the United States has not tried to impose. It has imposed other systems of government, specializing, and I say this sorrowfully, in dictatorship.

At Christmas time it is customary that the United States Ambassador send a Christmas message to Americans in Greece and to Greeks living in America. This would have been the ideal time to have asserted American faith in democracy in general, with free elections as a principle, without judging the rightness or wrongness of the opposition charges. Or he could have avoided any reference to the elections and sent good wishes and greetings. Instead, Ambassador Briggs sent a message that repudiated the fight of the Center and whitewashed the government—clearly, one more service to a government that America wanted to protect and preserve. Briggs was an elegant, cultured gentleman with a beautiful use of the English language. He chose his words to achieve a purpose. His message represented deliberate interference in the internal affairs of Greece, interference which by then, 1961, had become an ingrained habit of the Americans.

For the period 1947 to 1957, Americans poured into Greece one million dollars a day in economic and military aid in the effort to keep Greece in the western orbit. There is no doubt that starting from that point, the United States played an active role in the destiny of the Greek people.

In 1955, upon the death of Papagos, a former army general who led his Greek Rally party to victory in 1952, the Americans handpicked his successor, the young Minister of Public Works in the government, Constantine Karamanlis. This was done officially by the King, who gave him the mandate to form government, stepping over the man in line for the succession of the party leadership, Stephanos Stephanopoulos. With the King's and the Americans' blessings, Karamanlis got his party's vote of confidence, and later won elections on his own. The Americans argued at the time that Greece needed a stable government, a stabilization of the drachma, etc., for economic development, and that an uncontroversial, untried but capable man would do the job. It was not an honest argument, since economic growth during the period 1950-53, when governments came and went at the rate of one every six months, was a healthy 7 percent. From that point on Karamanlis bore the curse or the blessing of being considered "America's boy," "made by the Americans," the "pet of the United States," etc.

58

The normal functioning of the American Embassy in a country like Greece, particularly when economic aid is involved, makes the United States appear to be allied with the party in power. But this was not enough. Once having created the government, the United States took a paternalistic attitude toward it, protecting it, displaying it proudly to the world, collaborating with it. Slowly it seemed that the fate of the United States in Greece was tied up with the success of ERE, not with the people, nor with the strong democratic forces there.

The embassy ceased seeing members and leaders of the opposition parties in any public way, except at an occasional large reception (Fourth of July, for instance), where all political parties were included. The embassy argued that any contact on a social level was exploited by the opposition, that the Center press tried to claim that the embassy was "changing its policy." This latter was true. Whenever a contact was made, it became a big news item in the opposition newspapers, precisely because it was so rare it was possible to make it headline news. In one instance my father-in-law was invited to the ambassador's home for the first time in years. There was wild speculation on the part of journalists. If these meetings had been scheduled routinely, as a matter of course, and carried out through all stages of crisis or political trouble, so as not to show American favor or disfavor with opposition activities, the opportunities for "exploitation" in the press would have diminished considerably.

Some contact was made clandestinely by lower staff members of the American Embassy's political section with the minor lights of the opposition parties. Contacts of the American military and the CIA with their Greek counterparts were likewise clandestine, but for other reasons. However, when the Sixth Fleet anchored in Phaleron Bay, there was no doubt in the mind of the Greek as to where the cards lay. The professed stance of neutrality by the embassy was belied by its actions.

Ambassador Briggs' Christmas message of 1961 was the epitome of this identification. I quote: "We are among people who believe as we do in personal freedom and in the dignity of the individual: *elections here last October testified to those beliefs* [italics mine]; nearly two million Greek-Americans living in the United States multiply that testimony."

Some days later I ran into an acquaintance of mine, a fifty-year-old teacher of Greek and French, a wonderful Greek woman with a solid set of values, a no-nonsense approach to life, and that low, strong voice of a Katina Paxinou. She boomed at me from some distance on a street near Patission where I was shopping for children's clothes: "Kiria Papandreou! Ti kanoun? Ti kanoun, oi Amerikanoi?" "Mrs. Papandreou! What in hell are they doing, the Americans?" She ran up to me, grabbed me by the arm, and pushed me to a safe spot up against a building and shouted again, "What are the Americans doing? What does that 'Briks' mean in his message? Doesn't he have eyes? What do the Americans stand for?" I had no good answer. In fact, I had no answer at all. I wished I could defend what the embassy had done. There was no defense.

Eleftheria carried the Center Union's response:

> The Center Union, expressing the immediate reaction of the people to the message said the following: "The Center Union is deeply sorry for that part of the message of the Ambassador of the United States in which he said that the 'elections of October demonstrated faith to the ideals of freedom and human dignity.' This statement is doubly unacceptable. First, because it is an interference in the internal political life of Greece and the issue of a sharp fight, and, second, because it does not correspond to the truth. During the elections of October, exactly the opposite happened. The freedom and dignity of the individual was violated. Democracy—the common ideal of the Greeks and the great American people—was violated."

In addition to this newspaper statement, the Center Union took the only other action it could to demonstrate its opposition to the American Embassy: it boycotted the farewell cocktail party given for Ambassador Briggs, who was leaving for a new post.

CHAPTER EIGHT

A Man with Two Countries

ANDREAS and I were deeply troubled by the manipulation of elections of November 1961 with the use of the state machinery, the Greek army, and knowledge and support of the Americans.

The Christmas message of Ambassador Briggs appeared the day before Andreas was scheduled to fly to America to attend the American Economics Association Convention. His agenda was as follows: the convention in New York, a few days in Washington to see officials in AID to try to get additional funds for the Center of Economic Research, a flight to Chicago to spend New Year's Eve with my parents, New York again for talks with the Rockefeller and Ford foundations. He decided to add to this agenda a trip to the White House for private discussions with men close to President Kennedy.

Andreas was leading a schizoid life in many ways. Greek by birth, American by naturalization, he would see events one day through the eyes of a Greek, the next through the eyes of an American. He felt in this case, however, that in talking to American officials about America's role in Greece, he was doing something compatible with both his personalities. United States involvement in the internal affairs of Greece was harmful to both countries. One of President Kennedy's avowed aims was to put the CIA under strict control. Its special status as an independent body gave it prerogatives in foreign policy not necessarily sanctioned by the State Department. The formation of foreign policy in the United States is already remote from the people, but when it remains in the hands of the State Department, the people have some indirect control through Congress. In the hands of the CIA, they have no control. At the White House Andreas saw several members of the White House staff, among them Carl Kaysen, special adviser to the President. Carl arranged a meeting between him and Phillips Talbot, then chief head of Near East and Middle East affairs in the State Department. Talbot's reception was cordial, and he listened attentively to what Andreas had to say. Little did either know that they would one day be facing each other in different roles in Greece itself, for Talbot was to become Ambassador to Greece in 1965. Shortly after Andreas' visit to Washington, Laughlin Campbell was transferred to Paris, a move attributed to Andreas' intervention, which earned him the enmity of the CIA in America.

Rumors of Andreas' activities floated back to Greece. By the time he returned, a newspaper declared that he had made the trip to try to unseat the

Greek government. Any doubts the government had about working with the research center were nourished by this story. All contacts between the economic ministries and the Center were cut off, and the life of this scientific project was in danger. Although its financial contribution was not great, without the cooperation of the Greek government the center could not exist. Having been finally launched, with great difficulties, the research center now suffered a setback by the hostile attitude of the Karamanlis government.

The political picture was disheartening and murky. On January 9, 1962, a rainy winter evening, the Center deputies went to Parliament after Christmas recess to take their oath of office "with reservations." The government was annoyed with the stance of the Center Union, but it displayed a cocky smugness along with a paternalistic attitude: "Let the boys play . . . they will lose interest after a while and the fuss will fizzle out." ERE felt confident that the internal strife within this loose-jointed federation of Center parties would shatter the unity so necessary to fight successfully against the power structure. Those of us close to Papandreou felt with sadness that their appraisal was accurate.

With poor prospects, my father-in-law proceeded with the battle he had decided a few days after elections to wage, a battle which soon got the name "anendotos," or "unyielding fight," because of its intensity and uncompromising nature.*

We were reaching the first anniversary of our return to Greece to set up the Center of Economic Research. The children were settling down to their new life. George had transferred from the Psyhico public elementary school to fourth grade at Athens College, the school his father had attended as a boy. It was a private school, on 240 acres of wooded grounds, a few blocks from where we lived on Guizi Street, and the inspiration of Homer Davis, an American from California, who started the school with one building and a handful of boys in 1923. Under his dynamic leadership and with American funds, public and private, it grew into a huge campus and maintained high academic standards. Boys competed for entry through examination, but although Davis tried to be tough about this, government pressures were so great that boys with political connections were favored.

George was taken "on probation," his Greek still being rudimentary at examination time. Andreas had been one of Davis' first and best students, and so George was given a chance. By the end of the year George was on the honor roll, an academic feat which he was not to achieve later when his interest in school diminished. Because most of the governments had been rightist governments, and because the school had a substantial tuition fee, the majority of the boys were conservative politically, and although the teasing didn't seem to bother George, their value system did. He felt alienated from his classmates.

*Later it was to be called the "first anendotos." The second started with the overthrow of Papandreou by the King, when a fight for the constitutional rights of the Greek citizen began, this time under the leadership of Andreas. Greek workers and students living outside of Greece today identify themselves as the "kids of the first anendotos," or the "kids of the second anendotos," those who turned out for demonstrations and who worked in one or the other political movements. Many of these fighters for a progressive and democratic Greece have left their native land.

George is a quiet boy, a bit diffident, but with a great inner strength and an unswerving honesty, an honesty that eventually brought him in conflict with his grandfather. He never failed to state his opinions when asked about Greece, Greek political life, or Greece versus America. This he did in the face of an imposing and commanding personality—his grandfather. As he grew older, he didn't hesitate to criticize his grandfather's actions, and to a man accustomed to flattery, this was almost treason from a grandson. The relationship between them became distant. The traits that make him today a part of the young rebel generation, a distaste for what he saw as hypocrisy or dishonesty or servility, flowered surprisingly in a culture where deviousness and shrewdness, pulling one off on somebody, were ranked as admirable traits. He had one close friend, Pericles, also an Athens College student, who shared these attitudes.* If one asked George as a ten-year-old where he preferred to live, the answer was always America.

Sophia, who has two names—her American one, Gayle, and her Greek one, Sophia, after her grandmother Papandreou—seemed to be equally happy in one country or the other. A brown-eyed, sweet-faced child, she asked for nothing and gave much. She had a deep understanding of people, a wisdom beyond her eight years, and a cheerful cooperativeness in all activities.

The other two children were too young to have it make any great difference to them where they lived.

The question of where we were to live had come up again, and the unuttered question of the first winter, "Had we made the right decision?" was now part of our daily discussions. Andreas had come to Greece as a Greek-American to help develop a scientific research center, an activity which we had committed at least five years to—the length of time of the Rockefeller and Ford foundations grants. We had assumed at the time that it would be a more permanent move, but we were free to change our minds. Andreas had not severed his connection with the University of California and was on a leave of absence. Andreas felt he had given the Center a good start (in one year, in fact, it had turned out a prodigious number of excellent studies), and he hoped it would continue to produce fine work. He was not hopeful that any constructive use would be made of these studies. He felt that the entire political climate was negative, that the reactionary forces would do anything to maintain the status quo, that the fixing of an election was the mildest of measures they were prepared to take in order to halt liberal forces. The Palace, with its concept of Greece as a vassal state, the army with its tanks ready to overrun democratic forces, and the American-NATO contingent ready to back up both to keep Greece strategically under control, all worked against the possibility of a truly democratic Greece.

We were reluctant to leave the "old man," whose unyielding fight was an inspiration to everyone. The eighty-seven deputies were remaining together, and the people, after their first stage of shock and fear, were showing that

*The father of Pericles was forced to leave Greece after that fateful day of April 21, 1967, as have so many fine humanists, and Pericles is now attending school in Cleveland, Ohio.

they intended to continue to support the cause of freedom and democracy. In April of 1962 we got our first view of a police state in action. It was the 23rd of that month, and George Papandreou was scheduled to speak at an outdoor rally in Athens. The day before the speech, the government of Mr. Karamanlis announced that the rally was forbidden, in the interests of public order. The enthusiasm for the unyielding fight was beginning to concern ERE, and it turned to methods which generally tend to boost that enthusiasm—force and intimidation.

My father-in-law refused to call off the rally. Andreas and I joined with two friends and went downtown early to get a place near the square where the speech would be given. I brought my movie camera along and got some of the first shots of hordes of policemen trooping out of the downtown headquarters where they had been given instructions on how to handle the crowd. We wandered through the square, which was rapidly filling up, then walked to streets beyond it to see what, if anything, was going on. Up to then things had been peaceful. It was apparent now that a scheme had been worked out. At a certain time, the square would be surrounded by a thick cordon of police. From that square a mass of policemen would move out, in lines, like a big snowplow, pushing in front of them people who were approaching. When they reached the next block, a line of them would be left in a defense position, and the rest would continue with their sweeping. Eventually, they would clear the area for some four to five square blocks around the area of the speech, sealing off the square like a caterpillar in a reinforced cocoon. Anyone trying to reach the speech after that would have to pass the barricades, lines of helmeted, club-swinging policemen. The people had been gathering peacefully enough, but as they started getting shoved and pushed by the police, they reacted with shouting and cursing. They had not brought stones or weapons with them, nor were they asking for a fight.

Someone standing next to me at one point when we were being jostled by the crowd said, "You are an American. See what your country is doing to us? Tell your people!" I was disgusted with America's role in Greece, but I represented to that man a country, not an individual within that country. It was not pleasant to feel this hostility. When I held up my camera to take pictures, he said to me again in English, "Take pictures, take lots of pictures. Show them to your compatriots!"

I did take lots of pictures, until I had a run-in with the police. One officer saw me pointing my camera at a scene where fifteen policemen were chasing a young boy and trying to hit him. I suddenly felt a hand make a stab at my camera and try to pull it out of my hand. I didn't let go, and found myself in a tug-of-war with a member of the gendarmerie of the ERE government. It wasn't fun. As I tugged, his nails dug into the flesh of my hand and broke off three of my long fingernails. Andreas, who had gotten separated from me, turned up at the scene just as a second policeman shouted, "Let her go. She's an American!" He let me go.

We were not able to get to the square by this time, and we walked back to the offices of the Center of Economic Research. From a fifth-floor window facing Panapistimiou Street, we saw the skirmishes between police and young

Athenians who tried to break the lines. The streets had been cleared of civilian traffic and only Jeeps and army trucks patrolled up and down. In front of the Parliament building, a portion of which we could see from our windows, was a lineup of canvas-topped trucks, olive gray, waiting for orders in case reinforcements were needed. The Greeks I talked to were shocked. They said it reminded them of the time of the German occupation.

My mouth dropped as I saw the figure of a squat, squarish woman, streaks of white in her hair, approach a police line, argue, then turn around and point up to our office window, shouting "Kiria Margarita, yasoo!" She turned again and said something to the policemen; they opened up their line and she passed through. It was Louiza. She was on her way to hear my father-in-law's speech. After she passed the first barrier, she told me the next day, she merely told each new line of policemen that the last line had given her permission to go to the square. She didn't tell me exactly how she broke through the first line, right under our window, but I could guess that it was a combination of saying she belonged to the Papandreou family and had a right to be near the President, and her authoritarian manner. The woman who makes it in a male culture like Greece *really* makes it. I admired these women then—tough, competent, bright—and I learned to admire them more after April 21, 1967, when at times I felt they had more guts than the men.

We spent the rest of the spring and summer peacefully enough, falling in love with Greece more deeply as the knowledge that we were leaving her again hit home. The decision had been made, for the second time, to return to the United States. It would be hard to analyze the factors that went into making this decision, but I think primarily it was that the vision Andreas had of helping significantly his own country had turned out only to be a dream.

Toward the end of the summer we took a trip back to Skyros with Andreas' father, and one to Paros, and savored the beauty of the islands and these quiet, relaxed moments with the President. The spell of Greece was still on us, and when Andreas swore that he was leaving Greece "for good," it was an oath he took, like the Center Union party's, "with reservations."

Our year back at the University of California was fruitful. Andreas finished a book, *Economics as a Science,* and we had the pleasure of returning to a community of friends whom we loved. Despite this, our thoughts turned constantly to Greece, and we read with avid interest the Greek newspapers sent to our house, and any news on Greece in the local and foreign press. When Andreas got word from some of his colleagues at the research center that things were going poorly without him, that the promising start of the first year was now fizzling, he wondered whether he shouldn't give it a boost by directing it for one more year before turning it over completely to new leadership. Our home was still in Psyhico, rented out for the year to an American Fulbright professor. In Berkeley we ourselves were renting a professor's house. We pledged, however, to make only a one-year commitment, and as if to assure our return, we purchased a lot for building in the Berkeley hills.

Just shortly after we made our new decision, we heard the news of the conflict between the Palace and Karamanlis. It was spring of 1963. Karamanlis had advised Paul and Frederika not to make a trip to London because of recent antiroyal and antigovernment demonstrations organized by the Britishers protesting the continuing imprisonment of people involved in the guerrilla war of 1949. In addition, a popular deputy of EDA, Christos Lambrakis, had been killed at a political rally in Salonika, and word had it that this had received the sanction of official circles, including the Palace. This was expected to offer further provocation to the demonstrating forces.* Frederika did not heed the advice of the government and went anyway, only to be chased down a street near her hotel by a protesting group and forced to seek shelter in a private home. This experience undoubtedly did not make Karamanlis' advice sit any better with her. She had challenged Karamanlis' authority and judgment, and he had been proved right. It was, as well, a violation of the Constitution, since the royal family is supposed to move only with the advice and consent of the government in power. The Constitution, however, was never taken seriously by the Palace.

All of this led to a deeper rift between Karamanlis and the royal family. Karamanlis had been in power for eight years, had developed his own loyalties within the army, and was getting too powerful for the powerful Frederika. When Karamanlis offered his resignation and called for new elections, King Paul accepted this and chose a Palace man—Pipinelis, a member of the party of ERE, to form a caretaker government and go to elections. Under pressure from George Papandreou, and particularly from the American Embassy, which decided this time to tip the scales toward a liberal democratic government, King Paul dropped Pipinelis and chose a neutral premier, Mavromichaelis, a jurist, to take the country to elections. For King Paul it was not a difficult move, for he realized that as long as an ERE man headed the government, Karamanlis had a good chance of reelection. Shifting service government premiers was an anti-Karamanlis move. The former premier's challenge to royal power could not be accepted.

What caused the change on the part of the American State Department is hard to say. A cynical interpretation would be that it was the normal and usual support for the Palace. Papandreou was not considered a strong threat to the establishment, and next to him in the party was Sophocles Venizelos, a man who had good relations with the royal family and could be counted on to be their man within the Center Union. He had a large enough group of deputies to be able to break up the party at any moment. (His death in early 1964 would change this picture.) A kinder interpretation was that the United States government, taking all factors into consideration, felt that the country needed a more liberal government, and it was clear that the sentiments were strongly behind Papandreou and his unyielding fight. It was not inconsistent with a view that prevailed at the White House that progressive, reform-minded movements should be supported, *as the most effective means to fight communism,* for that remained the cornerstone of American foreign policy. Labouisse, the new American Ambassador in Greece, was a Kennedy appointment. So, too, was the recent new head of CIA in Greece, Jack Maurey. There were definitely fresh

---

*The story of the murder of Lambrakis has been told accurately and dramatically in the French film "Z."

winds blowing in the State Department under the brief leadership of Jack Kennedy.

When we returned to Greece—once again—in June 1963, the situation had changed vastly from the previous year. Karamanlis was out, and new elections were coming up before the end of the year. George Papandreou was hopeful for an election victory. And Andreas Papandreou was hopeful that in this atmosphere he could contribute considerably to the well being of his native land.

CHAPTER NINE

Andreas Moves into Greek Politics and Government

NO sooner had we arrived back in Greece in June 1963 than we found ourselves deeply involved in political talk and speculation. George Papandreou kept us apprised of everything and sought Andreas' opinion and advice. The bickering going on within the Center Union party as various subleaders jockeyed for position, feeling the reins of government almost in their hands, was a discouraging sight, and for the first time I felt distaste for the political game. Andreas, on the contrary, had moved much closer to becoming a Greek politician. Or I should say that he had come much closer to fighting for a cause, because he is more of a crusader than a politician. He maintained his theories about the determination of the power complex to maintain control—at whatever cost—but he felt the need to fight. He had seen enough of injustice, favoritism, and corruption to want to be a spokesman for the underdog, for the disenchanted, for the disenfranchised. He wanted to fight for human dignity and pride in nation. He had no political "system" he wanted to install or impose, but certain goals within the framework of parliamentary democracy. The goals he had when he entered Greek politics never changed, and he was still striving for them when he was dragged from our home, bleeding, on April 21, 1967. They were not radical goals by American standards, but they were "revolutionary" to the establishment.

On the economic front, Andreas wanted a fairer distribution of the fruits of economic growth, a strong, independent labor movement (not under the control and tutelage of the government, as was the case), a mixture of private and public investment within the context of a national plan, and a revision of the tax system. As for the Palace, he wanted the King to reign and not rule—the King out of politics, as is the case in Great Britain and the Scandinavian countries where monarchy still exists. He wanted education to be free through the university level, and to be modernized to meet the needs of a developing country. This meant developing technological and managerial skills. Regarding foreign policy, an area later to bring him into conflict with United States interests, he wanted noninterference in internal affairs. He believed in a military alliance with the West, but he wanted freedom to trade with the East, which was a natural market for Greek products.

The big question was when to take the plunge into politics. My own feelings were that Andreas should wait until his father had completed his political career. A powerful father and a dynamic son, separated by more than a generation and differing vastly in personal experience, functioning in the same party would be, I thought, explosive. Andreas agreed with this; he also felt that additional time at the Center of Economic Research would enable him to familiarize himself more thoroughly with Greek problems. So the decision was not to run in 1963, but to wait until the next elections, which would normally be held after three or four years.

Elections were held in November 1963 without Andreas' participation. These elections, in contrast to those of 1961, were relatively free and honest. The result was 43 percent of the popular vote for Papandreou's Center Union and 41 percent for Karamanlis' ERE. Fifteen percent went to the Left. Papandreou did not have enough seats in Parliament to form government. He could have done so in collaboration with the Right, but this was impossible after his spectacular two-year "unyielding fight" against ERE. He could have done so with the Left. This he refused to do. Always an anticommunist, he could not imagine such a collaboration. He also knew the attitude of the Palace and the army and the American contingent. He knew also that there had been talk of a dictatorial solution when it became clear that Karamanlis couldn't make it. (Sources in Washington informed us that spokesmen of the Right and the army had approached American officials with such a proposal.) An alliance with the Left could have touched off a military coup.

From a personal friend, Monty Stearns, recently reassigned to the Congo after a four-year stint in the political section of the American Embassy in Athens, we received the following warm letter:

> I am getting rather wall-eyed trying to keep one eye on the Congo and one on Greece. How I wish I could have been in Athens for the elections! I read somewhere recently that your father celebrated by dancing the night away, and it reminded me of the night after the rally in 1961. Two days ago we saw him in the newsreel, greeting the King at Chania, and he seemed younger than ever. His—and yours—is a remarkable achievement, and I don't know which impresses me more, the popular victory or the political skill and persistence that made it possible. In any event, I wish you and Maggie would write something on the Making of a Prime Minister—1963. The architecture of this election is classical and deserves to be recorded.
>
> The handwriting began to appear on the wall when your father stated his conditions for elections and made them stick. . . . The cabinet was not so difficult to predict after that, although your father's inspiration of keeping the Education portfolio was a masterful touch. Now ideas and programs seem to be exploding like rockets. I always thought you were a braintruster at heart (if that isn't a contradiction in terms). I hope our many friends, Greek and American, who spoke so often of the pressing need for ideas and programs and the need to tackle basic problems will not take fright. Fat, prosperous Europe can learn a great deal from Greece. We can all learn a great deal from your father.

It was a good period in American-Greek relations. The Americans had allowed the Greeks to express themselves freely, and seemed eager to see the progressive forces take the government into their hands for a program of reform. How much sovereignty they would allow this Mediterranean nation was to be seen in time. Nor can we ever know how much the loss of John Kennedy changed the course of events in Greece. What we do know is that the atmosphere under the Kennedy administration was warm toward the democratic forces.

The results of the 1963 election created a personal dilemma for us. Papandreou asked for new elections, and they were scheduled for February 1964. Andreas had said he would run in the next elections, but so soon? And what about the other condition, that his father be out of active politics? I held to my point of view that this was still not the time, sensing from the beginning that my view would be unheeded. The basic decision had been made, it was merely a matter of timing, and the argument forwarded was that the "old man" could not stand the pressure of the heavy burden as government head, that he needed a right-hand man whom he could trust and that it was perhaps a golden opportunity to enter public life in Greece. There is no point trying to explain the rationale. Andreas was not studying the pros and cons. He had become committed to a cause, wanted to get into the fray, no matter what the odds, and thus the decision was emotional, as are so many major decisions in one's life.

The campaign for election as a deputy was short—six weeks in all—carried on in the muddy mountain villages of Achaia in the Peloponnesus in rain, snow, and cold. I saw real poverty and hunger on the pinched faces of children and adults alike, and the look of hope on their faces as this new politician made his rounds. His opening campaign speech to party workers in a crowded restaurant on the seashore of Patras was a moving commitment to carry on the democratic tradition of his father and to dedicate himself to the task of building a modern and progressive Greece.

Until now we had been on a scientific mission in Greece, and our stay could always be terminated. Now we were citizens of the country. My feelings were mixed. For the first time faces looked strange in a strange land. We were moving into uncharted waters. The struggle was going to be hard. Still, in the years since 1959 I had grown to love this exotic country and now I was to become an integral part of it. If I had any doubts, they were slowly washed away by listening to Andreas' sincere pledge to fight for a better life for the people and by the people's warm willingness to support him in that quest.

Papandreou's party had a smashing victory—53 percent of the popular vote. Andreas himself had a personal triumph, gaining the most votes of any deputy in the electoral district of Achaia and the highest percentage of the district's total votes for any rural district in Greece. His father wanted him in his cabinet, which meant becoming a minister, but here he faced a delicate problem. All the deputies who had fought with him during the anendotos were expecting returns for their loyalty; Andreas was a freshman, out of Greece for many years since 1940, and furthermore, he was the Prime Minister's son. The obvious place for Andreas was in an economics ministry.

The Ministry of Coordination was the most powerful ministry in the government, and had been committed to George Mavros, a capable, conservative deputy from Athens. The Finance Ministry was considered the plum of Mitsotakis, the Cretan deputy whose newspaper *Eleftheria* had played an important role in the two-year crusade. There was a ministry called the Ministry to the Prime Minister, which was a true hodgepodge, overseeing such activities as tourism, radio and press, party matters, archaeological enterprises, and KYP, the central intelligence service. The minister who occupied this post was considered to be the right-hand man to the Prime Minister, which in theory Andreas was, but its importance, unless there was to be a reorganization of government, was minimal. Andreas' training and talents could not be put to good use here. But Papandreou was concerned about charges of nepotism, and concerned also that a higher post for his son would divide the party. With reluctance, Andreas accepted the Ministry to the Prime Minister and was sworn in with the cabinet two days after elections.

It was to provide the basis for his first clash with the American Embassy. Because the Cyprus problem had reared its ugly head again during the early days of the Papandreou administration, with a war between Turkey and Greece a real possibility, the sensitivities of the Greeks were high. Reports came in of abuse of the Greek radio by the British. When Andreas investigated these charges, he discovered that the Karamanlis government had given free air time to three countries—England, France, and the United States—for special programs, presumably having to do with cultural subjects. There was no control over the content of these programs, and Great Britain had been using part of its allotted time to read excerpts from British newspapers having to do with Cyprus, excerpts that were not compatible with the Greeks' view of the Cyprus problem. At a time when passions were high, this was offensive to the Greeks. Andreas felt that as a matter of principle, it wasn't acceptable for other countries to be given carte blanche to use the Greek airways, and rather than set up a censorship board, he decided to cancel the agreements with all three countries. He called in the appropriate embassy officials of France, Great Britain, and the United States. There was no protest from either of the first two, who were sorry, but felt it was a legitimate decision. The representative of USIS, (United States Information Service) Mr. Joyce, felt otherwise. He argued against it, and when he saw he was making no headway, he used threat—the usual: withdrawal of economic aid, support, etc. Andreas didn't budge and Mr. Joyce left in an atmosphere of cold hostility. The incident had a continuation which was unfortunate. The story leaked out to the press as a result of a discussion on the topic in a cabinet meeting and sometime later was printed in colorful and dramatic terms, finally sounding as if Andreas had literally "kicked out" Mr. Joyce. Given the new mood of the country, and the general attitude toward embassy interference in Greek internal affairs, this act received wide approval and praise, and gained the government popularity. On the basis of a cabinet decision, Mr. Joyce, in the States by that time on home leave, was asked not to return. It was the first time since World War II that an American official had become *persona non grata* in a western European country.

His second, and more sensitive, clash came when he discovered that American funds were being paid directly to the Greek KYP, without having gone through government control. This made the KYP a paid agency of the CIA, and although many of their goals may have been mutual ones, Andreas felt this represented limits on Greek sovereignty. He made an issue of it, and got nowhere. Before he was able to remedy this situation, his father made him acting minister of the Ministry of Coordination because George Mavros resigned to become head of the National Bank of Greece. The "acting" part of the title resulted from his father's reluctance to cut out Stephanopoulos, deputy premier, who had hoped to get the ministry initially instead of Mavros. Thus Stephanopoulos became minister and Andreas acting minister. If the initial ministry had been a mistake, this double-authority arrangement was a disaster. Andreas had a clear, concise plan for the economic development of Greece. For Stephanopoulos, the ministry was a grab bag of profitable economic deals.

While Andreas had his own clashes, I had one of my own, early in the Papandreou government, on the occasion of the funeral of King Paul. King Paul died within a month after the new government took office. He was a respected figure among the Greek people, considered simple and good-humored, his loud, hearty laugh booming out often in any gathering. The funeral would be well attended, and many governments had indicated they would send representatives. From the United States it was announced that Mrs. Johnson, wife of the President, would represent her country. My father-in-law asked me to be the official hostess for her stay in Athens, and I readily agreed. But I was very green, and I didn't know that these formalities were considered the prerogative of the Palace, not just for this occasion, but for any visiting dignitary. Everything I proposed to the American Embassy was somehow scuttled. When Mrs. Johnson finally arrived at the Hilton Hotel, I learned that I was not to be first to greet her and introduce her to the Greek ladies officially in her escort, but would be introduced myself by a lady of the court. It was suggested that I pick up this lady to take her to the Hilton, and I said I didn't have room in my car (the Prime Minister's Cadillac), and thus created friction between me and the Palace. Since I dislike formal functions, and feel that this is a duty which the government should be happy to be relieved of, I clashed on something irrelevant to me. The monarchy—if it does exist—can give the glitter and style, which so many people like, to such affairs.

In any case, I did accompany Mrs. Johnson on some activities, apart from the funeral itself, and arranged through Liz Carpenter, the marvelous, warm, and humorous personal secretary of Mrs. Johnson, a morning tour of the ancient Agora, without the ladies of the court. Several things I remember about Mrs. Johnson. One was her ability to pose for photographers to show herself at her best advantage, particularly obvious in pictures of us together, where I had my mouth open, or my long legs twisted unbecomingly around each other, or my arms dangling like foreign appendages at my side. Another thing I remember was a conversation we had in the car on the way to the Agora in which she asked about me and Andreas, and how we got involved in

72

Greek affairs. I gave a brief synopsis of the steps that led to our involvement, saying at the end, "Well, anyway, politics has its appeal." She answered with a smile, and a sudden burst of enthusiasm, "Don't ah know!" We established rapport, which continued in a later trip to Washington, entitling me, I thought, to write to her once in 1965 about the Greek situation, which turned out to be an explosive decision.

Much of my time during the days of the Papandreou government was dedicated to two projects I initiated, one a school clothing drive for the mountain villages of Achaia, the other a school feeding program with the assistance of CARE. For the first, I asked some of my friends in the States to collect old clothes and send them over, the key contributor being my former high school, York Community High School in Elmhurst, Illinois. I also tapped Greek sources—schools, churches, and manufacturers of knitwear. In collaboration with the education director in Achaia, we selected between twenty and thirty needy villages and got the lists of names of elementary-school students, and wrapped up individual packages with old clothing, one new sweater, and objects such as toys, pencils, crayons, and books. On my first Christmas distribution, I had merely delivered huge barrels of the items to the school and left the things to be distributed by the teacher or the local priest. I learned that it created many local problems and dissension, and so at Easter I arrived with plastic bags with the names clearly stapled on each. Each stop was a festive occasion, the entire village turning out for the event, and the youngsters were delighted to hear their names called out in such a personal way by "the lady from Athens."

Barbara Westebbe, American wife of Dick Westebbe, the foreign-trade director in the Ministry of Commerce, put me in contact with Phil Johnston, of CARE. He had started a pilot program of school feeding in several rural villages, and was hopeful that the Greek government would support this plan on a wide scale. We traveled together to many areas, along with Phil's Greek counterpart, a blond thirty-year-old, with organizational capacity unrivaled among the Greeks. We bumped and humped over gutted, poorly kept roads in an old station wagon to see what could be done in the villages of Achaia to develop a school lunch program, a program that required the participation of the community, the church, and the teacher. CARE would supply certain food products (powdered milk, canned margarine, flour for bread, a wheat-cereal product, and canned tomato paste); the local community would organize for bread making, assistance in food preparation, and local fresh produce for variety; and the government was to supply funds for administration, and some additional Greek foodstuffs. The Karamanlis government had allowed the pilot studies, but had shown no interest in supporting on a mass scale the aim to give all of Greece's elementary-school children a free lunch.

My old community organization instincts were roused. I was enthusiastic about the possibilities. I asked Phil along with Westebbe to work out the financial scheme, and one evening invited the Westebbes to Kastri to have Dick outline the plan. As always with Dick, he had all the facts available— number of schoolchildren to be fed, number of schools involved, areas most suited for initial stages, personnel needed, cost to Greek government. My father-in-law listened attentively, and when Dick concluded, and I had put in a few punch lines, he said, "We'll do it."

The school lunch program became a successful project of the Papandreou administration. School attendance increased: some youngsters had what they had never had—one good, nutritious hot meal a day; and local communities learned what they could do on a voluntary basis to improve their situation. By the time Papandreou fell, 400,000 children under the age of thirteen were eating these lunches at school.

In the spring of 1964, President Johnson took his first foreign-policy initiative to try to resolve the Cyprus issue, and invited the Turkish Prime Minister and the Greek Prime Minister to Washington on successive weeks for several days of conference. The Prime Minister was allowed to choose the cabinet ministers he wanted to bring along, and Andreas was chosen as acting minister of the Ministry of Coordination, as was Costopoulos, the Minister of Foreign Affairs. I was included, along with the wife of Mr. Costopoulos.

Washington was a fascinating and depressing experience for me. I was there as the wife of a Greek cabinet minister, and I was seeing my government, if you like, from the outsider's point of view. We were given elegant quarters in Blair House, just vacated the week before by the Prime Minister of Turkey, Ismet Inonou, and his wife. I found an itinerary for the Turkish delegation in the closet of our bedroom, along with a few items of feminine apparel obviously forgotten by Mrs. Inonou. The itinerary was identical to ours. Thoughtful planners had made sure that neither of the two hostile NATO countries was given special treatment.

My first social function was tea with Mrs. Johnson and Lynda Bird, along with Mrs. Costopoulos, Mrs. Matsas, wife of the Greek Ambassador in Washington, Mrs. Dean Rusk, and Mrs. Barbara Bolling, who was my hostess guide during my stay. We entered the Oval Room, recently redecorated by Jacqueline Kennedy. Mrs. Johnson was waiting and seemed genuinely pleased to see me again. The discussion was informal, and we got on the topic of underprivileged children in Greece. I told her about the school feeding program which I was then working on, and we talked about other possibilities of projects for the children. Lynda Bird joined in freely and easily, and we could have been in any American living room on a spring morning, chatting with the neighbors over a cup of coffee. After being shown the President's office, the living quarters of the First Family, and viewing the grounds of the White House from the Oval Room balcony, we left to return to Blair House.

Barbara Bolling asked me what I might like to do in Washington, and I told her there were two things: one was to visit my old headquarters in the Health Education Division of the Health, Education, and Welfare building, the other was to watch a session of the Senate or House.

We did both. First, we saw my headquarters, but the few colleagues I knew from the past had either left government service or were on assignments in the field. I was told that Mary Jo Kraft, who had fought to get me my job

74

without the educational requirements, would be coming through town for one day, and I managed a conversation with her from Blair House by phone.

We got passes to the House of Representatives, where I was introduced to the young guide at the gallery door as Mrs. Andreas Papandreou from Greece. About ten minutes after I sat down, he came and took the seat behind me, and in a soft voice began explaining to me the system of American government, executive, judicial, and legislative. I learned the terms of office for House representatives and Senate members, and how many came from each state. I felt as if I were back at Washington Elementary School in Elmhurst, Illinois, hearing my fifth-grade teacher, Miss Kline, giving us a lesson on American government.

Barbara looked at me and winked. We were enjoying it immensely. I winked back at Barbara, and so as not to distress a truly sweet and earnest young man, I muttered occasionally in my best Greek accent, "Oh, dat ees so? Eet ees only two years for thee Amairican raipresentateeves?"

Later, at a lunch given in honor of the two lady guests, and hosted by Senator Maureen Neuberger of Oregon, I had an opportunity to give my views on the American government—particularly as it functioned in a small nation like Greece. Among others present were Mrs. Robert McNamara and Mrs. James Reston. After the lunch and a friendly speech by Senator Neuberger, I was asked some questions about Greece. I started out by saying that I loved Greece, but that I often had the problem of feeling like a split personality; sometimes I managed to feel completely Greek and view the issues as a Greek, at other times I was an American in Greece, defending my country, but at the same time disagreeing with it.

As I started talking about some of the things "we" (the Americans) had done, I was aware of two things going on at the long lunch table at the same time. Mrs. James Reston was nodding her head in seeming agreement. At the other end of the table, however, Mrs. Matsas, the Greek Ambassador's wife, was whispering at length to Mrs. Costopoulos. It was more than just a translation, since Mrs. Costopoulos understood English well enough. I was talking about favoritism to the forces of the Right and the Palace and lack of support to the democratic forces, which did, after all, represent the majority in Greece.

After the lunch, Mrs. Costopoulos nabbed me in the rest room.

"You should not speak against the Palace to the American ladies," she said.

"You misunderstood me," I said. "I was not speaking against the Palace, but against an American policy of supporting the status quo to the exclusion of other political forces in Greece."

"Mrs. Matsas was very angry. She said you spoke against the Palace."

"Mrs. Matsas was wrong, and if she had listened carefully instead of jumping to conclusions and buzzing in your ear, she would have heard exactly what I said."

"Oh, I guess she didn't understand."

"That's right. She didn't understand."

Poor Mrs. Costopoulos. She was very nervous. I think she thought we were both headed for the chopping block because of my indiscretions.

This incident might explain why the cocktail party given in honor of President Johnson at Blair House and arranged by the Greek Embassy had a special stipulation: women were *excluded*. Essentially this meant me, for Mrs. Costopoulos and I were the only women in the Greek delegation visiting Washington. And there was no reason to exclude dear, confused, proroyal Mrs. Costopoulos.

Andreas in the meantime was going through his own Washington experience. He was struck first by the militaristic atmosphere in which events took place. Uniformed officers were everywhere and led the group in a file of twos down the steps to lunch, or to whatever activity was going on. But it was the meetings themselves that most distressed him. They had a totalitarian quality. There was no give-and-take, no real debate. The American government stated its point of view, listened patiently to the points made by Papandreou, with Andreas translating, then, as if nothing had gone on in between, repeated exactly the statements made at the beginning. Andreas described it as a drumbeat monotony, building in sound, but the beat remained the same. Papandreou would say something, and the answer would come back "boom-boom-boom-boom." He would try a new tack, and the response would be "boom-boom-boom-boom," the drumstick beating out the cadence. It was an overbearing pressure, and the most frequent "boom" had to do with the military power of Turkey. It was carefully pointed out many times that Turkey's military power was such and such and that Greece might have a staying power of ten days should a conflict break out between the two. In other words, Greece was in no position to bargain, and it better accept the initiative of the United States to resolve the Cyprus issue through a plan that had been proposed, to be called the Acheson Plan. All representatives of the American government in Washington with whom the Greeks had conversations maintained that line with one exception. Only McNamara seemed interested in listening and responding to the Greek point of view. Later, Adlai Stevenson in New York entered a true dialogue with the two Papandreous.

The second night, after a fatiguing day of such talks, Andreas returned to Blair House late, and in a black mood. "God damn Americans," he said. Then he told me the essence of the day's talks.

"Well, what would you do if you were the American government?" I asked. "What line would you take?"

"I'm not the American government."

Andreas was exhausted from butting his head against a stone wall, and was feeling the frustration of a small country which is being told by its "protector nation" what it must do—or else. He was absolutely committed to the fight for his country's rights. When he finally made the decision to go into Greek public life, he went into it with full dedication; that's the kind of person he is. He was no longer a man with two countries; he had made his choice.

I, on the other hand, was enjoying being "back home." And I was feeling defensive about Washington tactics. I put up some arguments about America's desire to maintain peace, their halting of a Turkish invasion of Cyprus, etc., and thus we started a nice verbal battle in Blair House, which got hotter and hotter and ended up with Andreas going to the other bedroom in our suite to sleep. Unfortunately for him, the other bedroom was unheated, and he caught a cold which by the time we reached Paris was accompanied by a fever, and he was forced to leave the delegation one day early to return to Athens and medical care. In New York my father-in-law had appointments with members of the United Nations; in Paris he had an appointment with de Gaulle.

In Paris, at the Crillon Hotel, I was introduced to Andreas Vahliotis, a classmate of Andreas' from Athens College. He came up to our sitting room, threw his arms around Andreas, and the two reminisced about old times. Vahliotis was a thin man, about the height of my husband, with glasses, shifty eyes, and an intense look. He didn't appeal to me. At some point he asked for a private conversation with Andreas, and they went into the bedroom for twenty minutes. Andreas later told me that the man knew quite a bit about Greek matters from the inside, and had expressed a desire to help Andreas. Vahliotis agreed, at my husband's suggestion, to send him reports from time to time.

Within a week after our return to Athens, we received a long-distance phone call from Vahliotis who, speaking in a mysterious way, said that Andreas must immediately send to Paris a man whom he trusted for critical and important information. When Andreas said he could not afford the expense and had to know the nature of the information, he was told that there was a plot to assassinate George Papandreou, and that it was extremely urgent that a man be sent out within hours. Because Vahliotis had connections with the Greek secret service, Andreas considered this serious enough. A complex plan was set up by Vahliotis for meeting a Papandreou representative at the airport in Paris, taking him to a secret place and divulging the information.

As it turned out, the scare was a come-on. It was a method to try to seem useful to Andreas and to work into his entourage. Alec, the man Andreas sent, reported that it had been a wild-goose chase, and advised him to stay away from this neurotic character.

Within a few days, letters arrived at our house, reports written in a big, clear handwriting, with changes in the color of ink to give emphasis to certain points. There were also many underlinings in strong straight lines. I told Andreas that without being able to read the Greek, they looked like the letters of a psychopath. Andreas did not respond to any of them.

The last time I saw Andreas Vahliotis was when he arrived at our home in Psyhico early one morning before breakfast, disturbed that he was getting nowhere as a confidant or adviser to Papandreou the younger. I remember vaguely the two of them walking together in our backyard, one of them—Vahliotis—talkin' incessantly with gestures, the other—Andreas— smoking and shaking his head from time to time. That was the last we saw of Vahliotis. It was not the last we heard from him. He was to turn up later as a key witness in the establishment case ASPIDA—against Andreas.

In the fall Constantinos married Anna Maria, a lovely teen-age princess from the royal family of Denmark, and pictorially they made an enchanting couple. It was a fairy-tale wedding. It reminded me of Sophia's remark back in 1960 when Andreas and I got into our fancy clothes to attend a dinner at the Grande Bretagne Hotel in honor of King Paul and Queen Frederika. She asked why we were getting all dressed up. "We are having dinner with the King and Queen," her father answered. "But that's for children!" was her reply. And then she got almost indignant; it was *her* world of princes, princesses, knights, knaves, royal balls, and sparkling palaces we were invading.

At the wedding I felt that I was one of the actresses (minor, supporting role) in an M-G-M spectacular—Ectachrome, Panavision, cast of thousands. There were many acts before the climax—the wedding—and we had to wear many costumes, and be on time on the stage set when the cameras started grinding. Andreas wore an Eisenhower jacket with black pants, black bow tie, and a collar that closed with a button in front that had to go through four holes, holes that maintained their rigidity along with the starched collar. The first time, it took half an hour of a hot fall day to get the collar properly on. I wore formals—some old ones I brought from the states, and a new glittering thing I had made for the wedding. Because Queen Mother Frederika had asked that all ladies wear sleeves and closed necklines, I had made a jacket to cover a dress which could later be used for a ball.

There were dances, teas, luncheons, curtsies, formalities. The most beautiful and dazzling event was the wedding itself with the Greek Orthodox priests in their splendid, rich robes. Considerably less attractive were members of royal families of yesteryear—for example Farouk's three daughters, fat and ugly. The Cinderella was Grace Kelly.

The Greeks had great hopes for this wedding, for Constantinos was marrying a member of a "democratic" royal family, that of Denmark. They felt that at last there was the possibility of having a modern monarchy.

During this period of our administration I understood some of the minor benefits of being in government: fresh lobsters from Spetses, rabbits from the Peloponnesus, eggs from a mountain village, crates of grapes from Crete, wine from Patras. There were other larger benefits which we didn't partake of. Attempts to "line Andreas' pocket" because of his position in the powerful Ministry of Coordination were frequent.

In November of 1964 he quit his post, finding his hands tied in putting through a dynamic development program by the strange arrangement with Stephanopoulos, and feeling that he could function better as a simple deputy. His father agreed to this with some reluctance, because he was having his own difficulties with the party over Andreas' growing popularity. It was one of the few times in modern Greek history that a minister resigned voluntarily. It was so unusual, in fact, that the Right manufactured charges of a financial scandal, which was nonsense, and the charge died its own natural death. Right after his resignation he was invited as an honored guest by Archbishop Makarios to visit Cyprus, which caused a flurry of concern among the rightists who felt this honor would gain him strength among their own nationalist youth, and within the army.

These were some of the personal highlights of the short-lived Papandreou government. The government itself, despite obstacles, started many reforms, particularly in the field of education, and Andreas himself was able to initiate programs of resource development which would have great dividends for the future. Probably the primary and great achievement of the Papandreou government was on the level of personal freedom and civil liberties. For the first time in modern times, the Greek felt himself a free human being, stripped of the yoke of a police state, unfettered by chains. The policeman was the servant of the people, not the master, and the psychology of the gendarmerie was changed in a short time, with its own approval, and to the joy of the Greek citizen. This taste of freedom, wiped out by the colonels who rule Greece today, was sweet and good, and will not be forgotten, just as those who stamped it out will not be forgotten—when the time comes.

CHAPTER TEN

The Ousting of George Papandreou

KING Constantinos was a Glücksburg on the side of his father, the dynasty that had ruled Greece on and off since 1863 when the British chose the Danish prince William George to be the new Greek King after the Bavarian King Otto's abdication. His mother, Frederika, born Princess of Hanover, was a granddaughter of Kaiser Wilhelm II (and a great-granddaughter of Britain's Queen Victoria, making her a third cousin of Queen Elizabeth). She spent most of her childhood in Austria. As a girl, she supposedly belonged to a Hitlerite youth group. In school in Italy during her late teens, at a time when three of her brothers served in the Wehrmacht, she was heard to defend Nazi Germany.

Constantinos had some of the characteristics of his father—the humor, the grace, and the simplicity. He was, however, raised by his mother, and she instilled in him the medieval attitudes of kingship, the blue-blood tradition, and thus he developed the arrogance that comes from believing he belonged to a very special category of human being. Extremely religious and mystical, he had come to believe that he was a descendant of the Byzantine emperors. Along with his arrogance—which one could see in the petulant expression of his mouth—was a wholesome, modern, almost American love of sports and a highly competitive spirit. Surely the articles that appeared in American periodicals after he disposed of George Papandreou which described him as "daring" must have puffed the sportsman's image he had of himself.

His image of himself in his role as King was a confused one. On the one hand, he wanted to be King of all the Greeks, that is, be politically neutral, and his first speech in Parliament in 1964 inaugurating the new government after the death of his father had that tone. On the other hand, he saw himself as the true leader of the country, a young de Gaulle, decidedly a King-politician. This version of his role as King was to grow after recovering from the loss of his father, to whom he was deeply attached.

The cornerstone of his political thinking was a blind hatred of communism, imbued in him from childhood by his mother, who always saw everything bad in life as a communist conspiracy. He was, in fact, very much influenced by his mother after he became King. Although he made the statement to my father-in-law in a private meeting, "You think that I am guided by my mother and she makes my decisions. Well, you are wrong," it was conceded by all who knew the domineering Frederika that she had great influence on, if not control over, her one and only son. She never trusted Papandreou, believing that deep in his heart he was an antiroyalist republican. With the death of Venizelos, who had had almost equal control of the Center Union party, who was proroyal and would have been the Palace's agent within the party, she got restless about Papandreou being Prime Minister, and urged her son to assert his power, particularly in the army. In this the King found little resistance. Papandreou was quite willing to make an accommodation with the Palace and not push for the changes all democrats were expecting him to make, in order—he thought—not to clash with the King. It can honestly be said, furthermore, that he had a liking for the boy. Many people said that remaining in the older Papandreou was an awe for royalty common to villagers, for he had had a barefooted boyhood in the mountain village of Kalentzi, four mule-hours away from Patras in the Peloponnesus. He always rejected this conjecture, but I suspect that it was true.

Constantinos, between squash games, sailings, and ceremonial functions, became more involved in the political life of the country. He met frequently with ministers of the government in his own office where he got reports on their ministerial activities and made his various requests and suggestions. He had frequent meetings with the heads of the armed services. He particularly had contact with the Minister of Defense, Petros Garoufalias. Spring, 1965, was too soon to dump Papandreou, but no doubt the plan was shaping up. To succeed, the Palace would need the support of the Americans, and the trip to Washington in June of 1964 brought this support closer to reality. In Washington, it will be remembered, Papandreou found huge pressure on him to agree to a Greek-Turkish dialogue, which he refused to accept. His argument was that in that case the country with the greatest military might (Turkey's was four times that of Greece) would win in the bargaining. He further argued that no agreement could be made without the inclusion of Cyprus representatives. He urged discussions under United Nations auspices.

The architect for the scheme of settling the Cyprus issue was Dean Acheson, and subsequently the scheme came to be called the Acheson Plan. Papandreou finally agreed to informal discussion in Geneva, laying down certain conditions, but after two months of such negotiations, the plan was rejected by Papandreou. It proposed partitioning the island into two sections, one Turkish, the other Greek. It was also rejected by Turkey, but the ire of the State and Defense Department officials was taken out on Greece. Papandreou and son, for son was depicted as the hard-liner of the two, were seen as obstacles to the solution of the Cyprus problem, a problem that was considered to be weakening the NATO alliance in its southeastern flank. It was under these circumstances that the song being sung privately by the Palace and rightist groups that "Papandreou Must Go" began to sound like a catchy tune to the American faction. Having been in the game of making and breaking prime ministers for a long time, American officials were in familiar waters.

It was not easy. The Center Union was enjoying its term in power, Papandreou was still a popular leader, and the people were experiencing true freedom for the first time in years. Panayotis Cannellopoulos sang the first note publicly in a speech in Klathmonas Square in Athens in February of 1965. In that speech he did not attack the Center Union party, but its leader. He claimed that Papandreou was leading the country to economic disaster and chaos.

After Cannellopoulos sounded the note, the establishment forces got the message and joined hands to help. The Greeks, keen to shifts in the political winds, understood that moves were under way to unseat Papandreou, and watched with awe, despair, and excitement as the game progressed. The case of ASPIDA, which will be described more fully in subsequent chapters, came into the picture, thus the issue of the army, and a collision course was set up between Constantinos and George Papandreou.

The King had insisted in June that all those said to be involved in the ASPIDA case be brought to trial, despite the results of a government investigating body which found the charges groundless. Papandreou said he would acquiesce to this wish, if the King insisted, but would also bring to trial those involved in Plan Pericles, the military plan for carrying out elections of 1961. This would have hit some of the King's most devoted officers.

A further point of contention, electrifying the atmosphere, was the role of Garoufalias, the defense minister, who, it turned out, was supplying the King surreptitiously with information from cabinet sessions where this delicate issue was being discussed. When Papandreou discovered this, he decided to remove Garoufalias from his ministry and to assume the ministry of defense himself, a move which the King could not oppose without challenging directly the Prime Minister and his government. Papandreou was legally within his rights because, according to the Constitution, he was entitled to choose his own cabinet. The conflict was a broad one, but was reaching its climax over the question of a presumed conspiracy in the army against the King, and the prime minister's rights and powers in choosing his own ministers.

We did not know exactly what would be the steps to the final confrontation. On July 8, 1965, we learned. It was Thursday, our regular dinner evening at Kastri. It was an unusually cool summer night, and we were eating inside at the oval dining room table, rather than our customary summer eating place on the terrace. The doorbell rang at 11:30 P.M., and Karambelas, faithful bodyguard, companion, and house manager, answered. He returned to tell the President that someone on a motorcycle had brought a message from the Palace and was waiting at the front gate to deliver it personally.

"You get it, my boy," the President said to Andreas, who walked out the front door and down the steps to the big white gate. The only thing George Papandreou said while we waited for Andreas to return was "It can't be good."

Andreas came back with an envelope bearing the official insignia of the Crown on the outside and handed it to my father-in-law, whose big hands fumbled as he tore it open. He put on his glasses and peered at the first line. Then he removed his glasses and handed the letter to Andreas.

"Here, read it out loud so that we all can hear."

It was a long rambling document of several pages with the big scrawling

82

signature of Constantinos at the end. My heart skipped a beat when I heard the accusation against my father-in-law:

> *The situation became abnormal from the time when the Central Intelligence Service, which answers personally to you and is run by persons who have your absolute confidence, organized a revolutionary, conspiratorial organization in the armed forces, having as a sole aim to overthrow the country's Constitution and impose a dictatorship of a wretched form, repugnant to every free individual.*
>
> *Unfortunately, I am in the unpleasant position to declare to you that you reinforce and urge these interventions [the King was arguing that Papandreou intervened in the investigations of the ASPIDA case] although, for reasons I would not like to mention, insuperable and objectively granted,* your position in conjunction with the case of conspiracy in the armed forces has long become extremely sensitive and delicate. *[Emphasis mine, reference to Andreas]*

When Andreas had finished, he handed it back. Papandreou, Sr., said nothing. I felt as if a spotlight had been turned on above our table, hot and blinding, the silence and darkness of the rest of the room clothing us like a black shroud. We were players at a poker game, the chips were all out in the center of the table, and we were waiting for the key player to declare his hand.

It was Andreas' voice that broke the silence. "Father, it is an ugly, pompous, slanderous letter," he said, then added, "and it is the end of your premiership."

Papandreou, slowly and thoughtfully, laid his strong fist on the table, clenched, then his hand opened up and reached for my pack of cigarettes and he took one, an unusual act, as he wasn't much of a smoker. Andreas lit it for him. He took a puff, then laid the cigarette down in the ashtray which I had pushed in front of him. He was thinking, and it was obvious that he was refusing to accept the notion that he had been given his walking papers.

Finally, he spoke. "It is a private communication," he said, "not public. I need some time to think." He stood up, which was the signal for us to leave. He kissed us good-bye with a sad tenderness, but there was no trace of defeat in his voice as he said goodnight and "kalo ipno," "good sleep," nor even a touch of irony in this last remark.

On the drive back to Psyhico, Andreas told me that it was all over, that he was sure his father believed that he might be able to reverse the decision, but that he, Andreas, was sure of the end result. I, like George Papandreou, held out hope. It was not that I really desired that the Center Union remain in government. I was truly fed up with the endless official activities, the jockeying for power, the bickering, the deceit. I was disgusted with the slanderous press. And I was horrified at the attempt to charge Andreas with a conspiracy, a charge that I thought would die as soon as he was out of power. But I was quite certain that the step was a disastrous one, and knowing as I did that no "plot" existed to overthrow the King, an unnecessary one from even Constantinos' point of view.

A panicky King was charging ahead, backed by his own army and an applauding American contingent on the sidelines.

My father-in-law answered the King's letter on July 9, replying to the accusations as if the letter were indeed a private communication, not his "walking papers," as Andreas saw it. The letter was delivered to Corfu, from where the first had been written, and where Constantinos was awaiting the birth of Anna Maria's first child. In it he enclosed the decree for the King's signature making him Minister of Defense. The lines were drawn.

On July 10 a girl was born to the Queen. The Prime Minister arranged to fly Sunday morning to the island to pay his respects to the King and Queen. He also arranged for a private meeting with the King. When he arrived at his hotel in Corfu, a second letter from the King, dated July 10, awaited him. It was similar to the first, but tougher.

Papandreou expected his private meeting with the King to be grim. It was not. It was, in fact, puzzling. None of the venom and anger of the letters was present. It was as if the letters came from another hand.

When he returned Sunday evening from Corfu, he was mildly hopeful that the differences could be worked out. The problem, however, was not a simple question of cordial relations between the King and the Prime Minister but involved a much deeper power struggle. These same forces could easily sweep both of the principal actors off-stage with equal indifference.

On July 14 a third letter arrived for Papandreou from Corfu. The attacks were continuing, despite the semi-friendly personal encounter, and the President asked, through the King's political secretary, Choidas, for an appointment with the King. It was made for the next afternoon at the Palace in Athens.

It was at that meeting that the King dismissed George Papandreou, the people's choice for Prime Minister.

It must be obvious that by now, midsummer of 1965, my personal involvement with the "Greek situation," as we often called it, was complete. I participated in discussions, sometimes as a listener, sometimes expressing my own views, in both Andreas' and my father-in-law's inner circles of decision making. Perhaps I was used as a sounding board more than anything else because I was considered to have good judgment and a balanced point of view. But such a close association with the nerve center of government did involve me emotionally. I was committed to both Papandreous' pursuit of a decent life for the Greek. The ugly attempt to frame Andreas angered me, and the consistent support the American forces gave to the establishment had embittered me. The deceit and treason within the party was abhorrent. The scheme to oust Papandreou from the leadership of the country, being hatched by the Palace, army, and Americans, could not have succeeded without party apostasy—the willingness of Center deputies to be seduced away from the party. Thus the personal ambitions or general corruption of people like Mitsotakis, Stephanopoulos, and Tsirimokos, not to mention the ridiculous vanity of Novas, who was to become the first Prime Minister after Papandreou fell, made them pawns in a bigger game of chess being played by the establishment forces.

On July 8, the same day the first letter by the King was sent to Papandreou, I sat down and wrote a long analysis of the state of affairs in Greece, and sent the letter to fifteen personal friends in the States. It was written without the knowledge of the King's letter and mailed that afternoon before we left for Kastri. I also wrote a separate but shorter letter to Mrs. Johnson on the basis of the friendship we had established during her brief trip to Greece at the time of King Paul's funeral and my visit in Washington. I was later asked by someone, did I think this would have any effect? I suppose the answer is no. There were two reasons for writing the letters. One was that it didn't seem possible to keep this rage to myself. That was the cathartic side. The other was an application of a simple rule in any battle. Do what you can personally in the fight. The letters were an attempt to enlighten Americans by pointing out what I considered disastrous mistakes in American foreign policy.

One week after Papandreou was thrown out, a paragraph from this letter appeared in Drew Pearson's column. His syndicated column appeared in over two hundred American newspapers. This was much more "enlightenment" than I had counted on, but I had no objection because it certainly fulfilled one of the purposes of the report. I had not sent the letter directly to Pearson, contrary to all news items in the Greek press, but I do know the "mystery" of how he received it, and it had my approval.

The *real* mystery was how the Novas-apostate government got my letter and published it on the front page of the Mitsotakis newspaper *Eleftheria* on July 23, 1965. I have not yet unraveled that bit of "espionage," but learned recently from a book written by Kyriakos Diakoyannis, a man who had worked with the Greek CIA in trying to frame Andreas on the ASPIDA case, and who escaped from the junta to tell his story, that one of the boys we used as messengers in our close entourage was a Greek KYP man. Since I had a messenger mail the fifteen letters, it would have been remarkably easy to steam an envelope open, photostat the contents, reseal it, and send it on. This would have happened on the day of the mailing, July 8, but could not have been used while Papandreou was still Premier.

This letter became a big issue in Greece, and in fact, an international story when the new Minister of Foreign Affairs, George Melas, called the foreign press to castigate this "scandalous act." My hometown newspaper, the Chicago *Daily News,* published a piece by George Weller with the headline "Maggie from Chicago Called Enemy of Greek Throne."*

> . . . She was just plain Maggie Chant back home and she's already "Maggie" to millions who eat olives with bread and drink resin wine.
> But Greece's new Royalist cabinet claims that this educated statuesque Maggie is an enemy of the throne. That's because she is now Maggie Papandreou, daughter-in-law and adviser of George Papandreou, the 77-year-old ex-premier fighting King Constantine. . . .
> A bitter attack in parliament against Maggie by Foreign Minister

*Reprinted with permission from the Chicago *Daily News* .

George Melas stopped Monday night's session in a near riot lasting 10 minutes. Maggie's supporters in the majority Center Union Party tried to maul the Royalist minister, threw paper balls and newspapers at him and drove him temporarily from the platform.

Maggie's defect is condoned by American men but unforgivable to Greeks: she knows too much about politics and shows it.

Melas, a withered 71-year-old diplomat with crafty eyes in a Mephistophelean face, condemned Maggie, who is low-voiced, tall and formidably kind-hearted, for writing what he called "ugly letters" to Mrs. Lyndon B. Johnson, Dean Rusk, Hubert Humphrey and assorted college professors. "The dear lady is strangely concerned," he said bitterly.

What soured the veteran minister—sometimes known as "the sweetest of Greece's molasses" was that Maggie foresaw the future too well. Maggie can prophesy trouble coming to King Constantine with more accuracy than any seeress since the priestesses of Delphi. Yet she learned her dark arts by campaigning for the late Adlai E. Stevenson and going to journalism school at the University of Minnesota.

"This gracious lady forecast with certainty," Melas angrily told a group of 100 foreign correspondents, "not only the fact that a divergency of view would occur between king and premier, but also with great precision what events would follow this clash. All her forecasts were curiously confirmed by events."

Maggie's Delphic cunning, Melas revealed, was actually due simply to her being tipped off beforehand by her father-in-law.

"This letter written by the hand of his daughter-in-law at dictation pace proves beyond any shade of doubt that it was he himself who laid down the plan of this dispute with the King in every detail and put it into application without any alteration whatsoever," Melas charged.

Melas attacked Maggie, whom he called "the gracious Mrs. Papandreou," for "representing the king as acting unconstitutionally and against the will of the people. She moreover exhorts an intervention of the U.S.A. to save democratic ideals in Greece."

Melas drew this conclusion from Maggie's White House letters, in which she said that if Constantine dumped her father-in-law, leader of the parliamentary majority "the king will be taking an unconstitutional, undemocratic act against the will of the people and the horrible thing for me as an American is to have Americans linked up with something so against our own democratic ideals."

Maggie, in her first letter to Lady Bird, declared that the American embassy was divided into two camps. In one were the CIA and military attaches, who favored the king and his armed forces. In the other were Henry Labouisse, ambassador until last March, and the minister counsellor, Norbert Anschuetz, who favored her father-in-law's majority.

Maggie's letter, as read out indignantly by Melas, closed with an appeal to Mrs. Johnson:

"If America has no involvement, and I hope she hasn't, then she must indicate she stands on the side of democracy. I write this letter to you personally because of our friendship, second because you are a woman of ideals of patriotism and deep concern that your husband succeed in expressing America—the real America—throughout the world."

The attack on Maggie opened up a new front for her overworked husband, 47-year-old Andreas Papandreou, whom she married in Nevada in 1951 after they met while he was a professor of economics at the University of Minnesota.

He has threatened Athenian newspapers with libel suits. Besides linking him with a leftist army plot, they claim that he is still collecting his professor's salary from the University of California.

The direct attack by Melas did not appear to have helped much a palace cabinet that is in its third week but still lacks any parliamentary support.

The essence of my letter was this: that the King and the rightist forces in the country were working together to oust unconstitutionally my father-in-law, the Prime Minister, and to attack and discredit my husband, Andreas, by linking him to a supposed conspiratorial group called ASPIDA. I pointed out the strong anticommunist stance of my father-in-law, and that he was, by the will of the Greek people, leading them toward real democracy, and that if the scare tactics of "communist infiltration" used by the Right succeed, the country would be plunged into turmoil, perhaps even civil war, which could result in a military take-over of the government. I did not accuse the United States of assisting the rightist faction, but said the CIA had a "negative attitude" toward the elected government; nor did I ask for American interference into the affairs of Greece. I asked on which side America would choose to stand, the side of "the minority, reactionary forces" of Greece or that of the popularly and constitutionally elected democratic Center Union party, headed by George Papandreou.

The anti-Margaret publicity continued for several days, and to my astonishment I found a picture of me in one of the Athens newspapers alongside a picture of Madame Nu of Vietnam. Our common crime had been to attack the CIA.

A week later, while sitting in the small hallway of our Psyhico house listening to Georgie practicing his guitar, the doorbell rang. It was a policeman asking for me. He handed me a small piece of paper, about the size of a 5 by 7 file card. I understood, by reading the tiny print and struggling with the official Greek, that it was a summons. My name and a date and place had been written in on a blank space. The date was August 11, and the place was a police station on Academias Street in central Athens. I was asked to sign. I argued that I couldn't sign anything that I did not completely understand and would have to consult my lawyer. The policeman told me it was just a matter of form, and I was not committing myself to anything. Wary of signing even a piece of toilet paper, however, I called Andreas, and asked the policeman to read the summons over the phone, to explain what I was to do and what it meant, and then to return the phone to me for directions from my husband. Andreas felt that signing was a formality and indicated merely that I had received the summons. What we would do after that could be discussed later.

It was obvious that this was a punitive act. Since those who were calling me in for questioning had manufactured the charges in the ASPIDA case, they already knew that my knowledge of Andreas' plotting would be nil. But they were angry that I had found an effective vehicle—powerful friends in the United States and a syndicated journalist of reputation—to expose their naked and clumsy scheme to grab the power from Papandreou. It was also a political act. Knowing the Greek's general repugnance to women involving themselves in politics, and a foreigner to boot, they felt a public "spanking" would be applauded. I cannot say I got very good support from the newspapers representing the Center Union, probably for the same reasons. The sudden decision to call me in for questioning and the haste to summon me (after all, where was I going?) had all the earmarks of the subsequent one-day judicial wonder in which the request was made in Parliament in February 1966 to remove the deputy immunity enjoyed by Andreas so that he could be charged with high treason.

The night before the investigation took place, Andreas and I went to Kastri to discuss the proceeding with his father and his father's lawyer. George Papandreou was tired, his face showing the strain of the preceding weeks, his usual healthy color whitened by fatigue. He was unsmiling and tense. I was also unsmiling and tense. A copy of my letter was on the table in front of him, and the four of us sat around trying to guess what the investigator, Army Lieutenant Colonel Laganis, might ferret out to question me on.

I argued that the letter was a political document, with only a one-paragraph reference to ASPIDA, and the questions surely could not pertain to political matters, but to the so-called conspiracy, and that the rest of the letter was irrelevant to the issue. I was to get a lesson in army justice. The others knew. As we read the letter through, the President sighed several times, and I regretted that I had to add this burden to his already troubled life. Still, I had written only the truth, and I was quite ready to defend it and present more facts if necessary. I couldn't understand why my interpretation of events, which most democratic Greeks believed in and which in fact had been discussed many times at this very round table, caused such consternation.

The next morning I went to the office of George Papandreou's lawyer, and his wife—also a lawyer—drove me to Academias Street. Andreas' lawyer, Menios Koutsoyergas, the day before had gone to the colonel in charge of the inquiry and made an issue of the translation problem, arguing that I should have my own translator. Having my own lawyer had not been considered remotely possible, although Menios also made an issue of that. Waiting at the door at Academias was Menios. He told me that he had finally gotten an agreement that I would be permitted to write my answers in English in response to the translated Greek question, rather than answer orally in English and have the translator give it in Greek to the recorders. This way I could be sure of no distortion of my answer.

With that bit of news, he led me up an old wooden staircase and to a door, half open, and told me to push on in. "I am not allowed inside," he said, "so you are on your own."

The room was not much bigger than an oblong bathroom. Tables were placed in a T shape. At the top of the T sat the investigator, short, balding, and looking like a clerk in a shoe store. To his left was a young, bonily attractive Greek in civilian clothes, who told me he was my translator. Along one side of the tables forming the stem of the T were two soldiers with impressive-looking recording books and pens, and I was to take the chair on the other side of the tables forming the stem, facing the translator. I was a contrast to their khaki and drab business suits in my lively green print silk skirt and jacket with pink blouse. It did seem festive enough for the occasion. We were a cozy group. The investigator stuck out his hand and pointed to the chair for me to sit down. A soldier got up and closed the door.

It was a hot Athenian day. A faint smell of sweat clung to the air. The noises of cars and trucks on the boulevard below could be heard through the open window to the backs of the soldier-recorders.

"Do you swear that the testimony you are about to give . . ." I recognized the Greek as an oath, but waited for the translation. The translator slipped a Greek Orthodox Bible under my left hand and gestured to me to raise my right.

"I do."

Laganis' voice was unpleasant in a whining, condescending fashion. The questions had been hastily put together, and were obviously in someone else's handwriting because of the difficulty he had in reading them. I wondered how it felt to be a cog in a machine that failed to emit warning signals to those accused. Those accused in the ASPIDA case did not see these machinations as the beginning stages of a military takeover. It was here that the army exposed itself, clearly and overtly, as a factor in the *political* life of Greece. We were all lulled by the crudity of the frame-up, the ridiculous charges, the preposterous statements, that we tended to look upon it as a painful comedy, rather than, as it turned out, a calamity. Here are the basic questions I was asked, and my answers:

Question In your letter to Drew Pearson you say that around February or March the army staff "discovered" a paramilitary organization of young officers called ASPIDA which was apparently organized some years back during Karamanlis' government as a democratic-minded, liberal force. How do you know about this?

Answer I want to make it clear at the very beginning that this was a *personal* letter I wrote to my friends. I do not know how it reached the hands of Drew Pearson. My source of information is from a newspaper article . . . [reporting] that such an organization existed. Because it was apparently formed while Karamanlis was in power, I made the assumption that it was democratic.

The next two questions had to do with specific ideas easily known to anyone reading the daily newspapers or living, as I did, in the world of politics and political discussions. The interrogater tried to make me out as a confidante of George Papandreou's—and somehow in the possession of secret information which I was not entitled to. The constant refrain of "how did you know" seemed to me more harassment than any belief that I was rifling secret files. The point of the interrogation came up in the sixth question.

Question You write that a real conspiracy was under way and was being handled by people skilled in the task, forces that had operated professionally for years of rightist regimes. What evidence can you give for this, and what persons did you meet who were the professional operators?

Answer My letter, in English, used the word "purported," which means that it falls in the realm of speculation, and remains necessarily as a theory. What I know is what my husband told me, that he has absolutely no involvement in ASPIDA, and I have great faith in my husband. When the newspapers were writing that he was involved, it gave the appearance of a plan against him. I think my husband believes that it was a political plan. I avoided saying military plan.

Question How did you have access to secret conversations between the King and the P.M., and how did you know there would be riots and demonstrations after the government crisis?

Answer If you read my letter carefully you will see that all the information appeared in one form or other or was talked about in general in political circles prior to the resignation of George Papandreou. My prediction that there would be demonstrations came as a result of my observance of political behavior here over a number of years and my expectation of a citizen's right to express himself freely in a democracy. I also know the love of the people for George Papandreou and anticipated their reaction to his resignation.

Question Are you aware of the possibility that you have offended the pride of the Greek nation by asking a foreign power to intervene in the internal matters of this country, particularly in military affairs?

Answer I am not aware of the possibility that I offended the pride of the Greek nation. I love Greece and I love the Greek people and if I thought that what you say were true I would be deeply hurt. Also, if you had read my letter carefully, you would see that I do not ask for interference *of any sort,* and never, also, in military affairs. My purpose was to enlighten public opinion according to my beliefs and what I believe are the beliefs of the Greek people.

Because I was getting no support from our own Greek newspapers of the Center, I had decided to write my own defense prior to the interrogation and get it published in the Athens *Post,* one of the two English-language newspapers published in Athens. I called Al Wagg, a funny little free-lance journalist, publicist, moviemaker, etc., an American always warm to the Papandreou cause, and asked him if he could get an article in the *Post* on the issue of my letter and interrogation. "You bet," he said. "Just write it up, and I'll submit it." So I wrote my own story—about me—and it was printed. I

90

must say that my defense of myself was quite eloquent. Fortunately, it was printed the same day as my session with Laganis. Had it been printed a day later, I would have been accused of giving information I was not entitled to give, since I touched on some of the issues I was questioned about.

The initiative of the King to dump Papandreou created a wide vehement public reaction. On Sunday, following the Thursday of the dismissal, Papandreou "let it be known" that he would visit his political office at seven o'clock Monday night. This meant a drive down the main trunk boulevard, Vassilis Sophias, leading into Athens from the northeast, passing by the Parliament building into Constitution Square in the heart of the city.

Masses of people turned out in a wild display of spontaneous support for the downed Prime Minister they had elected. For them it was also a matter of *filotomo*; that fine Greek word which has no real equivalent in English, called by some "love of honor," but which may be more accurately depicted by the words "pride" or "ego." They, as a people, had been treated like dust, like trash, like "subjects," by an arrogant King who was saying in essence, "Your votes mean nothing, your judgment is bad; I will choose your parliamentary leaders for you."

The one they had chosen, however, was at that moment driving into downtown Athens, and Vassilis Sophias was lined with roaring, shouting, crying people. He was a hero, mistreated, maligned, "the old man of democracy," kicked out by a punk. Constitution Square was jammed to its corners with waving, sweating, red-faced men and women. The mood was one of anger and hurt. It was my father-in-law's most triumphant moment. That night he also had an immense power, which he didn't use, and which was never to be his again. As the Ambassador of Egypt told us a few days later, "My secretary told me it was a prerevolutionary crowd."

Naturally, the Palace was scared. But when it started its series of letters to Papandreou prior to July 15, it had counted on one thing: Papandreou wouldn't bite. He might holler, he might address huge rallies, he might use all the accepted techniques of democratic operation, but he would not, for instance, instruct a crowd to charge the Palace, or set up a violent situation between Greeks. This was the splendid humane side of this man. It was also his weakness.

During this demonstration the King sat well guarded and protected in his palace at Tatoi, far from the madding crowd. He was beginning his business enterprise: the buying and purchasing of deputies; the trading, the cajoling and coercing; in short, the attempt to put together a viable concern which could be presented as a parliamentary majority. He had the commitment from his own party, ERE (the party of the Right was always considered the King's party), to vote for any government he set up with a splinter Center Union group. But ERE had only one hundred duputies, and fifty-one would have to be coaxed away from Papandreou to make the government legal. He felt pretty safe; he was sure he would get American assistance.

CHAPTER ELEVEN

Patching Together a Government — with the Help of CIA

THE NEXT two years, the second anendotos, saw the emergence of Andreas as the key political figure in Greece. All the attempts to attack him, to discredit him, to label him "communist," had failed to halt his growing popularity. He was called a "parachutist" by some newspapers—someone who had dropped from the skies into the midst of Greek politics. He was called "arrogant," "ambitious," and very frequently a "demagogue." Most of these appellations were repeated by United States Embassy and military personnel, and we got word-by-word reports from Greek friends attending cocktail parties or small gatherings where these Americans were present and the conversation turned to Andreas. The forces of the Right and the United States got assistance from a prominent American journalist and Palace sidekick, Cyrus Sulzberger. On August 8, 1965, he wrote a scurrilous article entitled "Handy Andy: U.S. Gift to Greece." Appearing in the prestigious *New York Times,* it carried weight, and helped form a hostile American public opinion toward Andreas among people not familiar with the Greek case. Here are some paragraphs from that piece:

> George Papandreou, a wily, eloquent old orator, is now fighting to get back the Premiership in a continuing crisis. He was dislodged in a fight with young King Constantine over the army. He symbolizes a very considerable movement which wants to restrict the Crown's political power and Andreas Papandreou, his 47 year old son, is unabashedly ambitious to succeed his father and to lead this country even further leftward. Many of Andreas' enemies say he wants to form a Socialist party and unite with the Communists in an outright popular front.
>
> Andreas lived in the United States more than twenty years and there, while making a brilliant career as an economist, he acquired an Illinois-born wife, Margaret, four children, and the nickname "Andy," by which he is widely known. Andy is very handy to his father because of his left-wing contacts and his talents as an operator.
>
> During the pre-war Metaxas dictatorship, Andreas began writing political pamphlets at sixteen and was associated with a Marxist movement. He was arrested and beaten by Metaxas police and is said to have involved some associates. At that time he had a close friend whose brother, Leonidas Kirkos, is now an important official of the

*legally permitted pro-Communist party, E.D.A. Kirkos and Andreas
know each other well and are suspected of collaborating in producing
the mobs that have been staging street demonstrations.*

*Andreas had no suspicious record in the U.S.A., but since his return
he has contacted important foreign communists on European travels.
His wife, Margaret, who is adored by her father-in-law, has tried to
help as a propagandist by writing chain letters to American women
proclaiming the Papandreou program as beneficent and Jeffer-
sonian. . . .*

*Andreas Papandreou has intellectual brilliance, personal charm, a
way with women, and a knack for intrigue. He opposes present U.S.
policy in Greece and probably suspects Washington wants to keep
him from gaining power—despite the corny letters his wife has started
writing to important Americans whom she fancies as her penpals.*

The technique of the article is not unknown to the dishonest journalist.
First of all, say something good about something irrelevant ("brilliant career
as an economist") so that when you say something more important
("unabashedly ambitious . . . to lead the country further leftward") it will be
believed. Secondly, use the qualifying phrase "according to his enemies" so
that you can say all the nasty things desired, and sound factual, knowing that
most readers will forget the qualifier and accept the substance of the
statement. Thirdly, and most important, damage him by linking him up with
the communists, knowing that for the Americans there can be no greater
crime.

In conjunction with this article in *The New York Times* Sulzberger wrote
one for *The New York Times Magazine,* printed on August 15, 1965. The title
of the piece was "A King on Trial." Perhaps it was the first public hint of a
dictatorship-in-the-making. "Young Constantine is a fighter. . . .If it comes to
an issue of crown vs crowd he figures that many . . . prefer royal stability to
left-wing domination."

Sulzberger's Greek wife is the niece of Queen Mother Frederika's closest
friend. He is one of the few journalists in the world ever given a private
interview with King Paul. He had easy and ready access to the Palace
whenever he wanted. He and his wife have property on the island of Spetses. I
am saying this to prove that he is not, and has never been, an objective
observer of the Greek scene. To the reader of *The New York Times* editorial
page, he was the roving reporter, commenting on and analyzing the situation
in various countries. The reader could not have known his special, highly
personal, and emotional involvement in Greece, as the reader of this book
knows mine. His damaging series of articles on Andreas—three of them—his
constant support of the King, and his exaggeration of the communist menace
in Greece assisted in creating the atmosphere for a right-wing take-over. He
was counting on its being a King's coup, the kind of dictatorship he could
embrace.

To complete the Sulzberger story, permit me to jump ahead to 1967.
Sulzberger arrived in Athens right after the coup. The King was still on his
throne and Andreas under lock and key. He was one of the first reporters

who with almost orgiastic glee—rushed over to see "the adversary" in captivity at Pikermi, the hotel where Andreas was kept prior to being taken to prison. After viewing the animal, and asking the two questions which were permitted: "How are you being treated?" and "Is your food all right?" he wrote his last column on Andreas—for the time being. (One has since appeared—August 23, 1968,—castigating Andreas again, and his deals with the Left, and giving limited praise to the junta.) Having long ago plunged the knife in, he used this opportunity to twist it.* He sent me, as he reported in his column, books for Andreas' reading pleasure. They were the following, and had these obvious implications: *The Splendor of Greece*, by Robert Payne—that Andreas had despoiled Greece politically; *Ethics*, by Dietrich Bonhoeffer—that he was a demagogue; *Judgment at Deltchev*, by Eric Ambler—that he was implicated in the ASPIDA conspiracy; *The Masque of the Red Death*, by Edgar Allen Poe—that he was faced with a maximum sentence of death for treason; *From Russia with Love*, by Ian Fleming—that he was a communist.

He must have sweated profusely charging around Athens bookstores to locate the appropriate titles. Needless to say, I did not send the packet to Andreas. But I have picked out some lovely reading matter for Cyrus in return, and when the time comes, I will send them. *The King and I*, play based on *Anna and the King of Siam*, by Margaret Landon; *Desperate Remedies*, by Thomas Hardy; *Huntsman What Quarry?* by Edna St. Vincent Millay; *The Decay of Lying*, by Oscar Wilde; and *Heart of Darkness*, by Joseph Conrad.

Immediately after the ousting of Papandreou, the King was in "his counting house," as the old nursery rhyme goes, and the "wheeling and dealing" period started. The method used was labeled by the Center press as the "salami technique." It was an apt description, and an effective technique. The trick was to pick up slices of the Center Union party until the combined slices could join the mashed potatoes (ERE) and become a full course. The slices contained (1) a prime ministership, (2) assorted ministries, and in some instances, (3) money. Thus George Athanassiadis-Novas became the first apostate Prime Minister. He had been waiting in full dress behind the heavy window drapes in the King's Palace to take the new oath of office when Papandreou was dismissed—according to some imaginative reports. It was true, however, that twenty minutes after Papandreou left the Palace, Novas was sworn in. Eventually, he brought his cohorts, led by the chief apostate, Kostas Mitsotakis of Crete, most of whom had formed the Club to Dump Papandreou, along with the Palace, the army, Americans, and the Right. The difficulty was that the slices were not enough, only twenty-four deputies, and the coalition failed to get a vote of confidence in Parliament. All of these deputies received ministerial posts. The second man to be offered the premiership was Elias Tsirimokos, the socialist-leftist and ex-EAM man of the civil war. (EAM was the communist-led guerilla movement.) This was almost too much for the Right to swallow, but they reasoned that they would control him by being able to withdraw their support at any time.

*See Gertrud Lenzer's analysis of Sulzberger's articles on Greece in *The Death of a Democracy*, by Stephen Rousseas.

His slice of the Center Union party was not impressive, however; and in the end Markezinis, leader of a minor rightist party, withdrew his votes, and the second King-appointed apostate Premier did not get a vote of confidence. The situation was getting desperate. The third man, Stephanopoulos, was chosen by Constantinos, and by now CIA men were dashing around with funds and promises trying to help the King patch together a government, any government, to end the crisis and dispose of the Papandreous for good.

On September 11 my father-in-law made a statement to the press, which contained the elements of the second anendotos (to be further elaborated and carried on by Andreas), the proper functioning of the Constitution, and the rights of the people versus the rights of the Kings. These are quotes from the first half of the statement. The second half contained an assertion of his faith in democracy and his conviction that "democracy will win."

> *Two months have passed. The anomaly continues and grows worse. The anomaly occurred when the majority leader was forced to resign. This is unprecedented in the country's political history. Now the question arises: Whose fault is it? It is the fault of those who provoked the anomaly and are now prolonging it.*
>
> *1. I address to expert constitutionalists the question: if they insist in finding justification for the first mandate given to Novas, how can they justify the second mandate to Tsirimokos? And after the voting down of Mr. Tsirimokos, how do they justify the adventure of the third round that has just been initiated? Is this use or abuse of a right?*
>
> *2. There is also the question, apart from the constitutional one, of moral order. The King, as Supreme Ruler, is also the despository of moral values, of the prestige of institutions. But what are the means used to try to get a successful majority number in Parliament? The immoral means of buying off deputies through the offer of ministries. No ideological defection has been effectuated up to now. All defections were accompanied by appointments to ministries. Parliament has become a trading place. How can this fact leave the Supreme Ruler indifferent? So much the more when these methods are used for the success of royal initiatives? Is it not correct that not only parliamentary votes be examined but also the means used to procure those votes?*
>
> *3. The fearful Herculeses of the Throne claim that elections would destroy the King's prestige. But why? Elections would be called among the parties. The royal prestige is destroyed by the voting down of royal governments in Parliament. And these governments are voted down because they do not derive from the people, but are products of the royal mandate. Parliament must express the will of the people.*
>
> *4. There is moreover another abuse of a right. It is the fact that the will of the majority in Parliament has been expressed in favor of*

its dissolution. Nevertheless, the Supreme Ruler has not responded to the will of this majority.

During this period, July 15 to September 24, there were demonstrations in the streets and workers' strikes. While the King was making a personal tour of the country, carrying his newborn royal princess in his arms to touch the hearts of the people, the citizens of his country were asserting their rights. The Center youth, workers, and other supporters were joined by the Left. There is no doubt that there was collaboration in this resistance to the violation of the Constitution. But the two political groups represented, after all, 65 percent of the Greek people, and it was they who were going to pay in the end for this act of the King: the Center by losing government and the possibility of putting in a progressive program, the Left by losing some of the freedoms it had enjoyed under the Papandreou government for the first time in twenty years. A common cry in the demonstrations was "ena-ena-tessara," one-one-four, the article in the Constitution that says the ultimate protection of the Constitution is in the hands of the Greeks themselves.

The foreign press, particularly the American press, got into the act and began writing its sensational headlines: "Leftist Youths Battle Police," "Riots in Athens Led by Leftists," "Police Fight Left in Hour-Long Confrontation; 31 Injured," etc. On one of these occasions Andreas and I arrived at City Hospital to visit the wounded. We had heard that Kaklamanis, former head of the party youth group during the difficult days of the first anendotos against Karamanlis, had been seriously hurt.

We found him in bed in a semicoma, a wicked-looking bruise over his left eye. He recognized Andreas and through swollen lips muttered, "the bastards," and fell back into unconsciousness. Andreas moved around from bed to bed and talked to the men, mostly young men, lying there. Of the twenty men in that ward, one was a communist. The rest belonged to various democratic organizations and were definitely ours. This ratio was probably the general ratio of Center to Left in most of the activities that took place that long, hot summer of 1965. It is apparently not very exciting to news editors in the States to have copy read, "Center Youth Fights Police" or "Democrats Battle for their Rights." It has to be that old bogeyman, communism, that makes the city desk do pirouettes and say "print this," and the reporter on the scene need ferret out only one leftist or one Leftist slogan ("Down with fascism!") to call it a communist-dominated rally.

Because the leftists participated in these Center-dominated demonstrations and because many pro-Andreas slogans were used, the appellation "leftist leader" was attached to Andreas, assisted by the quarterback on *The New York Times* editorial page, Cyrus Sulzberger. The Americans in Greece were quick to point out how justified they had been in their fear of Andreas, that his leftist associations were now out in the open and this was further reason, they argued, for rushing to the aid of the waterlogged King, floundering in the storm.

There was purpose in these demonstrations. The government representing the majority of the Greek people had been dismissed because it "didn't have the confidence of the King." It had, however, the confidence of the people.

Or if the King judged that it did not, since he was obliged to ensure that Parliament was in harmony with the will of the people, then there was one sure, democratic way to test it—elections. The purposes of the demonstrations were two: to make it difficult for the Center deputies to leave the party and join the apostates, seeing the public reaction to this act of treason to the party, and second, to get new elections. Orders were given by the political leadership that no weapons were to be carried and that this civil disobedience was to be at all times peaceful. It is most significant that for the first time since 1963, when Papandreou was elected Premier, the heads of Greek civilians were clouted by the police. One young boy was killed. Despite many demonstrations during the Papandreou government, not one man landed in the hospital. But acts of brutality were back, the real sign of a minority government in power against the will of the people. These acts were to increase over the ensuing two years and reach their peak in the tortures at Bouboulinas Street Station under the rule of the smallest minority ever to impose itself on the Greek people, the present-day junta of the colonels.

When Stephanopoulos squeaked through on September 24, 1965, with a vote of 152-148, the struggle to force the King to call new elections was over. All the King's horses and all the King's men had put Humpty-Dumpty back on the wall—for the time being. The King could go back to his squash game. American officials could stop nabbing deputies in the halls of Parliament to urge them to participate in the new government. CIA agents could stop paying bribes, making promises, and paying for publicity to castigate the Papandreous and build up the image of the King. The game had been technically a success. Instead of working to prevent the subversion of the Constitution, the Americans assisted in it.

How does a CIA agent bribe a man? It is very simple and very crude. One case: After the fall of Tsirimokos the need for additional deputies for the third round was extreme, and of necessity, some of those close to Andreas had to be approached. A Greek-American businessman, extremely influential in Greece, went to the house of such a deputy, and over a cocktail they discussed the Greek political situation in general. "Oh, I know you are close to Andy, and I know you like him. I like him, too. I knew him well in the States. But this is not his time. He is too new in politics and too inept. He should ripen up a bit. Meanwhile, the country has to be helped out of this morass. There will be other elections in a few years . . . let those be his. And that's what I want to talk to you about. You will need funds for those elections. You will be afraid that if you go with the apostate government you will lose your popularity with your people in Messenia, but with good money, and two years to repair the damage, you will be a sure winner. I want to help. I can write a check now. You understand . . . I'm doing this because I love Greece. I'd give my shirt for this country . . ."

In the second case, an attractive woman CIA agent came into Greece literally with bags of money. She was introduced as the friend of one of the bachelor deputies, one of the early defectors, and was seen around town with him to help promote the idea that he had the support of the Americans, and the means, to make payoffs. This was done, on a large scale. Part of the funds even went into the ASPIDA case for the framing of Andreas. A Greek girl was paid 50,000 drachmas to make a deposition against Andreas to be added to the fattening ASPIDA file. For some reason, unknown to us, when she went to make her deposition (a pang of conscience?) she charged she had been bribed, stating the amount of money and the name of the deputy turned CIA boyfriend who bribed her, with the date and place. This deposition was seen by Andreas' lawyers and remains now, or should remain, in the official file of depositions in the prosecuting attorney's office. It was not included, naturally, in the final indictment against Andreas. An ex-KYP man told me at a later date that all of their methods and techniques were taught to them by Americans, usually Greek-Americans who spoke Greek well. When I asked him what they were taught he said it varied, depending on the section an agent was in. He and his group were taught how to build up a network of informers. The Americans taught them what kinds of approaches were most effective with what kinds of people. Payment was an obvious technique, but there were others. In some cases the informer could be made to believe he was performing his patriotic duty. In other cases, blackmail would be effective. Or a simple threat might be enough. Other groups were involved in the study of wire tapping and bugging of conversations. He made eminently clear that the Greek KYP was under the tutelage of the American CIA, with little contact or responsibility to its own government.

According to the Constitution, elections did not have to be called until February 1968, exactly four years after the previous elections, and a one-month extension is constitutionally acceptable, which would make it March 1968. On such matters the Palace and the Right could be extremely constitutional. This gave legal time of two years to kill off whatever political life remained in the Papandreous after displacing them from government. George, it was assumed, would be too old by then to participate actively in politics, and Andreas would find it difficult to ever get a majority with the entire establishment against him, and thus his power would be limited.

So American diplomatic activities resumed: cocktail parties, dinners for the government, dinners for the King, contacts with American and Greek businessmen. (All the Center Union deputies boycotted all social functions given by the embassy, the few to which they were invited, with the exception of some budding apostates.) In any case, the Papandreous personally were not invited. A new ambassador arrived on the scene to replace Labouisse, whom I really liked, and who I felt did not relish the role he was forced to play in this corruption of Greek institutions. Phillips Talbot moved into the spot, a physically attractive man, tall, silver-haired, soft-voiced, and with the reputation of a liberal. He had long worked on Near East and Middle East affairs in the State Department, and was perhaps more factually knowledgeable about that part of the world than most of his predecessors had been. However, he arrived with a pot of prejudices from the State Department and not enough dynamism to impose himself on the CIA or military portions of the American contingent, nor perhaps the desire. One former American ambassador of another country, whose name I shall not use, told me that having a conversation with Talbot was like playing Ping-Pong with a marshmallow. In the many times I saw him during the dictatorship, with Andreas in jail, I remembered this description all too well.

A mild depression set in among our forces after the vote of confidence for Stephanopoulos. Stephanopoulos was a poor substitute for Papandreou. A man of the Right, who had been the legitimate heir to the party of ERE at the death of Papagos, he had been shunted aside by the Palace-American choice of Karamanlis, and had left his party in a huff. For a while an independent, he finally joined forces with Papandreou when the union of Center parties took place. Always miffed at this earlier affront, he felt the current turn of events was a righting of an historical wrong, and that it was his destiny to be Prime Minister of Greece. The contrast between him and Papandreou was pitiful: Panandreou was flamboyant, he was dull; Papandreou was warm, human, he was a cold fish; Papandreou was electric in his oratory, he was a fumbler and a stumbler. Never married, he was devoted to his mother, and it was a familiar story that he was called by phone from Pyrgos during cabinet meetings when he could be heard saying, "Yes, Mama, yes, Mama . . . don't worry, Mama . . . I'll call you later, Mama." Seemingly mild, he participated during his tenure in office in assisting in the ASPIDA frame-up by giving credence to the false Vahliotis testimony, and by offering a girl half a million drachmas in state funds to turn over a letter she said was incriminating.

From the moment of birth of the illegitimate Stephanopoulos government, Andreas plunged into a long, grueling, physically exhausting crusade to bring the issues to the people. His incisive powers of analysis combined with his ability to teach clarified the problems of the Greek nation. He laid naked the power structure, displayed its weaknessess, and optimistically pointed out the changes that could benefit the people and make the nation strong. He called it a "peaceful revolution." Three main themes emerged in this crusade: "The King reigns; the people rule," "Greece to the Greeks," and "The Army belongs to the Nation." He carried on a dialogue—with the farmers in Thessaly, with the workers in Piraeus, with the islanders of the Sporades, with the doctors in Athens, with the young people of the universities. They all taught him as well, and he was a good pupil. Their problems became his problems. They called him by his first name, Andreas, partly to distinguish him from his father, but primarily because this was the kind of relationship they had with him. As the people liked to touch and paw him, he also liked this physical contact, and I saw him often with his hand on the shoulder of a simple Greek, his head cocked to catch the words in the midst of a noisy crowd, hungrily trying to understand the man's complaint, or suggestion, or words of dedication. In villages where he intended just to drive through on his way to a speech, crowds would block the street, stop the car, pull him out and hoist him into the air. Then they would beg for a few words, and a hush would fall on the group encircling him as they strained to catch everything he said. It was possibly too much adoration, for he was not a saviour. One felt that the Greeks had so often been betrayed, had heard so many lies and half-truths, that their love and affection for him came from the appreciation of his efforts to speak the truth with all its un-niceties and hardness. It also came from his obvious respect for them, new in Greek public life. It was reported to me that a conservative newspaper editor said at one point, "He is a cultured, educated gentlemen. I wait for him to get tired of that pawing by dirty hands, that garlic-laden air, that simple oily eating in simple tavernas with the simple folk." As I traveled with him, I thought of this editor's comment, and his waiting. It would be a long wait.

In March of 1966 we had a setback. My father-in-law suffered a heart attack, and within a week Andreas too was down in bed with a severe cold and high fever and the spitting of blood. X rays showed he had contracted tuberculosis. For the rest of March and all of April I seemed to be sitting at the bedside of one or the other of the two Papandreous. My father-in-law made an initial rapid recovery, only to discover that it was to take months before he regained some of his old energy and verve. Even then, recovery was not complete. Andreas, on the other hand, got well by inches. He lost weight, slept fitfully, and his eyes, under his prominent eyebrows, took on a strange, bright glow which I had seen only once before when, in another sickness, he had been obliged to take massive doses of drugs. He was ordered not to see any of his political circle, just close friends. Twice a day a stooped, wizened little man came with a needle. We waited anxiously for some change in his condition. Slowly his drawn look began to fade, his fever descended, his night sweating lessened, and he began to eat more than a few bites of the food we placed in front of him.

By May he was back on his feet again, and not just standing, but running. We had described his sickness as pneumonia, and it wasn't until he was in jail, when I considered it necessary to make an issue of his condition, that people learned he had had tuberculosis. It was then assumed by many that he had contracted the disease while in his cell at Averoff. This was not true. What was true was that the dampness and coldness of his cell, the darkness, the foul air, and the cramped quarters were all conditions for a relapse.

May passed, June, July—July 15, the anniversary of the King's dismissal of Papandreou. A shaky, unstable government continued to survive, every renegade member of the old Center Union a minister—the payoff for leaving the party—with the deputies of ERE forming the underpinnings for one of the strangest deals in Greek parliamentary history. This unholy alliance could be broken by the defection of two deputies. Or ERE could withdraw its support and the edifice would crumble. Thus blackmail became a way of government. The Stephanopoulos group formed itself into a party called FIDIK (the Greek word for snake is *fidi,* and the name of the new party was considered appropriate), and was obliged to respond to many requests from ERE in order to keep ERE's support. On the other hand, FIDIK could remind ERE that withdrawal meant elections, for which ERE was not yet prepared. This seesaw of threat and blackmail continued. It was unclear what any one party or group stood for; certainly ERE voters were confused and angry, since the government held on through the votes of their deputies, yet none had governmental posts nor policy-making positions. Those who had voted for Center deputies under the leadership of Papandreou were dismayed at the realignment of parliamentary forces, and EDA, the Left, was silent, the victim of splits within its own ranks. Most likely these conditions added to Andreas' zooming popularity. His was a clarion voice in this babel, stating clearly the principles in which he believed and the program that he stood for. He was emerging as the real leader of the party, although his father still held the title.

In the fall of 1966 I wrote a letter to our friends, Barbara and Dick Westebbe, who had spent six years in Greece and were now in Washington with the World Bank. They had followed our strivings for a better Greece from close up, and I wanted to keep them apprised of developments. Here is a section from that letter:

> *So we returned glowing, rested and ready to face the onslaught [from a trip to Italy]. HMERA was writing that the strange explosions along the coast of Italy, some unexplained eruptions had happened while we were there, could be easily explained to the Italians. Mr. Andreas was in town! Others were reacting to his articles on foreign policy, which had been printed while we were in Rome (Kathimerini can't leave us alone for at least a week while out of Greece)—and he is being charged with Nasserism, treason, and the usual. . . . but the articles were exceptionally good, and he played a nationalist theme which made it tough for the papers of the Right. It is Andreas' theory that Greece needs a sense of unity of purpose, pride in nation, etc., in order to compete in the European world, to meet the challenges of the Common Market, and to face other problems ahead, after which its bargaining position in joining international agreements will be improved, and it can and should get the most that a little country can in competition in which it has a huge size disadvantage.*
>
> *In any case, I will send you the pieces as soon as the translations have been corrected. He also did a good piece on the economic future of Greece (perhaps you were still here then) and on educational reform, and has several others yet (land use-conservation, administrative reform, agricultural reform, etc.) which will make up the essence of the program of the Center Union party. (Where is the* constructive *approach to the problems of the country, the Americans used to say. . . . well here's the answer.) All pieces have been published in VHMA, which has given him a good projection.*
>
> *The situation with the American Embassy remains the same. A fellow by the name of Day seems to have picked up the Owens role . . . the task of going around the country and saying nasty things about Andreas. In Crete, Day visited the head of the Center Union youth group in his office. He saw a picture of John Kennedy on the fellow's wall and asked him how come. The boy said, "We Greeks loved Kennedy." "Yeah," says Day, "he was great. But his brother is a gangster type." (Pezodromio—leader of mobs—a word they have used about Andreas.) Then he asked, "What is this that I hear about a Kennedy in Greece?" "That's Andreas," said the Greek. After*

which started a tirade from Day . . . how could the Cretans support him . . . their liberal tradition . . . Venizelos, etc., etc.

We have had some long chats with Anschuetz [chargé d'affaires], who remains the warmest to Andreas of anyone in the Embassy. He is deeply concerned about the situation and wants, or hopes, to find some solution to recommend. But the two sides are adamant. The solution for us remains, and will always remain elections, the most democratic, logical way out. The solution remains for them the hope that something will break the power of the Papandreou forces. Essentially, the King is afraid for his throne, and he is putting the country through this dangerous adventure for the sake of preserving the Monarchy, not with the Nation's or the people's interests at heart. In the end he will not preserve it, but destroy it by his own acts. It seems incredible to think of this freedom-loving people buried under the iron fist of an Army, this magnificent, gay people. And yet, the signs, omens and inside information are there."

It was at this stage that a conflict between father and son began to smolder. It was a conflict in its classic form. A father jealous of his son's ability to gain power, his youth, his virility, his productive energy. Side by side existed also a pride in what his son was achieving. But the old man had all his life been stage center; he was unable to play a supporting role. For the son, the fight had become a crusade—an uncompromising fight for the rights of the people. It was an ambitious hope to democratize Greek life more thoroughly—to put the governing of the country in the hands of the Greek people—and to correct some of the stark inequalities. It was undoubtedly the same kind of motivation that had propelled Papandreou, Sr., to get into politics. Papandreou, Sr., was now seventy-eight years old. He had mellowed, had learned the art of compromise, made his way through the maze of intrigue, plot and counterplot, deal and counterdeal, to the top. Although he was no longer head of the country, he was still head of the party, and this position he hung on to tenaciously. Yet his illness had limited his stamina, and doctor's orders limited his public appearances. Under these circumstances it was natural that Andreas assumed a leadership role, often making decisions without consulting his father. Andreas' father considered him ungrateful, impulsive, and disrespectful. As his feelings in this direction got stronger, he began telling them to me, hoping I might act as a brake on what he termed irresponsible actions. This usually happened when I would arrive early with the children for our regular Saturday noon lunch at Kastri, or in the evening before dinners with him when I would arrive from home before Andreas left his office.

I would find him alone, since most political appointments were scheduled for the morning hours. He would be waiting for us, sitting in a maroon-colored upholstered chair, Greek music playing softly on his tape recorder, to which he seemed not to be listening. He would pull himself out of the low chair as I came in, now often not smiling, kiss me on both cheeks, and say,

"Yasoo, Margarita," in a resigned kind of way, which was a prelude to a long harangue on Andreas and his activities. First he would look behind me toward the door. "Andreas?" he would say.

"He'll come directly from his office. He had some things to do . . . "

In the past, he berated Andreas for being late. Now he had stopped saying anything either to him or to me. I would ask Christine, the maid, to bring some ice and soda so that I could make a whiskey at the small desk bar in the corner of the room. The room was the extreme of simplicity. Two plain-colored wall-to-wall carpets provided an imaginary division of the room for eating or sitting, one a deep maroon, the other a deep green. The upholstered furniture carried out the same color scheme. Two unimposing paintings of Greek landscapes, by Greeks, graced the room. Behind his chair at the dining room table in a corner were two framed photos, one of Sophia, the other of Nick. Above the record player which straddled the two rugs along the wall was a photo of Andriko, and on a side table next to the couch was a standing frame with a photo of George, a profile of a sitting pose with his legs tucked up near his chin. My father-in-law liked to turn on the lamp on the table to light up the photo, claiming that it gave the quality of a marble statue to George's figure. When he liked something he would return to it often, pointing out his special observation as if we hadn't heard it before. When he disliked something, he would do the same thing.

"You saw the article in *Ethnos*?" he would ask. Or the speech in Zographou. Or the interview to a foreign journalist. Sometimes I would feign ignorance in order not to have to respond to "What did you think of it?"

Then he would tell me that an action had been taken without his knowledge, and he had heard about it for the first time through a telephone call from a friend. Or that he was about to make a similar statement himself, but that it was a matter of timing and certain delicacies in the issue . . .

My response was always the same. "Why don't you call Andreas more often and have some strategy sessions with him?"

"Why doesn't he check with me before he does something?" would be his answer.

I would shrug my shoulders and agree with him that that would have been a desirable thing to do. Yet I knew that this in itself would have created great friction. Andreas had a far more liberal philosophy than his father and was far more direct in expressing his beliefs to the people. Add to this the fact that my father-in-law had never established any party discipline and each party member had always been free to make public pronouncements as he wished. Andreas, in that sense, was doing no more, no less, than the average Center Union deputy. Andreas was not, however, the average Center Union deputy.

"He is secretive," his father would say. "And impulsive. These are Mineiko traits."

Sigmund Mineiko was Andreas' grandfather on his mother's side. A Polish engineer and distinguished army officer, he had fought for Polish independence from Russia in 1863. He was captured, tried, and sentenced to death. His mother, a wealthy woman, paid vast sums of money to get the sentence converted to life. He was sent to a labor camp in Siberia where he worked under the discipline of a whip. At night he slept handcuffed to another prisoner. His partner died one day, and that night he found himself sleeping alone, unchained for the first time. He seized the opportunity and escaped from the camp. With much difficulty he reached Romania where he managed to make contact with his mother who sent him funds to travel to Paris. There he studied at the Paris War College, and when Turkey requested from France the services of a good engineer, he was recommended and moved to Yannina in northern Greece, an area still occupied by the Turks.

He met Andreas' grandmother there, a pretty young Greek girl, married her, and became an ardent Philhellene. He started drawing maps of the area and smuggling them out to Greek army headquarters, only to be discovered by the Turks who held a council meeting and decided to sentence him to death. One of the members of the council was a friend of his and warned him to escape before he was picked up. He left for Athens where the Greek government gave him a post as chief engineer. In 1912 he left for Salonika and a private conference with King Constantine I, to whom he presented a plan for attacking the Turks from behind in the Yannina area where fighting was going on. His intimate knowledge of the area and his ability to provide maps gave army headquarters in Arta the essential information for a successful attack on the Turks. For this he was to receive a high Medal of Honor from King Constantine I.

He was the father of nine children, one of them Sophia, the first wife of Papandreou and the mother of Andreas. Of the six daughters, two had married Polish princes, and when Sophia brought George Papandreou home, poor and a student at the University of Athens, to introduce him to her parents, he did not make a very happy impression on Sigmund Mineiko. Early in their marriage, when George and Sophia were living with Sophia's parents, Mineiko kicked George out of the house permanently when George made a comment on the loose morals of Polish women.

When George Papandreou was criticizing Andreas, he took out his hostility on old Mineiko as well.

Very often when Andreas arrived, nothing was said of the substance of the conversation between me and his father.

With the passing of time, Papandreou, Sr., began complaining not only to me but to close friends, and it was soon understood that a conflict existed between father and son.

104

CHAPTER TWELVE

How the ASPIDA Case Started

BY the fall of 1966 it was obvious that time had not reduced the strength of the Papandreous. From a friend in banking circles in New York came this letter (October 25, 1966):

> You may be interested to know that, according to some recent visitors from Athens (who incidentally are ideologically sympathetic to Markezinis), the oligarchy will use any means to fight Andreas, not excluding murder as a weapon of last resort. In spite of all this, the same source indicated that no one really doubts the fact that the political base of Andreas has been constantly widening and that if elections are held the Center Union will sweep the polls. On the other hand, they tried to gauge the reaction of the banking circles in New York for a potential dictatorship in Greece. At a luncheon meeting today this question was raised in the presence of a senior officer of a large banking institution in New York. The answer was unequivocal: "a dictatorship in Greece will be bad for the economic development of the country because foreign investment does not go to countries where political conditions will ultimately become explosive, and a dictatorship does exactly that."

This wise bank official was not a representative of the American government, unfortunately, but forces in Greece pushing for a dictatorial solution were still finding opposition in many quarters to this extreme step. Palace-army and rightist circles decided instead to put on the ASPIDA trial which had been kept on ice until now, as the means of delivering the coup de grace to Andreas.

Andreas was scheduled to give the annual Wicksell Lectures on October 2 and 4 at the University of Stockholm. This was an honor which had been bestowed in the past on such great names in economics as Tinbergen, Samuelson, Solo, and Machlup. His topic was "The Political Element in Economic Development." It was while we were planning our trip that news leaked out that the date of the ASPIDA trial would be announced and the indictment published. Rumors reached us that Andreas would be indicted for high treason along with the officers and would be arrested at the airport and barred from leaving for Sweden.

I watched tensely for men in uniform to emerge from the walls of the airport's international waiting room. We left as scheduled, but the Stephan-opoulos government timed the release of the indictment of the officers to hit the newspapers the same day as Andreas' departure, and the press of the Right declared that he had "fled the country." The timing was a move to detract from the honor given to Andreas, and to give the impression, even momentarily, that he had turned tail and run out. Instructions were given to the Greek Embassy in Stockholm to boycott his lectures.

I remember spending a long evening in Drottningholm with our good friends the Svennilsons and the Lundbergs in which Andreas gave them a picture of the political situation back in Greece. They were flabbergasted. "But it's wild," one said. Wild it was, and if I, an American, closely in touch with events had trouble understanding it, what about a Swede, so distant from the Greek scene?

During our stay Cyrus Sulzberger printed another article on Greece, having just visited his young friend Constantinos in Athens. It was a "trial balloon" and appeared in *The New York Times* on October 5. This is the passage that created a violent reaction in Greece: "If Constantine feared the country faced disaster I suspect he might even temporarily suspend some of the Constitution, should he think this necessary to meet the challenge." In the same article, ludicrously combined with the proposed suspension of articles of the Constitution, was the information that the King was a strong, athletic type who had won his black belt in karate! Again the picture of a daring boy, who could split bricks with one swift karate stroke on the one hand and put the Greek nation under his control on the other. About the same time, *Life* magazine published an assortment of flattering pictures of the King and his family, the King dining with Anna Maria, the King piloting his Dragon class sailboat, the King with his brother-in-law Don Carlos of Spain practicing their karate. Slyly included was a one-page piece by Peter Dragadze on the political situation implicating Andreas in the ASPIDA case. Sulzberger and *Life* magazine were softening public opinion in the States for a take-over by the King as a potential necessity against communism and the threat of a left-wing coup.

Here is the paragraph from Dragadze's "The Making of a Monarch" referring to Andreas:*

> *Evidently the combination of character building and general know-how in his education was a happy one for the making of a head of state. Within a year of his accession came the "Papandreou affair," in which the young King boldly stood up to the powerful—and popular—prime minister, George Papandreou. The prime minister wanted to take over immediately the Ministry of Defense, but as there was an investigation pending into an alleged plot in the army in which the premier's son Andreas had been mentioned, the king advised Papandreou to appoint somebody else for the time being. Papandreou refused and offered his resignation, confident that the*

---

*"The Making of a Monarch," by Peter Dragadze, *Life* magazine, October 21, 1966. © 1966 Time Inc. Reprinted by permission of the publisher.

King would back down. But Constantine called the bluff and let Papandreou go. He held to his decision in the face of parliamentary revolts and violent Communist-inspired riots. Two months ago a committee of inquiry presented a report charging that Andreas Papandreou had been a leader of a plot which had aimed at a take-over of the armed forces, to be followed by Greek withdrawal from NATO. *[Emphasis mine.]*

Passions were now roused in Greece. In support of Andreas and what he represented—a democratic way of life—people turned out in the thousands to meet us at the airport when we returned from the Scandinavian countries. We had also attended a student meeting in Oslo and a meeting of the Social Democratic party youth group in Copenhagen. In each case Andreas spoke about the dictatorship threat in Greece and revealed the plans that were under way. He asked for the vigilance and assistance of the democratic peoples of these countries to use their power to prevent such an eventuality. He said it would be a neo-fascist beachhead in Europe—a threat to all European institutions.

At Hellinikon airport at a press conference on our return, he described his trip and spoke of the support he found everywhere for the ideals of democracy. It took us three hours to drive the twenty minutes' normal drive to our home in Psychico from the airport. The streets were lined with people, the traffic lanes jammed with supporters in cars, buses, and motor bikes. What impressed me more than those people hugging our side of the street, the ardent ones who had come out to greet us, was the response of the people on the opposite side, ordinary Greek citizens returning home from work. When they spotted our car, they shouted and tooted a greeting with equal enthusiasm.

This was the pleasant side. The unpleasant was the presence of the police in hordes. Frankly I was frightened. The possibilities for bloody street clashes were obvious. The police were overwhelmed by and scared of the crowd. We picked up a young boy reeling in the street from a blow on the back of his head. He groaned until he heard he was in the car of Andreas Papandreou. Quickly he improved and at one point, saying nothing, he jumped out of our slow-moving car and joined the chanting mob. The crowds were angry. This was their answer to the King and his ASPIDA-mania, and the cry "one-one-four," that they, the people, would protect the Constitution, was everywhere.

But the King wasn't listening.

Twenty-eight officers, most of whom had been kept in prison for seventeen months awaiting trial, were brought to court-martial on charges of high treason. The indictment was brought against them, plus "other persons, known or unknown," for whom a separate investigative procedure would be held. It was meant to be a trial against Andreas in absentia. As a member of Parliament, he had deputy immunity which could be removed only by a majority vote in Parliament. Despite the antagonism toward Andreas, deputy immunity was highly prized, and not many deputies cared to start a precedent which might one day be used against them.

In February of 1965 an informal communication from General Grivas from Cyprus to the Palace started the ASPIDA affair. In May in a formal report he stated that he had discovered a conspiracy in the army. He added that there were indications that Andreas Papandreou was implicated. There were probably two reasons for the writing of this communication. One was that Andreas' visit to Cyprus at the invitation of Archbishop Makarios in November 1964 had been enthusiastically received—particularly among the members of the Greek army stationed on Cyprus. Grivas and Makarios were archenemies, Makarios looking upon the Greek troops in Cyprus as a mixed blessing: They were protection against the Turks and an occupying force. Makarios' dream was an independent Cyprus; Grivas' was *enosis,* or union with Greece. Andreas got along well with Makarios and was feted as a VIP. Grivas disliked this and the impact Andreas made on the young Greek officers and soldiers. The second reason for the communication was that some kind of loose organization of officers did exist, most of them from the same officers' graduating class, formed ostensibly as a mutual benefit society, each to help the other in getting army promotions. These groupings were not unusual in the Greek army. The means for getting promotions, as for getting anything done in Greece, were political connections. The group was "shopping around," one might say, for a strong political personality to whom they could attach themselves. Among the names being mentioned in the group were Mitsotakis, Vardinoyannis, Stephanopoulos, and Andreas, all ministers in the Papandreou government. Andreas was a rising star and had power in his father's government. He was also appealing as a new figure on the political scene, unfettered by past connections, associations, or deals.

No one in the group knew him. One of the members, Papageorgopoulos, was dispatched to make an appointment with Andreas and meet him. This was easy because Papageorgopoulos came from Andreas' constituency, and his family had long been political supporters of George Papandreou. The subject to be discussed had to do with a family problem in Achaia. Papageorgopoulos reported enthusiastically to Bouloukos, the alleged head of the ASPIDA club. He liked the man, he said.

Thus, according to the ASPIDA indictment, Bouloukos became a preacher of "democracy," and in all his meetings with other officers, he described the virtues of democracy and advertised its leaders. He is reported to have said that Andreas Papandreou is a "great economist, that he fully understands the Cyprus problem, that he is the incarnation of the ideals of democracy, that the country is not going well but that fortunately there is Andreas Papandreou who will govern Greece and for this reason we must organize around him so that he can put into effect his policies." Again, according to the indictment, other officers were saying that "Andreas Papandreou is a brain, he was Kennedy's adviser and the only one to lead the country out of the deadlock."

On this flimsy evidence, on the basis of his own jealousies, and thinking that it would serve the King's needs at the time, Grivas started the row which was then to be picked up by KYP, extreme rightists in the army, the Palace, and Palace-oriented judicial personalities. One of these latter was Constantine

108

Kollias, chief justice of the highest Greek court, close friend of Queen Mother Frederika, and eventual Prime Minister Number One of the dictatorship. They built it into a monstrous frame-up, eventually entangling some of the framers themselves in their own evildoing. (Grivas has been retired from the army; the King is in exile; Kollias has been stripped of his judicial robes; Socratides, Kollias' sidekick and investigating prosecutor, has been kicked out of his job; the Queen Mother is in Rome.) The KYP portion helping in the frame-up are in power in Greece today.

By the time the news of the army "conspiracy" reached the ears of Andreas and his father, Bouloukos himself had visited Andreas' office twice, on the pretext of asking for complimentary boat tickets for a trip he was to make to Cyprus, off-duty, which he did not get. There was nothing unusual in his visit. Political offices in Greece had arrangements with shipowners to enable them to hand out small political favors to their friends. He made a general tour during this time of many political offices, including those of Mitsotakis, Vardinoyannis, Costopoulos, and Papaconstantinos. Whether he was a conspirator in search of a leader, whether he merely wanted to prove to his boys that he had pull enough to be seen by members of the government, or whether he was just trying to advance his own personal aims, I do not know. Except for a few comments on the Cyprus situation with Andreas, he did not mention the existence of a group out to "overthrow the government, set up a Nasser-Tito socialist style dictatorship and take Greece out of NATO." In fact, the name ASPIDA, or "shield," was read for the first time by Andreas in a newspaper in April, 1965.

If Andreas *had* wanted to set up a conspiracy in the army, I think he would have chosen someone more qualified than Bouloukos. Captain Aristotle Bouloukos had been a member of the extreme-right-wing Grivas group uncovered by Karamanlis in 1961. At that time disciplinary action was taken against the members of the organization, and they were shunted off to new and widely dispersed posts.

In addition, if Andreas *had* been the leader of ASPIDA, he could not have written the grammatically bad, poorly phrased oath which was offered in the indictment as proof of the existence of such an organization. The oath offered had no signature on it, which hardly made it admissable evidence, but it is interesting as a document because nowhere can one conclude that the aims of ASPIDA were those later attributed to it. It reads as follows:

> *I take an oath in the name of my country, as the only supreme thing for me, after God, to offer myself to her totally, until my death, for the completion of the following objectives of ASPIDA:*
>
> *1. For the preservation of every security and freedom from all treacherous and belligerent foreign enemies.*
>
> *2. For the preservation of all values that constitute a nation of justice, for the safety from every Communist activity, anti-popular force and any other internal intrigue.*
>
> *3. For the preservation and maintenance of the democratic form of government in the sense of the Rule by the Worthy and rejection of every kind of superficial dignity.*

4. *For the indestructible struggle to create a Great Greece.*

5. *For the support of the democratic government, in the sense of the Rule by the Worthy, with all my strength and all means available, even if force is needed for the processes of democracy to function.*

6. *I pledge blind and unlimited obedience to ASPIDA and the commands of the representative leader, acknowledging ASPIDA as the only bearer of legal authority in case action is undertaken for the purpose of achieving its objectives.*

7. *I pledge to offer myself in every sense of sacrifice for the realization of ASPIDA's aims. To remain aloof from politics, to carry as the symbol of ASPIDA the moral integrity of the Greek Officer and to be considered dishonorable if I violate this oath.*

After having notified the Palace and high army officials of his suspicions of the existence of such an organization, Grivas ordered an administrative investigation by a brigadier general D. Kollias (not related to the junta's first Prime Minister), which was submitted on May 5, 1965, to the Minister of National Defense, Petros Garoufalias. At that time the Prime Minister, Garoufalias, and Andreas decided on a sworn administrative investigation by the Lieutenant General of Military Justice, J. Simos. It is hard to imagine that if Andreas had been involved, he would have been so willing to urge an investigation. The results of the investigation were submitted on June 1, 1965, and read as follows:

(1) It was indeed confirmed that a movement to form an organization by the name of ASPIDA was in progress by a team of officers with the selfish aim of serving their personal interests and those of the organization's members through the initiated officer's advancement into opportune and important positions, and a further aim, which was not, however, substantiated or revealed. (2) It was not confirmed that this movement had any political aspirations or any affiliation with political figures. (3) During the above movement, it was diligently sought to initiate primarily junior officers, with Infantry Captains Bouloukos, Aristotle Panoutsos, J. Papagiannopolos, and J. Theodosiou acting for this purpose. (4) Because of the loyalty of most officers, the faithful preservation by them of their oath and their devotion to military duty, the number of recruited officers in the aforementioned organization was minimal. (5) From the gathered evidence it was not verified that another paramilitary organization exists. [Emphasis mine.]

This should have been the end of it. Disciplinary action could have been taken and the case dismissed. It was obvious that it was not a serious development, that those officers said to be involved were captains, lieutenants, and adjutants, and none was in a key position or had sufficient authority to carry out any kind of coup.

When Papandreou proposed to dispose of the issue in this fashion, the King reacted, and so did Garoufalias, Minister of Defense. When a conflict developed, Garoufalias—a Papandreou appointee—sided with the King. The

King wanted an interrogatory investigation of the ten officers cited in the lengthier Simos report. Papandreou said the Simos report did not give adequate reasons for beginning something that would turn into a judicial process, eventual court-martial, and jail. The King insisted. Finally Papandreou said he would do so, but he would take a parallel action with it. He would bring under interrogatory investigation the officers involved in Plan Pericles, the scheme developed by the army to rig the elections of 1961, long a sore point for George Papandreou, and something he had refrained from doing in order not to antagonize the King and put on trial some of Constantinos' faithful officers.

This was the point of the real break. The King was concerned not only that there were officers in the army plotting against him, but that Papandreou was about to carry out a purge of right-wing officers loyal to the King. His advisers spurred him on to take action. His closest adviser, Constantine Hoidas, was in contact with Mitsotakis of the Center Union and assured the King that Mitsotakis had enough Center Union deputies behind him to defect should the King care to confront Papandreou, and that a new parliamentary government could be voted in quickly with the help of ERE. CIA agents and American Mission officers had been moving around Athens for some time expressing general disgust for the Papandreous, father and son. The stage was set, and when Papandreou moved to take over the Defense Ministry himself—not to protect Andreas as the foreign press reported, but to rid himself of a disloyal government minister—the curtain fell, and the last act was about to be played.

ASPIDA was put in deep freeze, twenty-eight officers were carted off to be held in jail pending trial, eighteen more than named in the Simos report (in order to give a weighty appearance to the conspiracy), and a diligent, fiendish secret process of concocting evidence began.

In October 1966, seventeen months after they were jailed, the officers were brought to trial as the establishment's "ace in the hole." Ironically, it backfired on them. Instead of proving the King's case, that he had had to take vigorous action to circumvent a take-over by a group of officers, headed by Andreas Papandreou, it proved only that he was immature, lacking in judgment and prone to panic. Evidence given to implicate Andreas would have thrown the case out of court the first day in any Anglo-Saxon system of justice.

An unimaginable assortment of witnesses was paraded before the court, including a man named Lalakis, owner of the Lucky Bar and convicted procurer of women, who made some monstrous claims about overhearing conversations among ASPIDA officers in jail (being in jail on a morals charge himself) which proved to him that a coup d'etat was being prepared by George Papandreou. Two of the accused officers stood up in court and stated that they had been offered bribes to give testimony against the Papandreous, to the tune of $100,000 per officer. They also said that a third officer had accepted a bribe of one million drachmas ($33,333) and had turned state's evidence.

Shortly after the trial started, Andreas paid a surprise visit to the court while proceedings were going on. It was an act of courage. Everyone else wanted to forget the whole affair and abandon the officers to their fate. This was particularly true of the politicians who preferred not to tangle with the King and the army.

But Andreas felt that basic principles were being violated. After his visit he explained his views in an interview with the newspaper *Ethnos*:

> *I wish to point out through my presence today in the Courtroom the flagrant violation of the Constitution and the Greek citizen's basic rights, that the ASPIDA construction represents.*
>
> *The King's letters to the lawfully-elected Prime Minister of the country are as such, independently of their insulting character, a violation of the Constitution of a crowned democracy. The Royal constitutional experts should tell us which article of the Constitution gives the right to the King to send such letters to the Prime Minister. Furthermore, which is the article of the Constitution which transforms the non-responsible Monarch into a prosecution witness against Greek citizens and officers, through the use of his letters in the report of the military committee of inquiry? This is the first violation in respect to the ASPIDA case.*
>
> *But there is a second one: the more than one year long preventive arrest of the officers is a violation of the Constitution and of the international rules on human freedom and other inalienable rights.*
>
> *There is a third flagrant violation of the parliamentary regime, of our parliamentary system: the notorious ASPIDA report contains conclusions concerning the alleged interference of deputies in the affair—a thing which is well beyond the competence of the military prosecutor.*
>
> *And fourth, despite the fact that regular justice is competent for political affairs, this affair, as far as the accused deputies are concerned, has been taken away from the normal judges of the accused and given to the Military Court, which does not have the right to judge, nor does it provide any constitutional guarantees for independent judgment.*

This last violation was referring to the fact that a good portion of the trial was devoted to determining the guilt of Andreas Papandreou.

Under the brilliant handling of Nikiforos Mandiliras, a dynamic forty-year-old lawyer representing one of the accused officers, revelation piled on revelation exposing the army machinations, and the accusers became the accused. Mandiliras earned the undying hatred of the military judges and the army in general which had an arrogant certainty that it could do no wrong. He paid with his life for daring to challenge this authority. One month after the military coup, his body was washed up on the shores of the island of Rhodes. The junta's explanation was that the captain of the ship Mandiliras was using to escape from Greece had put him overboard when wireless communication from a shore-patrol boat asked if there were any illegal passengers aboard, and that Mandiliras drowned trying to swim to the island.

The details of the way he really died were supplied later by a navy defector of the junta who said Mandiliras had been apprehended on the boat, taken ashore, tortured, then killed, and his body dumped into the sea to make it appear an accident. I remember him well, coming to our home with Andreas, a man of courage, energetic, devoted to democratic ideals and human rights, and a close collaborator of my husband's. He became the first known victim of the junta and a martyr to the cause of freedom and democracy.

As the trial went from bad to worse for them, and criticism from the daily press turned to derision, the tribunal of judges—army officers of high rank loyal to the King—decided to carry on the trial behind closed doors. The issues coming up, they said, involved national security problems. Reporters would be allowed, but anyone writing on the events of the trial would be penalized with a prison sentence. Here were embryonic junta tactics.

By now there was renewed discussion of a military solution in Greece. The decision to put on a show trial of the ASPIDA case had proved that the King was doggedly, stubbornly determined not to go to elections which would bring back father and son Papandreou. He reasoned that at the least elections would be a judgment on his act of July 1965, and at the worst, a plebiscite on the throne itself. A dictatorship was being prepared, but the King and the Americans were still hoping that by maneuvers that were pseudoconstitutional, a full-fledged open dictatorship could be avoided.

During this time Andreas and I were not invited to any embassy functions. Although the embassy made an effort to keep in touch with leading political personalities, excluding the Left, it made a specific effort *not* to see Andreas. This social snub was a means for the Greek world to know that Andreas was just not acceptable. Without the blessing of the American Embassy, a man's political career was considered doomed. One lone man, Norbert Anschuetz, chargé d'affaires, tried to keep the channels open to Andreas. This was done over cocktails in his home in Psyhico or, on occasion, at our place. One such evening occurred in the late summer of 1966 when Norbert came by for a cocktail with us on our backyard veranda. Since his wife was out of town, I suggested that he remain for dinner with us, and we were still talking at 11 P.M. when two professor friends dropped in to see if we were home. One was George Lianis, a Greek, professor of aeronautical engineering at Purdue University. The other was Stephen Rousseas, American of Greek descent, professor of economics at New York University. Steve later wrote an excellent book entitled *The Death of a Democracy: Greece and the American Conscience.*

The two of them machine-gunned questions at Anschuetz and put him on the spot. They asked him, for example, why Talbot did not attempt to keep contact with liberal leaders while he sought out secondary politicians. Anschuetz tried to squirm out of this one by saying he thought Andreas did not want such a meeting. When Andreas refuted this, he said he would arrange a dinner within a few weeks. The dinner never materialized. A Greek friend, Phillip Dimitriades, also present, responded to Norbert's insistence that the Americans did not advocate a dictatorship by asking why Talbot didn't make a public statement to this effect, that is, that it is not the policy of the United States to encourage the installation of a dictatorship. Norbert answered that this was tantamount to interference. But Phillip reminded him that United States ambassadors in the past had commented on the merits of the Karamanlis government, electoral laws of their preference, etc., without a similar sensitivity to charges of interference. Norbert protested that we were all asking too much of him, "a wage slave," to carry the responsibility of past ambassadors. It was an unproductive conversation.

A succinct description of American Embassy policy was made by an embassy man himself, an economist, to Herbert Kubly, who was in Greece to write a book. He talked to the economist at a garden party at the embassy about the same time we were talking to Norbert Anscheutz on our back terrace, and was told he could use the conversation on the condition that he not give the name of the embassy employee. He records his conversation in his truly beautiful, moving, and perceptive book, *Gods and Heroes*. He told the economist that everywhere he had been, in Crete, Macedonia, Epirus, and the Peloponnesus, the people were clamoring for elections and were blaming the Americans for the postponement. Kubly asked if there was truth in the rumors, and this is the answer he got:*

> The Embassy policy is one of passivity, of sitting it out. The weak, corrupt and decrepit government now in power is buying time which is absolutely necessary to save the crown. A semblance of government is, of course, better than no government. What the United States wants in Greece is a government that will be friendly to us, which will look warmly on NATO and which will have stability and effective leadership. If there had been an election this year, it would have been an overwhelming victory for Papandreou. This would have been a disaster. The army would support the King and civil war would result. Stefanopoulos is a puppet, but as long as the Papandreou party attacks him, the heat is off the King. Of course, there must be elections eventually but the longer they can be delayed, the less acute will be the situation.
>
> Papandreou's personal charm wins you. He has charisma, that mystical hold over people which is the strength of great leaders, leaders like Venizelos, Roosevelt, Churchill and Kennedy. He articulates all the vague yearnings, the aspirations of the Greek people. More than anyone else he is aware of the needs of the common man. He has consciously tried to lead his backward people into the twentieth century. A good example is his program for free education. He tried to raise Greek education up to European standards, to make it compulsory through the ninth grade, to raise teachers' and professors' salaries. Unfortunately, he is no longer the man to carry through, he is no longer capable of action. I admire him and like him

more than anyone in Greek politics. But unfortunately, he has come twenty years too late.

The plan is to ride out the crisis until George Papandreou dies, or at least until he and his son can be discredited, until the attitudes about them can be changed. The ASPIDA affair, with its purpose of suggesting Andreas as guilty of treason, is part of the effort to diminish the popular support of the Center Union. In the past winter the old man has deteriorated visibly, his health has failed.

The hope is that with Papandreou's death, the factions within the Center Union will come to odds and the party will fall apart. The death watch seems to be a fact. I look to the future with gloom and see nothing decisive ahead for a long time.

This brutally frank description of embassy policy proved we were not one thing that we were accused of from time to time: paranoid. The Americans simply did not want Papandreou, father or son, heading a Greek government, and the reason was that they were too independent. This embassy employee didn't even try to make the puerile argument that they were communists, but that they couldn't be counted on 100 percent to be loyal to NATO, thus adopting a principle not of just maximum control of Greece, but *total* control by Big Brother across the sea. It was often said that Andreas made too much of American influence and intervention in Greece, that he exaggerated it, and that I was somehow disloyal to America by arguing similar points—that we both had an obsession on this issue. Kubly's conversation was not the only one we learned about, nor the only proof we had. The reasons for our reaction to American intervention were different ones, actually. For Andreas it was the natural antagonism that develops between a colonist and the colonizer. For me it was an outcry of horror that my country was acting in this manner; it was, if you like, the lament for the breaking of an illusion, the smashing of an image.

The ASPIDA trial for the officers dragged on. In February sentences were passed out. Bouloukos and Papageorgopoulos, the two men who had visited Andreas, were given sentences of twenty years each. This was an indirect punishment of Andreas. It was a terrible, terrible travesty of justice. The military officers sitting as judges were the King's men, and these were undoubtedly their orders. I was appalled. I was also unhappy that people seemed so unaffected by the fate of these young men.

The trial had failed to discredit Andreas. At the end of the trial, an announcement was made that an investigation of "other persons, known or unknown, connected with the ASPIDA case" would be undertaken by the public prosecutor. This created the possibility of trying Andreas himself. The difficulties were overwhelming. His immunity would have to be removed by a majority vote of Parliament. Not only that, but his status as a popular hero had risen to such an extent that a public reaction could be expected and its force unpredictable. To make matters worse, *there was no case!*

But there had been no real case against the officers. Yet there had been wives, mothers, and relatives standing outside a court on Santarosa Street in downtown Athens waiting to get in to listen to the proceedings and have their few moments at court recess to touch and talk to the prisoners. I had seen them, their faces full of anguish and despair. The question came to me: Will I one day be one of those faces? And will no one really care?

CHAPTER THIRTEEN

Wanted for High Treason

AT THE dinner we had in Kastri the night after our return from Copenhagen, the President was clearly disturbed. He had been deeply impressed by the turnout at the airport and by the success of Andreas' trip. I also believe that he was scared. Such an obvious popular ovation was a rebuke to the King and all the shenanigans of the ASPIDA frame-up. My guess, although I had never discussed this with George Papandreou, was that the seed of an idea to topple the Stephanopoulos government took root at this time. His reasoning must have been that an arrangement that included concessions to the King and to the Right in return for elections which would resolve the anomaly in Greek political life, was the only way to prevent a military take-over. Others have argued that his overwhelming desire to become Prime Minister again in the waning years of his life was the key motivation for the scheme that developed. Although he was an ambitious man—what political man is not?—I cannot accept this as the real goal of his subsequent maneuvers. What I do believe is that his strategy, ironically enough, helped prepare the ground and speed the day of the junta's coup.

There was nothing in our conversation that night to indicate the "planting of the seed" I suggested. But his manner was unlike himself. His voice was subdued, his interest in Andreas' trip minimal, and his mind distracted. He neglected to fill my wineglass when it was empty, a host's task which he always performed with gusto.

For the next ten days or more, the press was full of stories about Andreas' welcome. From the Center press it was "hallelujas"; from the rightist press it was scorn and disgust at "sidewalk tactics." The Stephanopoulos government, teetering and tottering because of its weak majority and peculiar arrangement with ERE, reacted with a vengeance to Andreas' airport press-conference statements, in which Andreas had reported on the support of the democratic peoples of the Scandinavian governments for the fight of the democratic Greeks. It *claimed* he had said he had gotten the support of the Scandinavian *governments*. Their next move was to call in the ambassadors of Sweden, Denmark, and Norway and ask for explanations. The ambassadors were shown the newspaper stories of what Andreas had purportedly said, and two denied that their governments had given such support. Since Andreas' press comments were read from a written document, available to the press, and taped—also available to all and any who wanted to check—this rushing to the aid of the

Stephanopoulos government and responding to a falsified newspaper report was widely ridiculed and condemned by the Center press. It was perhaps the only "blooper" made by the Scandinavians who later, after the military take-over, were to take a continuing forthright and democratic position against the junta on behalf of their governments.

October and November passed. November 30 was Andreas' name day, and we had an enthusiastic parade of well-wishers at our home. Name's day in Greece is celebrated instead of the birthday, a tradition which I find quite palatable, since it avoids the reminder of age and the problem of keeping track of birthday dates. One knows that on St. Andreas Day, all Andreases are celebrating. Likewise for St. George, St. Nicolas, St. Sophia, etc. Unless one publicizes in the personal column of the daily newspapers that one's house will not be "open," all friends, relatives, friends of relatives, political colleagues, the grocery man, the butcher, and others can come and have an ouzo or brandy on that day and give wishes of good cheer.

People came in hordes. We ran out of both ouzo and brandy and sent out for more supplies. Groups came and sang songs with words praising Andreas and the national renaissance. The mood was great: optimistic and jubilant, even though elections seemed to be at least a year and some months away. As photos were taken, everyone tried to have his face next to Andreas' for posterity. Little Andreas (Andriko) welcomed everyone at the door, looking eagerly to see whether a special package was being carried in for him. He also posed—cocksure and poised—for the flashing bulbs.

While our spirits soared, the President's mood was alternately glum and manic. While we were relaxed and welcomed the coming year or so of campaigning, George Papandreou was restless and sometimes cranky. Friction increased between the two, father and son, and there were frequent spats and disagreements.

Sometimes on the scene was George Papandreou, Jr., a son by a second marriage to Kiveli, one of Greece's finest actresses. Half brother of Andreas, he was ten years younger, a six-foot-two handsome creature, with classical Greek features, a heart of gold, and a conservative philosophy. He would have been a real rival to both his father's and Andreas' political careers if he had not had encephalitis at two which had affected his central nervous system. He had not been able to finish any school, despite the ten or more tried, or hold down any job. Thus he was a ward of both his father and mother, who had separated in 1951. Before the invasion of Greece, he had been taken to Europe by his mother and subsequently to America where he showed up to visit Andreas, who was a gob in the American navy, in an American army air force captain's uniform. Andreas persuaded him to run back home and remove it before he was caught. He had tried to commit suicide many times, once in a spectacular attempt at the top of Notre Dame in Paris, when he shot himself through the left lung. He missed his heart by a quarter of an inch and was saved.

Despite George's difficulties, I had a warm feeling toward him, as did Andreas. Friendliness was reciprocated to some extent toward me, but not toward my husband. He looked at Andreas as his father's undoing, and as the conflict between father and son heightened, so did George's hostility toward

Andreas. This made for a snug family foursome—Andreas' father criticizing Andreas; George trying to advise Andreas, as if he were the older brother, not the younger; and I trying to keep some balance among all three. When the children were present, my father-in-law had the good sense to steer the conversation to nonflammable subjects. But enough tension existed for our children, George and Sophia, to know that all was not well in the Papandreou household.

Later, my father-in-law's shifting moods could be explained on the basis of the progress of the clandestine scheme he was working out. It was a most carefully guarded secret—to a degree that was almost unheard of in the political world of Athens.

On a few occasions during this period, my father-in-law made the comment that something had to be done, that the Stephanopoulos government was intolerable. We found it no more and no less intolerable than before, and Andreas had geared himself to a year of opposition with the fervent hope that a stronger party structure and a true grass-roots organization could be developed as a solid foundation for an electoral victory in 1968. We neglected to read into the President's comments a pending political maneuver.

It was my husband's belief that if the pressure was too great on the King, and he foresaw Andreas gathering too much popular strength over the year, he had one alternative: the dissolution of Parliament and the selection of a forty-five-day service government to hold elections. His continuing, unswerving determination to keep Papandreou from returning to power was a key source of the political anomaly in Greece. This, along with his blindness in pursuing the ASPIDA affair, was adding coals to the fire each day. There were others who argued that Andreas was feeding the fire with his "demagoguery." Among those in this camp were members of the American Embassy. One November day we were invited for a drink at Norbert Anschuetz' house. The conversation, after the preliminaries, went something like this:

"Well, Andreas, how do you see things?"

"I think things are great!" said Andreas in a buoyant mood.

"I don't agree with you. Things are lousy " was the answer.

"What makes them lousier now than in the past? Isn't it the same old situation?"

"No. Too much tension has developed, and too much danger for the future."

"The danger of a Center Union victory, you mean," smiled Andreas.

"Well, a variety of things." There was always a sparring around that was typical of our conversations with Norbert, a bit of teasing, some jokes, some nonsense. Today, there was less. He was Norbert, the worried embassy diplomat. In a somewhat nasal Wyoming twang, inconsistent with his eastern Brooks Brothers looks, he continued.

"For one thing, you are whipping up the people too much. You are creating a clash situation."

Here I piped up a bit sarcastically and asked, "Do you think Andreas is a demagogue?"

He turned to me and answered in one syllable, "Yes!"

"Did it ever occur to you," I asked, "that the man is sincere, that he believes in what he says? A demagogue is an exploiter of people's passions for his own personal or political aims and makes promises he knows he cannot fulfill. Andreas tells the people plainly and simply that they should be sovereign in their own country, and he has promised them nothing. Quite the contrary, he has told them the problems are immense and will require individual sacrifices." It was a defense of my husband, spoken with honesty and true belief, but Norbert was not really listening. Now we came to the heart of the issue.

"I think you ought to try to see the King."

"What good would this do?" was Andreas' question.

"Well, you know, he's not such a bad fellow. In fact, he is quite reasonable and more liberal than you think." This was new! The man who had thrown out George Papandreou and was chasing Andreas through the corridors of the court with the ASPIDA charge was really an all-right guy! Andreas said nothing.

"If you two got together," said Norbert, "maybe some things could get straightened out that have gotten all messed up. You're awfully good in face-to-face contacts, and it would be worth a try."

"You think my 'charm' as you have called it in the past is going to resolve the Greek crisis?" Andreas asked sarcastically. "What am I to tell the King? That I really love him, and let's bury the hatchet and all that?"

Anschuetz was getting a bit irritated, and he spoke in a much sterner voice. "Goddammit, Andreas, you won't make one concession!"

"I'll be glad to see the King," Andreas answered, "if he wants to call me in for a visit publicly."

"You know he can't do that. It can be a secret meeting, arranged at a home. Mine, if you like."

"Do you still function under the illusion that anything remains secret in Greece?" was the answer. "Such a meeting would seem to be a compromise. I would be seen crawling to the King when I have a potential charge of high treason hanging over my head, as if I were asking for clemency. But I state to you flatly that I will see him if he wants to invite me publicly."

Norbert continued to be distressed, and it was obvious that he was going to insist on this meeting.

I chimed in once again. "You are always putting pressure on Andreas to make a move in that direction. Did it ever occur to you to put pressure on the King? Why must he be protected and shored up in everything he does? After all, he is the man with the power, and supposed to be King of all the Greeks. Magnanimity should be easy."

I think Norbert said something like "shit!"

Clearly, Norbert was looking for some kind of political deal.

"There is only one way out of this mess," Andreas argued. "The King should give amnesty to all those officers in the ASPIDA case, and all those under investigation. This thing has become a cancer in Greek public life, and you know as well as I that it is bunk. After this occurs, elections can be called and a new Parliament assembled which reflects the mood of the country."

"He wants the simple proportional system." (This system would give no extra benefits to the majority party and would tend to encourage formation of many small parties.)

"Let him get it. It's his government."

"You know damn well that the Mitsotakis forces don't want it. They'll be wiped out in such an election."

"They should be. In any case, the King made his bed, now let him lie in it."

Once again Norbert brought up the idea of a meeting between Andreas and the King. Once again Andreas agreed to such a meeting under the conditions that it be public.

"You both speak in circles," I ventured. "Why don't you try a new tack, Norbert? That a representative of Andreas' see the King?"

Norbert looked at Andreas. "Is that possible?"

"Perhaps" was the reply.

I wasn't sure that my initiative was appreciated by Andreas. I think he felt that any contact would be hopeless and unfruitful. But he agreed to give some thought to the name of a person whom he could trust to handle this matter.

This is how our "cocktail hour" ended. Before any thought could be given to a name, other events took place to make this proposal obsolete.

The "solution" that was supposed to take Greece off its clash course had the following components: (1) the King would not be made an election issue by the Center Union; (2) acceptance by George Papandreou and Panayotis Cannellopoulos of a transition government of six months to be chosen by the King with a nonpolitical figure at its head; (3) the voting in of the simple proportional system, desired by the King to reduce the strength of the Left and the Center in Parliament; (4) at the end of the six months elections would be held—May 28, 1967. The people interested in such a scheme were the Americans, the King, Cannellopoulos, and George Papandreou. Also supporting the scheme were Eleni Vlahou, the capable and shrewd publisher of two conservative newspapers, and Christos Lambrakis, the young publisher of two Center but anti-Andreas newspapers. Each one of these interested groups or persons had his own reasons for liking the scheme. For the Americans it seemed to be a resolution of the two-year-old anomaly, an avoidance of an open dictatorship, and the country in the hands of rightist and Center-Right elements. For the King it had the same attractions, with the additional one that for six months he would have his own government in power, and the army under his control for the preparation of a dictatorship in case it appeared that despite all the measures, George Papandreou (or Andreas) would win a clear majority. For Cannellopoulos, it was the expectation of a collaboration government, ERE-Center Union, in which he and his party would share the power in a meaningful way, not as the props of a lame Center splinter group. For Vlahou it also meant more share of the governmental power, newspapers being what they are in Greece. Lambrakis would defeat his chief rival newspaper, *Eleftheria*, which supported the apostate government, and would also clip the wings of Andreas, whose more progressive forces would not be happy with such a collaboration.

As for George Papandreou, what would he get out of it? He would get elections, a demand he had been making since July 15, 1965.

Despite the fact that we were having our regular weekly dinners with George Papandreou, *we were not told of this plan*. The night before the underpinning was pulled from the Stephanopoulos government, my father-in-law presented at the dinner table theoretical solutions to the present state of affairs, all of which Andreas rejected as not solutions, but "deals" which in no way solved the social conflict and political anomaly, deeply disturbing the country by this time. He insisted that the game of musical chairs by the party leaders, along with the King and the Americans, should be passé, that the parties themselves had to be consulted, and under those circumstances obviously no secret arrangements could be made. When my father-in-law argued that a primary target should be the getting of elections, Andreas answered that elections were not a gift to be handed out under certain circumstances, that they were a constitutional right. It was a conversation held without anger, more like an academic debate in which the old man was the professor, and we the pupils. We were presented with alternatives for Situation y at Time x. He asked my opinion frequently. This was a habit with him only when he felt my silent opposition, or suspected I might be in disagreement.

For some reason, I was rather satisfied with the conversation. I felt that if he were harboring any thoughts of political machinations, Andreas had certainly clarified where he stood. Andreas was not so satisfied. As we left the house, he suggested that we call up Kiveli and Tito and ask them to meet us at the Blue Pine Inn for a midnight drink.

These two people were close social friends of ours. Tito was an excellent student of political affairs, as well as a man of sound judgment. He had been an officer in the Greek Coast Guard for twenty-five years. His wife, Kiveli, had been a childhood playmate of Andreas' at Kastri, which was natural since her grandmother was married to George Papandreou at the time. A vivacious brunette, she is one of the kindest, most uncomplex Greek women I have met.

Andreas told the two about our evening conversation and expressed his fear that a deal was in the making. I argued that if this were true, certainly the possibility had been scotched this evening by Andreas himself. Tito tended to side with Andreas, expressing concern. Troubled, we drove home silently on that misty early morning of December 12, 1966. Late in the same day I got the news from Petros that Cannellopoulos had withdrawn his support from the Stephanopoulos government and that Stephanopoulos had just gone to the Palace to submit his resignation.

I was shocked, sick, and disgusted. I was furious. And my anger was directed primarily against one man, whom I was bitterly calling the "enemy within"—George Papandreou. I was less angry at the deal at the moment than I was at the fact that it had all been done behind Andreas' back, that we had sat at the table in Kastri the night before like neophytes (certainly I), smiling at an interesting intellectual exercise.

Since we were invited for dinner at the Nickolaus' and Andreas was expecting me to pass by his Souidias Street office to pick him up, I simply dressed more quickly and drove over.

At the office there was bedlam. Koutsoyergas, Andreas' trusted friend and lawyer, was talking on the phone confirming the news to someone. There were other angry young men: Mandiliras, the ASPIDA case lawyer; Stratis, Andreas' political secretary; Koulourianos, economist friend; and some of the deputies of the Center Union. All were trying to determine what deal had been made, and what the outcome would be.

By now my anger had turned into hurt and pain. The conflict between father and son, with all its psychological, emotional, and political components, had burst into an open discord. When Andreas had called his father on the telephone to express dissent, his father had hung up on him.

The news came in that Paraskevopoulos, director of the National Bank and a Palace man, had been sworn in as Prime Minister. In short order we heard the names of the cabinet ministers, all royalists. There was one glaring irony in this: the transition government would have to get a vote of confidence in Parliament to run the country for six months. ERE had 99 votes and 52 more would make the majority. But anything fewer than the 126 votes of the Center Union meant a split-up of the party, and the two dissident factions would be headed by father and son!

The mess was a cruel absurdity. Because no one in the party had been consulted, the entire structure was shaken up, and the deputies started a parade between the house at Kastri and the office at Souidias, each one with his own motive—to keep party unity, to push for a split, and to try to figure out, if there were a split, which Papandreou he would join. If it hadn't been so serious and so personally brutal, the scene would have been a riotous bit of low comedy. It wasn't the first time, nor the last, that I didn't know whether to laugh or to cry.

Andreas was cautious and made no statements to the press. His problem was monumental. Had he been other than the deeply kind and sentimental person he is, his choice would have been obvious. He was convinced that the six months of a Paraskevopoulos government would be used for the preparation of a dictatorial solution. He was sure that his father had given too much and gotten too little. He felt that this imposed solution was not settling the problems of the country. He suggested that we spend a few days at Lagonissi, a small seaside resort thirty miles down the coast south of Athens for some opportunity to assess the situation.

I felt truly sorry for him. No blows of any sort, then or later, were to depress and disturb him so completely. A breakup of the party meant an election victory for the Right, at a time when the country was vastly pro-Center. Everything he had fought for for a year and a half was being ground to dust. But in a culture like Greece, a schism between father and son was repugnant and incomprehensible. Some Greeks even said that the two were playing charades in their obvious dispute, so that Andreas could keep the progressive forces and his father the conservative forces. A vote for the Pareskevopoulos government was a vote against his better judgment in terms of political instinct. A vote against the Paraskevopoulos government was a vote against his father. The dilemma was extreme and acute.

In a short time, forty deputies declared their desire to join with Andreas if he wanted to fight the Paraskevopoulos solution. A failure to get a vote of confidence would have forced the King to choose among three alternatives: (1) a service government and elections within forty-five days; (2) a new parliamentary rearrangement with a politician at the head; (3) instant dictatorship by the King's junta. The first was the most desirable, the second most difficult and unlikely, and the third the most probable.

No matter what road Andreas chose, the prospects for Greece were not bright. There was no action he could take which would help the country off the path of dictatorship. In the end I was dispatched to Kastri to act as intermediary—with great reluctance—between Andreas and George. Marjorie Schachter, an American friend from my Minnesota days and now living in Athens, rushed over with tranquilizers prior to my trek to Kastri to narcotize my emotional world and allow me to carry on a sane conversation. The argument was drearily pat by then; I had heard it from the paraders who were visiting both homes. It went as follows: The great victory and joy for us was the attainment of elections. The King had at last given in! When I asked the President what arrangement had been made about ASPIDA, that Sword of Damocles hanging over Andreas' head, he answered that it would be impossible for any action to be taken by a government which he was supporting. I reminded him that once we went into the preelection period of forty-five days with Parliament closed, he would no longer have any special bargaining power and that Andreas' immunity as a deputy to charges of high treason would no longer be in force. He mumbled that it wasn't a problem, and I suspected that some agreement, at least with Cannellopoulos, had been made on the issue of Andreas' arrest. This was not adequate. Andreas considered the ASPIDA case far more important than his own personal fate. The judges in the original ASPIDA military trial were all the King's men. No fair trial was possible. And the prosecutor of the Supreme Court, Constantine Kollias, was a close personal friend of Queen Frederika's. It was he along with Socratides who was now carrying out the civilian investigation of nonmilitary persons suspected of being connected with the so-called conspiracy. The civilian courts were becoming political instruments, and personal freedoms could no longer be guaranteed; all protection of human rights could be swept away at the strong man's whim. It was these general developments with ASPIDA as a focus, that disturbed Andreas.

George Papandreou argued to me that if Andreas stayed with him, Andreas could determine the candidates for the electoral lists and thus take his own party to elections. When I said there would be no elections, that this course was a huge one-way street to dictatorship, he fervently declared that it was the opposite, a way out of the impasse.

The meeting was unpleasant. I could do nothing but report it word for word to my husband. Andreas made a difficult decision—to vote for the royal government.

On January 13 I wrote to a friend in the States:

> *Well, the ugly and incredible thing has been done—the vote for the Paraskevopoulos government. The main aim of the government will be to reduce the power of the Center Union and of Andreas, and to prepare the country for dictatorship. It was like voting to send oneself to the gas chamber.... Cannellopoulos talks about another phase, a "governmental" phase that is, before we reach elections. Andreas thinks the trick there is to withdraw their confidence from Paraskevopoulos, get the mandate from the King to form a government, find it difficult to form a political government, get the right to dissolve parliament and go to elections with himself, Cannellopoulos, as prime minister for 45 days, with his own people in the ministries. In any case, many games can be played, but the most dangerous is the dictatorial game—and there is renewed talk about it, either for threat purposes, or because it is meant seriously....*

So there we were, early January 1967, sitting on a powder keg, predicting developments quite accurately, yet crossing our fingers in the hope that the country would actually reach elections. Although Andreas had voted for the Paraskevopoulos government, primarily to avoid an open father-son split, and to keep the party united for the elections promised (on Constantinos' word of honor) for May 28, he had never entered a deal and hence was not bound by any agreements. His father refused to discuss any of the conditions of the deal, as if no behind-the-scenes maneuvering had happened. This freed Andreas to chart his own course of preelection campaigning. Feeling that the only protection against a King's coup was a show of strength and the threat of a popular revolt, Andreas continued the battle he had begun, taking his crusade to the people. He neither heightened nor reduced his attacks. He tried to present a program that amounted to a platform for a revitalized Center Union party. He spoke to business groups about a plan for economic development, to doctors about a medical and health program, to the youth about education. With a date of elections now given, the country's interest in politics heightened, and Andreas' popularity continued to rise.

From a Washington source, we received the following note on January 21, 1967: "Circles here close to the Palace say that the King will never allow a Papandreou victory."

By now all attention was focused on Andreas, the bête noire of the establishment forces, the idol of the young, the farmer, the intellectual. He was new, exciting, and his straight talk refreshing. He was a true charismatic leader. A theme developed, "Get Andreas," as if this were the only means to stop the snowballing movement. We started to receive threats, either directly, by telephone, or through friendly couriers who had gotten wind of schemes and plots under way. It was during this time that Andreas purchased guns in case of a sudden attack or an assassination attempt. It was not unusual for me to be at a social gathering, dressed in evening wear, necklace, and dangling earrings, carrying a revolver in my beaded purse. We were urged to take precautionary measures. We watched for cars tailing us day or night. When we approached our Psyhico home, we circled around to check the environs before entering Guizi Street. We never jumped out of the car before the driver had a chance to walk up to the entryway and unlock the door. Many, many nights Andreas slept away from the house. Sometimes I joined him, in weird out-of-the-way places—empty apartments, homes of friends, or friends' friends, the latter the wisest because they were the most remote. There were some hideouts I knew nothing about. In case of torture, I could reveal nothing.

This was the atmosphere in which we were living those winter months of 1967. Hatred, threat, intimidation, were part of our daily diet. Georgie, who had been much affected by the schism between his father and grandfather, lost weight and showed a listlessness in school. Sophia grew much more serious and worried. We tried as much as possible to keep the children removed from this turmoil, but they heard snatches of conversations, read the Greek newspapers, and occasionally saw the guns.

In a sudden, lightninglike move on February 24, the investigating attorney, Socratides, working directly with Kollias, the Palace man, requested that the Speaker of the House ask Parliament to remove Andreas' immunity so that he could be charged with high treason. Another deputy, Pavlos Vardinoyannis, was also to be charged. This action against Vardinoyannis, a conservative Center man, was judged to be a smoke screen in order to avoid the impression that Andreas was the sole target. The formal preparation of the charge took nine hours from the time the order was given to proceed, an unprecedented speed in court bureaucracy.

"New and startling" evidence was given as the reason for the speed. Andreas Papandreou, the charge read, had spent the weekend of June 25, 1965, at the Xenia Hotel in Nafplion and had held a secret meeting in a nearby village close to Tolo with officers A, B, and C, at the home of Aristotle Calligas, a resident of that village.

I checked my 1965 calendar book. Although we sometimes went to the Xenia, on that specific weekend we had gone with the children to the Lagonissi Hotel in Attica, six hours away from Nafplion. I sent Petros to check with the Lagonissi Hotel register, and they found Andreas' signature and reservation for those days. In the court's trumped-up story, they hadn't bothered to give a semblance of truth to the charge by at least being able to prove that we were in Nafplion.

Within a few days we had a nice surprise. Five members of the village, political supporters of ERE, as they pointed out, and hence in no way connected to Andreas, sent a signed letter to the newspapers and asked that it be included in the evidence piled up in the court offices, that Andreas Papandreou had never been in their village and that Aristotle Calligas had been working in Macedonia on the dates cited, and his house closed down. Later Calligas himself said that he had never met Andreas and never given him use of his home. Supporters of ERE were themselves fighting the efforts of the junta to impose a dictatorship on the Greek people.

Despite the fact that we could prove the charges false, I was deeply affected by this move. Blatant lies on the part of the highest court of the nation for the political aims of the Palace and its allies were signs of deep sickness and a passionate determination to put Andreas out of action *at any cost*.

We were with Tito and Kiveli the evening the Speaker of the House made his request, and much as they tried to buoy up my flagging spirits, I felt the handwriting was on the wall. Any tiny hopes I had nurtured for normal developments died that night. We slept away from home once again, and in my dreams I saw huge black newspaper headlines: WANTED FOR HIGH TREASON!

CHAPTER FOURTEEN

All the King's Horses and All the King's Men

THE FOREIGN PRESS ASSOCIATION in Athens invited Andreas to be the guest speaker at their monthly luncheon meeting in the Grande Bretagne Hotel. The date was March 1, 1967, less than a week after the new developments on the ASPIDA charges. Andreas' speech was a lucid analysis of the situation in Greece at the time. Because I think it gives better than anything the atmosphere at the time, and points up the substantive issues involved, I would like to quote from parts of it.

> When I accepted your kind invitation to address you, I did not suspect that by the time I delivered this address, political events in Greece would have taken such an unfortunate turn. For there can be no doubt that the political problem immediately before us has the dimensions, once again, of the crisis of July 15th, 1965.
>
> On Friday, February 24th, the disclosure in the Athenian press of the deposition at the trial of ASPIDA of General Tsolakas, the man who heads the Greek Armed Forces, exploded as a "bomb" to validate the charges of the democratic camp, charges that have been made ever since this unsavory matter attracted the attention of Greek and international opinion ... that the so-called "conspiracy" of ASPIDA was in fact a "frame-up" involving Army officers who have been used as scapegoats in an operation that has dominated Greek public political life for almost two years, and which has reached by now the proportions of the Dreyfus case. As a result of this development ... the government of Mr. Paraskevopoulos proceeded with the speed of lightning to process, through the judicial machinery of the state, the papers necessary for the request on the part of the public prosecutor to the Greek Parliament for the removal of my immunity, in order that I face charges of high treason. All relevant papers bear the same date, namely the date of February 24th, a feat which has never been equaled by Greek bureaucracy.
>
> ... The parliamentary members of the Center Union party have unanimously decided to vote against the removal of my immunity, and this for two reasons: first because this attack on me constitutes, according to the view of the Center Union party, political persecution rather than prosecution for a crime. Secondly, because, again

according to their view, Greek justice in this instance is acting under directions from the executive branch of the government.

The ASPIDA case is but an aspect of the current Greek political problem. It is a symptom of the deep political crisis, of the deep conflict that is under way in Greece. In a nutshell, however, it contains the evidence for diagnosing the ailments of the Kingdom of Greece. For it discloses the ease with which a sector as important to the country as the Army may be shaken to its foundations, may have its morale destroyed, in the service of some tactical political advantage.

It disclosed the ease with which the King (in his letters to the Prime Minister) not only concludes that there has been a conspiracy against the State, before any evidence had been brought to bear on the matter, but also the ease with which he charges the Prime Minister and his immediate colleagues for being involved in it. It discloses the extent to which military justice in Greece is but a tool in the hands of the Right. It discloses the utter disregard for human dignity. For the treatment of the officers during the one and a half years of their imprisonment prior to trial violates all standards of civilized human conduct. And it discloses finally the ease with which the Establishment that dominates Greek political, social and economic life can use the smear, the slander technique, and finally the state machinery to combat a politician when it cannot defeat him in the political arena.

In a nutshell, the ASPIDA case is living proof of a most important fact, namely that in Greek political life the cards are stacked, the deck is fixed. In this light it is not surprising that the Right has been almost continuously in Government for over 30 years, even though it represents a minority of the Greek electorate.

. . . The cards are stacked in Greece for an additional reason. Greece, ever since it became a free nation, has been under the tutelage of one or more friendly powers. The sponsor nation has always seen fit not only to direct political developments within Greece, but also to shape its foreign policy, more or less independently of vital Greek interests. Since the Greek civil war the United States has replaced England as a sponsor nation. It poured funds into Greece both for the purpose of guaranteeing the success of the then-government forces, and for the purpose of assisting in the reconstruction effort that followed the civil war. This gave it an all-powerful place in Greek political life. In a very real sense it participated in the process of government formation. . . . Of course it is a mistake to think of American foreign policy in Greece as monolithic. Present in Greece are at least three distinct American agencies: the State Department, the Military Mission, and the CIA. American policy in Greece has displayed the basic characteristics of the cold-war foreign policy which dominated the world scene since the death of Franklin D. Roosevelt.

. . . Greece, as a developing nation, a nation barely emerging from a semi-colonial status, is extremely sensitive about its national independence, its freedom to chart its own international political course, its right to pursue freely its own national interest without placing in quandry its allied relationships. We do not raise the question concerning the participation of Greece in the NATO alliance. But at the same time we demand that Greece be recognized as an independent nation, which pursuing its own particular interests has chosen to be a member of the Western Alliance. Greece refuses the status of a poor relative, of a satellite. It insists on its right while executing its obligations as an ally, to determine its own course. It affirms its right to expand its commercial, economic and cultural relations with all other nations, independently of the bloc to which they belong. It assigns special importance to developing good relations with its Balkan neighbors, the countries of the Near and Middle East and the new nations of Africa.

. . . Surprising though it may seem, the relegation of Greece to a semi-colonial state, the fact that Greece belongs to the Middle East desk of the State Department, has something to do with the conflict that is developing between America's insistence on dominating its Western allies and with France's reaction, which has gone almost to the point of breaking away from NATO. For it is this situation that has forced America to seek a more solid foundation in its South-eastern NATO flank. It is this that has led to its peculiar attempt to link together Greece, Turkey, and Iran. Indeed, it is interesting to note that Johnson's recent budget address indicated that $234 million, or almost half of the total army aid going to 70 nations around the world, will go to these three countries. It is this that creates the impetus on the part of America to force a solution of the Cyprus problem in the context of the NATO alliance. And it is this finally that makes it essential for America to demand an allied security in Greece which goes way beyond the norms of an alliance with an independent nation such as Greece. The disclosures that are going on now in America concerning the role of the CIA in foreign policy should leave no doubt as to what we mean when we insist that Greece should belong to the Greeks.

Two members of the political section of the American Embassy, John S. Day, political officer, and Richard W. Helgerson, information officer, walked out in the middle of the speech. Apparently the frankness with which Andreas presented the power factors in Greece and the way he and the Center Union looked at the situation was too much for the young American diplomats to stomach. They later put out a public statement that they walked out because their country had been criticized. Quite expectedly, the incident created a riot in the Greek press. The Right, who cherished for itself alone the title of "nationalist," did not know quite what to do because Andreas' stand had been so clearly nationalist and because the vision of a little country standing up to its big sponsor power was appealing to the Greek. The Center press berated the diplomats for unacceptable behavior. One can imagine what the leftist press did with this. Since this was a foreign press meeting, it got its share of foreign coverage as well.

I knew that a friend of ours, a professor, was going to Washington on a brief visit away from his American college academic duties later in March, with the intention of warning the State Department about the pending dictatorship. Figuring that he would have to answer some tough questions about Andreas' statements, and knowing his intention to see Senators as well, I wrote and suggested what he might say. My letter is dated March 12, 1967:

> *...Andreas' purpose in attacking US foreign policy was to expose to the world prior to any coup, the role of the US in Greece. He wanted to warn them that they would be held accountable, and in that sense make them think twice about getting involved in any adventures here. It has worked in this sense: Anschuetz has come to see Andreas and he is obviously worried. You should certainly throw in the bit about a NATO supported and equipped Army being used as an internal political force, and in no way against communism or a communist leader, but against the popular leader of the democratic camp—at this stage a national hero. Such action can only lead to a clash, and a dictatorship, to years of instability in Greece. It will finish off the monarchy, and the far Left will be the only benefactors. Look through Fulbright's* Arrogance of Power, *if you have a chance. He has much in the first few chapters and the last that would be consistent with Andreas' points in his speech. Ask him whether he thinks the Embassy people here displayed the magnanimity and tolerance he asks of our diplomats in dealing with a small, friendly allied country. Their action reminds one of the Russians in Red China who periodically march out when their country is mentioned in a critical fashion. In other words, these are totalitarian methods, hardly democratic.*

At the same time, I wrote a letter to Steve Rousseas to congratulate him on his article in *The Nation*, entitled "Greece—Elections or Coup?" and I asked him if he could see Carl Kaysen, who knew Greece from his year here in 1959-60, who had been coresponsible for the idea of an economics center in Athens, and who might have influence in the Johnson administration, although his government experience had been confined to the Kennedy administration. We had not seen Carl for several years, and I was sure his thinking about Andreas and Greece had been influenced, as had the thinking of many of our friends, by the Sulzberger pieces in *The New York Times*, and by other editorials and pieces in *Time* and *Newsweek*. Thus arguments to him through Steve took on an argumentative tone, as if I were responding to a hostile barrage of criticism:

> *I would like to add for Carl's sake, that as of this date, Talbot has had no private conversation with Andreas.... You see, they have*

discounted entirely Andreas' sincerity, nor do they understand his sense of values. They fail to understand the people of Greece, nor the needs of Greece. Furthermore, Dan Brewster arrived on the scene, who is head of the new Greece, Turkey, Iran desk, and although Anschuetz had said he would arrange for a meeting with Dan and Andreas, it has become apparent that Dan came with instructions from Washington not to see Andreas. If C.K. can explain how and why the Embassy avoids like poison almost any contact with the most popular and powerful political figure in Greece today, then he can tell me that the State Department is functioning properly and wisely. But it has to be an acceptable explanation—and I'm sure none exists. If Kaysen could begin to understand the atmosphere here of conspiracy, plot and counter-plot, of harassment of the people, of CIA activity, including involvement with the Army—maybe he could better understand Andreas' fight. It's a fight against a gang, and normal low-key politicking would never develop a force strong enough to present a formidable obstacle to the gang. By the way, Andreas believes that most of ERE itself is outside the junta activities. Maybe two or three characters are in. It is truly military-palace—plus some dark characters from the journalistic world*—and that's about it.

... In the meantime, we try to live a fairly normal life. We are constantly beset by rumours and warnings of imminent arrest, assassination, midnight attempts to throw dynamite on our lawn, etc. Among the children only Georgie seems to understand the nature of developments here. Nick asked one day, in a very matter-of-fact way, when did I think Daddy was going to jail. So he couldn't be less concerned.

How does one stop a military coup? The snowball had been pushed, and we were rolling down the hill, speeding toward disaster at the bottom. We were shouting, but our words were heard only by us, echoing our desperation. Andreas was informing the people, and giving instructions for immediate resistance, but he had made only slight headway in the development of a grass-roots party organization, which would have been an instrument for quick action. With the unions, the situation was the same—just the beginnings of a European-style labor organization. It wasn't that he envisioned that Greek citizens could keep the army at bay, but massive reaction would have brought a split in the army and a failure of the coup.

The force that could prevent a dictatorship was the foreign power, the sponsor nation—the United States. That accounted for my "cries in the wilderness" to friends in positions of power in the United States, and Andreas' warning in his press speech that a dictatorship would be backed by the United States.

*One of these was an ex-communist editor of *Eleftheros Kosmos*, considered by everybody to be a paper financially supported by CIA.

On the morning of March 9 I suggested to Andreas that we ask Anschuetz over and tell him our fears. Andreas shrugged his shoulders as if to say, "Maggie, it's hopeless," but he agreed.

Anschuetz' first remarks had to do with Andreas' speech. He called it "ill-advised" and wondered what the motivation was.

"To place the blame for a dictatorship squarely where it belongs, on the shoulders of the Palace and the Americans."

"You don't think there could be a coup without the involvement of these two?" he asked. This was an intriguing question.

"Inconceivable" was Andreas' categorical answer.

Then I told Anschuetz that I, as an American citizen, felt it was a duty to report information we had about a junta clique, that it came from an informer who sat in on their meetings, and that it was planning a dictatorial solution. And I didn't think this was in the interests of the United States.

Anschuetz looked concerned and serious. He asked for details. I told him where they were meeting, and I told him the names of the key people. He wrote this down.

After this he had a discussion with Andreas about the general situation and suggested that a postponement of elections seemed almost mandatory. Andreas rejected this as a continuation of the same game and insisted that elections were the only means for getting out of the impasse—if we reached elections.

It was a tense discussion, and afterwards I felt disheartened. I felt that Anschuetz had been upset, but I also felt that he might have been disturbed by the fact that we had inside information on the dictatorial scheme, which included a representative of the King. After this talk, the King's representative disappeared from the junta meetings. I attributed this to an action on the part of Anschuetz, but I couldn't ascertain its reason. From the point of view of the King, of course, it was unwise for him to be associated with an unconstitutional act, for in the future he could be held accountable. Otherwise the meetings continued, and we were apprised of the progress being made. As the days passed, it became apparent that there was confusion within the junta (later to be called the Big Junta), and they moved closer to acceptance of elections on May 28, with the reservation that if the results were too devastating, and if old man Papandreou did not stick to his commitment for a government of national unity, which would include ERE, they would act by force.

These developments allayed our fears somewhat. The fact, also, that we had almost daily reports of their conversations made us feel that we would have advance notice of the date of a coup, should it be decided on by the Big Junta, and could make at least some rudimentary preparations for it.

Andreas continued to take his crusade to the Greek people. In every speech he outlined his program for a new Greece, and castigated the extremist elements in the country who were proposing a dictatorial solution. He gave instructions to the people to gather in the squares of their cities and villages en masse in silent protest in case of a coup. "Greek boys carrying the arms of the army will not fire on their own people," he said. In Larissa in March he drew hundreds of thousands of people from all over Thessaly at a public speech, but there were bad signs. The government had ordered all bus companies to refuse to charter their buses for the occasion, and more ominous yet, army Jeeps were on the highways leading to Larissa and turned back farmers traveling to the speech in their farm trucks and cars. Totalitarianism was creeping closer.

Cannellopoulos had made a statement when he announced his support of the Paraskevopoulos government that "there will be a second phase." This was not considered a mysterious remark by the average Greek citizen. It meant simply that he was going to try to maneuver himself into the position of being the service premier for elections. The party in power is considered to have the advantage at election time. And there were always possibilities of an election like the one in 1961 under Karamanlis, the one that started my father-in-law on his unyielding fight.

But to make this "second phase" feasible, one or the other of the two parties supporting Paraskevopoulos would have to topple the government and force the appointment of a new premier and a service cabinet for elections. To make it look better, since Cannellopoulos as a party leader, and a minority one at that, was not an impartial candidate for election premier, it was preferred that Papandreou bring down the government and break the "deal" with the King. This would somehow justify the choice of Cannellopoulos.

Shortly after General Tsolakas had declared at the ASPIDA trial that the whole affair was a frame-up, he was fired from the army by the Paraskevopoulos government. At the same time, the head of the gendarmerie, the lone Papandreou man in a high position who had survived the changes of governments after 1965, was fired. These were provocative acts against George Papandreou, and it was thought that he could not continue to support the government. Papandreou did not budge, however. He castigated the act of firing, but said he would not withdraw his vote of confidence. (By this time we felt as if we were all standing with our pants down and asking for more and more swats.) Everything Andreas had predicted about this lovely solution to Greece's political problems, this transition Palace government, was coming true—and worse. They were grabbing more and more control for the coming confrontation with the people.

With an adamant Papandreou trying to hold on to the Paraskevopoulos government and get to elections, it was obvious that Cannellopoulos himself would have to pull out. He found his opportunity when the Center Union proposed an amendment to the electoral bill for the coming elections. The Center Union was concerned about the possibility of an arrest of Andreas during the forty-five-day election period when deputy immunity was no longer in effect, and decided to request an amendment to the electoral law, extending immunity. Having defeated the request for the removal of his immunity, they judged that the strategy of the Right was to arrest Andreas during this period.

There was an extremely good basis for proposing this amendment. In January 1966, when the apostate government was functioning, the judicial committee of Parliament preparing the electoral law accepted a proposal made by Cannellopoulos' ERE party that a section protecting the deputy from arrest during the preelection period be included. It was voted on unanimously by the committee, on which Deputy George Rallis, ERE's expert on the constitution, sat at the time. But when Paraskevopoulos presented his electoral law, approximately the same as the Stephanopoulos law, *this section was removed.*

At the time ERE had made the proposal, they must have considered it important for giving protection to the ten or more deputies of their own party who had charges hanging over their heads, not knowing as yet what government would have control during the election period. When they saw that they and the Palace had the government, the section was no longer necessary—in fact, it was an obstacle to the arrest of Andreas. When the electoral bill (simple proportional, favored by the smaller parties) was introduced for debate, the Center Union brought up the same section word for word, in the form of an amendment. Cannellopoulos started screaming that it was unacceptable, that he would withdraw his vote of confidence, etc. When he saw that the Center Union party was insisting on its amendment, he argued that the amendment was unconstitutional and asked the government to rule on its constitutionality.

This in itself was irregular. The Parliament legislates and votes. The constitutionality of measures can only be challenged by the proper judicial body, if someone brings it to court. Nevertheless, Paraskevopoulos got a ruling from Stratos, a businessman-minister, who said it was unconstitutional. ERE said therefore it would not discuss the issue. At this point the Center Union asked that Parliament take a vote on whether or not the issue should be discussed. It knew it could get a majority because the apostates and EDA would vote for discussion. Because ERE didn't want a vote defeat in Parliament, it asked Paraskevopoulos to announce that because of a disagreement between the two major parties supporting his government, he would have to resign.

Whether Cannellopoulos had second thoughts or the King didn't like this state of affairs is unclear, but the following day, March 30, before submitting his resignation to the King, Paraskevopoulos telephoned Papandreou and asked if the President's stand was still the same, that he would insist on the amendment. Papandreou answered "definitely." That evening Paraskevopoulos went to the Palace and officially submitted his resignation.

Associated Press reported the new government crisis as follows: "King Constantine began looking for a new government today after attempts to bring Andreas Papandreou to trial for treason resulted in the resignation of Premier John Paraskevopoulos."

The King started a round of talks with party leaders on March 31, beginning with Papandreou. As I understood the talks, Papandreou told him simply and directly what were the possible solutions. The first, and correct solution, was to form immediately a service government which would stay in power forty-five days and hold elections. The Parliament, he said, was a dead body, and only elections could bring some meaning back into political life. Second, however, since it was the desire of the King and several small parties for a simple proportional system, and since the Center Union had declared itself willing to vote for such a system, he could choose a caretaker government which would come to Parliament for a vote, pass the electoral law, and then go immediately to elections. He added, however, that there could be no normal elections with ASPIDA charges dangling in the air. He remarked that every day new summonses were issued and people called in, that four of the officers who were declared innocent were to be summoned back for another trial, that discussion of investigating ex-generals and air force officers had started, and that the whole affair was a malignancy that should be cleared up by any caretaker government—by a simple act, declaration of amnesty for all said to be involved. The superior way of handling this, he told the young King, would be for Constantinos himself to declare amnesty and get the credit as a magnanimous King who wished to bring peace to an embattled political world.

Papandreou continued by saying that these were the two possible correct solutions, but if, by any chance, the King was thinking of naming a political government, then the mandate would have to be given first to the majority party in Parliament. He further stated that it would be unconstitutional to do otherwise, and if by chance he were to give the mandate to ERE, he, George Papandreou, would charge the King with ceasing to be a King and becoming a "party boss." In other words, he warned him very clearly that such an act would intensify the attacks on the court and the King himself, not lessen them. We were told that when someone later asked the King how he could have decided to give Cannellopoulos the mandate, he said that this way he could manage to get out of the political picture and the parties would be battling among themselves. That statement calls for at least three exclamation marks.

On Sunday, April 2, the King, after finishing his round of talks, including talks with Tsirimokos, who had organized his own party and thus was a party "leader" (his one member was his nephew), asked his political secretary, Mr. Bitsios to call my father-in-law and ask him to join with the other leaders on Monday for a further discussion, a "King's Council" on internal affairs. He didn't say what proposals might be made at the meeting, just that it was to be a discussion. The President said he would not participate, that he had stated his views to the King and would be at his disposal for a second session, if the King desired. He refused to play out the comedy of the King's Council.

The key issue, the absence of elections, remained after almost two years. On Saturday, April 1, the King got an assist from the American Embassy, toward further delay. Anschuetz met with Andreas. The theme of Anschuetz' proposal was the Palace theme, postponement of elections through the device of a national unity government which would get the support of all the parties except for EDA, and include in the cabinet representatives from all parties. Given the absolute decadence of Parliament by that time, the passions that had been aroused by defections, interference of the King, and the role of the party of the Right in supporting these maneuvers, the proposal was unacceptable. My father-in-law's conviction, as Andreas', was that only elections could make an honest institution out of Parliament and the likelihood of return to normalcy very strong. During this discussion with Anschuetz, Norbert said surlily to Andreas, "Many people call you a walking corpse." Was this meant to frighten Andreas, or to warn him of things to come?

Then a dirty move was made. The radio on its 9:30 P.M. broadcast said that the King had called in all leaders to discuss a government of "national unity" and that Papandreou had refused to come. This was to put the onus of the continuing crisis on Papandreou's shoulders; in other words, his stubbornness and obstinancy were creating new problems for the Greek nation. It was also an attempt to give some justification for the King's next move, for on Monday he gave the mandate to Cannellopoulos to form a government.

The mandate to Cannellopoulos was not to take the country to elections. Given the fact that he controlled only one third of Parliament and the other two thirds were violently against him, it required more than the magic of Circe to get a vote of confidence.

Papandreou did charge the King with being a "party boss," as he had promised to do. *Aktuelt* in Copenhagen wrote a strong editorial attack on Constantinos for his appointment of Cannellopoulos, and from reports from the Palace circle, we heard that this seemed to disturb him more than the press attacks in Athens. Because of Anna Maria, he considered Denmark his second home.

Within a few days it was obvious that a vote of confidence on the new government would be tabulated at 101 for Cannellopoulos (the one deputy outside his party who would go along was, naturally, Garoufalias), and 199 against. This was a real defeat for the King and a strong slap in his face. Frantic activity began to try to get Constantinos off the limb. In the two-hour discussion Papandreou had with Constantinos, he had presented a second possible correct solution, a caretaker government which would come to Parliament for a vote, pass the simple proportional system, declare amnesty for the ASPIDA case, dissolve Parliament, and go immediately to elections. Such a scheme would get the vote of two thirds of the Parliament, since the smaller parties wanted desperately to go to elections under the simple proportional system. The makeup of such a government would necessarily have to meet the demands of the parties supporting it, thus would be more balanced than a strictly ERE service government. Would the King turn to this second solution?

On Saturday and Sunday, April 8 and 9, Andreas and I went to Lagonissi for swimming and rest. The turmoil, the chaos, the feeling of the inevitability of a dictatorship, in short, a sense that one was in a meat grinder, necessitated an escape. We were having dinner alone in the Lagonissi dining room, which was virtually empty, enjoying, as I remember, grilled fresh fish and the quiet of the dining room. It was 10:30 P.M. when Kostas, a political secretary of Andreas', came with news. A representative of the King had seen him to ask him to reach Andreas and determine whether he would support a caretaker government with Tsakalotos, a retired general, not a democrat. It was a gesture, however, to the democratic camp, as an anti-Cannellopoulos move, assuming it was genuine. Andreas indicated he was interested, depending on the makeup of the government, but added that the decision would have to be made by his father who was head of the party.

A meeting was set up for the representative to meet and talk personally with Andreas on April 11, late afternoon, in our home. I remember the date because I was preparing for a cocktail party we were giving for establishment figures (the first of two such activities we nicknamed our "establishment parties") to try to ease the tension which had built up between Andreas and the conservatives. With a nation racing toward the precipice, we were searching for ways to veer it off this chilling course. It was undoubtedly naïve, but then our weapons were few. Some of the Americans we invited, businessmen and educators, were told by the embassy not to go. It is to their credit that they refused to accept this pressure.

At this discussion, which took place with George Papandreou's approval, Andreas made the proposal of a "mini-government," which would have neutral ministers in the cabinet, and one member from each party as minister without portfolio to represent political interests during the election period. The King's representative promised to report the proposal to the King. A subsequent telephone call set up a second meeting for breakfast in Psyhico on the morning of April 21.

During that same week, we had another message—a most serious and shattering one—from a different source. It was Thursday, April 13. A group of friends, including Andreas and me, had been invited to dinner at Kiveli and Tito's house. It was eleven o'clock when the phone rang and my son George asked for his father. George told him he was coming to the house, and asked if his father would still be there. The answer was a puzzled yes. Already accustomed to not asking questions on the telephone, nothing more was said.

George arrived by taxi and took his father into the bedroom for a talk. The sister of a dear friend of ours in the United States had come to the house and told George she had received an extremely urgent phone call from her brother. She wanted to speak only to Andreas, but George said we were out for the evening. She asked to see Andreas' mother, but his mother was sleeping. George told her that in any case, if it was something serious, it would just upset Mrs. Papandreou. He offered to take the message to his father. The message was clear and unmistakable. *There was to be a coup in Greece within the next five days!* What gave this message particular authenticity and importance was that our friend had reliable contacts with the American CIA.

The following day Cannellopoulos requested that Parliament be dissolved, without having tried to get a vote of confidence, and his request was granted and a royal decree signed to that effect. Since no other Premier had been appointed, this left Cannellopoulos holding power to conduct the elections. As my father-in-law said, "The worm was in the apple." The worm, I believe, had been in the apple for some time.

This action didn't jibe with Palace contacts with the Center Union party. We had heard that when Cannellopoulos had gone to the King for the formalities of submitting his resignation, the King had tried to force him to step down for a service government, and that Cannellopoulos had refused. What power Cannellopoulos had to refuse is a mystery, unless he had gotten a prior commitment from the King, which he was insisting the King honor.

Despite this new development, the date of the meeting between Andreas and the King's representative was reconfirmed, and it was clear that the King didn't consider Cannellopoulos the final solution. A *New York Times* editorial on April 17 wrote of "King Constantine's Dilemma" and said: "... It is the King, however, who has wedged himself into a political corner, where the only option to the return of a Papandreou government may be an army-backed dictatorship. This is not an acceptable option and Constantine must know it."

For the next six days, Andreas slept away from home. Our information from within the Big Junta was not consistent with the emergency telephone call from the United States. The Big Junta was considering dates for a coup closer to the elections. They were also spending considerable time arguing about whether they should have Andreas arrested or not. Now that Parliament had been dissolved, Andreas no longer had his deputy immunity. Thus two threats hung over our heads—an official arrest, carried out by the party of ERE which was in government, or a military coup. The first would have produced a violent reaction and would have solved nothing, for the people would have united more solidly around the party of Papandreou in the elections. Andreas would have become a martyr as well, and a Center Union government would have dismissed the charges as being political persecution.

The contacts with the King's representative could have meant two things: an attempt on his part to reconcile differences, accept his bitter cup of tea, and hold elections, or it could have been a smoke screen for more evil intentions. We believed that the King was in control of the army and that a coup could be only a King's coup. If avoiding a dictatorship could be done by abridging the differences and burying some of the antagonisms and hostilities of the past few years, it was a national duty to do so. That is why Andreas encouraged the contact.

The week starting April 16 had these features: the army generals were called into Athens for a staff meeting; Cannellopoulos put men of his confidence into key posts in the government; three civilians were arrested by Socratides, the investigating attorney, and charged with treason for participation in ASPIDA; the State Police Station went completely under the control of ERE; vast preparations were being made by the Center Union party for its campaign kickoff in Salonika the following Sunday; we had our second "establishment party" on Tuesday; and Andreas started sleeping at home, having passed the five-day deadline and because we had faith in our own inside information. We waited for the breakfast appointment with King Constantine's representative on the morning of April 21.

The day of the 20th, Andreas suggested that we call Kiveli and Tito to join us for dinner somewhere. He was exhaused from meetings, speeches, organizing. That evening he was scheduled to speak to the heads of the Democratic Clubs, units of a larger organization which were the beginnings of a modern-style party system, and which he had also organized to be ready to confront a dictatorship.

At 10 P.M. I met him at a hospital where we visited a friend who had just had a baby. By 10:30 we were in the Hilton Hotel taverna to join our friends. Kiveli looked a bit strained and asked me immediately, "Why did you tell me on the phone to meet tonight to celebrate Andreas' last night out of jail?"

"I said that?"

"Precisely."

"Well, there's so much talk about it, I guess I just thought I'd make a joke out of it."

"I thought maybe you had some special information."

"Oh, Kiveli, I'm so sorry," I said, as I saw how seriously she had taken my attempt to be funny, and how she had apparently suffered during the day, not daring to call me and ask for details. "I guess it was some joke."

"Some joke," she repeated. Then she flashed a relieved, warm smile, and we turned our attention to finding a table and trying to forget our anxieties.

By midnight we had finished dinner. For the fun of it, we had a photographer take a picture of the four of us. Andreas suggested that we go up to the Hilton Skyroom to hear some music. Kiveli said that they would love to, but she thought we both looked tired, and maybe it was an opportunity to get to bed early and get some sleep. I looked at Andreas and concluded that she was right. Andreas didn't insist. We kissed them good-bye in front of the Hilton. As we drove home, we were silent. The streets of Athens looked normal. There was nothing particularly ominous about that night, no more ominous than hundreds of nights preceding it.

The Athens *Post* managed to circulate some copies of its papers the following morning before its presses were seized. Down in one corner, next to a résumé of the speech Andreas had given to the heads of the Democratic Clubs was the following item:

STOP PRESS

Tonight, around 3 A.M., military putsch was held in Athens. Tanks and paratroop units keep the strategical points of the town. Telephones, radio and other communications are cut. Till now is known only about Andreas Papandreou, Glezos, Kirkos and other personalities arrestations.

Some days afterward, I thumbtacked the photo of Kiveli, Tito, Andreas, and me taken at the Hilton taverna on the bulletin board on the wall above our telephones, and underneath I wrote across the photo in sprawling script: *Last night of freedom, April 20, 1967.*

140

PART TWO

The Dictatorship

CHAPTER FIFTEEN

The Day of the Coup

DAWN finally came to a shattered household. Except for restless dozing by the younger children on the living room couch, no one had slept. We were all physically and emotionally exhausted, but worse than that, we were lost. The dynamic force in our lives, the man around whom activities swirled, had been barbarically dragged from our home. Andreas' mother had sat the night through in one spot, staring into nothing, her face white and lined with anxiety. My mother, seventy, had tried to keep busy around the house. Now, at seven in the morning, she was on the verge of collapse, the color drained from her face. Antigone continued to huddle in a chair in the corner of the hallway, not hearing or seeing anyone.

Since six o'clock I had been considering turning on the radio. This had not occurred to the others, and in my fear of what I might hear, I had not mentioned it. Taking a deep breath, and trying to sound natural, I asked George to switch it on. The first thing that greeted us was a blast of military music. The music stopped suddenly, there was a long pause, then just as suddenly a new march came on. I was pacing the floor now, my hands wet with perspiration. I didn't want to hear any announcements. The music was bad enough. Would I hear the name of my husband? And what would they say—Andreas Papandreou, shot at dawn, convicted by a military court on charges of high treason?

Another pause. The Greek national anthem. What right, I thought, what right do they have to play the national anthem? Briefly, I felt a slight hope. As long as there was just music, the coup was in an unsettled state. The words "abortive coup" came to mind . . .

A voice. I half listened, walking away from the radio and onto the terrace where I could catch just a few words. They were words about the national army and the nation, and then a list of numbers of articles of the Constitution that had been abrogated. At the end the announcer said, "Constantinos, King of the Hellenes."

So it was the King's coup. But who were his collaborators, and whom would he name ministers? The King in charge, I thought. What did that mean for Andreas' fate? Would he want to take the direct responsibility for ordering a firing squad to do away with Andreas? One thing I was sure it meant was a trial on the ASPIDA charges, a conviction, and a maximum sentence. It would be by military court. A fair trial was out. Then I wondered. What articles of the Constitution had been canceled out, and did they perhaps reinstate the death penalty?

Petros was sitting at the radio waiting patiently for me to stop my pacing.

"Petros, you heard it," I almost whispered as I walked into the room. "It's the King."

He shook his head slowly. "Maybe yes and maybe no. But the arrest of Arnaoutis is puzzling."

"Maybe it's a cover-up." It was conceivable that the King wanted it to look as if he had been forced into a dictatorial solution, and what better way than to have his secretary pulled from his home in the same manner as others.

"Yes, but if he wants to be covered, then why have his name signed to a proclamation abrogating portions of the Constitution?"

There were too many questions, and my mind was unclear. There was just one question that really mattered—what about Andreas?

My father came in to ask what the radio had said. He had just taken my mother upstairs, virtually carrying her to her bed. I told him approximately what I had heard. He made no comment, but turned to me and said, "Marg, I think I'll go to the embassy."

"I'll go, too," said my son George, who appeared somehow from the walls.

"I was thinking I should go," I replied.

My father thought just he and George should go, that I was recognizable to the Greeks, and he didn't know what he would find in the streets. Both George and he, especially he, looked like Americans and had American passports and could probably get through if there were any barricades. They would surely stop me, he felt, if they saw me, and then we would be blocked from any contact.

"They must find out where Andreas is," I said, "and they must take immediate steps to protect his life. Tell them I will kill the ambassador himself if anything happens to Andreas."

My father looked at me in a strange manner, studying my face to determine whether I meant this literally or was just trying to communicate determination to him. He saw that I meant it. "I know where the guns have been hidden," I added.

My father knew me well. We were both Anglo-Saxon types with similar temperaments. We never exchanged many words, but there was a deep bond between us. His traits—honesty, courage, strength of character—were formed by his immigrant English-Scotch parents, and nurtured through farm living in the Midwest. A hard worker, he was throughout his life on a weekly wage, except for one entrepreneurial fling at a garage-car-agency business, which was crushed by the depression of 1929. He never made money an aim; his values were nonmaterial. It was my luck that he and my mother were visiting me when the coup took place. They sustained me emotionally, and assisted me in countless—and dangerous—ways.

"Take your American passports and hold them high if you get into any trouble," I told them. I was hesitant about Georgie's going, but I knew he wanted to fight for his father as he had done earlier that morning when he boosted him up on the study roof. His father was his idol, an invincible giant who was fighting for a cause, and the shock of seeing him treated like a common criminal was to haunt George for months to come. Too, he felt that had he managed to climb down from the terrace instead of being huddled in the corner when the soldiers crashed through the terrace door, his father would have escaped. Nothing I could say dissuaded him from this belief. I am sure that he spent long hours going over the experience in his mind, reforming it in fantasy in which he did all the right things, and his father was free.

After they left, friends began to arrive. Popi, a young, attractive twenty-year-old secretary from Andreas' political office, was the first. She had started early in the morning to try to find public transportation, but no buses were running. After walking some distance, she hitched a ride, and the unknown driver, hearing she was coming to my place, brought her to the corner of Guizi Street. She arrived breathless and worried, and close to tears. Angela was next. Angela had been the secretary to Andreas when he was Minister of Coordination. After the Papandreou government fell, she was hired by my father-in-law to be his personal secretary at his home in Kastri. She was thoroughly dedicated to both Papandreous. Stratis, one of Andreas' political secretaries, burst in through the back door, hugged me, and said he had to take off again. When I asked him what we must do, what could we do, he simply said, "We'll see, we'll see" and left as abruptly as he had arrived. Having spent two years in prison during the German occupation, the specter of iron bars must have loomed large in his mind. Those in Andreas' close political circle were in heavy danger.

Two men I didn't recognize rang the front doorbell, asking if there was anything they could do. When they mentioned their names, I knew I had heard them before, but the faces meant nothing. Two neighbors, a lawyer and his wife, came on their heels, and I walked out to the front gate to talk to them. Their son was a classmate of George's in high school, although I had not met the parents. They were extremely kind and offered to take the younger children to their home for the day and night, if I liked. Sometime later they returned with bags of canned goods and groceries, saying that queues had formed, and they wanted to be sure I didn't have to spend the day queuing for food.

Everyone asked what he could do. Everyone wanted to help. And I needed help. My only request: Find Andreas. Save his life. Protect him. Go hang the dictators. In the early hours of the morning when I had tried, through a lone soul calling from kiosk to kiosk in Piraeus to get the people to resist, it had been a plea of desperation, and doomed to failure. The grass-roots organization which Andreas had begun was a fragile web, vulnerable and easily broken by a few scissor snips here and there. Those snips had taken place during the night: arrests of union leaders, journalists, mayors, leaders of democratic youth clubs. With telephone communications cut and lines of soldiers guarding key arteries through Athens, a mass reaction was unlikely. I am convinced, however, that such a reaction would have forced the junta leaders out within twenty-four hours. They were a tiny clique, using an already prepared NATO plan called Prometheus for the take-over, but on the morning of April 21 they held only Attica, that is, Athens and surrounding area, and a portion of Macedonia. The rest of Greece was essentially free. A powerful reaction on the part of the people would have given the majority forces of the Greek army the necessary excuse to form an immediate countercoup. And the Americans, sitting on their hands at the moment, would have intervened to prevent civil war in a NATO country. I do not mean military intervention. They would have played the arbiter's role. Some act of resistance was needed. None occurred.

In less than an hour my father and George returned. On the way to the embassy, they had had to circle around Lykebettus to avoid a blockade, and finding themselves near the apartment of my close friend Marjorie Schachter, they decided to stop and pick her up. Marjorie was asleep, oblivious to the night's tragic events. The news was a shock, even though she knew the tension the recent weeks had contained for us. It was to her apartment that Andreas and I sometimes went when a threat to his life was made. She dressed in two minutes and ran to the car to join the committee of protest going to the embassy. Marjorie, a stunning blonde, proved to be a help in intimidating a cordon of young Greek soldiers. The trio now consisted of a Gary Cooper, a Dorothy Malone, and a teen-ager, and if they couldn't get through guns and tanks to the American Embassy, no one could. Had I arranged it with cunning, I couldn't have done better.

They reached the embassy, and were soon ushered in to Ambassador Talbot's office. Anschuetz was also there. My father reported that the two looked tired and seemed genuinely not to know much more than we did. He then said that I feared that Andreas would be killed, and that I expected the entire power of the American contingent to be used to prevent it. Marjorie told me my dad was very effective and very tough, and that she didn't think it would have added anything to tell Phillips Talbot that he would be killed if Andreas were killed. Later I was kidded about this passionate statement. I had meant it.

Phillip Dimitriades arrived at our house. A tall, thin intellectual with glasses, sandy hair, and a reddish moustache, he was a close friend and political supporter of Andreas'. He was one of the three men reached by Petros by the time of the break-in, but he had misinterpreted the call and thought that Andreas had escaped, and he came ready to help Andreas out of Greece, or to keep him hidden in the underground. When Andreas had told Petros on the telephone, "Call our friends," he meant to warn them for their own personal security and to set a prearranged plan into motion. When Phillip went to the assigned house and no further messages were delivered, he left and reached Psychico late that morning. Even the rudimentary communication system we had organized for such an emergency had misfired.

I was very fond of Phillip, and I used to tease Andreas that he belonged to the "party of Margarita," not the party of Andreas. My other member was Tito. Sometimes we would have mock meetings in friendly social gatherings in which Tito and Phillip always took opposite points of view, and then ask me, as president, to break the deadlock. The man whose point of view I sided with would declare himself second in line for the leadership of the party. The debates were held in recessed spots, away from the larger gathering, and we would usually end the meetings in loud laughter. These were always friendly entanglements, but once in a while I had the distinct feeling that they gave significance to my vote, not because of me, but because it was a form of competition, and neither could stand to lose. I told them on these occasions that I was delighted I had a small Greek party, and only two members to deal with!

Phillip tried to reassure me that Andreas wouldn't be touched, arguing that those who were already in were safe; the danger was for those who were out. I could not agree that anyone in the hands of barbarians was safe. About those of us out, I couldn't care less. He then wanted to talk about organization for resistance, methods, techniques, people to be trusted. It was a debate without my vote. I heard the words, but they did not reach my brain. I needed time to find the broken threads of my life and patch them together again, to look at the new environment, to learn what it meant. Subconsciously, I knew that what Phillip was saying would be part of the new world, but I was unable to respond in any coherent fashion. I suggested we talk about it in the afternoon.

Spyros Angelopoulos, a young teacher from Philothey, came by, looking as if he had already joined a militant antijunta movement. Soon after that, Virginia Vardoni was in the backyard, walking back and forth with me, trying to comfort me. Virginia's husband, who had been a resistance fighter against the Germans, had died in a Swiss hospital a year earlier after an operation, and she understood more than anyone my sense of loss. Virginia was a top journalist and had been using her pen effectively to espouse the Papandreou cause for the now extinguished elections. She also wanted to talk about resistance.

Now and then the radio was switched on by one of the aimlessly wandering visitors. We would hear the same announcement, by the same voice (who was the radio announcer conscripted into serving the junta?), reading over and over again the numbers of the articles of the Constitution that had been blacked out by the military. And always at the end, "Constantinos, King of the Hellenes."

"Turn that damned thing off!" I would shout, and we would have silence until the next curious visitor snapped the radio on again.

We went through the motions of lunch about 2:30 P.M. The children had disappeared into the homes of friends, except for Georgie, who refused to leave my side. There were seven of us at the table: Marjorie, Popi, the two mothers, George, my father, and myself. My stomach turned at the sight and smell of food. This was to go on for days, until Antigone discovered that I could sip a banana blended with milk and sugar, and she would appear, unasked, wherever I might be, with a glass of this mixture, at least four or five times a day. I couldn't touch anything to drink, even Tito's gift of raki from Crete, which was a favorite of mine. I increased my number of cigarettes.

My body ached and my eyes were burning, and from time to time a hot pain filled my lungs and throat, giving me a momentary sensation of suffocation. It was afternoon and there was still no news of Andreas.

I was nervous and jumpy and with the approach of evening, my fears heightened. I asked my father and Marjorie if they would go back to the embassy, even though friends told us that the Athens area was getting more and more difficult to travel in.

They climbed again into the Taunus, without a word of protest. I begged them to be careful, for things were getting tighter and the tension building up. The radio had announced a curfew at sundown, after which anyone found would be "shot on sight." Three names had been announced for government posts: Papadopoulos, Makarezos, and Pattakos. Everyone speculated that the coup leaders were having trouble forming a government. In this atmosphere, I watched my father and Marjorie walk the short distance to the car parked in front of the house. I saw my father struggle with the stub of the gearshift, broken off by a soldier at the time of the manhunt for Andreas early that morning—centuries ago. He forced the shift into first, and the car lurched off.

I did not know how to react to the news friends were bringing me of an uncertain and unstable state of affairs. Since I didn't know yet Andreas' fate, I forced myself to believe that he was alive. Was he perhaps safer than he might be if a new shake-up took place, if there were a countercoup? A shift situation might offer more opportunity to shoot him. Chaos, passion, hatred, rivalries, were hardly the conditions for predictable events. While I wanted more than anything for the dictatorship to fail, I was terrified contemplating the changeover. Much of this thinking was the product of a confused, distraught mind, now filling again with foreboding.

Information during that day was contradictory, distorted, and inaccurate. We heard that Crete was on fire and that it would rebel. We heard that there were skirmishes in the north and that the Third Army of Macedonia was marching toward Athens to put down the dictators. We heard that Queen Mother Frederika had shouted, "Save my son! Save my son!" when the King had left the Palace in the early morning. We heard that someone had seen the King driven down Vassilis Sophias about ten o'clock sardined between two army officers, looking very grim and angry. We heard that the Sixth Fleet was steaming toward Phaleron Bay, near the port of Piraeus.

The worst—and happily erroneous—news was not reported to me until sometime later. Popi had come from upstairs looking ashen white. She called Angela to one corner, and I could see them whispering together from the other side of the room where I was talking to Phillip. When they saw my eyes glance their way, they walked together into the dining room. I knew it was bad news. I was too scared to ask. Like a child, I thought that if I didn't know it, it couldn't have happened. At the same time, I braced every muscle and nerve for the impact of horrible news, should the two move in my direction. Some days later I was told what their dark secret was. Popi had gotten the Voice of Truth from Bulgaria, a Greek-language broadcast, on Georgie's shortwave radio. It had announced that Andreas Papandreou had been executed by a firing squad early in the morning.

On Vassilis Sophias Street, on the way to downtown Athens and the American Embassy, Marjorie and my father were stopped at least six times in their car. Each time they held up their green passports and pointed in the direction of the embassy. Each time, after some discussion, they were directed to the next barricade, where someone else would take the responsibility. The fact that the Taunus had a Greek license plate didn't help matters any. At the sixth stop, about a half mile from the embassy building, a gruff officer turned them back. My father took a side street, parked the car, and they started out the last half mile on foot. The area was completely clear of cars and people. The shutters on the apartment buildings along the way were closed tight. Twice they were stopped and waved on. The third time, at a checkpoint, the group of soldiers said nothing, just sullenly watched them walk by. Two bullets cracked over the tops of their heads. They stopped abruptly, their motion frozen as in a movie when the hold switch is flicked on the winding reel. There was dead silence. When my father turned to try to talk, a burly soldier pushed him off the boulevard and pointed him toward a side street. They were at this stage on the opposite side of the street from the embassy, at least two blocks away. Typically, my father refused to give up, and Marjorie, hanging on his arm, continued right along with him. They skirted the two blocks on a street parallel to Vassilis Sophias, then headed back toward the long, hideous boulevard. This brought them directly across from the embassy, separated by the wide boulevard. There was no sign of life outside the embassy. Taking a deep breath, the two started across, sole targets on an empty street. Perhaps the soldiers in that area felt anyone who had gotten that close to the embassy must have had clearance from the forces surrounding the area at a greater distance. Whatever the explanation, no one shouted at them or tried to stop them, and after walking what seemed like a mile, they reached the door of the building.

Talbot and Anschuetz were surprised to see them again. Much of the embassy personnel had not made it in, despite embassy cars and diplomatic permits, even in the morning when the restrictions were easier. Those who were in were planning to stay the night.

"How did you get through?" Talbot asked.

My father said very simply, "We got through because we have to find out about Andreas." For him it was just that simple. He had come because his daughter was in need and his son-in-law in danger, and the whole blasted Greek army couldn't have kept him from carrying out this mission.

They told him what they said they knew, that politicians from all parties had been arrested (that word "arrest" a euphemism!), including Cannellopoulos, Prime Minister at the time of the coup, and were being held at the Pentagon, Greek army headquarters. This bit of news about Cannellopoulos jarred me. Assuming it was the King's coup, which I still did, why would the rightist premier be arrested?

About Andreas they were unable to get any information. They assumed that he was there also. They insisted that they were not in contact with whoever had been responsible for the coup, and despite efforts, had not been able to make contact. When Talbot was pressed by my father to see that Andreas' life was protected, he repeated that they were isolated and not able to do anything yet.

Marjorie told them we had heard rumors of skirmishes in the north.

Anschuetz was interested. "Where?"

"Somewhere near Salonika."

"The army and the people, or divisions within the army?"

Marjorie was not clear. "I don't really know. Margaret said the information came from a reliable source."

"Do you know from whom?" Anschuetz continued.

"No."

The source was as reliable as any source that day. But many stories were based on either fear or hope. The subject was dropped.

There was not much more to say. My father had told them that he and Marjorie were shot at, and as they were leaving to go back into that jungle, Marjorie asked, "Do you have any advice?"

Talbot said nothing and looked at Anschuetz.

"You can stay at the embassy if you like" was Anschuetz' answer.

"That's out" was my father's immediate reply. He knew what a state I would be in if neither one showed up for the night.

"And what about Margaret's children?" Marjorie asked. "They may all be in danger."

Norbert's reply to that was "Doesn't she have any friends?"

Feeling forlorn and unsuccessful in their mission, the two left for the elevator. At the elevator the young man sitting outside of Talbot's office caught up with them and reiterated the offer to have them stay for the night. On that note, they started out for the car. They reached it without any incidents, and my father returned by back roads, until he reached beyond Embolokopi, the point at which they had encountered their first blockade.

The news they brought with them hardly fostered a spirit of hope. The embassy, always hostile, did not seem inclined to make any special effort for Andreas. Certainly they had given no assurances to my emissary, my father.

Popi had decided to stay for the night, and a boyhood friend of Andreas' came over before curfew to have supper and sleep in the study. Nick and Andriko were at the Kouratoses', fighting their own dark thoughts as the terror of the previous night became vivid again in the lengthening shadows. Disobeying the curfew, Takis' driver sneaked over around 8 P.M. with a promised hot casserole of stewed beef, potatoes, tomatoes, and garlic. The other visitors had left for home before the time when they could be "shot on sight." The naked crudity of this order had made me chill and sick.

Everyone tried to get me to eat, to take a sip of wine, to join in some conversation. I could do none of these things. At ten o'clock I went up and put on my bloodstained robe—an act of defiance—took one of Marjorie's Miltowns, and tried to sleep. Within an hour I was back downstairs, talking to Marjorie. I had not slept for twenty hours, but my nerves were keeping me awake. Marjorie suggested that I lie on the couch with my head on a pillow while we talked, thinking I would drop off to sleep. She and I talked alone until 3 A.M. Twice after that I fell into slumber, only to awaken in a sitting position with my arms stretched out and screaming, and Marjorie trying to soothe me. Between five and six I slept. When I woke up, Marjorie was sleeping close by, stretched out on the carpet beside the couch, with a chair cushion under her head.

I went into the kitchen and made some strong coffee and decided that the fight for Andreas' life and freedom would have to begin, and that I was the only one who could lead it.

CHAPTER SIXTEEN

A Fight for Life

IT WAS eight o'clock when the other members of the house began trudging downstairs. I awakened Marjorie long enough to get her to climb from her floor-bed to the now vacated couch. I closed the door to the living room and admonished the others to keep their voices low. It was unnecessary. Marjorie would have been oblivious to a tank rolling through the room, exhausted as she was from a night of standing by a jumpy, nerve-wracked, battered friend.

The two younger boys, Nikos and Andrikos, came in the kitchen door from the neighbor's house, looking as if they too had suffered a sleepless night. I kissed them both and held them close, feeling their bodies taut under my embrace. How to explain to an eight-year-old and a ten year-old the brutalities of man? Their big blue eyes reflected troubled thoughts and and their faces had lost the gaiety and ready smiles of normal days.

"Anything about Daddy?" Nick asked.

"Not yet," I answered, trying to give the impression that I wasn't worried.

"You really screamed after they took him," he added. "I couldn't understand why. They won't do anything to him."

I looked at his serious face. He was not trying to comfort me. He sincerely believed what he said. An extremely bright child, Nick always had faith in his predictive abilities, arguing that he "sensed" things of the future, and he had proved himself right. Who could say what sixth-sense capacity he had? In his earnest expression of a conviction, he gave me solace.

"I was scared, too," chimed in Andriko.

"You mean that I scared you more than the soldiers with guns?"

"Well, no, not exactly," he answered. But it was clear that my momentary hysteria had frightened them. I was their shield; I remained behind while their father was pushed into the night, and my collapse gave deeper significance to the drama they had not understood. It was the first time I had really talked to them since the event. The day before had passed in a fog of agony and confusion, my thoughts glued to Andreas, and only Andreas. They told me their own story. They had been awakened by the flood of the ceiling light, and opened their eyes to see their father and mother frantically dialing the telephone. They heard the shouting and pounding downstairs, listened to our telephone conversations, by now sitting up in their beds, and then saw me suddenly disappear downstairs, and their father and George go through the terrace door. Left to their own resources, they tried to hide. They opened a cabinet door at the bottom of the wall-high bookcases and crawled behind it, using the door and a chair they pulled along with them to form a barricade. The two of them huddled there for a few seconds, then Andrikos, feeling the insecurity of his haven, whispered sagely that they might be mistaken for something else and could be shot. He proceeded to climb back out and got into the safer place of his bed, despite Nicky's protests. Nick, finding himself alone, quickly followed suit, and promoted the idea that they start reading their books. It was at this point that two bleating soldiers burst in, machine guns in hand, and if it weren't for their own state of confusion, they might have wondered at this strange sight: two young boys nonchalantly reading their books at 2:30 in the morning, lights ablaze, while a mad cacophony filled the house.

They were asked where their father was. Behind the two soldiers was Manoli, the night guard, not yet having been beaten, and he made one simple facial gesture known to all Greeks to mean "no," the raising of his eyebrows with a slight upward motion of his head. The boys answered they didn't know.

When the soldiers left, Nick made one noble attempt to get help. He went to the phone and dialed 0 to reach the police. The line was out.

I didn't want to hear more. The events were too recent and too painful, and I was affected by the picture of desperation and fear of my youngest children as they faced these unknown invaders alone.

They asked if they could ride their bikes. Remembering the boy on the bicycle, the shots over Marjorie's and my father's heads, and the "shoot on sight" order of the night before, I urged them to stay in the backyard with Blackie and Gilda, our two mongrel dogs. Apparently having been frightened off by the gunshots and noise, the dogs had come sneaking back a day later. I suggested that the boys give the dogs some comfort.

When my father finished his breakfast, I asked him to drive me over to the Anschuetz house. Mrs. Anschuetz let me in, expressed her concern, and asked me to wait in the salon. I studied her face to see if it revealed anything. Was her concern for me for a woman whose husband was somewhere under arrest, or for a woman whose husband was dead? She might know by now. A whole sinister day and night had passed. I could read nothing.

"Norbert is shaving," she told me. "He was at the embassy until early this morning. He'll be down in about ten minutes."

I had forgotten my father. "Have you met my father?" I asked, turning to him.

"Yes, of course," she said, nodding her head. "Hello, Mr. Chant. We talked early yesterday morning when he came by with your son."

I had almost forgotten. Yesterday seemed like years ago.

We sat down and were having our first cup of coffee when Norbert came down in his lounging robe. I stood up, and we went through the formality of shaking hands.

"Oh, Norbert," I said. "Do you have any news? Do you know anything about Andreas?" My mouth was dry again.

"I'm afraid I have no information, Margaret," he answered.

"I don't understand why you can't find out. You must have some means. Haven't you talked to the King?"

"We're unable to make contact."

This I could hardly believe. "But time is passing, and they may kill Andreas. I will hold you responsible." I wondered whether I should threaten, as I had asked my father to do with Talbot. Looking at his cold, handsome face, I felt I knew what he would say, in his best sardonic manner: "Oh, come, come now, Margaret," with the intimation that we're not in some Grade B movie.

"We're doing all we can," he said.

"For Andreas?"

"For all the political prisoners."

"But Andreas is not just *a* prisoner; he's *the* prisoner!"

"We're hoping it will be a reasonable bunch. They have made the judge of the Supreme Court the Prime Minister."

Yes, I knew. We had heard his name announced the evening before, and his speech to the Greek people. It had struck us dumb. Constantine Kollias, Queen Mother Frederika's close collaborator, and architect of the judicial charges against Andreas on the ASPIDA case! Norbert's comment had the tone of approval, as if somehow Kollias (judge, and all that) was an island of sanity in what otherwise might be madness. It was more simple than that. Kollias was a Palace man, and support for the Palace—no matter what—had been a cornerstone of American policy in Greece for time unending.

"You can't be serious," I retorted. "He's a wild man. He hates Andreas with a passion. For the democratic camp he's a red flag. The King couldn't have chosen a worse man."

"I don't think the King was in on the coup."

Now it was my turn to have said, "Oh, come, come now, Norbert." Instead I just stared at him.

"What do you know about Kollias?" he asked me.

I told him many things which he must have known already. I told him how my father-in-law had charged him with malfeasance in office, in his position as prosecutor general of the Supreme Court, because of the terrible cover-up of the Lambrakis case under Karamanlis. Lambrakis was an EDA deputy who had been murdered by two men on a motorcycle while coming out of a building in Salonika where he had spoken to a large rally. The court given the case on malfeasance declared itself incompetent to judge, and Kollias eventually resumed his duties. Kollias' hostility to my father-in-law for this attempt to discharge him was transferred to Andreas as Andreas' popularity rose and his attacks on the role of the King gained support. Under his auspices the investigation of political persons in the ASPIDA case was carried out, finally culminating in the request from his office that Andreas' immunity be removed.

There was not much for Anschuetz to say. After a pause, I told him, "Good God, Norbert, the coup was so unnecessary!" What I wanted to say was "You damned fools . . . Why did you do it!" but I needed help. I thought Anschuetz was it.

I sounded half-dead, and I felt it. A combination of no sleep and frequent tranquilizers had slowed my speech and dulled my intonation. I plunged into a recital of why this was a monstrous, unforgivable mistake of judgment, that the embassy had misjudged Andreas, that they had misjudged the intentions of the Center Union had it achieved government, that in their anticommunist phobia they were killing the only healthy, democratic forces in the country. Then again back to Andreas, that he was not a demagogue, that he was not an unreasonable man, that he had done everything to try to prevent this insane thing from happening, including warning the embassy and the State Department of the existence of the Big Junta and its intentions. And that he had further tried to reach a détente with the King to forestall action of this sort.

"That was a wily move of the King," I said, "to have arranged a morning breakfast between his representative and Andreas' the morning of April 21. That was the reason we were at home that night."

"I said the King wasn't in on it." In Norbert's insistence he gave away the fact that he had more information than he was disclosing. There was no rule that said he had to tell me, yet I was desperate for information which might give me some clue about Andreas, and some indication of what effective next move I might make.

Information I had gotten the afternoon before about one of the leaders of the coup gave Norbert's statement some credibility, although at the time I heard the story, I had assumed that the man was working in conjunction with the King. I proceeded to tell Norbert what I had heard about Colonel George Papadopoulos from a friend of Andreas'. His ambitions to take over Greece could be traced to 1958 when he organized a group of friends from his officers' graduating class and held long talk sessions with his buddies on the ills of Greece, the "theory" of dictatorship, and the need for an incision. When I used this word, I didn't realize that Papadopoulos' subsequent announcements and speeches would be peppered with medical terms and analogies, a hangover, it was said, from his interest in medicine and his frustration at not becoming a doctor. He was nicknamed "Nasser" by the other officers, a name that pleased him. He was a conspiratorial type, and in 1964 had reported an act of sabotage among his troops in the north (sugar in the gasoline tanks of army trucks) and termed it "communist-inspired." This was an attempt to give proof to the stories—initiated by the Right—that communists were infiltrating the army under Papandreou. The act of sabotage was traced to him. Disciplinary action was taken and he was transferred to a lesser post. (This was later reversed by Stephanopoulos who moved him into a key post in Athens in the intelligence service, KYP.) My father-in-law had been urged to kick him out of the army, by many people, including the man from whom I got the information—an ex-officer in the same officers' class as Papadopoulos. My father-in-law chose the transfer instead because Papadopoulos' father had been an old schoolteacher friend of his from a village near Kalentzi! What an irony of fate!

"I don't know what involvement the United States has in all this," I continued, "but one thing I feel sure of. He couldn't have done this without American support or expectation of American support."

"We haven't given our support."

"In a way you have. The atmosphere that was built up prior to the coup, the expressed distaste for the Papandreou government—all of these things— what would an army clique conclude from that?"

"It's always the Americans," Norbert said in obvious irritation. "Damn it! Don't the Greeks have anything to do with it? I have followed the Greek situation for ten years, and I can defend every American action during that period. I think our policy has been good and right."

He had stated this once before in our living room to Andreas and me. Then I believed that he truly meant it. Now, under these circumstances I wondered how he could repeat the statement.

He added, "We don't have that much power here anymore. We have been pulling away from involvement in Greek affairs." (That was a familiar tune.)

"If it were a communist take-over . . . ?"

He shrugged his shoulders. He wasn't being hostile. He was tired, and he was sympathetic to my agony as a human being. He let me ramble on some more. My vague goal was to try to convince him that American support for the dictatorship would be a ghastly error, that a solution which might bring the Center Union into power was not the end of the world for the United States. It seemed to me that the only chance for Andreas' life was the overthrow of the junta. But Norbert was just one man. Even if he accepted my thesis, there was a whole bureaucratic structure behind him, a huge machinery of Pentagon, CIA, and State Department. My sense of futility was further accentuated by the fact that my Greek friends considered this an American-inspired dictatorship. If they had done it, why would they undo it?

When I left, I begged him to do something for Andreas. He said he would let me know the minute he got any news (and he kept this promise). He gave no false assurances of help. I suspect that he thought we might be talking about a ghost.

When I returned home, the house was bulging with people. They were discussing the pronouncement of Kollias, broadcast the night before. Kollias had put on his preacher-man robes and officiated at the christening of this Gorgon, naming it the Greek Government, and absolving it of sin. The ruthless gang which had turned arms against its own people and abolished the Constitution and all human freedoms were present at the ceremony, listening with glee, according to my friends, like the characters in an Addams cartoon, to the thin, cold, monotonous voice of Prime Minister Kollias. Here is what was said by the highest man of law of the land:

People of Greece:

> *For a long time now we have been standing by witnessing a crime which was taking place at the expense of the society, our society and our nation.*
>
> *The ruthless and miserable partisan dealings, the irresponsibility of a large segment of the press, the systematic attack against all institutions, their corrosion, the total humiliation of Parliament, the slander of everything, the paralysis of the mechanism of the State, the total lack of understanding exhibited toward the burning*

problems of our youth, the mishandling of our students, the lowering of moral standards, the confusion and the fogginess, the secret and open co-operation with the insurgents, and finally, the continuing inflammatory slogans of conscience-less demagogues destroyed the calm of the country, created a climate of anarchy and chaos, cultivated conditions of hatred and division and led us to the edge of national catastrophe. There remained no other means of salvation than the Army's intervention.

This intervention, of course, constitutes a deviation from the Constitution, but it was necessary for the salvation of our country.

The country's salvation is the supreme law.

The elections which had been proclaimed would not have given a solution to the impasse. First, because under the present conditions it was impossible for them to be carried out in a normal manner. Second, because no matter what resulted from them, we would have been led inevitably to bloodshed and chaos.

This is why the Army intervened. To cut off the march forward to catastrophe just a step before the abyss.

Absolute calm and order prevail throughout the country.

The president and the members of the government have been enlisted for the execution of their duty toward our country.

Who are we? We do not belong to any political party and we are not prepared to favor any political camp at the expense of the other. We do not belong to the economic oligarchy which we are not disposed to allow to provoke the poor. We belong to the class of toil. And we shall stand by the side of our poor Greek brothers. We are moved exclusively by patriotic motives and will strive to eliminate corruption. To sanitize public life. To remove from the country's organism the decay from which it had been endangered. To prevent division and fratricide toward which we were being led by malicious Greeks and to create healthy foundations for the country's early return to the truly orthodox parliamentary life. We proclaim brotherhood. From this moment there do not exist members of the Right, Center or Left. There exist only Greeks who believe only in Greece—who believe in a nobler, greater and complete ideal of a true democracy and not the democracy of the sidewalk, the mob and anarchy. When the Greeks are united they are miracle makers. There exists of course a very few traitors, demagogues, conscience-less opportunists and professional opportunists. They tried to divide us. And they call us leftists, centrists, center leftists and rightists.

They have tried to instil in our soul through every means the hatred of the ones toward the others. They have tried to fanaticize us and to push us to bloodshed. Those few arsonists we shall isolate and all of us, the other Greeks, united, we shall move forward on the path of duty toward the country and virtue. Toward the radical change. Toward well-being and progress. Our basic target is social justice. The just distribution of income. The moral and material

156

uplifting of society and especially the farmers and the workers of the economically poorer classes.

The benevolence of the government will be turned without limit toward the youth and his problems.

Following the establishment of the normal rhythm and the creation of the appropriate conditions, the country will return to parliamentarianism on a healthy basis the soonest possible. Then the mission of the government will have come to an end.

For the prevention of national division and of the civil war which was ready to break out, which would have led to bloodshed and to social and national catastrophe, the government has had to proclaim martial law over the whole country.

The government declares categorically that it is committed to carrying out successfully through all means and with a rapid rhythm the heavy mission which it undertook. It is decided to carry out to the full its obligations toward the population for the realization of its aims. It demands total discipline to the State. As is the case in all the civilized countries. Because real freedom exists where the law exists. It exists where the liberty of one person extends up to the point where the liberty of another person begins.

The government is bound to warn in the most categorical manner that whatever reaction to its national task of change coming from whatever quarters will be crushed immediately through all the means at its disposal.

> *Long live the Nation!*
> *Long live the King!*
> *Long live eternal Greece!*

Long live the King. It seemed irrelevant whether or not the King had ordered the coup. He had joined them.

Kiveli arrived in the midst of the discussion of Kollias' speech, her thick black lashes wet with tears. How different things had been the last time I had seen her and Tito! She told me that they had gone directly home after saying good-bye to us in front of the Hilton, and immediately to bed. They, like we, had seen no signs in the streets of anything unusual. In the morning Tito had gone down to the concierge to find out why their newspaper was not outside their apartment door, thinking only that there had been a delay in delivery. When he heard the news, he raced back up, burst into her room, and awakened her with a hoarse shout: *Dictatorship!* Startled out of sleep by one of the most brutal words known to man, she lurched up in bed and asked the big question: Andreas? They must have gotten him, was the response. The two sat dumbfounded, the starkness of the news emptying their minds, and the horror of the event and all its ramifications slowly seeping into their consciousness. Seven hours earlier we had kissed and said good-bye, free men. Now we were slaves. They decided that Tito would go to his coast guard job, and she would try to reach me. As she lived near the American Embassy, she was blocked on several attempts to get to my house. Nor did she have any green passport to swing back and forth high over her head as a possible means of getting through. Tito had not returned that night. On Saturday she started out again, this time with success.

Someone came in with the rumor that the political prisoners were being held at the Hilton Hotel. For the first time I smiled. "Along with the tourists?" I asked.

Our house was full, and I was annoyed. Was it a wake or a cocktail party? There were many people conspicuous by their absence, and many people who surprised me by daring to come by. But there were some I barely knew, just loitering around, perhaps out of curiosity. The question they seemed to be asking was how does a woman act whose husband has been the target of a military coup and who is charged with high treason? Suspicion that they might be informers entered my mind. That awful sickness—suspicion, which infects a whole population living under a reign of terror and intimidation—was spreading its germs around already.

"Erasumus," I whispered to my father-in-law's lifelong chauffeur, who had earlier pulled me into the dining room and sobbed like a baby. "Please help me get some of these strange people out of here."

He suggested that I leave the room, and he would handle it.

As people were moving through the front door, I saw Marjorie dash past me and look frantically at the departing faces. She asked someone, "Where is Douglas?" and was told that my father was in the living room. I gave no more thought to this until I returned to the living room, now emptied of strangers, and saw from my chair through the terrace doors the figures of two people working on something in the corner of the garden. I recognized them as Marjorie and my father. Then I saw Georgie in a guard-position stance between the kitchen and the front door. It was obvious that he had been stationed there to keep people out of the backyard. I waited, too tired to investigate. When my father returned, he called me into the dining room and closed the door.

"Did you know about the machine-gun bullets in the backyard?" he asked.

I nearly shouted. "Machine-gun bullets in the backyard!"

"Yes. Blackie dug up a box with his paws and was pulling on it with his mouth when Marjorie went to see what he was doing."

I was flabbergasted. That pine-scented haven of serenity and peace, my garden, contained an incriminating and deadly treasure. I put my hand to my forehead. "Did anyone else see you?" I asked.

"No. I don't think so. Just Marjorie and me and George at the door."

"How? Why? Who?" I asked in rapid succession.

"I don't know" was my father's reply, "but anyway there's a bunch there."

"What do you mean, 'a bunch'?"

"There is more than one box. When we reburied the one Blackie found, we found some more."

I didn't know what to say. Did Andreas know about it? No, he would never have allowed such a thing—not with children always around. I kept thinking.

"How many boxes?" I asked.

"Six all together."

"Were they recently buried?"

"Rather, but I can't say."

"Dad, it's a plant," I said. We looked at each other and our eyes asked the same question: When could it have been done? The night of the coup? Before the coup? Since the coup? And by whom?

"Dad, they want to catch us with weapons, or ammunition, or anything to prove their case against Andreas. Oh, God, Dad, what am I to do?"

"They're reburied now, and we put some heavy potted plants over them."

The tension in my body, which I thought had hit its peak, reached an alarming intensity. "Ask Antigone to bring me a glass of water," I said. I sat down at the dining room table and tried to compose myself. Antigone came in behind my father, a big glass of cold water on a small tray in her hand. I drank it all and remained as dry as before. I looked at Antigone's disappearing figure and wondered how long she would stay around to help. Surely she understood that all of those close to me and Andreas would be subject to intimidation, and perhaps worse. She had come two years earlier, saying she had heard I was looking for a maid. She was an attractive, short brunette of twenty-seven. She came from the island of Samos. In Greece it is said that island girls are the best—even-tempered, hard working, gentle with children— and Antigone was all of these things, and more. She had waded through all the island superstitions and old wives' tales of her birthplace and emerged a modern girl—probing, questioning, doubting, and determined. She had little formal education, but during the time she was working in our house, she learned to speak English and read American cookbooks. She had an unusual judgment of people, she knew what and what not to say, and I could rely on her for anything. I needed her for these latter reasons, more than for help in the house. I hoped she would stay, but I would understand it if she left.

My mind had wandered, and I'm sure that my eyes had a look of bewilderment.

"Dad," I sighed, "we'll have to figure out what to do about those bullets. But I can't think any more about it now. All I want to know is what's happened to Andreas . . ."

I returned to the living room and sat down next to Phillip and lit a cigarette. Kiveli was talking to the two mothers. Georgie gave up his watching post and plunked into a chair, his slim body lost among the cushions. Marjorie wandered in from upstairs, shaken by her recent experience in the yard, but putting on a noble act of self-containment. It was noon by now. I counted the hours. Thirty-four. It seemed like thirty-four years. What should I do now? See the King? Ask to see Kollias? Go into the lion's den? I could visualize spittle forming on Kollias' lips as I made my plea for the life of my husband.

I hadn't noticed that Marjorie had left to answer a ring of the doorbell. She came back looking rattled, her earlier cool façade gone.

"There are some soldiers at the door," she whispered to me. Kiveli heard her and her hands tightened. My legs changed to rubber. My first thought was of the machine-gun bullets in the backyard, and with the thought came a prickling sensation in my stomach. Then I thought: They've come to take me!

Although I am an American citizen, according to Greek law I am also a Greek citizen, having married a Greek. Women had been arrested the first night. Now they were getting to me. Then I thought, no, they've probably come to check on who is here, what we are doing. I looked at Phillip and Virginia, sitting in the room with me. "You'd better get upstairs," I said, rather panicky. For a moment they looked about to obey my order, then they hesitated.

"Hell," said Phillip. "I'm not running from anybody. I'm a friend. I'm here with you, and I have a right to be here with you." With that he picked up the *kamboloi,* a string of beads like a necklace, on the table next to his chair, and started playing with them with indifference.

"Act natural," Kiveli said to everybody, a forced smile on her face.

I got up and walked to the door, Marjorie alongside me. The sight of the two young soldiers in battle dress, holding their guns partly toward the door, shocked me. In front of the gate on the road was a large army truck, and two soldiers, also with guns, had positioned themselves on each end. A driver remained in the truck. One soldier was saying something to me very politely. With effort I tried to understand what he said. The words swirled around me like heavy sea around a rock. He handed me a card. I saw my arm reach out to take it in a robotlike gesture. For half a minute I simply stood there staring at him, hardly realizing I had something in my hand. Then I looked at it. It read: "Please send me pajamas, shaving kit, underwear, handkerchiefs and a suit. Love, Andreas."

I unrolled my tongue from the roof of my mouth and stammered, "When? Now? You will take these things?"

"No, ma'am. You are to send them to Goudi." That was the camp headquarters near the Pentagon.

"Tell me. How is he? Is he all right?"

"Yes, ma'am."

"Where is he? Where are they keeping him?"

"I don't know, ma'am. I came from Goudi."

So he was at Goudi, I thought. The soldier saluted and left quickly. I held the card tenderly in my hand and burst into the living room, where family and friends were waiting, not breathing, in near-theatrical poses of nonchalance, anxiety and fear hanging in the air like mist over a quagmire.

"It's a card," I announced. "From Andreas. He's alive!" My eyes filled with tears, and Kiveli jumped up and hugged me. I read and reread the card. It was in his handwriting, no mistake about that. The back of the card was scratched out, but I could see the name "John Alevras" through the scribbling. He was with Alevras. Alevras was a Center Union deputy and close friend. I passed the card to Andreas' mother, who sniffled as she read it. I watched it pass from hand to hand and waited for it to be safely back in mine.

Marjorie, Kiveli, and I went upstairs to pack the items. I added a few things: slippers, two mystery stories, and a bottle of wine. Erasumus was coming back in an hour. I would ask him to drive to Goudi with the red plaid zipper bag, and the suit, which I had carefully covered with plastic and hung on a hanger. Momentarily I considered tucking a note in the pocket of the suit ("with infinite love"), but I decided against it for fear that it might delay the arrival of his clothes. It was a strange task. Packing for a man in jail is not an occasion for great joy. But it meant that he was alive.

Now I wanted desperately to see his lawyer, Menios Koutsoyergas. He had been in Patras campaigning when the coup came, and I had no word from him. Had he, too, been rounded up? His brother had come by the first day, full of anger and passion, and said he would be by again this afternoon. There was nothing we could do but wait until more reports came in. I wondered also about Andoni Livanis, who was Andreas' chief organizer in his political office, and loyal to the point of death. He had been in Salonika getting things ready for the Center Union rally which had been scheduled for Sunday. I was positive he had been arrested, for he, more than anyone, knew Andreas' political machine and key people. His wife had sent a message that morning that so far she had no word of him.

That afternoon reporters started arriving at the house. I decided to see them on one condition, that they not quote me or write that they had visited me. Any information I gave them which could be used without giving the source, however, was okay. Marjorie stood at the door and screened those coming in. I had also given orders that no Greek journalists were to be permitted, only foreign. Any foreign reporter accompanied by a Greek journalist friend was also to be turned away. This was wisdom learned from past experience with Greek journalists, and now, under these conditions, common sense. It would have been an easy, sly tactic of the junta to send an agent in the guise of a reporter and catch me saying all manner of nasty, vile, and violent things against the dictatorship. My big worry was that I might be deported. Having endeared myself to the army through the letter I wrote in 1965, I feared they might use this opportunity to kick me out. They needed no excuse, but it would have been very helpful to have proof that I was engaging in "antinational" talk.

Marjorie was perceptive and tough. She asked for the name and the paper represented and would ask several questions to get a "feel" of the person. Then she would say, "Mrs. Papandreou is very tired, but I will ask if she will see you." We would then have a discussion to decide yes or no. She would return, lay down the conditions for seeing me, get a promise of adherence, then usher the reporter in. No photographers were allowed, this being proof of an interview with me. I talked at length and in detail. Most all of them wanted a description of the arrest. But others were interested in background information, events leading up to the coup, what I knew about the dictators. One of them asked if I would remain in Greece. I answered that I would remain until my husband was free, but I would not allow my children to grow up in a totalitarian country. I expressed this with passion, without knowing what this meant in practice. If my husband were in jail for twenty years, would I send the children elsewhere? How long would I let them be submitted to the brainwashing which would be inevitable in their education in Greece? And what would I do for money over such a length of time?

My thoughts dwelled fleetingly on these questions. Instinctively I knew, however, that a fight for Andreas was a fight against the junta, and although I had not worked out a strategy, I believed that the first reports coming from Athens would set the atmosphere and determine the attitude of the western world to the take-over. There were important points to make: ASPIDA was a pot of lies, a real frame-up; the junta's claim of an imminent communist take-over was sheer propaganda to appease the Americans (how did one explain the fact that all EDA deputies were in bed when arrested though plotting a revolution?); the colonels were simply a gang of ambitious, power-hungry army men with no ideological commitment; yes, we would have won the elections on May 28 and killed their ambitions. A Danish reporter asked me if I foresaw bloodshed. My answer was yes, eventually. He asked if I thought the Americans would intervene in case of a civil war. I answered yes, on the wrong side.

By 7 P.M., after talking all afternoon, I was weary and beat. I had two tasks yet to do: take care of the buried objects in the backyard and write some letters for help. The Danish reporter offered to take out anything I wanted on his flight back home Sunday noon. On the problem of the ammunition, I located an old trusted friend of Andreas', Stavros Papadimitriou, who sent his brother that evening, and we dug up the six boxes of machine-gun bullets to be taken to another hiding spot, outside of Athens. Then, some weeks later, on a moonless night, my father dropped them in the sea on the road to Sounion.

I asked Popi to bring me my typewriter and paper. I felt limp, battered. I was sure I had a slight fever. Sagged over the typewriter, I started to write my letters. I decided to write first to Kenneth Galbraith, Ambassador to India during the Kennedy administration, president of Americans for Democratic Action, and ex-colleague of Andreas' at the Harvard University Economics Department. I felt I could turn to him for help. I began as follows: "They have taken Andreas." Then I told him of the brutal and inhuman manner in which Andreas had been arrested. I continued:

> The Greeks feel the dictatorship cannot stand without the backing of the United States. America's role in Greece, along with the Palace, are considered major determiners of the fate of this country. There is no question that the U.S. can topple this regime. *Does it have the daring and courage to stand up for* the people *for once, and in this fashion redeem its image in the world today?*

I ended with a plea to help Andreas.

My next letter went to Stephen Rousseas, the New York University professor and a close friend of Andreas', who had been in Greece from summer 1966 until January 1967, and had written about the political developments of the time.

My letter began: "We are living a black, ugly nightmare." I told him some of the same things I wrote to Galbraith. I pointed out in my second paragraph that

> *America is the only power at this point that can do something about the situation. Later the Greeks will do something about it*

themselves. And then it will be America's headache and anguish for years. Another Vietnam? How do they like that? Despite all our warnings, our special emissaries, our clear call that danger existed here . . . the only reply we got was that the State Department did not consider the situation in Greece particularly dangerous or at a stage of crisis!

In giant, ink-penned letters at the bottom of the page I added:

DO WHATEVER YOU CAN FOR ANDREAS AND GREECE!

I sent a carbon of this to George Lianis, professor of aeronautical engineering at Purdue, the man who had worked for a year in Greece with Andreas trying to organize a new university at Patras.

My last short note went to Siggie Mineiko, a cousin of Andreas' living in Paris.

Dear Siggie. . . . Get the International Red Cross in Geneva to intervene on behalf of George Papandreou, who had the flu when he was taken, and who needs constant medical attention; and get them to protest a jail cell for Andreas who is still under treatment for TUBERCULOSIS!

Marjorie walked in at the moment of completion of Siggie's letter, and seeing my head drooped within inches of the keyboard, suggested I take one more pill and try to sleep. As soon as the pill went down, she took me by my hand and led me, unprotesting, to my room.

That night, with one hour's sleep in forty-four, and with the knowledge that Andreas was alive, I slept quietly. I awakened at 6 A.M., dressed, and walked out to the sunlit backyard. A terrible sense of loneliness and helplessness welled up within me. There, amidst the churring of the cicadas and the aroma of jasmine, I had my first cry.

CHAPTER SEVENTEEN

The Searches

I STAYED an hour in the backyard that Sunday morning, pacing around the ten-foot-square clump of bushes growing in the middle of the yard, sitting on the redwood bench, smoking, patting Blackie and Gilda. The yard was enclosed by a thick fence of stone and concrete, whitewashed, eight feet in height. In one corner stood an adobe-style garage, used as a storage place and practice room for the children's guitars. Matted vines covered one side of the garage and lined the fence. Rising above the fence was the foliage of a string of trees whose slender trunks were lost among the vines, but whose tops cast gentle shadows across the garden furniture in the early morning light. It was an area for the children to play, for the dogs to romp, for lamb roasts at Easter time, and for summer buffets.

Now the yard was dead. Without Andreas it had lost its meaning. He was the exotic component for us in what otherwise would have been ordinary, middle-class living. His mood was invariably gay, and even in very serious moments he would find humor in the situation. Could I now, on my own, find the humor in this situation? I already missed his touch, his voice, his call as he would arrive at the house, "Margaret! Come join me on the terrace!" And this would be the signal for a talk about the day, and I would be treated to a spellbinding hour or so of description and analysis. His mind would slice through the superficial outer bindings and get to the heart of the issue. In this respect he was much like his father. Both had a sharp, clean, mathematical precision to their thinking. They could take the most difficult of issues and reduce them to their bare elements. The difference was in their language. Andreas' maintained a one-to-one relationship with his thinking—simple, direct, and stark. His father's was more flowery, had flourish, and often a poetic style. In brief, he dressed it up. Their difference when they spoke to large audiences could best be described from the point of view of the listener, who felt that Andreas was talking to him personally, that George was talking to the mass, and for posterity. Both men were kind. George's kindness had an all-enveloping, priest-to-his-parish paternalism. (I had often heard shouts along campaign trails, "You are our father!") Andreas' kindness was an empathy, an understanding.

Because of his quick decisions, Andreas was considered by many as impulsive. He relied to a great extent on instinct, and 90 percent of the time he was right. When he was wrong, it was usually because he decided something out of a feeling of warmth for a friend or colleague. The most ridiculous adjective used about him in the foreign press was "arrogant." I can only assume this came from his unwillingness to compromise on basic principles. He is an extremely human, informal, and unpretentious individual.

In our married life we have had our feuds. One point of conflict was my (admitted) level of disorderliness, although I always defended myself by saying that my interest was in *people,* not *things.* Little "things," like socks out of place in the drawer or a button missing from his shirt, could start a barrage of accusations of slovenliness or disinterest. This would generally occur in the morning when he would awaken, full of energy and exuberance, and I would be plowing through morning rituals with one eye open and barely communicating. Another point of contention was the children. He was always anxious about their health and thought I should run to the doctor for a minor cut, a splinter, or a slight fever. He also thought I was too relaxed, too permissive in their upbringing, yet he never failed to respond to a child's plea for something. Generous to a fault, he would get upset about our finances only when we were low on cash and measures of economy had to be inaugurated. Then we would sit down to a stormy session of budget analysis, during which time he would write out a set of rules, hand the paper to me with a sense of relief, and then go out the next day and break one of the rules himself. In the end he would add to our depleted resources by giving a lecture here or there, picking up a summer session of teaching, sign a book contract, rather than cut down on our style of living. At one point in my thoughts I heard the back door of the kitchen open. I recognized Antigone, who, seeing me saddened and contemplative, discreetly closed the door again without disturbing me.

By 7 A.M. the house was astir, and the smell of boiling coffee and fried eggs laced the outdoor air. I came in to find Popi, pale and worried, still suffering, she told me later, from the impact of the Voice of Truth broadcast of Andreas' execution. Although we had received the card in Andreas' handwriting, we could not be sure that the junta might not at any moment hold a murderous kangaroo court.

By nine o'clock, friends and reporters started arriving again and the house began to look like a political rally at Madison Square Garden. The rules still held: no direct quote from me, and cameras outside. One photographer took a picture of Nick tossing a baseball to his friend Alexi, and Marjorie raised a big fuss and made him swear he wouldn't send it in for publication.

Popi knew I had the problem of getting my letters out that morning, and offered to take them to the Danish reporter at the Grande Bretagne Hotel. I was reluctant to involve her in anything that might put her in trouble. My daughter, standing nearby, offered to take the letters. I agreed. I decided that a twelve-year-old, along with my Gary Cooper style father, would be a good cover. She wore one of the boy's corduroy jackets which had an inside pocket, and the four letters were tucked in there. When she arrived at the Grande Bretagne, she found a group of men with cameras standing in the lobby and went up to one and asked for the name I had given her. The group turned immediately, like a row of trained penguins, and walked away. Puzzled, she stood—hesitant and wondering what to do. My father was waiting in the car outside, so she was on her own. One member of the group broke the line, breezed past her, and not looking at her, spoke quietly from the corner of his mouth, saying, "Follow that group to the elevator, but don't act as if you know them." She obeyed, and when they all got into the elevator, she joined them. Inside, one of the young men said, "You are the daughter of Mrs. Papandreou?" (Actually, he had seen her at the house the night before.) She was uncertain how to answer when the man continued, "I am Björn Neilsen." That was the name, and she asked, "Shall I give you the letters now?" He said to do so, and the letters were transferred from her pocket to his. They told her to continue two floors higher than their floor, then push the button for the main lobby and walk out. This was how Ken Galbraith, Steve Rousseas, George Lianis, and Siggie Mineiko received letters postmarked "Denmark" within the next few days.

During Sunday morning I saw and spoke to one Italian reporter, a sweet and sensitive young boy, terribly sympathetic and concerned about my welfare. He gave me his card with his name, and I wish I had it now to express to him my appreciation for his kindness and words of encouragement. But that card, along with others like it, was burned in the metal bowl on our living room cocktail table, where the flames these two days not infrequently ate up the bits and pieces of tell-tale evidence of "subversive activity," turning them into twirls and wisps of harmless smoke.

Because of the impression this reporter had made on us, Marjorie, who sat in on the interviews, was feeling positive toward Italian journalists. When a Mr. Artieri arrived at the door, she greeted him warmly. Then he turned and introduced the man with him, a Mr. Agnostopoulos.

"Greek?" she asked.

"Yes."

She looked at Artieri. "Why have you brought him along?"

"I need him as an interpreter."

"You mean, he will interpret Mrs. Papandreou's Greek to you?" she asked, rather disdainfully.

"Well, yes, ah, no . . . I thought . . ."

"Mrs. Papandreou speaks perfect English. In fact, she does amazingly well in her native tongue."

"I know she is an American. I just wanted to interview her and I thought it would help to have Mr. Agnostopoulos along."

According to the rules, he should have been automatically turned away, but Marjorie was under the spell of our earlier Italian contact.

"Just a moment."

We decided to tell him that I was exhausted and would not see any more reporters that morning, but suggested that he telephone at six that afternoon.

"Be sure to get the name of the paper," I called after Marjorie as she went back to the front door.

"Yes, of course."

The name of the newspaper was *Il Tempo,* a far-right publication. When he called at six o'clock, I spoke to him personally and told him that I wasn't seeing any reporters and was staying secluded in my home.

This brief contact gave him a marvelous opportunity to manufacture a myth. He wrote in his article that he had talked to me on the phone, that I was a very shrewd and cunning woman, and that I had been involved in mysterious activities in the Middle East during World War II. He added that my name was not really "Chant," but had been shortened to this from my Bulgarian father's name of "Chantioff" or "Chantiev." This article was reprinted on the front page of the Athenian newspaper *Estia,* and was frequently referred to after that. Because this has been repeated by hostile elements (ministers in the junta itself refer to me as "that Bulgarian" to foreign journalists), let it be known that my father's name *is* Chant, from his British-born father. His Scotch-English mother's name was Douglas. My mother's Swiss-born father was named Pfund, and her Swiss-born mother, von Braun. To the junta's warped mentality, calling me a Bulgarian would immediately discredit me with the majority of the Greek people.

At noon, I welcomed into my home Bernard Nossiter, a correspondent for the Washington *Post.* He had visited us on other, saner occasions, and I was pleased to see him. He listened sympathetically and quietly while I told him the events of April 21 and nodded in agreement at my interpretation of the developments. Before he left, he told me he was planning to see Cannellopoulos, who had been transferred to his home.

"You will be able to see him?" I asked, surprised.

"I think so. Anyway, I'm going to try."

"Give him my greetings," I said. "Tell him we are not antagonists anymore and that now it is a mutual fight." I really meant it. I felt strongly that the political world, from left to right, would have to unite if any activity was to be meaningful against the junta, and that even then, the cards were stacked against us.

Bernard would have stayed longer, but just at that moment Marjorie came to tell me that two policemen had arrived and were turning people away at the gate.

"It is best that you go," I told him. "It seems that I have been put under house arrest."

He left, wishing me good luck. His article in the Washington *Post,* also published in the *Congressional Record,* was one of the most perceptive and clear analyses of the coup and causes of the coup that I had seen. In a letter to a good friend, Dick Holton, professor at the University of California, who had inquired about us, he wrote: "Maggie and the kids are at home. She looked shell-shocked, but otherwise controlled. Starting Sunday noon, newsmen were turned away from the house by guards."

Still in the house at the time Nossiter left were Kiveli and, at long last, dear Tito. Always elegant and proud in his uniform, he had discreetly changed into civilian clothes before coming to my home. He was sure that despite an excellent twenty-five-year career, he would be booted out. His association with Andreas was well known. I suspect his greatest concern was that they might not release him. I was sure he had ceased wanting to have anything to do with the military.

Since the guards outside had not laid down any rules, I urged Kiveli and

Tito to stay for lunch. We discussed many things, always getting back to Andreas. These two people loved Andreas, and their concern, as mine, was for him. Whether it was to buoy me up or not, I do not know, but Tito was optimistic. He said that whatever length of time the colonels remained, they would have to release Andreas. They couldn't dare go through a public parody of a trial. The general opinion, also shared by my parents and Marjorie, was that the dictatorship could not last. It could not be tolerated on the European continent.

Thus the afternoon was talked away. The house was quiet now. The word had gotten around that people were being turned away, so there were no longer those who tried, as had been the case in the early part of the afternoon. Andriko was with his American friends who lived next door, and would stay the night. Nick and Sophia were with Greek friends. Only George hovered about, silent and brooding.

We decided that Kiveli would stay the night; Tito would have to return to his house and job the next morning. Kiveli wanted to go home to get her nightclothes and prepare Tito's dinner, so we agreed that I would walk out with them and explain to the guard that she was the children's governess and teacher of French, and would be coming back to stay the night. He agreed with some reluctance to let her pass when she returned.

By evening the silence in the house was frightening. From early in the morning of the 21st until now, voices and sound had filled the rooms, annoying me at times, but providing a din and an activity that masked reality, that blocked thoughts from reaching the sensitive corners of the brain. Now the silence flushed clean the passages, and pain thrust in like a dentist's drill hitting a raw nerve. I thought about Andreas who might be isolated in a room or cell. How does one tolerate such silence, such aloneness?

At nine o'clock I was startled by the doorbell. In came Lefteris, our druggist, with a box of pharmaceuticals and a police permit for entry held in his teeth. He had gone to the local police station and told them I was in need of these medical items for the children, and he merely wanted to carry them in and leave immediately. He motioned me to follow him to the kitchen. In the small room off the kitchen which we used for stringing beans, peeling potatoes, or ironing, he took off his shoe, pulled up the inner sole, and handed me a small piece of thin paper with writing on it. I could barely read the tiny hand-printed Greek letters. It was the writing of Petros; he had remembered that I had difficulty reading script in Greek. It read: "The people who are hiding your things are scared and want them out of their house. What shall we do?" The files and guns back to haunt me again.

"Can you get them out?" I asked Lefteris.

"I think we can."

"Get them somewhere else, at least temporarily, then we'll figure something out. But it should be done tonight if they are frightened. Can you do it tonight?"

"I think so."

"Will you try?"

"We'll try, Mrs. Margaret."

"You must."

Lefteris slipped out quickly, leaving behind the tiny scrap of paper, which we subjected to the flame of a match. Afterwards I sat, assessing the day. I had, and always was to have, the feeling that I wasn't doing enough. I had talked to reporters—until that was stopped. I had gotten four messages out. I had solved for the moment the new problem which arose about the files and guns. My thoughts turned to an issue which had concerned me several times during the day—Andreas' health. If there were some way I could raise a fuss about his tubercular condition, then maybe at least I could make them sensitive to the dangers of a damp, cold, clammy cell—assuming, naturally, that they would have some sensitivities to this. It had the danger of giving them the means of slowly killing him off. My judgment was that if he had not been shot during the heat of the coup, when a justification of his death (tried to escape while being arrested) could be made, that he would be their responsibility and his death by any means would be a cold-blooded, carefully contemplated murder. Not that I was so naive as to think this impossible. But with a few more days of grace, I was counting on the mobilization of international opinion to tie their hands. A central theme was beginning to emerge in my thinking about ways to gain Andreas' freedom. It was simply this: Make Andreas the bane of their existence. Stuff him down their throats until they gag and turn purple. Don't let a day go by without their hearing, breathing, and reading his name from every possible source.

I talked it over with my advisory committee, consisting of Marjorie, my mother and father, and George and Kiveli. We decided that my father and George should once again try the Embassy, but this time see several more (Danish, Egyptian, French) with the information about Andreas' condition, and strong emphasis on the need to protest against an environment which would endanger his life. For this we needed Andreas' X rays, and to be more effective, his doctor. I would have to talk to him and ask him to accompany my father and George. But how? Having decided to take this action, I wanted to do it immediately. The telephone was out for the simple reason that I couldn't talk freely, and I doubted that the two gunhands marching up and down in front of my house would let me out that night. We concocted a story, and Marjorie called Michalis, the doctor, speaking in French to create an obstacle to the listening ears. She explained to him that Margaret was sick and was getting pains in her left arm and chest, and asked him to come as quickly as possible. Then George told the guards outside that his mother had apparently suffered a mild heart attack from all the anxiety, that the doctor would arrive soon and should be permitted up.

Not knowing whether or not the guard would accompany Michalis on the visit, I undressed and got into my bathrobe (still bloodstained) and went to my bed, propping my head up with the two pillows. Michalis, a man of gold, came in carrying his bag, looking very perturbed and frightened. Coming two days after the coup to the Papandreou house was not easy, and I shall always be grateful to him, and to the many friends who did come (and dismayed at those who did not).

Fortunately, no guard followed him. This simplified matters for me. I had been trying for the last hour to rehearse a means of talking to him in the presence of another, thinking we might not be alone. The story I was going to give was the following: Andreas' X rays which I had dug out from the upstairs bookcases were to be X rays of my own chest, and I was somehow to indicate that they should be taken the next day to a specialist (although he himself was a specialist), and that he would meet my father and George at Syntagma Square in front of the American Express office in order to go with them. Once he met them, they would explain the task ahead. None of this was necessary. My first words were "I'm all right, but I had to see you!" He gave a weak smile and pulled up a chair next to my bed. I asked him whether he had any word from the President's doctor, whom he knew, and whether the doctor had been allowed to see the President. He said he had heard nothing. Then I explained what I wanted him to do, and he agreed readily. He looked over the X rays and told me which ones my father should bring along. He stayed on for the appropriate length of time for a doctor's visit, and we covered rapidly the whole situation, both of us feeling a sense of horror and helplessness.

At midnight I received a phone call from the United States. It was Leo Hurwicz and John Buttrick, professors at the University of Minnesota. They asked how I was, and in a guarded fashion, how Andreas was. It was obvious from some of their questions that they had heard the story of the firing squad. Leo, a World War II refugee from Poland, knew the terror and methods of dictatorial regimes. He was standing by to help. John, a conscientious objector in World War II, a pacifist, was naturally strongly antimilitary. He was also standing by. In few words, they let me know that the academic world of the United States was being mobilized, and would spare nothing to help. I felt weak, and thankful, and full of gratitude. The fight was on.

The next day while George, my father, and Michalis were making the rounds of the embassies, we had the first invasion of our home since the coup. The Psyhico policemen came to search, under orders of the junta. They insisted that I or someone I designated accompany them around the house to see what they took. They also said I would be told what they were removing. I had the feeling that they were functioning under some old rules of search behavior. The search warrant was missing, but the rest of the rules were followed. One policeman beckoned me over to my bedroom side table to show me 3,000 drachmas ($100) he had found in the drawer, taken out, and was putting back. I was impressed—and depressed—at the thoroughness of their search. Their hands were everywhere. All the natural places: drawers, desk tops, closet shelves, cabinets, bookcases, file drawers. And all the unnatural places: under the floorboards in my bedroom closets, into the toes of all the shoes, inside the envelopes of music records, in the accordian sections of my nylon stocking holder, inside the water closet behind the toilet, inside the holes of the children's guitars.

In Georgie's room they found a page of verses in Greek, critical of Frederika, to be sung to the tune of "She'll Be Comin' 'Round the Mountain." A classmate of George's had passed it on to him sometime in the past. In George's room also was a small index-card file box of Nick's with cards labeled C.A.D.E. at the top, and a Greek male name on each, with some additional notations. This was Nicky's own boys' organization—Committee Against Destructive Evil. They took this, too.

Upstairs in the study they looked through my carefully culled out files. One policeman stood reading some pages he had pulled out and was laughing out loud. He had found in my files a script of Karagyozis, that fabulous character in Greek shadow plays who invariably puts one over on his Turkish masters. Karagyozis was a product of the Turkish occupation, and was surreptitiously performed to give a feeling of revenge to a frustated population. The script in my file had been specially written to fit the political situation after the fall of Papandreou in 1965 and had been submitted to Andreas for use, if he wanted a popular means of parody. I was annoyed at this sign of joviality in the midst of the invasion of my privacy—in fact, I found the laughter obscene. After flipping through several pages, he replaced the script in the file drawer. Here and there they found letters that hadn't been filed and got tucked away in books or under stacks of newspapers. The search took about two and a half hours. Kiveli had accompanied part of the group down to the basement, where she said they almost dismantled the oil furnace. In Antigone's room, right above the furnace, they pulled off the linoleum floor covering and jimmied up a floorboard. Something intrigued them about that area. I wondered, were maid's rooms traditional places for hiding secret documents?

All of the time this was going on I had the feeling I was doing a forced striptease. Disgusted and helpless, I watched strange hands and eyes pry into my most personal possessions—photographs, old love letters, sentimental mementos, underclothing, cosmetics, the medicine chest—all the things that are an extension of one's self, or a loved one's self.

When they finished, they had gathered up a cardboard carton of materials. They called me to the front hall. The captain held up a mimeographed book prepared by EDA on the crisis of 1965.

"We thought we would take this," he said.

"Why?" I asked.

"We didn't find much of anything."

"What did you expect to find?"

"We're under orders, ma'am."

"Yes, I know. But what did you expect to find?"

"It was just a general search."

He was obviously not going to answer. I asked him again why he wanted to take the EDA publication.

"Does it matter?" he asked. I had the feeling he was playing with me, and I didn't like it.

Antigone was nearby, and she spoke up. "Mrs. Papandreou thinks you will use it against her."

"Would she like to keep it?" he asked Antigone.

I couldn't make out the game, but I answered the question myself. "I would like to take it and burn it so that no one can use innocent materials to prove I am subversive."

To my surprise he handed it to me. Then they all walked out and mysteriously left the cardboard box on the floor behind them.

I closed the door and locked it, and heaved a sigh of relief. What they

171

hadn't found were six precious antijunta letters which were inside the candy-striped panty girdle being worn by my friend Marjorie. I had typed them early in the morning to six more people in positions of influence, including two in Washington, D. C., to ask them to join the fight against the dictatorship and for Andreas' freedom. They were similar to the one I had written to Galbraith, but stronger. Marjorie had put them in her purse in preparation for a meeting with a foreigner leaving the country, but shifted them to her girdle when she heard that there were policemen at the door. They were safe, and they went out the next day on an SAS flight.

Later that evening we looked through the box. Most of it was nothing, but I came across one letter from a friend in Washington, D. C., dated July 1963—just after the resignation of Karamanlis over the dispute with Frederika, and before the election had been declared. It said that agents of Markezinis had been in Washington testing the ground for a dictatorial solution. Also parading through Washington about the same time was Mr. Farmakis, deputy of ERE and fanatic rightist. He was raising the same question. The answer, according to the letter, was a resounding rebuff. The State Department wouldn't listen. One of the first-named appointments in the Papadopoulos dictatorship was to the post of public-information officer—Mr. Farmakis. Had the State Department finally listened? Or was it true what had always been said about Farmakis, that he was a CIA agent? Farmakis was dumped about a month later as Papadopoulos started moving CIA agents away from posts near the inner circle of the junta. Those who had made him could unmake him as well.

My father took half of the materials outside to burn. Marjorie took a sheaf of letters upstairs to the bathroom to burn and flush down the toilet. If an instruction manual is written for amateurs who find themselves in this dire state, it should warn them *not* to use this method of disposal. It is smoky, messy, and unsatisfactory. How the technique managed to be considered a standard means of disposal—in spy stories and detective movies—I do not understand. As the burning paper is dropped into the toilet, the water puts out the fire, and a substantial portion of the letter is left unburned and slowly soaking up water. It does not flush down the toilet in that condition. This means dipping into the water, fishing it out and tearing it into tiny bits, which still create problems going down the pipe. I found Marjorie, half an hour later, in a blackened, smoky bathroom, window wide open and tears running out of her eyes, cussing and desperate. What was left we gave to my father in the backyard, who was having better luck. During this time I had concluded that the Psyhico policemen, acting as my friends, had separated out those items that might be used against me and left them behind for me to get rid of. This was partially true, as I learned later, but they had taken some items away in their inside coat pockets, perhaps as proof that they had done a search. A week later, when the captain brought an itemized list of papers taken for me to sign, I refused, saying they had not shown them to me, so I could not "authenticize" their report.

After the mess was cleaned up in the bathroom, I sat down and wrote a scathing attack against the junta, rage growing in me like a brush fire on a

172

windy day. I made five copies in all and signed them *Democratic Resistance.* Then I addressed them to five major correspondents in Athens from the United States and Europe. I took them upstairs and placed them against the small vase on my night table. I knew that if I could get them out to Dimitri, a close friend, he would find a way to get them into the hotel boxes of the reporters. Relieved that the search I had been waiting for was finally over, I tumbled into bed.

The next morning, Tuesday, I made my first attempt to leave the house by going shopping. I had not been told I was restricted to the house, although that had been my initial assumption. I carried two shopping bags and got in the car with my father. The guard said nothing. Relaxed about the house search being over and done with, and engrossed in the act of playing the busy, preoccupied housewife, I forgot completely about my five letters on the upstairs night table. We returned two hours later to find a new crew of men, mostly in plain clothes, crawling over the house like spiders. The man who answered the door told me and my father to get into the living room and stay there. He was gruff and unsmiling, not like the semifriendly policemen of the day before. As I walked through the hallway, I had to step over machines, wires, cameras, and suitcases. Inside the living room, sitting like anguished, anxious patients in a doctor's waiting room, were my mother, Andreas' mother, Antigone, Kiveli, and Marjorie, and Sophia—home from school with a slight cold. I glanced at the typewriter on the round glass-top table near the bar which had contained a portion of a letter I had started, and saw the typewriter empty. When the door closed after me, Marjorie pointed to her stomach and said, "It's here, but I ain't got my girdle on, and things are not very secure." Indeed, one could see the clothes didn't match the occasion. She had on wide, bell-bottomed flower-printed pajamas, with a knee-length unbelted housecoat on top. There was nothing to contain the papers, and already she indicated something had started down her leg. This was certainly a problem, but it suddenly dawned on me that I had a bigger one: my rebellious propaganda upstairs! It was all the junta needed to send me out of Greece, or imprison me.

"Oh, my God!" I uttered quietly. The pale faces around the room looked up at me. "I have something upstairs," I said slowly and in a low voice, "that if they find . . ." How was it, I asked myself, that they had come for a second search? How could I have been so stupid to go out without making any provision for such an event? I was kicking myself and trying desperately to think.

Sophia piped up. "I'll get them, Mommy, I'll get them!" I looked at her wonderful, earnest, and concerned face. She was ready for orders.

"No, darling . . . not you . . ."

"But they won't understand. I'm a child . . ." And what a child, I thought! I had to think fast. As far as I could determine, there were men in the backyard using machines, which sounded like minesweepers. They had closed the shutters in the living room so that we couldn't see out. Another group sounded as if it was upstairs on the third floor in the study.

"How long have they been here?" I asked.

"About ten minutes" was the answer.

"Have they been in the bedrooms?"

Antigone said she thought they had gone directly to the study. There was still time, I thought.

"Mom," I said. "You're going to get sick. You're going to have a pain in your heart" (how valuable an organ this was turning out to be). "You have to lie down upstairs and take one of your pills, and I have to help you. Okay?"

My mother was game. Seventy years of fighting hard for everything she got in life had made her a resourceful and courageous woman. She was a worrier, but when you broke the gloom, she would burst forth in a wonderful, warm laugh that invited everyone to join in. Her life had been dedicated to her five girls, and for them she would do anything. There was no question about her answer to my plea.

We opened the living room door, my mother leaning on my arm and breathing heavily. As we crossed the entryway to the kitchen to reach the stairway, one man in police uniform standing in the kitchen near the door to the backyard looked up. I recognized him. He was from the Psyhico police force and had accompanied today's group—obviously secret service men of KYP—probably at their order, on the second search. I pointed to my mother, made a motion to my heart to indicate trouble, then pointed upstairs. My own heart beat wildly as he hesitated a moment, then indicated with a quick scoop of his hand to go ahead. He also meant, move fast.

As we made our way up the stairs, I kept murmuring to my mother, "You'll be all right. Don't worry. We'll take care of you." Then in a tiny voice, "Take the letters and put them in your bosom as soon as we get in the room..." More loudly, "Please don't worry... I'll get you your pills and a glass of water..." Whispering, "They're on the right side of my bed... soon as we've got them in your dress, fall on the bed and close your eyes... Does it hurt that much, Mother?" We reached the second floor. Voices were coming from the study, but no one was on the second floor. We made the door. We quickly shut it behind us and dashed for the five envelopes conspicuously propped on the table. A quick grab and a thrust and they disappeared into the recesses of my mother's ample bosom. I sat for a moment beside her. She was white and breathing hard from the effort. My dear mother, I thought—why must you be made to suffer, too? I asked her if she was all right, and got a glass of water from the bathroom faucet and set it next to her on the same spot where the letters had been.

"If you're okay, Mom, I think I'd better go down. My presence here might raise some questions. Pretend you are sleeping when they come in."

"I'll moan," she said, and gave a wan smile.

"I'll send Dad up to check as soon as I think I should. I don't believe they'll find that odd."

I thought I heard footsteps just above me in the hallway leading away from the study. I patted my mother on her arm, moved out of the room with speed, leaving the door slightly ajar, and resumed my place in our downstairs prison. The drone of the machines continued in the backyard, like giant vacuum cleaners. On my descent from upstairs I again saw photographic equipment, and I began to worry that something phony was being cooked up. Nothing prevented them from placing materials in my study among other papers, photographing them, and claiming they had been found in the house of Andreas Papandreou. I was completely aware of what was going on in the backyard, and it confirmed my notion that the machine-gun shells had been a plant. I felt at the time a smugness at having outsmarted them. It didn't dawn on me until later, thank God, that an entire arsenal could have been down there, buried, since I didn't know the origin of the bullets in the first place. Also, what was true for my study was true for the backyard; they could have dumped things at the time and claimed to have found them there.

For two more hours we sat, trying at times to be witty to break the pall that hung over the room, but mostly sitting silently, heads somewhat drooped. Marjorie had managed to solve the problem of the sliding letter by shifting its position from below to above—her brassiere. She sat on the colorful, Persian-style rug of our living room playing solitaire. My father walked up to check on my mother and brought the news that the searchers had arrived in the bedroom seconds after my departure, and had searched the room on tiptoe when they saw her on the bed and heard her low groans. She was feeling very proud and would hold the fort upstairs until they left. The envelopes must have been burning a hole in her chest while the room was being searched. Later I told her that we blessed her courage, her fortitude, her daring, but most of all we blessed her bountiful bosom.

The search lasted a total of three hours. When they finished, they called me into the hallway. A stocky, crude-looking man with black hair said to me, in the presence of four others, "We have locked your husband's study and will come later for the files."

"First of all," I said, "it is not my husband's study, it is mine."

"It belongs to Andreas," a slender, fair-complexioned Greek interjected.

"No," I insisted, "it belongs to me."

"It has Andreas' files there."

"No, those are my files, and I need them to work."

The blond smirked. "Work on what?"

"I am a professional woman," I answered. "I must keep up my work."

"What kind of profession?" was the question, sarcastically.

"I am a writer. I write articles on public health."

"We know it is Andreas' study. But if there is anything you need, you can go upstairs and take it out before we lock it."

"I don't only need my materials, I need the room. I have two beds there, as you could see. My children sleep there."

"They can sleep elsewhere. You have a big house."

"And I have a big family," I retorted.

"There's no point in discussion," the blond continued, a note of annoyance in his voice. "We are locking it up."

"Then I will go up and take out my materials," I answered defiantly.

There was nothing special for me to take out, but I had said that I needed them, so I had to follow through. In addition, I was curious to see what had been done upstairs before the door was locked. The blond and a man in uniform accompanied me, silently, up the stairs. When I got in the room, I went directly to the big three-drawer file cabinet and pulled open a drawer, starting haphazardly to pull out files. The blond watched me, standing to one side and behind me. Three files were in my hand when I reached for one marked "Logii" in Greek which contained a public speech of Andreas' in 1964. A hand clamped down on my wrist. I turned and looked at the blond.

"Why do you want that?" he asked sharply.

"It's a speech of my husband's, and I want to keep it."

"You can't read Greek."

"Yes, I can."

"You're not Greek."

"In a way I am. According to your law, I am a Greek by virtue of being married to one."

"O-ho," he smiled. "Then you make things easier for us."

I stuck my foot in that one, I thought. Obviously the less I said, the better.

"Perhaps you'd like to be put up in a hotel," he continued.

"For what purpose?"

"You might be safer there."

"And my children?"

"They can be put up there, too."

Was this a coy way of telling me I could be locked up? Or did he mean I might be shipped out?

"Do you speak English?" I asked.

"Yes."

"Then can we talk like two human beings in English and drop this nasty approach in which you speak in riddles?"

He moved back a bit to sit partially on the edge of the desk, folded his arms across his waist, and said in a more soupy voice, "Yes, of course. What would you like to talk about?"

Now I was stuck. What did I have to say to a bastard of KYP?

"I would like to keep the speech," I said, "because it has sentimental value. It belongs to my husband. I love my husband."

"We love him, too" was the response.

"Then why don't you help me?"

"What would you like us to do?"

"Stop this goddamned stuff." Watch it, Maggie, I thought. Say something against the dictatorship and they have you.

"What goddamned stuff?"

"All this going through *my* papers."

He shrugged his shoulders.

"You won't let me have the file?"

"No."

I turned and walked out. As I walked down the stairway I heard the study door being closed and locked.

I felt dirty and unclean. Why had I bothered to try to converse with an underworld character of KYP? The three hours of search had shaken me, however. Nothing seemed secure or safe. Even after they left, there was a ubiquitous presence in the air of many pairs of eyes of secret police. Uncertain how long it would take to find Dimitri for the distribution of the letters and feeling that searches were now a way of life, I took the five statements from my mother and sorrowfully burned them, mentally chalking up a failure in an act of resistance.

CHAPTER EIGHTEEN

Andreas at Pikermi

ALL during the first week of the coup—as the rape of Greece continued with new arrests, searches, lists of orders by the military, and brainwashing through radio-controlled propaganda—the Greeks tried to put the puzzle together: Was Constantinos in on it? His mother? Had he initiated it or inspired it? Did he oppose it?

A photo published on the front pages of the Athens newspapers and later in *Time* magazine taken at the time of the swearing-in by the King of the new government gave credence to the latter theory: that he had opposed it. He stood stony-faced and stiff, staring straight ahead, his hands clasped tightly in front of him trapped in invisible handcuffs. Short middle-aged uniformed men stood in lines on either side, their bodies pressed toward him as if to keep him from bolting.

There were rumors that the King had refused to sign the decree emasculating the Constitution. Nevertheless, he had sworn in the colonels, and he bore the historic responsibility of legitimizing the take-over. The details of what he accepted to do or what he refused to do were academic. As the supreme defender of the Constitution, he was in a position to stand up to the usurpers of power. A threat to abdicate unless constitutional government was restored would have sent the trio of Papadopoulos, Pattakos, and Makarezos scampering like rats to a hole. Instead he chose to play a waiting game, to see how the engagement period came off. If he and the junta got along, if his powers remained untouched and the dare came off well, he could marry it; but if the junta proved to be incompatible to live with and failed, he could say he never liked the idea in the first place.

Clayton Fritchey said on April 26, 1967, in the Detroit *Free Press* that it was relatively beside the point to wonder how much Frederika or Constantine or both had to do with the coup. The fundamental fact was that "it was the throne which provided a royal climate for a military seizure."

> *The Army had been packed for years with a pro-monarchist, anti-democratic, officer corps, and everyone in Greece understood there was an unwritten agreement that the military would move in and take over if the democratic forces became strong enough to curb the monarchy or depose it in favor of a republic.*

He concluded as follows:

To protect themselves in a land where they have been strangers, the royal family has consistently aligned itself with the military, mostly in defiance of popular opinion.

The present crisis is only the climax of a delayed showdown which was precipitated in 1965 when Constantine, prodded by Frederika, dismissed Premier Papandreou, even though his party controlled Parliament. Since then every royal maneuver has inexorably led toward army intervention.

As a few more details of the coup leaked out and as the histories of the nonentities who had organized and performed the coup emerged, Greeks began using the terms the "Big Junta" and the "Little Junta." The Big Junta had been the King, his generals, judicial royalists, and extremist members of ERE. This is the one we knew about and had been following. This is the one I reported to Anscheutz. And it is the one Andreas warned the people about. But like its chief, Constantinos, it was Hamlet-like in reaching a decision, and it was trying to the last minute to use all possible means within a stretched framework of the Constitution to frustrate a Center Union victory. The military scheme to be used if all schemes failed and a military take-over was decided upon, however, had been worked out well in advance and was a ready, handy blueprint. It was Plan Prometheus, the NATO contingency plan for a communist threat against Greece from an external force. Part of the plan was to arrest communists within the country who might want to assist the invading enemy. These names were in the security files of the Greek police for years, some of them old, decrepit men and women who had long ago given up political activity, but who may have been active in the resistance against the Germans or during the Greek civil war. Since the definition of "communist" in Greece stretches from left to right, a name may have been in the files for having voted for the "wrong" person or for having said the "wrong" thing. This was List A to be rounded up the night of April 21. It was necessary to do this to appear consistent with the cover story to be used—threat of a communist take-over, thus the army intervention. But the real target of the Big Junta was the Center Union, so a list of political figures from the ranks of the Center Union was added to the Plan Prometheus scheme. The main blueprint was there, and a single command could set it in motion. Wax-sealed envelopes were located in key spots in the army, the navy, and the air corps to be opened, when the code name Prometheus came down from headquarters, and the instructions therein were to be followed *immediately*. Such a message could mean only one thing: threat of war, and the officers were to follow the orders without question.

In view of the fact that the Prometheus Plan had been kicking around for years, prepared by NATO experts, the Big Junta had little to worry about in terms of mechanics. It merely had to choose the right time, add a few touches, and work for minimum public reaction. What it forgot to worry about was *a coup within a coup*. There were lower-level officers in on the scheme, among them the ambitious, devious KYP man, Colonel George Papadopoulos. He and two others, Stylianos Pattakos and Nicholas Makarezos, formed the nucleus of the Little Junta. Their group they called EENA, the initials standing for the Union of Young Greek Officers. Annoyed at the namby-pamby strategy of the Big Junta, and eager to seize power, the lackeys of the generals turned their guns against their masters and the Greek nation and took over. Conveniently, the generals had been called to Athens that week for a meeting, so they were simply surrounded and presented with a fait accompli. On the night of the 20th, Makarezos was in charge of army communications and sent the coded signal to set Prometheus in motion. A tank battalion rolled in from Eleusis, five miles northwest of Athens, to secure the city. Soldiers and tanks sealed off the center of Athens, seized the principal ministries, and cut all communications, including the King's. They also moved in on the Pentagon, army headquarters. By using Plan Prometheus, they deceived many fine officers in the army who thought they were facing a threat of war and carried out their orders unquestioningly. Greece was always in a state of preparedness for a new Cyprus crisis, and an emergency was a real possibility. It was the first deception by Papadopoulos and Company, but not the last. Deception was to become a way of governing in Greece.

The King as well as others was their prisoner, the difference being that they needed him. Since foreign governments presented their credentials to the King as head of state, the question of diplomatic recognition would arise without him.

The King had demanded on the morning of the 21st to see Cannellopoulos, the captive Prime Minister. This was granted, and Cannellopoulos is said to have argued vehemently for the King to resist the coup-makers. In the morning, according to reports I got from the grapevine—a phenomenally fast and fairly reliable communication system in Greece—Constantinos was in a resistance mood. In the afternoon, after being told he could have Kollias as Prime Minister, and could speak about return to parliamentary procedures as soon as possible, he decided to go along with them.

The King's cards were being played out. Did he know it?

As the various pieces began to be put together, the people took solace in the knowledge that there was a rift between the King and the Little Junta and felt some vague stirrings of hope that the King might topple the colonels and reinstate parliamentary rule. Despite their criticism of the political world and their feeling that it bore some of the responsibility for the final denouement, they much preferred the freewheeling political bombast and the right to resolve dispute through open debate than the criminal enslavement of their nation. The spirit of freedom dies hard. In the Greek, if history has any meaning, it never dies.

Apart from the worry I had for the life of Andreas, the most difficult emotional experience I had that first week was the sudden shift from being a free person to being a shackled, chained animal. What was this? Not to be able to stride down the street, master of my own life, expressing my own dreams and hopes, speaking my own free thoughts? Who were *they* to tell me what to do and what not to do? By what divine right had they set themselves up as the spokesmen for the people? They had wrenched the soul from a nation and were filling in the gap with mud and slime!

My most persistent physical feeling was nausea. When this was overcome, I would feel a roaring fury build up in me and the desire to rip things up and pound the walls and kick the furniture. I felt hate in its most brutal form. When I was informed by a friend on the police force that a listening device had been put in my home during the second search, I tore through the house like an angry animal, looking for something I couldn't even describe. And not finding it, resorted to whispering to friends and writing notes for communication, which were immediately burned—and then despising myself for bending to this intimidation.

Not to be free is to be watched, followed, harassed, to have unknown men paw their way around my home, to be always suspicious, to be forced to crawl, to be at the mercy of cruel, sadistic tormentors, while decent men, like my husband and others, are locked up in dark filthy rooms and guarded over by younger editions of the leaders of a police state.

It was such a blow to one's sense of human dignity that the acceptance of it was impossible and the tolerance of it unbearable. Now I understood emotionally what I had understood intellectually up to then—the cries and the anger of the oppressed peoples of the world. It was because of this inner cry of frustration and rage that the early efforts of resistance were doomed to failure. Responding with passion and unlearned in the ways of operating in a totalitarian regime under the eyes of skilled secret police, the resistance rings that formed were to be discovered and broken up, their members beaten and tortured and then sentenced to prison.

It was during this week that I read a note from the underground resistance. It was brought to me by Virginia on Saturday morning, the day before Easter. I was in the backyard trying to decide where to roast the Easter lamb. Most Greeks had canceled their lamb roast festivities, preferring to make it a day of mourning. I had debated this alternative, but decided for the sake of the children to keep the custom with just the family and a few close friends. My goal was to try to give the children as normal a life as possible under the terrible conditions in which we found ourselves. I suggested that they invite some neighborhood children to have company of their own age.

The day was sunny, like most days in Greece, and the rustle of the breeze-brushed leaves on the trees and the twittering of birds, muffled the soft sound of Virginia's footsteps as she approached me in the garden.

"Oh, you startled me!" I exclaimed.

"I'm sorry," she answered. "Can we talk here?"

"I think it's the best place. But talk quietly."

She looked around, then pulled out of her blouse a piece of onionskin paper on which was written in ink a full page of text. She gave it to me, but after glancing at it I turned it back and asked her to read it to me.

"I'm not very good at reading Greek handwriting," I said.

In a low voice that had a tremor in it she read me the paper. It was a beautiful document, poetic in style. It expressed the feelings we all had about the tragedy that had befallen Greece. Then it said that an organization was being formed to cut across all political parties to fight the junta. It asked her to think about membership and to wait for further contact. It was signed "Mikis." Mikis Theodorakis, the splendid songwriter of Greece, the man who had written the theme song for *Zorba the Greek* and other even more magnificent numbers. A talented artist, he was also a deputy of EDA, the leftist party in Parliament, and had managed to escape capture the night of the coup.

"You carried this here?" I asked, surprised. "Why didn't you burn it immediately?"

"I wanted you to see it."

"You could have told me what it said."

"No, it's all right. I had it hidden."

"My dear Virginia, nothing can be 'hidden' if the KYP people want something. We can burn it now."

She was hesitant. I couldn't insist. Perhaps she had her own reasons. "All right," I said, "but promise me one thing—you won't keep it in your house."

To this she agreed.

"What do you think? Should I join in?"

I smiled rather weakly. "You are already in," I answered. I urged her to be careful, and to keep me informed. I suggested that she and her son have some roast lamb with us on Sunday, but she demurred. Her thoughts were elsewhere.

As she walked away, I thought of big Mikis, six-foot-five, shaggy dome of a head, restless, kind, temperamental, hidden somewhere in the vast recesses of Athens, the net of the Greek KYP working twenty-four hours a day to close in on him. He was an important political personality not captured on the night of April 21. He was not a political man in the true sense of the word. Politics was his hobby, music his passion. But he was important as the political head of the Lambrakis Youth Clubs, a group of leftist young people's organizations which took the name Lambrakis in honor of the EDA deputy murdered in 1963. Theodorakis had written a song called "My Bitterness," a haunting, sad melody which summed up all the anguish felt by the downtrodden at the loss of someone they had pinned their hopes on. "With my blood so bitter, I kiss your mouth" was the line repeated several times in the song. In Greece it is a village custom to kiss the mouth of a dead man before he is buried.

Mikis had spent two years after the civil war as a very young man on the island of Makronisis. He was accused of being a communist. I don't think he had any particular political philosophy. He was liberal, humane, and always espoused progressive causes. What was to be his fate now? Another island of barren, craggy, heat-soaked rock—Yaros? Or would he manage to remain underground—undetected?

Earlier that week I had seen Andoni Livanis, the loyal, energetic, and nervous head of Andreas' political office. By some miraculous luck, he had not been picked up, but was living in constant expectation of an early morning pounding on his door. None of Andreas' close inner circle of political workers had been touched, and Andreas told me later that this was done purposely in order that they be followed and expose the key second-string people in Andreas' movement.

It was the evening five days after the coup, the same day as my second house search. I had left the house to get away from the stifling atmosphere and to spend a few hours with friends who had a small child they couldn't leave. About 10:30 the doorbell rang unexpectedly, and we all waited with concern to see who was there. It was Andoni. When he saw me standing there in the center of the room, he gasped, ran to me, took me in his arms and held me tight, his body heaving with silent sobs. It was for Andreas he was crying. As soon as he got himself under control, and I had wiped the tears from my own eyes, he started talking in his quick, breathless way—and it was all about how to fight. I stopped him.

"Andoni, let me see Andreas first before you do anything."

"Yes, yes, of course. But you agree we must fight?"

"I agree, but I don't know how and when. I need to talk to Andreas." I was also wondering how what we did would affect the fate of my husband. He was their captive and at their mercy. Might they retaliate against him for our activities? It was the question that was to haunt me for the duration of Andreas' imprisonment.

Andoni was not the only one with this commitment. On the previous Saturday, prior to the stationing of the guards at my door, a thirty-five-year-old by the name of Stamatis arrived at my house barking out words and flailing his arms. I brought him into the dining room and closed the door.

"Mrs. Margarita, we could have beaten them! The first day! I went all over Athens. They were few—and the people were milling around on the streets waiting for instructions!" He was desperate and angry. He said he couldn't find anyone to move, to make a decision, that he had walked miles that day, only to find the best of the Center people arrested or in hiding. He talked about the deputies who were free, and here he spat out his words as if he were belching out their shriveled bodies. He called them cowards and worthless opportunists. He was the owner of a small cement factory, he told me, and had met Andreas only twice, but was dedicated to him, as were the majority of the people. He told me that if he had known I was free he would have taken me and carried me on his shoulders down the main streets of Athens, and when the people saw me I would have been the flaming torch of resistance—and we would have won. I smiled briefly at this image and inwardly agreed that I would have been a flaming torch, period. He wanted to be in touch with someone close to Andreas, and I told him to return the next night and I would have someone in the house. Unfortunately, the next night my house was closed to everyone by the uniformed pigeons strutting in front of the gate, and it was a few weeks before Stamatis turned up again, with the same passion, but much more caution.

Then there was Phillip, one of the two members of the "party of Margarita." For him it was a question of pride. He could not stand the notion that a nation of freedom-loving, proud, fighting people had allowed themselves to be penned up like sheep. He argued for something to be done fast, even at the sacrifice of lives, to show the world what stuff the Greeks were made of. His despair was uncontrollable. He could not bring himself to argue for anything but immediate action.

On Wednesday, my guard was lifted. In its place came surveillance of the house of a less obvious nature, although there was no attempt at finesse and subtlety. Men in plain clothes stood at the corners of the block and down at the square, which had to be traversed to get to Guizi Street. In addition to that, my street suddenly became a favorite for strollers who wandered by in ones and twos, chatting to each other when together, their eyes checking out the license numbers on any cars parked near my home. The young people who rang my doorbell took great chances. When I told them that, they shrugged it off, honestly unconcerned, as are the young, with danger. It was for them I felt the most compassion. It was their future that was being thrown into the gutter. It would be their fight, their lives, and their ability that would determine the fate of Greece, and they had lost the one man they had put their faith and trust in—Andreas. Their determination was clear; their confusion pitiful. Neither they nor I had had any experience with fighting an invader with the tactics and strategy of resistance. If I had directed them, it would have been the blind leading the blind. I asked them to be patient, and to keep in touch with me, but I could see this did not satisfy them.

As for Menios, the lawyer, he had returned from Patras late Sunday afternoon and had come immediately to the house, only to find his way barred. Luckily, I saw him and his brother at the front gate from the broken glass door and walked out to talk to him. When Menios saw me walking out, he turned to the guard and asked for permission to have a few words with me, saying he was my husband's lawyer and needed to discuss some legal matters with me. We were brief, aware of the police guard walking back and forth, his hand on his gun. He told me two things, that Sakeleropoulos, head of the Athens Bar Association and key lawyer of the team of three for Andreas' anticipated ASPIDA trial, had been picked up the night of the 21st and shipped off to Yaros. About Mandiliras, the other lawyer, he had heard nothing. That left only him, of the three, and he said he would add Stavros Cannellopoulos, a brilliant trial lawyer, who had been a reserve. The next day he expected to go to Socratides and make arrangements to see Andreas. I asked if he thought there would be any trouble. He answered in the negative with assurance, but I knew that he himself could not predict what luck he would have.

He was granted permission, and it was through Menios, on Wednesday of the first week, that I got information on where Andreas was being held, his physical condition, his room, and details of his confinement. On the night following the coup, the night of the curfew, Andreas, along with other Center deputies and deputies of the Left, had been taken to Pikermi, a small hotel on the road to Marathon. His leg wound had been a serious one and doctors had operated on him during that day at Goudi, prior to his transferral. Thirty-two stitches were necessary to sew up the jagged gash. He had been given a tetanus shot, the old-fashioned type, and had been put on a ten-day nonprotein diet. His spirits were good. I couldn't be sure of all this until I saw Andreas. Menios played the role not only of lawyer but of family friend and morale booster. We were to develop a close association as my respect for him grew into open admiration at his courage, decency, and devotion to Andreas.

The more unpleasant part of his visit was the reason he had been given permission to see Andreas. He had to be present when Andreas was subpoenaed to testify in the ASPIDA trial on charges of high treason. It was the first legal action taken against any of the ten thousand prisoners by the junta government.

Andreas also told him news about his father. He had occupied a room across from him the first night at Goudi, and then was transferred in a separate army truck to Pikermi the next night. He had been given a special, private, spacious room at Pikermi in honor, apparently, of having been Premier of Greece in the past—a touch that no doubt galled my father-in-law. On Sunday night he was transferred to a hospital in downtown Athens, under guard, in deference to his health. He was allowed no visitors.

This is the way eight garish days passed after the coup: first the flurry of reporters, then the dramatic news that Andreas was alive, then guards, then house searches, then legal action against Andreas—and all the visits from friends, relatives, and fledgling resistance fighters.

Some pieces of the puzzle were falling into place; much was still to be learned. Colonel George Papadopoulos was actually the liaison man between the Greek KYP and the American CIA. His official title at the time of the coup was director of the "Psychological Section of the General Army Staff." Colonel Makarezos was a KYP man. Only Pattakos seemed to be straight army with no intelligence-services background or connection. Savvas Constantopoulos, editor of the newspaper *Eleftheros Kosmos*, considered a CIA-financed newspaper, had been brought in by military car the night after the coup to the political office of Papadopoulos where they had a discussion. This fell in the category of rumor at the time, but many months later Constantopoulos himself wrote of this rendezvous, saying that Papadopoulos had asked him what he thought of the "revolution," and the reply was that they had moved just in time to prevent a civil conflict, and were to be congratulated. A full tape of this conversation between these two shady characters would be much more revealing.

One of the civilians placed in government as Minister of Public Order was Paul Totomis. Initially a TWA representative, he had been involved in a scandal in 1951 and shortly afterward left Greece for a stay in America. Upon return, he became a Tom Pappas representative for Esso.

Pappas' connections with CIA were well known as far back as the period of the apostate governments, but he himself later confirmed this to a Greek newspaper reporter in an interview in *Apoyevmatini* (July 17, 1968) in which he declared he was proud to be a member of the CIA, and that everyone has the right and duty to work for his country. While "working for his country," he managed a package deal with the Greek government in 1962 when Standard Oil of New Jersey went into partnership with him. Esso-Pappas forms the major part of a $190-million complex that includes a $15-million petrochemical plant run by Ethyl Corporation, a fertilizer plant, and a steel mill in which Republic Steel has a 15 percent interest. Altogether there are seven companies which have about $120 million in sales. The most lucrative part of this is Pappas' own contract to transport oil for the refinery in his own tanker fleet—Maritime Enterprises Company, flying Greek and Liberian flags.

It was not surprising, then, that in the States in July 1967 Pappas made one of the first public statements supporting the coup. He was not the only American. During the week after the coup, the Greek armed forces radio station carried the following statement made by Cyrus Vance, Assistant Secretary of Defense:

> It is not possible for peace to exist if we turn our backs on the invaders. Greece clearly and inexcusably was in danger of becoming another Vietnam. And America today would have to contend with chaos in that corner of the Middle East if at the right moment catastrophe had not been avoided.

As the mosaic took on shape, form, and color, it began to look more and more like the germ for this production had come from the States. If they hadn't conceived it, they were pleased with those who had, and wished to indicate their favor for this illegitimate creature.

Menios called me on Saturday afternoon, saying he was on his way to get a written visiting permit for me to see Andreas the next day—Easter—at Pikermi. I could take two of the children along. I felt myself getting choked up as I asked for how long. The answer was half an hour. Menios had trouble getting the permit that day, and my spirits sank. The next day was Sunday; the ministries would be closed. For the first of many such times, Menios came through. He hounded, pounded, telephoned, shouted, and finally Sunday noon he brought me personally the slip of paper which was to give me half an hour with my husband.

Tito volunteered to drive, and as soon as George and Sophia had finished their spit-roasted lamb and coal-roasted potatoes, they got ready to accompany me to see their father. It was the first Greek Easter that I couldn't touch food. Nick and Andriko had objected to being excluded, but I promised them they would be next for a visit.

Kiveli sat in the back seat with the two children; I sat in front with Tito. We had started early and drove slowly. My visit permit specified the time 5:00 to 5:30. On the way we passed a small taverna where just two weeks earlier we had listened with pleasure to the lugubrious singing of an old Greek, his gnarled hands nimble on the guitar and his voice strong and resonant. That night when Andreas came in, the crowd in the taverna had stood up and applauded. "Remember?" was all I said as we passed.

Finally around a bend on the opposite side of the road appeared the sign "PIKERMI," and set back among pine trees was a small, squarish two-story hotel made for couples, not prisoners. Its innocent-looking appearance was jarred by the presence of tanks in front of the white wrought-iron gate and inside in the yard, and men with tommy guns at the corners of the fences which enclosed the hotel. A long, wide stone path led from the front gate to the entrance of the hotel. The shutters on the windows facing the highway were closed. In one of those rooms was Andreas. We parked in the cleared gravel parking area in front of the fence. George and Sophia, looking uncomfortable, climbed quietly out of the car with me. "Give him our love and kisses," whispered Kiveli. Tito was still on active duty and was taking a risk driving us there. But that was Tito.

186

At the gate a guard examined my permit and waved me on to the hotel. There were soldiers sitting at tables on the terrace, eyeing me with interest. As I came in the door, Mrs. Mitsotakis was leaving, and I was about to greet her when I saw that she had no intention of greeting me. I marveled at the peculiarity of human emotions. We had been adversaries in a political battle after the defection of Mitsotakis and the formation of FIDIK, when my father-in-law fell from power. But now we were two women whose husbands had been brought to their knees by the barrels of guns. We had a common adversary, using nonpolitical means—force—against us. I felt no animosity toward her. Just sympathy.

Inside in the tiny hotel lobby stood a young officer behind the registration counter who silently took my permit, then asked for my identification card. I pulled out my American passport. He looked at it carefully, then asked for my Greek I.D. card.

"Do you doubt my identity?" I inquired. "Do you doubt that I am Margaret Papandreou? I have no I.D. card." My stomach was knotting up again as I foresaw the possibility of losing the chance to see Andreas. He told me to wait and went upstairs. Within a few minutes he came down and beckoned the three of us up. On the second-floor hallway at each end were guards with machine guns. I tried to pretend I didn't notice them, as if they were orderlies in a hospital and I was visiting a sick man.

We passed three closed doors and went to the fourth. The officer opened the door and I was staring straight into the eyes of Andreas, who was standing with outstretched arms. He had seen me walking up the pathway through the slats of the window shutters and was waiting for me. I threw myself into his arms, tears blurring my vision, and held him close to me until I could speak without a tremor in my voice. Sitting on one of the beds was John Alevras, one of Andreas' staunchest deputy friends. I greeted him as Andreas kissed each of the children, and the first emotional moment of our reunion since the night of horror on April 2 was past.

The guard came in and stood at the door as we started to talk.

"He understands English," Andreas told me, "so we can speak in English." This was a warning.

I sat on the bed next to Andreas after he got back on his bed in a sitting position. Sophia pulled up a chair, but George said he preferred to stand. Then I looked at Andreas carefully. He had lost weight and his face looked pale. His eyes were shining like bright coals. Where had I seen that look before? He began to talk in a rather loud voice, enunciating his words carefully. I tried to talk, but he seemed to want to do all the talking. He asked about the children, how they had been after the arrest, and when I told him they were great kids, his face screwed up with emotion, as if he might cry out, but he did not. I told him about the efforts of his friends in the States, but feeling the presence of a listening ear, I automatically became devious and vague, and when I told him about Leo and John's call from the States, I said—which was silly since they were in no danger—Evelyn's and Anne's husbands. He looked at me with a blank expression. I repeated the names. He ultimately said, "Yes, yes," but I knew he had not understood. His

187

responses seemed very slow to me, not clear and quick, as they usually were. Toward the end of the half hour he told me that he had had a visit from Pattakos, and that after some brief exchange of words, Pattakos had said, using an ancient Greek expression, "Where the word fails, the stick will serve." With that Andreas winked at me. He never winked. I had a growing feeling of horror and terror in me. Of course Andreas had suffered and had been through a violent emotional experience. Was this enough to explain this strange meeting we were having? I kept looking at his eyes. They dominated his face like the spectacular eyes of children in the paintings of the California Keanes. Before we left, as I kissed him, I managed to tuck some newspaper clippings from the foreign press under his pillow, articles that would make him feel good. I had pulled them out of my purse at the same time I had reached for my last cigarette and waited for the chance to give them to Andreas. But the activity was automatic and mechanical. I was panicked at a growing suspicion I had, and it was with the greatest of effort that I put on a bright smile.

In the car, Tito and Kiveli waited patiently for me to give them details of the visit. I said he sent his love, then fell into a black silence that lasted the entire return trip. The few friends and relatives who had joined us for Easter were waiting at the door upon my return to hear news of Andreas. I tore past them and ran to my bedroom. I sat on the edge of my bed and tried to sort out my thoughts. That look, that look—only twice had I seen it in my life on Andreas, and in both cases he was being given massive doses of *drugs*. Once was when he had a blood reaction to Buscopan, a mild stomach pill, but to which he was allergic. Result: Loss of most of his white blood cells, a disease called agranulocitosis. The second time was after he took huge units of streptomycin in his fight against tuberculosis in March of 1966.

Marjorie turned the handle of the door and asked if she could come in, knowing something was troubling me deeply.

"Marjorie," I said. "You know me. Am I prone to hysteria?"

"Why, no, of course not."

"Do I see things pretty clearly and objectively, even under great tension?"

"Yes, Margaret, but what—"

"I have the terrible feeling that they are feeding Andreas drugs! And that he may be under threat of beatings!" I put my face in my hands and bent my head down.

"Let's talk about it," said Marjorie. She sat down next to me on the bed. I told her about the whole interview with Andreas, his strange way of speaking, his appearance, and the inexplicable wink that was supposed to mean something. In the midst of my story Kiveli came in and sat down on the other side.

"What shall I do, what shall I do?" I kept asking.

"Let's talk to Tito" was Kiveli's answer. We walked down to the dining room and called Tito in. Kiveli told him my suspicions and Tito paled.

"Menios felt he was all right," he said. "Let's call him and ask him to come over." There was no answer at Menios' house.

"Let me call his doctor, Michalis," I said. Again no answer.

"I will have to call Angelis," I told them. Angelis was the senior doctor in charge when Andreas had agranulocitosis, but he was a man I found cold and had little respect for. He was home, and when he heard my name I could almost feel the telephone quiver. I told him my concern and asked what could happen if Andreas were getting a drug he was allergic to. He confirmed my fear that it could spark off a reaction which would kill off his white blood cells.

"Then I want you to do one thing for me," I asked. "Meet me at the American Ambassador's residence and describe what Andreas had and what danger there is to his life should he be getting drugs."

"Oh, no, I couldn't do that" was his answer.

"Why not?"

"Oh, no, no, no. . . I have nothing to do with the American Embassy." He was scared silly.

"I won't involve you in anything except the medical side," I offered. "Please come with me."

"Impossible" was the only thing he said.

I turned the phone over to Kiveli. "Ask him to give you the exact medical term for his illness," I said. "Write it down and then hang up on him." Kiveli did exactly as I asked her.

With Tito again at the wheel, we drove hurriedly to the home of Phillips Talbot. A group of young people, Americans, probably friends of his daughter's, were winding up their Easter festivities with music and drinks, and Talbot asked them to go out in the yard and motioned to Marjorie and me to follow him to the library.

There I told him the story in a tiny, dried-up voice, fighting to maintain the appearance of control. When I told him about Andreas' problem, he said almost with irritation that he thought he had a history of tuberculosis. "Now," he said, "you tell me about something new." It was as if he were protecting himself from future weekly visits during which I would reveal fresh medical problems of a serious nature. Marjorie bristled at his attitude and started telling him about the use of drugs to break down resistance and described experiments done by psychologists (which was her field) to test these possibilities. Talbot listened to her patiently, a queer little half-smile playing on his face, then asked some questions about her background, finally being curious about this friend of mine who kept popping up in the embassy on my behalf, or in this case, with me.

He offered us drinks, and then asked the most amazing question. "Don't you have someone who could go and discuss this with the government?"

"Who?" I asked, disconcerted.

"His doctor."

"Do you have the slightest understanding of what fear exists among the people today?" I retorted, losing some of my control. "I asked a doctor to join me here in this meeting with you. You think he had the courage to do a simple thing like that? You want me to ask him to throw himself to the wolves? Do you know what fear exists?" I repeated.

He said nothing. The marshmallow bouncing back and forth on a Ping-Pong table.

He pulled out a pad of paper from the desk and asked me to spell the name of the disease that could be initiated by drugs.

I spelled it. Then I added, "My husband gets strange diseases." "So that you won't argue that I didn't tell you his whole medical history, you can also write down "lupus erythematosus," a serious illness he had in Minnesota which in its acute form kills. It is a metabolic disorder usually triggered by overdoses of the sun, but there can be many agitating factors."

Patiently and slowly he wrote it down. Then he sat and said nothing. I assumed the interview was over.

"There is nothing you can do?" I asked.

He shook his head and said, "I don't know."

Suddenly I saw him as an enemy. What was the good of giving all this information to him—only to present it as a gift to a gang of desperados who could be looking for ways to eliminate Andreas?

"Never mind," I said. "I will talk to his lawyer. Don't do anything unless I give you the go-ahead." (Not that he had offered to do anything.)

With that we got up and left.

When I arrived home, Kiveli had reached Menios and he had rushed over and was waiting for me. He told me he hadn't seen Andreas in the bad condition I had described. Andreas was weak from loss of blood and from the emotional experience, and he was also on a diet which may have weakened him more. His eyes? Possibly his general condition. The way he talked? He was probably concerned that you might say something to get yourself in trouble and decided to talk himself to avoid this. Furthermore, he must have been very moved to see you and the children after what you had all gone through. And the stick business? Some stupid remark of Pattakos' without meaning.

It all sounded so reasonable, and I so unusually nervous. But he too was concerned about my seeing Talbot. The Greeks all felt the Americans had just as much desire to get rid of Andreas as the army. We decided that Marjorie would go out to a kiosk, so as not to use our phone, and reach Talbot and tell him to forget the whole thing, that Margaret had found a means of handling it.

The joy at being able to see Andreas had turned into a nightmare.

190

Hope and Despair

IF IT were possible for governments to fall from the pressure of public opinion outside their countries, the military dictatorship in Greece would have collapsed within the first week. Although suppression of foreign publications had been ordered the first few days, this was soon rescinded in deference to the tourists in the country, and the Greeks were eagerly buying up foreign papers to find out what was being said about their fate. About 90 percent of the articles, editorials, and news stories written about Greece were violently against the dictatorship. There was a general refusal to accept the trumped-up charges of the junta that military intervention was necessary to prevent a communist take-over. Herblock came out in the Washington *Post* with the first of a series of excellent cartoons lambasting the dictatorship. In this one a small cradle labeled "Greece" held a monstrous, uniformed officer labeled "Military Junta" sharpening his sword with his thumb, fangs hanging out of a grinning mouth. The title was "Cradle of Democracy."

In Washington, Americans for Democratic Action gave out a press release entitled "Galbraith Opposes Greek Coup, Urges Restoration of Civil Liberties." The statement read as follows:

> ADA expresses grave concern over the replacement of the civilian government of Greece with a military junta and the arrest of Greek civilian political leaders. We do not accept the suggestion that these leaders, many of whom in these days are as well known in America as in Greece, are communist or pro-communist. [Emphasis mine. Obvious reference to Andreas.] We join with others in rejecting the effort so as to associate political disagreement with communism. We are especially appalled by the arrest of these leaders and threats to their personal safety. ADA stresses the deep-seated dislike in the United States among our own members for a military dictatorship, and this is especially so in the case of a military ally. It urges the human treatment and release of the political prisoners and the prompt restoration of constitutional guarantees and civilian authority in accordance with the oldest and most vital of Greek traditions.

On the yet more personal front, I drew strength from a copy of a memorandum to President Johnson written by Walter Heller, an old friend, and head of the Council of Economic Advisers under both John Kennedy and Lyndon Johnson. He started out in the following manner:

> I am one of the legion of alarmed friends of Andreas Papandreou. In twenty years as an outstanding economist at Harvard, Minnesota and California, "Andy" developed a very large and devoted U.S. following.

He finished with the following eloquent statement:

> U.S. efforts to protect the life and liberty of a man who has voiced some anti-U.S. opinions would vividly demonstrate to the Greeks and the world that we mean what we say about those "inalienable rights."
>
> Our concern is for the life and safety of personal friends. Yours has to be for America's defense of freedom in the world. I hope you will agree that the two coincide in the case of the Papandreous.

At the same time that the junta was being condemned by all decent people of the world, and the machinery to work for Andreas' release got started with key Americans helping, there were disturbing signs that the regime was going to be recognized and foreign governments would carry on where they left off before the coup interrupted their normal activities. Bernard Nossiter chronicled this on April 28 in a release from Athens:

> The United States has taken several small but significant steps, moving toward a business-as-usual relationship with Greece's new military dictators. After a three-day delay, U.S. Ambassador Phillips Talbot was instructed by Washington Thursday night to acknowledge a letter from the Junta's Foreign Minister, Paul Economou-Gouras.... Senior Western diplomats explained today that Talbot's acknowledgement means that the United States is looking forward to working relations with the new government and expects to continue to treat with it.

On the 29th, Rusk issued his first comments on the Greek coup through his press office. He said he was "encouraged to see that King Constantine in his first public statement . . . has called for an early return to parliamentary government." In addition, Rusk said that he was pleased by a statement that Greece would "continue its strong support of NATO."

The latter was the key. Talbot's primary responsibility during the days after the coup was to determine the nature and color of the faceless triumvirate which took over. American services knew the Big Junta and could count on its loyalty. But the Little Junta was a little-known body. If the CIA did know about it, it was taking some time to sift the facts. When the report came in that it was clean—that is, anticommunist and pro-NATO—the authorities could embrace it. This was to be done slowly and with decorum, like a bashful boyfriend wooing a shy maid, so that the neighbors wouldn't understand that he had already decided to sleep with her. There was to be some holding back of arms shipments as a means, it was explained, to pressure the junta toward the return of parliamentary government. It was also explained to me at some time later in a session I had with Anschuetz that the question of recognition or nonrecognition had not really come up since the head of state remained the same. That was King Constantinos' contribution to the cause.

On May 8 a story appeared in *The New York Times* under the caption "Johnson to Appeal to Save Jailed Son of Papandreou." It stated that President Johnson had assured academic leaders in the States that he would intercede on behalf of Andreas in an effort to make certain that he would not be summarily executed. According to the story, J. Kenneth Galbraith had asked the President the week before to "do everything possible" when it appeared that Mr. Papandreou was in danger of execution, or at a minimum "in real trouble."

Johnson had commented, "This is the first issue in history in which all the American economists seem to have agreed."

Also, according to the story, a group of demonstrators headed by Professor Stephen Rousseas of New York University appealed to Secretary-General Thant at the United Nations to intervene on behalf of Mr. Papandreou. A few days later, an American-Canadian University Committee for Andreas Papandreou was established in New York.

In an open letter to the editor of *The New York Times*, five outstanding economists of the United States declared the following:

> *We hope you will join with us in stating unequivocally that Greece cannot be regarded as a nation with which the United States should maintain close political and military relations until the Papandreous and other arrested political leaders are released; until King Constantine reappoints a government based upon a parliamentary majority; and until elections are scheduled to permit the Greek people to express their political preferences by the only means legitimate to a democracy—the ballot box.*

The signers were Ken Arrow from Stanford, Walter Galenson from Cornell, Harvey Leibenstein and Roy Radner from the University of California, and Henry Rosovsky from Harvard.

And yet another hopeful sign, "Reuther Asks Suspension of Aid to Greece." In Detroit, Walter P. Reuther, president of the United Auto Workers, urged the United States to halt military and economic aid to Greece until "a trigger-happy military" put aside its "dictatorship." The union and its 1,500,000 members, he said, "are deeply concerned and disturbed by the recent military coup in Greece where thousands of opposition leaders now have been jailed, freedom suppressed and other democratic institutions suspended."

In Geneva, Switzerland, the International Commission of Jurists issued a press release on May 9. Here are some extracts:

> *Until April 21, when the coup d'etat took place, a lawfully constituted Government was in control and elections were due to be held on May 28th. This coup d'etat was clearly intended to overthrow*

the Government and to prevent the Greek people from expressing their will at an election. This is in complete violation of the Rule of Law which the International Commission of Jurists seeks to protect. Indeed at the Athens Congress of the Commission, in 1955, it was laid down:

"The will of the people is the basis of the authority of public powers. This will be expressed by free elections.... The legislative power must be effectively exercised by an appropriate organ, freely elected by the citizens. The laws and other legal measures taken by the legislature cannot be abolished or restricted by a governmental measure."

...Having seized de facto power, the military regime purported to issue a decree "suspending" all those articles in the Constitution which protect the rights of the individual and provide the guarantees necessary for the maintenance of the Rule of Law. This group of military officers had, of course, no authority to nullify the Constitution. In case of grave public danger, the King on the advice of the Government, and subject to subsequent ratification by Parliament, could have suspended some Constitutional guarantees. The military officers went even further than the King, the Government and Parliament were entitled to go in that they purported to suspend Article 18 of the Constitution which cannot be suspended even in an emergency. It is the Article which forbids torture, capital punishment for political offence and total confiscation of property. The following fundamental constitutional safeguards are among those that have also been abrogated: freedom of the press and of expression, protection from arbitrary imprisonment, prohibition of special tribunals, freedom of association, inviolability of the home.

It was Frank Newman who brought me a copy of this press release. Frank was dean of the law school at the University of California where he and Andreas had fought together for many liberal causes. I had met him briefly at a party near the campus and didn't recognize him immediately when I opened the front door on that Wednesday morning, May 10. He acted as if he thought maybe he was intruding, and I had to assure him that I welcomed him. (Welcomed him! I was ready to throw my arms around him and plant fat kisses on his cheeks!) He explained that he and family were living in Geneva and would stay there until classes started in the fall in order for him to complete some work on the Human Rights Commission. Somebody I could talk to! He was the first friend to see me in person, and he had come, I soon discovered, to help. I had to ask him how he broke through the bars surrounding the land of Greece, for in my mind we were all penned in, a nation of sheep, herded here or there according to the master's whim. A barrier had been erected between us and the world of free men, and Frank breezed in with the air and confidence that is the mark of a free man.

Frank told me that he and his wife had been planning for a long time to visit Greece and had made arrangements for a week on a Greek island with another American couple. When the news of the coup came, they were tempted to cancel their reservations, as so many people did, but decided to come in order to see me, find out about Andreas, and judge what could be done to help.

We talked for more than an hour and agreed that it would be helpful to have a session with Andreas' lawyer, Menios. The arrangement was made to meet at his hotel the next evening. I promised to reach Menios, and since Menios spoke no English, to have him bring along his law partner, John Lambrinides, who spoke English perfectly. The next evening, sitting on the beds in Frank's seventh-floor hotel room, Lambrinides gave a concise, clear description of the ASPIDA frame-up, answering Frank's questions with precision and eloquence. Frank took notes and when the discussion was finished, I remember him saying, "It sounds like a bag of worms." That is exactly what it was. It was also during this meeting that Lambrinides told Frank that an American client of his had recently run into an American Embassy official, unnamed, who told the client, "Well, I hope they at least get Andreas." To the client's question "What do you mean, 'get'?" the answer was "Execute!" The client later said to the lawyer, "Never have I been so ashamed of my nationality."

I heard this story with my heart in my throat. Between the time I had seen Frank at my home and then at his hotel, I had had a soul-shaking experience. The radio gave a special announcement at 11 P.M. May 10. "Andreas Papandreou has been moved to Averoff Prison." I had been expecting it, but not so soon. Frantically, I had gotten in the car with Marjorie, and we drove round and round the prison, peering at the ugly structure of concrete with its tiny cell windows and guard parapets on the corners of the roof. It covered more than a block of land, its front a façade of large windows and parklike lawn with trees facing a main street near downtown Athens—all this to hide the stark, primitive quarters behind. The road to the rear was of mud, gutted by rain and hardened into mounds and pits. The Taunus had bumped along valiantly many times around as we peered up into the dimly lit structure in a vain effort to determine where they might have put Andreas. I wanted to shout his name to let him know I was nearby but the best I could do was to toot the horn each time I traversed the main road in the front of the building where the sound of a car honk might be considered natural, hoping he would recognize the sound. I found out later that he had heard nothing, concentrated as he was on adjusting to a black cell.

Frank left the next day for a remote island, having arranged ahead of time for an appointment upon his return with Phillips Talbot to discuss the legal defense of Andreas on my behalf.

About the same time that Frank and his friends left for their island stay, around ten o'clock in the morning of May 11, I received a telephone call from the director of Averoff Prison. In a guttural voice with an accent from the provinces which I could barely understand, he told me I was to prepare food for the prisoner Papandreou (the Greek word is *kratoumenos*, which literally means "the held one") each day and bring it to the prison at noon and in the evening. He told me I could bring along with the food a thermos jug of coffee and one of juice or water. They wanted me to have the responsibility of the food so that no case of poisoning could be passed on to them. If this were so, I reasoned optimistically, then the food would have to be passed from my hands directly to Andreas, and I had visions of being led to his cell each time and setting his meal in front of him. I immediately called Menios to learn what he knew of this procedure and to verify that I had correctly understood the village Greek. He said that he had been told the same thing, and that he would meet me at the front entrance of the jail at noon when I arrived with the food. Marjorie and I decided that she would accompany me so that we would establish from the start that a friend would be along to help me.

It is hard to describe my feelings as I approached the entryway of that ominous structure. Guards patrolled the yard and the long, wide sidewalk leading from the street to the door, their tommy guns held low, but ready. Menios was at the street end of the sidewalk pathway, and I learned from him that Andreas was in a cell with one of the big windows facing the highway, second floor, just to the left of the entrance. I looked up, but no one was there. I had the strangest feeling that the place was completely dead and deserted, a place outside of life. Menios was exuding optimism and assuring me that the quarters were not bad, and Andreas' spirits good. He had seen him just an hour earlier and was pleased to find him taking the new situation so well, etc., etc. When we reached the big iron door, Menios reached up and tapped the peep-window, a face appeared, a key turned in a latch, a bar was lifted—and I was inside.

It was my first time in a prison. As my eyes got accustomed to the dim light, I could see that I was standing in a long, high-ceilinged entryway, about twenty feet wide, with a cement floor extending to double doors on the other end. Pencil shafts of light came through the cracks of that door, and I surmised that behind it was the prison court. From my circling of the night before, I knew that cells surrounded the court. To my right was a small booth with an opening like a ticket window at a train depot. A large ledger lay open on the counter, apparently the "guest book." Just beyond the booth to the right was a door leading to offices, and directly opposite to the left an analogous door, standing ajar. I glimpsed desks and counters. A large passageway opened up on both sides at about the halfway mark of the entryway, apparently the way to the stairway for the upper quarters. The rest of the entryway was caged by chicken wire, and two large doors of wire the same size as the courtyard doors stood open. I couldn't make out what this section was.

I was ushered into the door at the right, without Menios, and led through outer offices into the inner sanctum—the office of the director. Mr. Tournas, the prison director, sat at his desk, rising reluctantly as I came in. He waved the guard out and asked me to take a seat. He was short, paunchy, and balding. The fringe of hair that remained was jet black. His age I put at fifty-five. What impressed me most were his hands, tiny and slender, incongruous appendages on a bulging body, remnants of a slender youth, somehow unaffected by the oils, pastas, and bread stuffed into the system over a period of years. The face didn't impress me one way or the other. I couldn't read cruelty, kindness, intelligence, or stupidity into it. It was the face of a weary bureaucrat, with a rubbery flexibility in expression, the result of years of watching for cues from higher authorities to reflect quickly the proper attitude of the moment. He was the kind of man, I was sure, who would bow and scrape to his superiors, then take out his hostility on his underlings.

He briefly told me the rules. I was to bring Andreas his food at twelve noon and at seven in the evening. He could have no alcoholic beverages. That evening I should bring sheets, a blanket, towels, and clothing. Books would have to go to the Ministry of Justice first for checking. There were to be no notes tucked in his food or clothing. I was to have four visits a week at 12:30 for half an hour each. The children would be allowed to see him once a week. I asked him about the food that Menios was holding in the hallway outside the office. He said it would be checked and sent up to the prisoner. I argued that I could not let it go through someone else's hands because of the threat that existed to Andreas' life. For a moment I saw him uncertain and undecided. It seemed that for a split second he considered this logical, and perhaps best of all, relieved him of a heavy responsibility, the true aim of any good bureaucrat. This was a criminal jail; its prisoners were dope peddlers, petty thieves, rapists, and the like. A political prisoner of Andreas' level was a new phenomenon for him and the special arrangements broke into his routine. He finally answered that a special guard would be detailed to carry the food to the prisoner (he liked to use this word) and in one sentence smashed the hope I had of being in contact with Andreas twice a day.

My nerves frayed from the experience, I drove home with Marjorie, intent upon flopping on the couch and sipping a cool drink. Antigone opened the door, her face and lips colorless, her eyes frightened.

"Mrs. Margaret, they're coming again."

"Who?"

"The KYP people. I got a phone call from Iakovos in the police station and he told me to hurry and lock the study door." When the searchers had left the last time, I had allowed the study door to remain locked for several days, but finding it impossible to operate without the children's beds, had sent Georgie to buy a skeleton key to open it up.

"And what happened?"

"I ran up to lock it, but there was no key in the lock. I searched all over Georgie's room and didn't find it. At that point the doorbell rang, and I thought we were lost." She was spilling out her words in a breathless torrent. "It was Iakovos who asked if I had locked the door and when I told him my trouble, he ran upstairs and locked it himself."

God bless the police, I said to myself—untamed as yet by their army masters. It didn't occur to me until later to wonder how they knew I had unlocked the door!

Antigone wasn't through. "Ten minutes after he left, a man in plain clothes rang the bell and asked me if someone from the police station had stopped by here. I said no, and he looked at me for a few seconds, then left."

Oh, good God. Iakovos in trouble; Antigone in trouble. And I didn't really give a damn if they learned that I had opened the door. Yet I had given no instructions, and these people had merely been trying to protect me.

"Marjorie," I said, "you have some letters in your purse. Let's take no chances with girdles and brassieres this time. You and Dad take the car and leave the house. Don't return without telephoning."

Two minutes after they drove away, the KYP men drove up. Once again we were herded into the living room, those of us who were home: my mother, Andreas' mother, Sophia, Antigone, and I. The other children were out playing. The door was closed, and I heard once again—for the third time—the sound of strange voices and footsteps tramping through my house. I recalled a phrase in the International Commission of Jurists' press release: *the inviolability of the home.*

After about half an hour, the same stocky, dark-haired man who had been leading the search the last time came to the door and said, "I want to talk to you alone, upstairs."

Sophia gave a gasp and said, "Oh, Mommy!"

"Don't worry, darling," I managed to say. "They won't do anything to me." I carried with me a glass of wine I had been drinking and followed Mr. KYP into my mother and father's bedroom. His face was surly and black.

"You opened the door to the study," he said.

"Yes, I needed it."

"You were told not to."

"No, that's not true. I was just told it was being locked."

"You were told not to unlock it," he repeated.

"No," I answered again, "I was just told that it was being locked. You can ask your colleague, the blond, if that was not the case."

"You took things from the room."

"There was nothing to take," I said. "I needed the room for my younger children."

He was rough and unfriendly. All of a sudden he stood up, pulled some keys out of his pocket, and shook them in front of my face, almost scraping my nose with them. I didn't budge.

"What are these for?" he asked.

I recognized them. They were two sets of keys for two apartment hiding places. One had a white tag with the letters L-E-S printed on it, and the number 37. It was in my handwriting and was a means of identification.

"I have no idea," I replied.

"What do you mean, you have no idea? We found them in your husband's briefcase." Something I had missed the night of the coup and the days thereafter. They must have been picked up in the second search.

"I don't know what my husband keeps in his briefcase."

"He's your husband, isn't he? What do you mean, you don't know? Take a good look at them." He again shook them at my face, so close that I would have had to look at them cross-eyed to read the writing. I took a sip of wine and didn't answer. He glared venomously at the glass. I had the feeling he wanted to punch the glass into my face and grind in the pieces. Outwardly I was cool, but my legs were trembling. Already the stories of beatings had gotten to us, and we all knew that anything was possible.

He changed the subject. "I want to ask you about your personnel. Who works here?"

There was no use saying that Antigone didn't work here. This he knew, and in any case she was sitting in my living room downstairs. He wrote the name. "Who else?"

"No one else works here, unless you mean a cleaning woman who comes in from time to time." He didn't seem interested in her name.

"What about a driver?"

"My father or I drive," I answered.

"Somebody by the name of Stelios."

"He was my husband's driver when Andreas was Minister of Coordination. I haven't seen him for ages."

"The gardener, the old man."

"Nikos."

"Nikos what?"

"I don't know his last name."

"You're lying!" he shouted. I wasn't, but I would have. Let them work for their information. I knew they could find it and as much as I was revealing was not particularly helpful. In talks I had later with friends who had been grilled in this fashion, or worse, I discovered that we all had tried the same technique—to give enough information, already known, to appear to be cooperative, but not enough to help, or to betray.

"Perhaps my mother-in-law knows," I said.

"Where is she?"

"Downstairs."

"Go ask her."

I left on my wobbly legs, surprised that he did not follow me down. When I came into the living room, I found Sophia sitting on the floor next to my mother, tears streaming down her eyes.

"Don't cry, Sophoula," I said. "It will be all right."

"Oh, Mommy, Mommy," she sobbed, "they're going to take you!"

"No, no, no, honey. They just want to ask me a few questions. Put such thoughts out of your mind." I kissed her on the top of her head and walked over to her grandmother Papandreou.

"What is the gardener's *first* name?" I asked.

"Nikos," she replied.

"That's what I thought." I refilled my wineglass.

I returned to the bedroom and told him the only name we knew was "Nikos."

He asked who did our carpentry, our plumbing, who was our milkman, grocery man. To all I replied that I never really paid attention to names, that Greek names were always hard for me. I didn't have the feeling that he expected to get information from me. He was trying to rattle me, for what purpose I couldn't ascertain. These people are skilled interrogators and have worked out effective techniques through long practice. I thought I could stand up to psychological pressure, but not to physical torture.

Suddenly he changed the subject again.

"When you talked to my colleague upstairs last time, you asked him to help you. What did you mean?"

And what do *you* mean? I thought. That damned, wormy conversation.

"I was distressed. I'm not accustomed to people invading my home. I don't know quite what I said."

"You have a bad memory," he barked.

"I'm afraid so."

"Think now. You meant something by that. What did you mean?"

What in God's name did he expect me to mean? Did he perhaps think that I was offering to become a collaborator with KYP? It was the only possible explanation I could think of. But if that were the case, wouldn't he be approaching me in a different manner? I was lost.

"I told you, I don't remember."

"Are you saying that you didn't say it?"

"Maybe I did. I was emotional. I could have said anything."

He watched with disgust as I sipped again from my wineglass. It occurred to me that normally in such interrogations people are not even given water to drink.

He said nothing for a few seconds, then waved his hand and said, "You're released." In his mind I had been his captive.

I returned to the living room and tried to soothe a frightened Sophia. In another hour they were gone, having carried down file cases and boxes to a waiting truck. I went immediately to the telephone and called the American Embassy. Three searches were enough. I made an appointment with Norbert Anschuetz for the following day in his office.

The next day I drove the Taunus to the parking space behind the embassy, parked the car, and walked down the wide white steps to the rear entrance. The building is a stately structure, designed by Gropius and opened in 1959. The architect designed it in Greek style, but with enough humility not to try to compete with or copy ancient classical architecture. Its lines are straight and simple, the effect noble and masculine. In the yard on my right I could see the American flag, high atop a tall slender pole, its "banner unfurled" in gusts of spring wind, symbol of the land of the free and the home of the brave. My country, my country—this flag a mockery, this building a mortuary for the embalming of a democracy in the very land in which it was born.

I announced to the man at the desk my appointment with Anschuetz, and he directed me to take the elevator to the third floor. I found Norbert waiting for me in his long, elegant office, and we sat in one corner, he in an armchair, I on a narrow, black leather couch.

"How is Andreas?" were his first words.

"He seems to be all right. He's been moved to Averoff. I will see him this noon."

"I heard about your concern when you visited him at Pikermi."

"Oh, yes, that. I guess I was overdistraught. I think I misjudged the

200

situation." I switched the topic. "Norbert, I came here for several reasons, but primarily to make a protest."

"Yes?"

"I would like to point out that, although some of us are also Greeks, in my house on Guizi Street there are nine Americans: myself, four children, my mother-in-law, Marjorie, and my parents. Furthermore, the house is owned by my mother-in-law who is a naturalized American citizen. Despite this the house has been invaded three times for searches, and yesterday's, which occurred just before I called you for an appointment, included an interrogation. All my personal papers, files, photos, and films have been removed from my study. I want a note of protest to go the junta. And I want my papers back."

"Nine Americans," mused Norbert. I couldn't tell if he thought it was funny or if he was just overwhelmed.

He poured some coffee from the coffee tray on the table in front of us, and stirred some sugar into his cup thoughtfully. "Mrs. Schachter is living with you?" he asked, as if he were trying to sort out the menagerie.

"Yes, thank God. She helps me in many ways, not the least of which is moral support." I waited. He had not answered my request.

Finally, he said, "I'll see what I can do, Margaret."

"I have another request. I am being attacked incessantly in the Greek press as a Bulgarian communist. If this were a democracy, I would have my own means to fight this dishonest attack. I wouldn't come to you. But there are no means for a voice other than the military to be heard. The press and radio are controlled. All you need to do is deny the charges on my behalf. You know my background, my family lineage, and that I have no communist record. I want you to ask the junta to print the truth and take back the accusation."

Again he said, "I'll see what I can do."

I sat back and lit a cigarette. I saw that my hands were still trembling from the experiences of the past few days. Norbert saw it, too.

"Take your time, Margaret," he said quietly. "Are there some more things?"

"Oh, yes. I'm only half through."

I continued. "I read in *The New York Times* that President Johnson had intervened on behalf of Andreas' life. Nobody from the embassy informed me of this. It is of interest to me, you know," I added bitterly.

"I don't know of any communication" was his answer.

"You mean nothing came through from the President?"

"I think I would have seen it if it did."

"That's strange, isn't it?"

He opened up his hands in a gesture that said maybe-it-is-maybe-it-isn't. "I'll let you know if I see something." I have never learned where the snafu came in. Did the underlings countermand an order, or did the "intervention" never get off the grounds of the White House?

I had immediately sent to President Johnson a short letter of appreciation after reading the story in the newspaper. Sometime later he mentioned to Walter Heller that he had received my letter. Apparently *he* thought his orders had been carried through.

"They say they are going to try Andreas on the ASPIDA charges. You know and I know that this is a case of political persecution. The charges are fake and the evidence concocted. You have been listening and reading for months now *their* side of the story. I think you should hear *ours*. I would like you and the ambassador to have a session with Andreas' lawyer."

Norbert looked a little surprised, about as much surprised as a capable diplomat can allow himself to look.

"I think that might be arranged," he answered, reaching for the pad of paper and pencil on the coffee table. "Could you give me his name and how he can be reached?"

"I can give you his name—and I will—but I can make the appointment for you. I see him almost every day."

"Better that we make the contact directly. Have you his phone number?"

"I know it by heart. I call him often from kiosks."

Although probably Menios' and my phones were both tapped, calling from a kiosk cut the risk in half at least. I gave Norbert the name, plus the name of his partner, who would accompany Menios for the discussion.

I spelled the names for him: K-o-u-t-s-o-y-e-r-g-a-s and L-a-m-b-r-i-n-i-d-e-s. And the phone: 727-518. I watched his pen form the letters and numbers on the pad, feeling a slight twinge of hope that I was making some progress. I had discussed this with Frank Newman and the reasoning went like this: If the American Embassy were supporting the junta, they would want to have it minimize the gaffes, reduce international interest on "returning democracy to Greece," and avoid a big political trial of a man of Andreas' stature and prestige which would bring the press scurrying from the countries of the world. If they had not decided as yet to support fully the junta, surely the junta would be seeking full support, and embassy interest in the case of my husband might cause them to reexamine the advantages and disadvantages of having such a trial. Although the meeting between Andreas' lawyers and the American Ambassador would be secret, there were ways of letting the junta know of the session.

We talked about the situation more generally. I remember telling him. "It was a big, shiny dream we had—along with the youth of this country—for reform, progress, and more opportunity, but it was stopped by metal."

We talked on a bit. I thought of him as a friend. I may have been wrong. My friends, even Andreas' lawyers, were convinced he was CIA. This made him automatically bad. I used to wish sometimes that people like Anschuetz *were* in the CIA. Since we are plagued with this parallel authority in the United States, and until the day its actions are put under congressional control, let it be peopled by men of intelligence, vision, and judgment. In the years we had known Norbert and in the bits of information we picked up from other sources, I always felt he pursued a policy of urging moderation. He gained the enmity of all sides this way, but the American factor with its strong voice in Greek affairs could have played an effective, moderating role when the King went off on a toot and maintained an equilibrium that would have made a dictatorial solution impossible. I knew that in the weeks after the coup he was doing two things: one, trying to find resistance somewhere so he could strengthen his position that the United States must not stand idly by; two, he was privately seeing members of the Center Union who were still free to examine what possibilities existed for a restoration of liberty. He was perhaps committed to the idea of a firm stand on the part of the King, but this was not unrealistic. There was no other force to stand up to the military. The people had remained silent. One of the Center Union deputies who saw me after he had seen Anschuetz told me Anschuetz asked the question "What would be the effect of the King's going to the radio and announcing to the people that he was taking over the country temporarily to reinstate parliamentary government and needed their backing for this effort?" It may have been a "pie in the sky" idea, because, among other things, it needed a gutsy King, but it gave me the feeling that Norbert was searching for a reversal of the tragic events of April 21.

Anschuetz told me he had something to tell me. The embassy had received a wire from the State Department that James Schwartz, a lawyer, and Pat Brown, former governor of the state of California, were coming over as legal representatives for Andreas. I already knew this, because Jim, the husband of a former roommate of mine at the University of Minnesota, had telephoned sometime after the coup, proposing that he come. I had urged him to do so, but had heard no more. I was overjoyed that it was being done in this fashion, through official channels. This also meant that it had gotten the okay of the White House, for Pat Brown was a close friend of Lyndon Johnson's. He told me that the ambassador had asked that I urge them to be discreet and cautious in their dealings here. Old don't-stir-the-waters Talbot!

As I was leaving, he went over to his desk and pulled out of a drawer a long sheet of paper, a copy of an ad that had appeared in the Washington *Post*.

"You have friends. This may cheer you up."

I saw big letters: "An Open Letter to the President, the Congress and All Americans." I stuffed it in my purse, murmuring a thank you to Norbert, and waited until I was sitting in the car to open it up and spread it on the seat next to me to read. It began with Harry Truman's message to a joint session of Congress on March 12, 1947. The document was signed by George Vournas, Washington Committee, Friends of Greece. I read:

> At the present moment in world history nearly every nation must choose between alternate ways of life. . . .
>
> One way of life is based upon the will of the majority, and is distinguished by free institutions, representative government, free elections, guarantees of individual liberty, freedom of speech and religion, and freedom from political oppression.
>
> The second way of life is based upon the will of a minority forcibly imposed upon the majority. It relies upon terror and oppression, a controlled press and radio, fixed elections, and the suppression of personal freedoms.
>
> I believe that it must be the policy of the United States to support free peoples who are resisting attempted subjugation by armed minorities or outside pressures. . . .

I stopped reading, turned the key in the ignition, and drove slowly away from the American Embassy. I felt like starting the windshield wiper. I was having difficulty seeing.

CHAPTER TWENTY

Resistance and Arrests: The Greeks Fight Back

FROM the embassy I drove directly to Averoff Prison. It was still early—around noon—and my visit was to be at 12:30, but I decided to drive directly to the prison, five minutes away from the embassy, to give me time to park the car and survey the situation. I was tense from my long session with Anschuetz, from the personal ugliness of the last few days, and from anticipation of my meeting with Andreas. I just wanted to have him hold me in his arms, kiss me sweetly on the lips, and tell me everything was going to be all right. The knowledge that I would soon touch him and hear his voice calmed me somewhat.

I parked the car on a street a block beyond the jail, on a hill, and I observed that at one point where there was a separation in buildings, I could see in the distance the window of Andreas' cell. A large palm tree on the lawn of the prison obstructed a portion of the window and made a clear view impossible. In time, I learned all the spots and angles from which I could get an unobstructed view of the window.

I twisted the rearview mirror of the car to look at my face and discovered that my tears had streaked the tiny bit of mascara I had applied and would not do as a sight for Andreas to see. With tissue and saliva I worked on the blotches under my eyes, then with an eye liner pencil and an unsteady hand, redrew the black line on my upper lids. Powder on my nose, lipstick, and a fluffing up of my hair with my hands put me back into shape. Ha. What shape? That lonely-looking lady with hollow cheeks and an anxious look—was that really me?

Marjorie and I had agreed that if I had not returned home by noon, Tito would bring her and Andreas' hot lunch at 12:15, and we would meet at the sidewalk café on the corner just before reaching the prison. She would carry the food and walk with me to the wide iron doors, wait for me on the bench outside the jail door, then walk with me to Tito's parked car. This was a ritual we established from the first day, either coming together from home or meeting each other when I had some activity elsewhere, and it continued in this fashion almost without exception.

I walked slowly down the side street to the highway corner café. Along one side of this street was a row of small shops—an ice-cream shop where they also sold pumpkin seeds (which I bought from time to time), a hardware store with pots and pans hanging in the window, a grain store, and a two-story

205

apartment building in a state of disrepair. It was a poor neighborhood, one of the many slum areas in the back streets of Athens unseen by the tourist. Curious eyes from the shops watched me with interest. When I reached the corner of the highway, I peered down the wide boulevard fronting the jail. Again I saw shops and several apartment buildings with the usual balconies on each floor. There were two grocery markets, one with a large faded green canvas top propped up by poles as a shelter for the colorful array of fresh fruit and vegetables in boxes on counters below. There was also a bakery shop and a store selling plumbing fixtures. The window display in the latter—toilets, bathtubs, sinks, bidets—I got to know well since it was one of the three spots from which Andreas and I could see each other. The second spot was the bakery, and the third—and best—the grocery stall. In the evening, when it started to get dark early, a naked bulb hanging by a cord from the canvas top lighted up my face and faces of friends for a companionless man watching in solitude from the fortress across the way.

I saw Tito's car pull up on the other side of the street and Marjorie jump out holding a white thermos bucket with the hot food and a net bag with thermos jugs, cold accoutrements to the meal, and, hanging out of the bag, a bright red rose, one of the first from our front yard. The night before I had sent Andreas a one-flower glass vase from our bedroom along with the blankets, sheets, and clothing, and remembering my father-in-law's belief—a rose must be seen singly in order to appreciate its beauty—decided to bring one daily, a spot of color in Andreas' bleak existence.

Marjorie asked about my visit with Anschuetz.

"I can't say," I answered. "The inscrutable one remains inscrutable. I'll tell you about it after my visit."

I walked up to the door and tapped on the small square peep-window, as I had seen Menios do. The window was pulled open and the face of a guard appeared. He turned and said something to someone, then unbarred the door and motioned me in. He asked me to put the bags on a wicker chair next to the booth and tell him what food I had brought. He walked around to the other side of the ticket window and pulled out an 8 by 10 ledger. Its pages were blank except for vertical lines which separated the page into one large column and three smaller ones. I watched the guard write the date, look at his watch and write the time, then draw laboriously a heavy black line under both. He stood with his stub pencil poised, waiting for me to list the items in the containers.

"Keftedes." (Meatballs—a favorite of Andreas'.)

The guard wrote slowly and with difficulty, and gave a grunt when he was ready for the next item.

"Purée." (Mashed potatoes.) "Horiatiki salata." (Literally "village salad," similar to tossed salad, but with pieces of feta cheese and black olives added.) "Fruita."

"What kind of fruit?"

I wasn't sure what fruit Antigone had put in. "May I look just a moment?"

"Yeah," with annoyance.

"Kerasia." (Cherries.) "Biskota." (Cookies.) "Tselo."

"What's that?"

"It's a gelatinlike substance, good for the stomach."

He had never heard of Jell-O and was at a loss to know how to record it. I offered a solution. "Call it American dessert," I said. He wrote it out as I said. I soon discovered that from time to time I could pass through orange juice with vodka in a thermos jug this way—American canned orange juice—"has a kind of tinny flavor."

This recording completed, I was asked to read the list and okay it by putting my initials in the next column. The third column, as it turned out, was for Andreas' initials, and the last for the guard who had checked the food. "Checked" is a euphemism. According to Andreas it was virtually chopped up by the time it arrived in his cell. As time went by, I used to glance at his initials of the day before to try to determine from this tiny bit of handwriting what his mood was, how his spirits were. When it occurred to me sometime later that he might be doing the same thing, I started signing in flamboyant style with large scrawling letters and a flourish at the end. I was sure it gave the feeling of someone optimistic, confident, and lacking in fear. It could also have been the signature of someone mentally unbalanced. If Andreas noticed these changes, he never said anything to me in our visits.

From the ticket window I was guided into the outer office of the director and shown a chair to sit on. It was situated close to a window, and I looked through the bars trying to imagine what it would be like to be told I was not to leave that room and *not to know when I might get out.* Everything outside looked normal: cars were speeding by, buses were making their stops on the corners, people were making purchases in the shops across the boulevard; in short, life was going on. I looked at the thick concrete wall and the black bars and couldn't quite comprehend how rocks and iron occupying a width of air space two feet wide could take on such significance, the difference between life and quasi-death. I was staring at it, rage growing, and my heart beginning to thump as I felt an uncontrollable desire to try to bend the iron bars apart and scream, "Andreas, let's get out of here!" when the guard appeared and told me my visit was to begin.

I hadn't thought much about where I would meet Andreas: possibly his cell, since he was the only prisoner in the front quarters of the building, or maybe a room nearby—one of the offices where he saw his lawyers. Thus I was surprised to see that I was being led into the chicken-wire structure from which the doors to the court opened. As I stepped in I heard a voice greet me with "Hi, Margaret!" I turned my head left to see a row of cages and, behind thick mesh, the silhouette of a man from the waist up, his features indistinguishable, but the outline of his head recognizable, as well as his voice. It was Andreas.

I was shocked and shaken, and unprepared. In an attempt to gather all my powers of self-control and give a bright "Hello, darling" in response to his greeting, I didn't even notice the clustering around of three guards behind me, one holding a tommy gun in his hand. There was an iron railing three feet from the cages, about the height of my waist, which I banged into in trying to get close to the mesh wire. Then I noticed there were openings on either end of the ten-foot-long rail, and I slipped through and reached the cage. The structure was cement from the floor up, again to waist level, with a half-foot-wide wooden counter jutting out at that point. I had my dark glasses on and removed them, thinking that this would help me see my husband more clearly. It didn't help. Andreas told me immediately that I would have to speak in Greek, and it was then that I became aware of the listening ears surrounding me. Behind Andreas, slightly to the left, I could make out another figure, that of a guard, the shape of a tommy gun vaguely visible at the end of his arms. I strained to see Andreas, putting my nose on the wire, pulling back to a different position, turning my head at an angle, blinking my eyes.

"How are you, darling?" I managed to ask.

"As well as can be expected. How are the kids?"

"I—I didn't expect to see you this way," I blurted out, detesting the quaver that insisted on entering my voice. At least, I thought, he can't see my eyes, undoubtedly stained again, and shadowed, or my dry lips under this brave red paint.

"I know. I know. I'm going to talk to the director about it" was the reply. That was Andreas. He would try to do something, even as a captive.

He told me about his arrival at the jail from Pikermi, his quarters, the furnishings (iron cot with thin mattress, one table for writing, one chair, a small table next to his bed, a sink for washing, and a dresser with three drawers; there were hooks for hanging his clothes). He asked about everyone in the family, about Marjorie, my mother and father, his mother, about Tito, whom we referred to as "the chef" because of his expertise in barbecuing, and about Kiveli, the "wife of the chef." With every bit of conversation being listened to, it was obvious that our subject matter would be restricted. Through these subjects—the family, friends, the children's health and school activities—I would have to learn to convey things that were going on outside. But it was too soon to think of this. Emotionally I was being torn apart with feelings of sympathy, love, frustration, concern. At one point a dizziness overcame me, and I clung to the wooden counter edge, hoping it would be unnoticed.

"Are you all right, Margaret?" Andreas asked immediately.

"I'm fine, fine . . . it's just that . . ." and I struggled to push down the wave of darkness that was washing up from the cement floor beneath my feet.

"Yes, what is it?" The note in his voice suggested that he thought maybe I was hiding some information I had, something ominous.

"It's nothing, honey. It's just that I love you so much, and this . . ." I couldn't finish. Yet I was determined to hang on to the corner of consciousness that I possessed, not to let Andreas see me faint or break down emotionally and, above all, not to give that satisfaction to the swine behind me.

"Don't feel pessimistic!" Andreas' voice came through with a sharp enough ring to shake the swimming parts of my brain back into place. The undertones told another story, and I thought of what the last forty-eight hours must have been for him, the shock of being taken, without notice, from a relatively comfortable hotel room to the isolation of a jail cell. I had resolved to leave him with a feeling of hope and confidence, but now I was confronted unexpectedly with this inhuman contraption and a shadow with a familiar voice. It had ripped my thin wall of courage and resolve and left me stammering. Now it was he giving me confidence.

Then I did something odd, on impulse. I took a cigarette out of my purse and lit it. I was absolutely sure this was against the rules, but I needed a moment of respite, and, perhaps, a small act of defiance. It worked. The guards were taken by surprise. Since Andreas was a special prisoner and I a special visitor (with three armed men assigned to me!), they were uncertain what to say, and hence said nothing. There was no ashtray, so I flicked the ashes—with gusto—on the floor. This enabled me to get through the last ten minutes with remarkable aplomb. I told Andreas about Frank Newman's visit and intent to help, and Andreas suggested some things to have Frank do. I told him about Jim's intentions ("the husband of Ruthie, my university roommate"—I didn't want to give too much information for fear Jim's visit might be stopped). I told him Jim was planning to bring along Pat Brown. I told him I had a long talk with Norbert at the *American Embassy* (loudly), and that it was most satisfactory (lie). I said clearly and many times—"American Embassy," as if I were constantly running around with the higher-ups, and on the best of terms with all. I spilled out all the good news I could think of—and then some. I stumbled over my Greek, and we both laughed. Andreas knew what I was doing, that I was giving the impression of a bubbly, talkative scatterbrain who moved around in powerful circles as if it were her native habitat, and that I was exaggerating the positive side for the listening ears as well as those to whom our conversation would be reported. I was cheering us both up. He knew me well, and I wasn't fooling him, but we both needed the exercise.

The guard told us our time was up. Resentfully, I shambled off, throwing kisses to the hazy figure in the vile cage, a headache piercing my skull and worsening in the hot sun as I stepped out of the iron doors. I walked with long deliberate strides away from Averoff Prison, chatting and smiling with Marjorie. (See that tall, blonde woman—she is Andreas Papandreou's wife. See, she walks with confidence and talks with gaiety. Obviously she knows Andreas can't be kept behind those walls for very long.) In a childish way I was playing a game, feverishly hoping that the pretense would become reality, that my act would influence the decision of Andreas' fate. I drove home with Tito once again, as from Pikermi, in gloomy silence.

When I saw Frank Newman a week later, he told me about his visit with Ambassador Talbot. He described him as "hospitable, careful, noncommittal, curious." When Frank told Talbot that Andreas could not see his lawyer privately—which was the case—Talbot asked, "What's your direct evidence that this is so?" This was indeed a hostile question. Obviously the only *direct* evidence one could have would be the word of a neutral observer, or my word that Andreas had told me so, or the word of the lawyer present. This issue became a source of friction between me and those at the embassy, who argued that the government had assured them that Andreas was having private consultations. Although I reported regularly that he was being given no chance to prepare his defense for the trial, Talbot and Kay Bracken, chief of the political section, continued to assert to my friends who inquired, either in person or by letter, that "we have just been told by the Minister of Justice that Mr. Papandreou sees his lawyer alone." Or "Prime Minister Kollias reiterated that Mr. Papandreou has private consultations with his lawyer." It was obvious that they wanted to be relieved of the responsibility of pressuring the junta on anything that had to do with Andreas Papandreou, despite the fact that he was the husband of an American citizen.

Frank told me he had one solid proposal. We should immediately begin to insist that official observers be invited to watch the trial. I was in absolute agreement with the suggestion. My own feeling for some time now had been that the louder noise and splash we made about the ASPIDA trial, the more difficult for them to stage it. Or, if they did stage it, the more extreme would be the consequences in terms of world opinion. I asked if he could take on the coordination of the observer's activity, looking into names of well-known people in the judicial profession who could be asked to participate, as well as the question of funds for this purpose. He agreed to do so, saying he would contact Ken Galbraith for assistance.

I said good-bye to Frank with sadness. He was sanity in an insane world, a man whose values I understood, liberal, humane, decent. He told me how to reach him, and we agreed on a method to keep in touch. He also said he would fly down again if the need arose, or if, for any reason, I wanted him in Athens. He left me with this comforting thought.

In the midst of this turmoil, fear, arrests, and intimidation, an American company, Litton Industries, announced it had signed a contract with the junta for Greek development. It was written up in the *Herald Tribune* on May 17, 1967: "Litton Industries and the new Greek government have agreed on an ambitious project for developing Crete and the Western Peloponnesus. The accord was hailed as the first major economic achievement of the three-week-old government of Prime Minister Constantine Kollias."

Litton had approached Andreas in early 1965 when he was acting Minister of Coordination with an attractive proposal that they bring investment into Greece according to a development program which would be carefully worked out by American and Greek economists, within the framework of the government's five-year development plan. The Papandreou government agreed to pay for a preliminary study, after which the proposal would be brought to Parliament for consideration. The proposal turned out to be an exploitation of the Greek nation. Parliament turned it down. Thus it was lying around as a scheme when the tanks descended on Athens, and in the wake of the tanks came Litton Industries in vulgar haste to wrap up a deal with the colonels. The colonels obviously couldn't have cared less for the Greek nation and they were hungrily searching for some item of prestige, particularly on the economic front, to show that investment was welcome, on any terms, and that the government was considered stable. What Litton neglected to consider was that development required people, not only businessmen outside of Greece willing to invest in this precarious situation, but people inside Greece

willing to cooperate. The Greeks did such a magnificent job of noncoopera-
tion and sabotage of the efforts, and the company ran into so many snafus,
that it found it impossible to come anywhere near their promised scheme to
raise and manage $830 million.*

As for my requests to Anschuetz for help, I had received no word by the
end of the following week. I then wrote up my first two requests, even
suggesting appropriate wording I wanted the American Ambassador to use in
protesting to the junta the "Bulgarian-communist" newspaper attacks. In the
second request, to remonstrate against the searches of my home, I also
included a long list of items taken.

When I next saw Anschuetz he told me, "Oh, yes, about your requests. I
saw Markezinis at a cocktail party, and since it was his paper *Estia* which was
doing most of the attack, I asked him to tell them to lay off." This was not
the point. I wanted the junta to know that I had embassy support; I wanted
to press the junta again and again with something having to do with the
Papandreous, and I wanted a denial of the Bulgarian-communist smear printed
in the Greek-controlled press. Of course, it was a lot to ask of a helpless
embassy from a powerless country to demand that they ask the truth to be
printed about one of their citizens. The attacks stopped, but the damage had
been done, and I heard reverberations of this from many sources, including
American, for months to come. As for the searches, all that had been done
was to turn my list of confiscated items over to Mr. Peterson in the visa
division of the embassy to try to get them returned to me. As for the lawyers,
he asked me to write the names again. He had misplaced the note.

In the general atmosphere of oppression and helplessness, resentment and
desire to resist developed. As the intentions of the colonels became more
clear, it became obvious that no return to democracy was contemplated and
that Greece was going to be turned into a "banana republic," with the new
military elite pocketing the profits that used to go to the old establishment, at
the expense of the people. Hatred and disgust became the emotions of the
day. I cannot say that this clairvoyance on the aims and prospects of the
dictatorship was general. Some felt that the ridiculousness of the colonels and
their ineptitude at governing would be their downfall. Others put their hopes
in the King. Still others felt that the pressure of the western world,
particularly Europe, would force them out. And there were some who thought
the corruption in government would stop, forgetting that these were primarily
village boys who were tasting power, the excitement of bright lights, publicity,
and easy money for the first time.

Certain acts of resistance started to take place. One of the first had been by
Eleni Vlahou, the editor of two large newspapers, who closed down her shop
and refused to publish. No cajoling on the part of the colonels could change
her mind. She claimed she could not publish unless freedom of the press were
restored. This hurt the colonels because Vlahou's papers, *Kathimerini* and
Mesimvrini, were conservative, rightist newspapers, and this refusal to publish

---

*In October, 1969, the deal between Greece and Litton collapsed.

belied the colonels' contention that they had acted to thwart a communist coup.

During this time a group of Center Union men, particularly those close to Andreas, started meeting secretly to determine what action could be taken on the political front to show resistance. Some, indiscreetly, turned up at my house to discuss their plans, and asked me to try to pass them on to Andreas. Two schemes developed. Neither was to be successful. One was to organize an extraordinary session of Parliament with all deputies who were out of jail, from Left to Right, on the lawn of the American Embassy on one evening, not yet chosen. The session would begin at seven, normal starting time for the Greek Parliament. Foreign journalists were to be contacted and asked to be present to follow the meeting. They were aware that it would mean the arrest of the entire Parliament, but it would show courage and determination, and a unity of the political world. To stop any possibility of deputies becoming active or to carry out their plan of a parliamentary session, nine from the Center Union were arrested on the night of May 24.

The second scheme was to organize passive resistance of all the Greek people for May 28, the day elections had been scheduled. With no radio and no newspaper, instructions would have to be circulated through "whisper." The instructions were to *stay home* on that Sunday from sunup to sundown. Some "whispers" I got said from sunup until noon. Nevertheless, the general theme began to get around.

During the month after the coup the junta applied a technique of arrests—then some liberalization, relaxation, release. As the mood of the people hardened toward resistance, particularly under this purposely wavering policy, as the bodies started popping up from under the water, looking as if they were about to swim, they were pushed down under again. This meant new arrests, new restrictive measures, new harassment. The theory must have been that this method would cull out the natural opponents of the regime. They were encouraged in some sense or other to make themselves visible. The expectation was that each time fewer and fewer heads would pop up. (My expectation is that at some point, bursting their lungs for fresh air, they will pop up all at once.)

On Sunday, May 21, Virginia came by. It was the first time I had seen her since our conversation in the backyard. Her face looked yellow and drawn. Dark rings of perspiration showed under her arms on her pink blouse, a sign of tension. When I offered her a cup of coffee, she shook her head. "It's my stomach," she said. "There's a constant pain in it, and nothing seems to sit right."

I opened the door to the terrace, and we moved into the golden sunshine and the deceptive feeling of safety in the enclosed backyard. Virginia was a beautiful woman, about thirty, lustrous brown eyes thickly lashed, jet-black hair worn in a short, boyish fashion, and just a slight tendency to overweight. Even in the harsh sunlight and with the expression of fear permeating her face, she was a stunning sight. I admired her greatly because, although terrified, she persisted in her antijunta fight.

"I have a document from Mikis," she told me.

"And you insist on bringing it here?" I asked her in surprise, and some annoyance.

"No, no, I haven't brought it. It is hidden."

"Hidden well?"

"Yes."

"Please, Virginia. Keep nothing in your house. Listen to someone who has experienced three searches."

She nodded in agreement. "He has announced the formation of an organization. It's to be called the Patriotic Front."

"He has announced it to whom?"

"People are circulating it as much as possible, particularly among foreign journalists."

"Then we should read about it soon in the foreign press."

"He wants me to become a member of the board, and wants suggestions for more Center Union people to participate."

"You sound as if you have seen him," I commented.

"I have."

"You were careful?"

For the first time the corner of her mouth lifted in a tight smile. "I changed cars three times, was walked for half an hour through crooked little streets, entered an apartment building from the rear, was asked to close my eyes in the elevator so that I wouldn't see the floor number, and the same process occurred when I returned. Not only would it have been impossible to follow me, but it would be impossible for me to describe how the hell I got there."

"How is he?" I asked quietly, as if talking about a doomed man.

"He's awful. There are dark circles under his eyes, he has a bad cold and cough, and his eyes are red from the smoke and stuffiness of the closed-up apartment he is in. He is like a trapped animal, but he is fighting. He even composes music from time to time."

"You want some suggestions for names of Center Union people to participate, I take it."

"That's what I've been asked to do."

"Virginia, I can't take any initiative without consulting Andreas, and the conditions under which I talk to him are so restrictive that it is almost impossible to convey anything more than the simplest bit of information or thought. Furthermore, I know that the Center people are organizing a resistance group. Maybe it should be the other way around, that is, the Patriotic Front should join forces with them and participate on their national board. If we assume that the Center forces represent most of the Greek people, shouldn't they take the leadership in the fight, and wouldn't that make it more likely to succeed?"

Virginia looked thoughtful and worried. "I frankly don't care how it's done—just so it's done."

"I know how you feel," I said, and I was surprised to hear the passion and bitterness in my voice.

We walked around the yard for a while saying nothing. I was sharply conscious of how alone we were, how difficult the task, what odds were against us. Two women—I a Midwesterner, simple product of the University of Minnesota; she a Greek, valedictorian of her high-school class in Larissa; mothers, both of us—caught in this Byzantine nightmare, victims of a gang in the army, trying to use our brains and pitiful resources against this rape of Greece. For me it was combined with the fight for my husband. For her it was pure gut reaction to the crushing of the soul of this beautiful country. But that gang was ready to kill. Were we ready to kill, assuming we had the means? It seemed to me that this was not only an essential but a necessary ingredient of an antidictatorial fight. Our way of winning a battle had been through political means, through persuasion, competence, and ultimately the ballot box. Our means were open, direct. Could we function in the swamp of spies, secret service, lies, deception, torture, brutality—and with no respect for the human being?

"Virginia, we're babes in the wood," I told her.

"What did you say?" Virginia's thoughts were clearly elsewhere.

"What I said means that we are inexperienced, naïve tender, if you like. We are sitting ducks, and we are going to get hurt. More hurt, that is."

"I understand what you mean. But is there any other way?"

"No," I sighed. "There is no other way."

I agreed to try my best to get instructions from Andreas. She suggested that I send her a note with Georgie on a day when Georgie would be going into town after school and could easily stop by her house in Kolonaki to deliver it. This way we would minimize our own contacts. I started to walk back with her, planning to take her through the house and to the front door, but she told me she preferred to go out herself and could always argue that she had dropped by to see my mother-in-law. Bit by bit she was learning caution, excuses, subterfuge—as we all were. I kissed her on both cheeks, and whispered "Take care," then watched her short, plumpish figure—which somehow looked frail now—vanish into the shadows of the house. I wondered when I would see her again.

Eventually I sent her a note with the man designated by Andreas to have discussions with the head of the Patriotic Front. It was concluded that they would maintain separate organizations in what Andreas called a "parallel fight," with some contact and eventually an agreement for collaboration. The Center forces represented at least 53 percent of the Greek people, and it was there that the resistance leadership belonged, Andreas said. It was against the Center Union that the coup had been staged, not against the Left, as the colonels purported. The problem was that the Center people were less knowledgeable in organization than the Left and far less experienced in clandestine activities. This is why the Left had a good chance of eventually taking over the leadership of the antijunta fight, and why the colonels dealt such a heavy blow to the democratic forces of the West by their sinful deed of the night of April 21. They attacked and tried to kill off the healthy forces of the Center, the only force that can fight extremism of either Left or Right.

While resistance movements were taking their first baby steps inside Greece, a resistance movement was building up outside of Greece. The democratic, liberal elements in the European countries and in the United States were joining hands in an attempt to use whatever means at their disposal to thwart the colonels in their attempt to enslave the Greek people. Most of the negative reaction was from the West, shocking the puzzled colonels who had expected to be applauded for halting a communist take-over. They finally explained this by saying it was the communist elements in all of these nations who were leading the antijunta battle, drawing in others more innocent and unaware of the truth. It was only the colonels who were in possession of the truth, of course. Eventually just about everyone fell in this category and was attacked in the government-controlled press: Jens Otto Krag, Prime Minister of Denmark, Tage Erlander, Prime Minister of Sweden, Wilson of Great Britain, Eric Rouleau of *Le Monde*, Cedric Thornberry of the *Guardian*, the London *Times* (as a whole), *The New York Times* (as a whole), all the professors of the United States—just to mention a few!

From the East there were blasts from Radio Sophia on the Voice of Truth, but that was the only regular squeak. One statement was made by the Soviet representative at the United Nations condemning the military take-over, saying that it would have "unforeseen consequences." Young people of the Soviet Union gathered in front of the Greek Embassy in Moscow in protest, but the truly vigorous protesters were the youth of the western European countries.

Leading the fight in the early stages was a country that had some special significance for the Greeks—Denmark. Young Anna Maria, Queen of Greece, was from Denmark. When Constantinos had married eighteen-year-old Anna Maria, the Greeks had hoped it would mark a change in the history of kingship in their country, that it would make the royal institution a more democratic one. Their hopes were soon dashed, but the people of Denmark were keeping the faith.

The Sunday before the coup, a remarkable young Dane by the name of Mogens Camre had come down to Greece to spend the week with us, and then would have joined us on the trip to Salonika where my father-in-law had planned to open his election campaign. Mogens was a member of the Social Democratic party, a close collaborator of Jens Otto Krag in his post in the Ministry of Finance, and the former head of the party's youth group. We had met Mogens the year before during our much-touted and maligned Scandinavian tour and since then had been in close touch with him, developing ambitious plans to have closer ties between the Center Union party of Greece and the social democratic parties of Europe. Andreas was hoping to be able to send some of the young political leaders of Greece to European countries for training in party organization, and some of the union leaders for training in trade unionism, and the Danish party had indicated its willingness to support financially such an activity.

Mogens had also sniffed out the coming Greek dictatorship while in Denmark, which is not too surprising in view of the tie between the two royal families. Surely Anna Maria was aware of the Big Junta conniving. But even without this means of information, any astute political leader in the West knew of the threat to Greek democracy. As a result, and with Krag's blessing, he came down to see what could be done—if anything—to help avoid this

Greek tragedy. He felt that if stopping a military take-over was impossible, then at least one should be prepared for the steps to be taken immediately thereafter to fight the tyrants. It was he who pointed out the significance of NATO on this score and read us its preamble: "the protection of freedom and democratic institutions within the countries belonging to the Alliance."

The night after we had discussed this very point, Mogens was awakened in his hotel room by the sound of rumbling, clanking tanks and looked out the window on Constitution Square to see liberty being defiled. He took some memorable pictures from his balcony in the eerie, unearthly light of early morning as the tanks, jeeps, and soldiers occupied the square, as mighty Acropolis in its awful, glorious sculptural stillness stood a silent observer to this latest bit of human insanity. It was also Mogens who had arranged for the Danish and Swedish reporters to interview me the evening of April 22 and to arrange for one of them to take pictures and letters out.

Andreas had asked me in one visit I had in Pikermi to get a note out to Mogens, who left Greece on Sunday, April 23, urging him to pursue the NATO line we had discussed.

In my letter to him written May 3, carried out, and mailed from New York May 5, I wrote the following paragraph:

> But the truly most effective and important weapon is NATO—as you so rightly understood. If NATO takes a stand and indicates to the US that this may foul up the entire alliance and make every country reconsider its position vis-à-vis NATO, then I believe the US may be obliged to take stronger measures to pressure return to democratic government. Their attitude is not a good one. They feel somehow that they can deal with these military minds better than the "corrupt" minds of the politicians. And they also seem to feel that the military government can accomplish things within the country that could not be accomplished otherwise. They do not understand the Greek people. But they pale when NATO is mentioned. Since they look at Greece primarily as a military base, this is one item that scares them. If you were to succeed on this crusade I am positive the situation would change here.

Mogens and his Prime Minister had already been thinking along these lines. On May 5, the same day my letter was mailed from New York, a news dispatch to *The New York Times* bore the following headline: Denmark Rebukes Greece at NATO over Army Coup; Norway Concurs. The report read as follows:

> Diplomatic manuevering today averted a potential crisis in the North Atlantic Treaty Organization over denunciation of the Greek military coup by Denmark.
>
> The Greeks had threatened to walk out if Denmark was permitted to read its attack at the regular meeting Wednesday of the NATO Permanent Council. Italy's Manlio Brosio, secretary general of NATO, had cancelled the Wednesday session and sought to placate the Danes and the Greeks.

> *Instead of pressing for the meeting, Denmark today circulated a White Paper to the NATO ambassadors, blasting Greece for squelching civil liberties.*
>
> *Norway, in a letter to Brosio, which was circulated to all delegations, associated itself with the Danish condemnation, saying it hoped Greek political prisoners would be released, democratic rights restored and conditions normalized as soon as possible.*

On the personal battlefront, the fight for Andreas' freedom, I initiated some steps. Andreas had been invited to attend the Pacem in Terris II Peace Conference in Geneva being held May 28–30, sponsored by the United Nations and organized by the Center for the Study of Democratic Institutions in Santa Barbara, California. His original plan had been to stay in Greece through election day, May 28, then fly to Geneva for the second and third days of the convocation. Representatives of western and eastern nations were participating. Andreas was the only Greek to be invited, and the Greek people were excited by this honor. Now Andreas' participation would be from a distance, from a different podium—behind the iron bars of a jail cell window. But it was, I thought, an excellent arena in which to denounce the Greek dictatorship, to point out the absence of the "delegate from Greece," and the reasons for that absence.

I wrote on May 3, to Professor George Lianis:

> *I think the best way to make use of this would be to call Alexander [Professor Alec Alexander, chairman of the Department of Economics at Santa Barbara, California, a fellow Greek and friend] and ask him to go see Robert Hutchins, chairman of the convocation from the Center for the Study of Democratic Institutions, and recommend the following:*
>
> *1. An empty place at the conference table with A.'s name and word Greece on a placard at the table.*
>
> *2. A special, extra session on the first day on militarism, taking away of human rights in Greece and the threat to the peace of Europe by the establishment of a fascist regime. I would like to recommend that Galbraith participate in this session—he was an invitee and he knows something about the situation here. It would be good to have an outstanding conservative from some country participate as well so that it doesn't take on a special leftist color. Alex can go into this thoroughly—but he should insist that it be included on the agenda.*
>
> *3. Ask that Pacem in Terris II under Hutchins' leadership wire the Greek government and ask that A. be given permission to attend the three day conference. Such as the following:*
>
> > *Your Excellency———. On behalf of the Pacem in Terris convocation, we would like to request your government to release A.G.P. for purposes of attending this conference in Geneva on May 28, 29, 30. We would consider it an honor to have him participate and an honor to Greece to have him come.*

Send copies to:
Stylianos Pattakos, Minister of Interior
George Papadopoulos, Minister to the P.M.
Constantine Kollias, P.M.
Copy to the American Embassy and the Greek Embassy in Washington
And, of course, publicity in the newspapers.

On Thursday, May 25, the "Fighting Group of Guizi 58," as we tabbed ourselves, were all out on the terrace watching Tito prepare the grill for the cooking of baby lamb chops. Kiveli was chatting with Andreas' mother, her voice raised to overcome the hearing weakness my mother-in-law had, and doing her usual bit of morale-building propaganda. In the most desperate of situations, Kiveli and Tito always found the positive side, or the elements of hope, and inflated our flattened spirits. The week had been a tense one and a sad one as we approached the day that was meant to be our day of victory, May 28. Although I had written to several others—Frank Newman, Siggie Mineiko (Andreas' cousin in Paris), Mogens Camre—about the need to make use of the Pacem in Terris II·Conference, I had heard nothing and felt a sense of futility.

I don't remember hearing the doorbell. Probably one of the children opened the door. Suddenly in our midst, filling out the entryway to the terrace with his height and breadth, ears sticking out like handles, a boyish grin on his face, was someone introducing himself by saying, "My name is Stanley Sheinbaum." He walked forward out into the terrace, hesitated a moment as he looked at Marjorie and me, then said tentatively, "Margaret?" his hand extended, but wavering between the two of us.

"I'm Margaret," I said, getting up. "This is Marjorie, and Tito and Kiveli. . ." and I went through the introductions.

"I'm sorry I just busted in like this. I thought this was perhaps the best way, rather than use the telephone."

"It's the only way," I said grimly.

"I'm on my way to Pacem in Terris in Geneva, and came round to Athens to see you before getting there. Alexander sends his regards."

At last a squeak from the outer world. I was sure this meant that Alexander had gotten my message. Now I remembered who Stanley Sheinbaum was—a member of the Center for the Study of Democratic Institutions. Some weeks before the coup we had received a note from him saying how pleased he was that Andreas would be at the peace convocation and that he would be through Athens the week before and would enjoy having a chance to see Andreas. Andreas had told me at the time that Stan had been a student at Stanford when they had met, and later they both had attended a conference at Santa Barbara. We had decided to drop him a letter and suggest that he have dinner with us while in Athens, a letter which he received in Santa Barbara the morning of April 21! Since that time I had forgotten all about our dinner invitation.

"Stanley," I said, "excuse my bad hospitality, but I forgot completely that we had invited you for dinner with us. I realize you are not showing up to honor that invitation, but could you join us for a simple barbecue on the terrace?"

Stanley said, "With pleasure" and settled himself on the settee next to me, and we started a five-hour session of talk which lasted through Tito's perfectly grilled lamb chops, Antigone's tossed green salad, a bottle of retsina and on into the evening until a cool May breeze came up and chased us inside, where we completed the conversation in the living room.

We went over all the things that could be done at the convocation. Stan had already set the mechanism into motion and promised to see it through. We discussed a campaign of letters that would flood the Greek post offices, directed to Papadopoulos, Pattakos, and Kollias, demanding the release of Andreas Papandreou. I told him that I had been in touch with Leo Hurwicz and George Lianis about this, and suggested he reach them on his return to the States. We discussed the life expectancy of the dictatorship, and there Stan was brutally frank and pessimistic. He was convinced the United States would do nothing to shake it up, and would eventually come around to supporting it, hoping it could take on enough of a veneer of democracy to stop the Europeans from hollering. I suggested that he might try to get someone to do a deeper story on the ASPIDA case. I pointed out to him that ASPIDA had been in the foreign press for two years, always as something sinister associated with Andreas, but never had anyone tried to put the story in its proper perspective. As one of the founding editors of *Ramparts* magazine, Stan was the person to promote another story that would tell the truth. Neither of us knew at the moment how deep an involvement Stan would have in uncovering the ASPIDA frame-up.

As we were beginning to unwind, about midnight, the doorbell rang. My stomach did its usual flip-flop. Marjorie gave me a startled look of apprehension, then nervously thrust her feet into shoes she had kicked off and went to answer the door. Tito and Kiveli had left an hour earlier. She returned to tell me that a young fellow, about twenty-seven, was asking to see me, and looking rather excited. He wouldn't give his name but said to tell Mrs. Margaret that Aristotle sent him. I excused myself and called him into the dining room, turned up the tape music which had been playing softly, and waited for him to talk. He had a frown between his brows and seemed not to have his full attention on me, but to be listening to sounds in the distance, his neck stretched like a bird ready to take off into flight.

"Were you followed?" I asked, bringing his eyes into focus on me and the room.

"No, no, I don't think so," he answered, but his voice did not have a ring of absolute certainty. He identified himself as a member of a Center resistance group. He pulled out the small white paper that covers cigarettes in a Greek package and wrote a number on it—114—then hastily scribbled them out as if he might at that moment be caught with his pencil forming the name of an illegal organization. Then he looked up at me, it suddenly dawning on him that I might not even have seen what he wrote.

"Did you see it?" he asked, concerned.

"I saw it. Is it the name?"

"We call it Democratic Resistance One One Four."

One-one-four. How often I had heard that shout in the streets during George Papandreou's rallies, the number of the article of the Constitution that entrusts the safeguarding of the Constitution with the Greeks.

"It's a good name," I said, now feeling my nerves tighten, an inevitable accompaniment to any resistance under the long black shadow of tyranny.

"Mrs. Margarita," he said breathlessly, "we have prepared a resistance manifesto and we want it circulated at the conference that Mr. Andreas was going to speak at in Switzerland. Can you get it out?"

"Do you have it?"

"Yes, here." He tapped his chest, indicating an inside pocket.

"Is it in English?"

"Yes, one of the fellows translated it into English."

"It's rather late, you know. And who should receive it there and circulate it?"

"Yerondopoulos."

"He'll be there?"

"That's the information we had earlier. He can be reached at the number we wrote at the top of the paper."

"Can you show the paper to me?"

He took out a piece of onionskin paper that had been folded into a tiny square, about the size that could be swallowed in a moment, or turned to ashes with the flame of one match. I saw my own hands shaking as I held it toward the light to read. To avoid this, I flattened it on the table, smoothing out its creases, and saw a typed, single-spaced document appealing to the countries of the world to comdemn the Greek dictatorship and to take immediate action in demanding the restoration of the Constitution, the release of political prisoners, and the reinstatement of civil liberties. One long paragraph was a vicious attack on the United States and its policy in Greece. In some ways it was not dissimilar to Theodorakis' Patriotic Front bulletin, but it was less poetic and had a more precise appeal. Someone with a good pen, strong views, and an understanding of what makes an effective appeal in the West had worked on the composition.

"I will get it out," I said.

His face was transformed from anxiety to relief, the frown faded, and his entire body seemed to drop about two inches into a more relaxed pose. I knew that feeling, too. He had transferred the responsibility of handling this hot piece of paper (one could almost see the price tag dangling from the corner—ten years in prison, or more) to someone else. His part of the mission was complete. I undoubtedly underwent the same transformation when I handed the paper some minutes later to Stanley Sheinbaum. I told Stan to call Siggie Mineiko in Paris as soon as he got to Geneva and tell him that he had a resistance document, that Mineiko should come to Geneva, reach Yerondopoulos and prepare it for mimeographing and distribution. And this is how a statement signed "Greek Democratic Resistance" was distributed at the Pacem in Terris II Peace Conference.

Stanley left with a promise to return in two weeks after completing European activities of his own.

By now we were getting close to Greek election day, a day of shame for the dictators. On May 27, the day before, the thugs of the security police arrested a onetime secretary of Andreas Papandreou, Helen Hahnikian, age thirty-one and mother of a nine-year-old girl, on charges of "harboring communists" in her home. The wheel of tyranny was turning, and the liberties of the Greek people were being inexorably ground beneath it.

CHAPTER TWENTY-ONE

One-Two-Three-Ziss-Boom

ELECTION day, May 28, 1967, was gloriously warm and sunny. I awoke early, as was now my habit, and propped my head up with two pillows in order to gaze through the open French doors which led to the balcony. From this position I could see the top needles of an aged pine tree whose branches provided shade for the ground-floor terrace below, and the sky of azure blue with puffs of white clouds floating carelessly by.

It was a day that would have smacked of excitement and promise, under different circumstances. I permitted my mind to imagine what the day would have been without the junta. Andreas would have dressed in a business suit to go to his constituency to vote. This election he had planned to place his candidacy in Athens instead of Patras. Ordinarily on Sunday the children would sleep late, but this Sunday they would have been up to accompany their father to the voting area, to enjoy the tingling entanglement of the race. We would have had breakfast together, soft-boiled eggs (a Sunday must), toasted village bread, hot coffee and hot chocolate, and Ymettus honey. Undoubtedly we would have had only momentary peace, as people from Andreas' political office, friends, and relatives, would have arrived to make their last-minute predictions on the outcome, and to be near a winner.

By 7 P.M. we would have been at the President's house listening to the first returns on Athens Radio, and if results were as predicted, by midnight we would have had victory in our hands, and the crowds would have swelled to thousands, intoxicated by a people's victory, and eager to shake Andreas' and George Papandreou's hands.

Instead there was an empty place next to me in bed, a household of fatherless children, my father-in-law lying in a hospital bed under guard, and a nation in bondage.

I sighed, wishing I could get some pleasure out of the fabulous beauty of Greece and find again that deep sense of joy that a May morning on rocky, flower scented, clear-aired Attica can bring. I flung my bare feet to the floor on the blue carpet, not more than a few steps from where the bloodstains from Andreas' torn knee were still visible, an ink blot that could be interpreted only one way: brutality. I walked over to my wardrobe closet and chose a dress with disinterest, avoiding too long a gaze at the closet next to it containing Andreas' clothes. I had the feeling one must have looking at a dead man's clothes. I would tell myself Andreas is alive. It's a fight with possibilities, a battle not lost. This morning lecture to myself was the shot I needed to give me the strength to face the day.

On the side table on Andreas' side of the bed was his photograph taken three years earlier and used on posters in his first election campaign. I liked the picture. Apart from showing to advantage his good looks, it brought out two of the characteristics I liked most in him: his strength of character and his deep kindness. As I glanced at it that morning while dressing, I became aware that in prison his hair had gotten much grayer. I was aware of something else, that with the passage of time I was ceasing to look at his photo, just as I avoided looking at anything that reminded me too poignantly and vividly of him, and of our life prior to the dictatorship. Slowly, slowly, I was closing up my emotional world, putting it on ice, so to speak. My senses had dulled and stimuli were recorded as through an anesthetic. None of the things I loved awakened in me the sense of being alive, that vibrant life force that surges through the soul when seeing the play of color on a mountain landscape, the smell of pine after a fire, the impish smile of a naughty child, the nonsense words of a swinging tune. Gone too was sexual desire—cold, numb, dead.

But just as I was aware of these things that morning of May 28, my awareness itself was muffled. I felt indifferent to this narcosis of my senses. I made a mental note of this phenomenon as if I were recording items on a patient in a clinic.

I was finishing my dressing when a tap came on my bedroom door.

"Mom?"

"Yes?"

"It's George. Can I come in?"

"Of course, Georgie." A tall, slender fourteen-year-old in wrinkled pajamas and uncombed hair pushed his way in.

"What are you doing up so early?" I asked. George was the family's best late morning riser.

"I couldn't sleep very well. I had pains in my side. Here. Do I have fever?" He walked over to me to have me put my hand on his forehead.

"I don't believe so, honey. But we can get the thermometer to make sure. You may have a slight one. What seems to be the trouble?"

"When I went to bed last night I had these awful pains in my kidneys."

"Your kidneys? How do you know it was your kidneys?"

"Well, here," he said, putting his hand on his back by his hip. "Isn't that where the kidneys are?"

"More or less," I answered, "but that doesn't mean that a pain in that area is in the kidneys. It could be caused by a number of things."

"I probably have some awful kidney disease," he said, looking at me as if he wanted me to think he was making a joke, but I saw too much anxiety in his face for him to carry it off.

"We can have it checked, George," I said, trying to lighten his mood a bit. "It's probably just gas. Don't go getting romantic about it." George didn't smile. I suggested that we go down and have some breakfast together, and he readily agreed, obviously not interested in the delights of late morning slumber.

We talked for about an hour in the dining room, the sun streaming in from the doors of the side terrace, laying long fingers of light across the dining room table and swelling into the sun-drenched hallway. The doors to the living room were closed in order not to disturb Marjorie, who had usurped the couch for her bed. Marjorie had become a resident of the house by now, the transferral of essential belongings almost complete, although we still hung on to her apartment for whatever use might be made of it.

Georgie wanted to tell me about a dream he had, which still remained vivid to him. His father was coming out of Parliament, and everybody was waiting in excited anticipation, thrilled and happy to be able to see him again. Andreas came out and everyone cheered. Then they all turned toward the pillars and stairway again, waiting for his grandfather to come and to speak to them. He appeared in the doorway, a wizened old man, looking like those starvation pictures, George said, of people in India. He walked slowly down the white steps and as he reached the bottom, he opened his mouth to speak. Instead of words, a bark came out, and then another, and as the barks got more rapid, his body was transformed into that of a dog, until finally he was a small, scraggly mutt, lying on the ground and yapping. Everyone was embarrassed, according to Georgie, and he himself quietly sneaked away. I told George not to give great importance to the dream, that there was nothing particularly significant about it; it just proved that he was restless and disturbed.

We talked about many things, including the night of the coup. George still insisted that somehow his father should have been able to escape, but he did not say this time that if he had not been huddled there in the corner when the soldiers came, his father would have gone undetected. I didn't know whether he was finally convinced that he bore no blame, or whether it was now something he didn't talk about openly. He told me school was a bore, and, anyway, the atmosphere was lousy. He thought the world was a mess—all fouled up—and another world war inevitable. When we finished he told me he was going up to play his guitar. I told him to come and play for me later in the morning, and he gave me a big, broad, happy grin of pride—and I realized I hadn't seen that bright smile of his for a long time now.

I was expecting Tito and Kiveli any minute. It was the day that we were staying at home in protest at the loss of a basic right in a democratic society, the right to vote. We had decided that they would spend the day at our house until sundown, when Tito was planning to grill something for Andreas' dinner at Averoff. Ordinarily Andreas' hot food was prepared for noon, but I had taken to him on Saturday evening enough food for breakfast and a cold lunch so that I would not be out on the streets on the day of protest. When I managed to convey to him during the week the scheme for passive resistance, he was pleased, and excited and hopeful for its success. He told me that I, of all people, could not be seen on the street on Sunday, May 28, and we made the change in the delivery of his food. For Andreas, though pleased with the planned resistance, it would be a lonely, melancholy day.

At that moment, Spyros, young friend of Nick's, came into the house through the back door.

"Where's Nick?" he asked.

"I think he's sleeping," I answered.

"Can I go up and talk to him?"

I looked at my watch. It was eight o'clock, and Nick was an early riser, in contrast to George, and wouldn't mind being awakened by his friend. "Go ahead," I told him.

In a few minutes the two of them were down, Nicky rubbing the sleep out of his eyes.

"Mom, Spyros wants me to go with his family to their beachhouse."

"He does what?" I almost shouted, looking from one to the other.

Nick's eyes suddenly lost their sleepy look as the meaning of the proposal struck him. He turned to Spyros. "I can't," he said firmly.

Spyros looked puzzled.

"We are not going out today," he continued. "This is the day Greece was to have elections." I saw that Nick was embarrassed by his friend's "treason."

"You know, Spyros," I intervened, "everybody who believes in democracy is supposed to stay at home today. Hadn't Nick told you?"

His face reddened. "Yes, but I forgot." He now wanted just to get out. A sensitive boy, he loved Andreas, who had always stopped and exchanged a few words with him whenever he came by the house. He scuttled off on his fat legs and returned about ten minutes later to give an explanation to Nick. His parents had told him that they were leaving early and wouldn't return from the beachhouse all day until sundown. To get to their house, however, which was near Corinth, they would have to be on the road an hour and a half. I felt a sinking feeling. Spyros' parents were close friends and good democrats. If everyone was using this kind of reasoning, the protest would flop.

When Tito arrived, I asked him what he had seen on the road. "Cars" was his laconic answer. He thought there were fewer than normal for a sunny Sunday, but he wasn't sure.

At 7 P.M. Tito drove me to the jail. Andreas was at the cell window waiting. He had probably sat there a good part of the day trying to assess the success of the protest. As I got closer to the window, I looked up and smiled in a vain attempt to indicate that I was satisfied. Through the bars I saw him shake his head slowly "no," and shrug his shoulders. Was it a lack of organization, was it a lack of understanding of what unified action could accomplish, or was it that the people had not fully comprehended what life under a dictatorship would mean? Whatever the case, the Greeks had enjoyed their lost election day at the beach.

The day was drawing near for the arrival of Jim Schwartz and Pat Brown. Excitement was mounting in our home. By now we envisioned them as two Galahads on white horses who would come charging in and with expert flourishes of their swords take off the heads of Papadopoulos, Pattakos,

Kollias, and others, then ride to Averoff to throw open the prison doors and speed off with Andreas and his family to receive the Holy Grail at "the castle of Carbonek." Andreas' mother often asked me, "When will come Jeem?" and my father, with two feet always planted firmly in the world of reality, told me once, "It's a good thing Jim is coming," as if this would settle the whole issue and we would be freed from our iron web.

Excitement was also mounting in the government. Pat Brown was an old friend of Greece who, together with Mayor Christopher, Greek-American, of San Francisco, had carried on many crusades for the Greek people and helped in health and education programs. Brown was also a close political friend of Lyndon Johnson's. It was unlikely that he would be coming without the knowledge, if not the agreement, of the President of the United States. It must have come as a shock to the village boys of the junta, who had painted the word "communist" in bright, dripping red letters all over the name of Andreas Papandreou, that Pat Brown was willing to associate his name in a humanitarian cause on behalf of that same man.

On the evening before their arrival, May 31, Pattakos called a press conference and issued the following statement: "Mr. Andreas Papandreou may be deported after his trial whether he is convicted or acquitted." To a small group of Greek journalists who remained after the main portion of the press conference, he pointed to a locked drawer and said, "There is the paper removing his Greek citizenship. It is all ready. All it needs is my signature."

It was hard to understand the psychology of the junta. Their actions were so erratic, their decisions so sudden and inconsistent, their moves so contradictory, that analysis was impossible. One had no guidelines, and to draw conclusions on the basis of logic was the wrong way to proceed. This particular announcement made on May 31 bore no relationship to developments in the ASPIDA case, nor to any internal political developments that one knew of. It was necessary to conclude that the Schwartz-Brown trip had motivated it, and the most likely explanation was that they wanted to give the impression that they were planning to release Andreas at some point, but this decision did not rest on any pressure from a couple of lawyers from the United States. They wanted to belittle the mission and assert their independence and omnipotence in matters internal. That they were the strutting peacock rulers of Greece—this they could agree on—but the junta was not a homogenous unit, and opinions varied as to what to do with the chief bête noire. The press statement about Andreas was not an assertion of a position, but a declaration of a likelihood. It was during the visit of Jim and Pat Brown that I got more insight into the views within the junta about Andreas, and an understanding of personalities within the cluster of people that called itself the Greek government.

On the same day that Pattakos held his press conference there was an additional development—an increase in police surveillance over my house and movements. Psyhico was blanketed with police and plainclothesmen, making no attempt at subterfuge, watching me from the corners coming and going into the house, tailing my car, parading up and down Guizi Street, and flooding the area around the jail. I began to think that they too believed the myth we had manufactured in our house of whisking off the entire Papandreou entourage and were taking countermeasures. It gave me a perverted pleasure and a feeling of strength. They had called out their dogs and sat shaking in their heavily guarded ministry towers, and for whom? Jim Schwartz, Pat Brown, and me!

At 10:30 P.M. on the 31, the phone rang, and I heard a voice say, "Hi, baby! This is your old boyfriend, Jim!" His voice was warm and clear, and more important, close.

"Jim, darling!" I responded in my most theatrical voice. "Where are you?"

"At the Grande Bretagne with Patricia. He sends his love and says he'll see you tomorrow. He's pooped. But, my dear chanticleer, I'd like to see you tonight."

"Hang on, Jim-O, my sweet. We're flying down to get you and then we'll sock it to 'em."

It was a good comedy act. Our tone was wild and delirious, our lingo nutty, and we had handed a fine bit of nothing to the phone tappers to scrutinize and sweat over.

The Grande Bretagne was considered the hotbed of informers, secret service agents, and intrigue. Jim really picked the spot! Tito, Marjorie, and I reached the hotel at eleven o'clock, two cars trailing not very far behind. Tito and I agreed that it would be foolish to try to drop them and give them the impression that we were up to something secret and dangerous. But after we picked up Jim, I did want to drop them. It was my custom, in agreement with Andreas, to drive by the prison every night at 11:30 to signal him a goodnight. He would be at the darkened window watching for the car, and when we passed, I would light a match to a cigarette, and Andreas would respond by lighting his own cigarette. On nights when I was feeling bold, or when I was simply terribly, terribly lonely for Andreas, I would ask Tito to park the car in the block beyond the jail, and I would walk down to the store with the toilets and plumbing fixtures, and light a cigarette there. This night I wanted to do this with Jim, so that Andreas would see from his lonely lookout that he had arrived. I was sure there would be extra police protection around the prison, but I didn't want to add to this by dragging two secret service cars along with me.

We ditched them in a very simple fashion. Tito dropped Jim, Marjorie, and me off at the Hilton Hotel, as if we were stopping by to have a nightcap, drove off and around to the rear of the hotel. By the time the secret service men had parked their cars to come and observe us, we were back with Tito and on our way through side streets to the jail. It was not always so easy to elude a tail, but for this night we had success. At the plumbing store window, lighting a chain of cigarettes, I described to Jim with great care the virtues of the various pipes and bathroom facilities we saw in the shop window of the Flenzeri Brothers. Jim saw Andreas' responding flame, and we headed back to the car.

Jim and I talked until morning. I filled him in with all the details I had, including the background of the coup, what I knew about each junta member, the role of the American Embassy, etc. Then I told him about something I had mentioned to nobody as yet—an indirect contact I had had with the King. I said I didn't know what to make of it, and I wanted another opinion. A close friend of Andreas' had seen the King's contact man, the same person who was to have breakfast with Andreas on the morning of April 21. He had asked him what were the chances of Andreas' trial, for release, for amnesty—in other words, what were the prospects. According to him, the King had expressed regret that Andreas and other political leaders were in jail and said he didn't see any likelihood of Andreas' getting out soon, unless he could get out under false pretenses. These pretenses, according to Constantinos' contact man, could be ill health—that Andreas was in such a physical state that a trial was impossible and he would have to be sent off for medical care to Switzerland!

I remember saying, "Jim, I feel I'm in a madhouse! If I play this little game, I may be playing right into their hands. If something happens to Andreas in jail, they can argue that even his wife Margaret had reported that he was desperately sick, for in order for this ruse to work, I will have to make a public declaration through whatever means I have. I will have to let the outside world know that he is critically ill so that a demand can be made for an examination and his release for health reasons."

Jim was as astounded as I. "It's a dangerous game," he told me.

"That was my feeling, but everything is so crazy here that one cannot think in the traditional manner. There are no rules. It's jungle warfare, and a fight to the finish."

"How will they determine his illness? Who will make this decision?"

"There's the rub. Supposedly Andreas is to begin to have dizzy spells, lose weight, and call in the prison doctor frequently because of pains and dizziness. In brief, he's to become a malingerer."

"Have you told him this yet?"

"I haven't been able to find the means. There are four guards listening, and I have to do it in a way not obvious to them, and yet clear to Andreas."

"And then what is to happen?"

"A team of doctors will go in and examine him, and recommend his release for medical reasons."

Jim whistled. "Good God! And they will be the King's doctors with instructions from him?"

"None of these things is clear to me. Obviously they would have to go in under instructions, or the plot cannot work, but, frankly, I have my doubts that the King has the power anymore to determine these things."

"Are you sure the King said this?"

"How can I be sure, Jim? It could be some fake hotshot idea of the friend, or the contact man, a kind of child's dream of how to help Andreas, and nothing more. I will try to get more information and more explicit details, but I do not want to toss it out as a possibility, because we have ceased to live in a sane world, and one must take the attitude that anything goes. My sole aim is to get Andreas out of that miserable cement structure. He is useless in there. Out he can fight."

My voice was cracking. We were talking in false whispers over the sound of a blaring tape recorder, the one means of scrambling listening devices which might be somewhere in the house. I had also turned on the kitchen and downstairs bathroom faucets because somewhere I had read that water running through the pipes of a house creates a barrier to listening devices. In addition to this, we wrote down some words in the midst of our conversation to add a further difficulty to someone trying to untangle the gist of our conversation. The most important part of our long night of talk had to do with the strategy for Jim's and Pat's anticipated talks with the junta. We agreed that the approach should be that this man they had in captivity was an intellectual, an excellent teacher, and a highly respected economist in the academic community. Since his political life had been cut short by the action of the colonels, he should at least be allowed to pursue a productive life and offer his talents to education somewhere outside of Greece. Jim felt that he should be able to indicate that this was the desire of Andreas as well.

I hesitated. "Andreas hasn't said this. In fact, my fears are that he is stubborn enough to sit out years in that damned place in defiance of their dictatorial take-over. He won't give an inch."

"You have to persuade him to be realistic. He must think of this as a method, as a means to give him a chance to be active again."

"I know all the reasons, all the arguments, Jim. I've gone over them in my mind tens of thousands of times. I find myself checking my thoughts with my value system—or what I thought was my value system. This is a terrible, harrowing trial of one's beliefs, and one's image of oneself. If you had asked me before the coup how I would behave under such circumstances, I suppose I would have said, with some humility, of course, that you can count on brave ol' Maggie—she'll spit in their eye! Now I find myself listening to devious plans, willing to enter into a game with a former antagonist, eager to promulgate lies, just so I can see that man walk free out of those doors. And at times I don't even know where the lie ends and the truth begins. And my powers of rationalization—oh-ho—my powers of rationalization: I can't do this because of the children, I can't do this because it might hurt Andreas, I can't do this because I'm just a woman alone. And if I hesitate to act—with some protection because I have an American citizenship—isn't it understandable that the guy down the street doesn't act for whom an action means livelihood, his job at the bank, his kids accepted in the university—is he to be castigated or blamed for not standing up to an overwhelming force?"

"And what about Andreas? How do you think he's feeling?" Jim asked quietly, and with an understanding of what I was trying to say.

"You know Andreas, Jim. He's a kind of all or nothing at all kind of guy. It took him a long time to decide to go into Greek politics, but once he made the decision, he went into it fully, with a commitment to fight for what he believed in, and what he thought was good for the people. As he was once quite completely American, he became quite completely Greek—even his language and his gestures changed. He identified himself with the cause of Greece—as a nation, as a people. Maybe he was even blind at times in this commitment. I remember a governess we had, Louiza. She told me once that what Greece needed was a man who would hurt a little for the people. Well,

Andreas hurt a little. And then some. That is why I am afraid that I won't be able to persuade him to use a ruse to get out of jail."

"Damn it. It would be twice as effective if I could say that I know that Andreas wants to return to academic life."

"Why don't you say that his wife feels he would like to return to the academic, and that she and the children are tired of politics and want a normal existence."

Jim liked this. "Also," he said, "I will try to get to see him. Then I can report my own conclusions of what I understood from our conversation."

The first rays of dawn were creeping through the slats of the shutters. Our eyes were stinging and bleary from cigarette smoke. Despite the two pots of coffee, we were both drowsy and near collapse. Jim suggested that he fold up on my living room couch, which Marjorie had vacated for the night, sleep a few hours, and take off for breakfast with Brown at the Grande Bretagne.

"You will be illegal," I told him.

"What do you mean?"

"I'm supposed to report to the local police station any overnight guest I have."

"That sure limits your sex life, sweetie," he smiled.

I smiled, too. Banter felt good for a change.

"Well, anyway, legal or illegal, I'm done. I couldn't drag this body out if you put a fire under it." As he was saying this he was already heading for the couch where he sat down and pulled off his shoes.

"Goodnight, old dear." Jim yawned. "Call me at seven."

"I will . . . and, Jim . . ."

"Yeah?" from the muffled depths of the couch.

"Thanks."

"Remind me to tell you in the morning about one-two-three-ziss-boom. That's when I get you all on a plane and take you out of here."

I didn't say anything. He wouldn't have heard it anyway. I turned out the light, with a lump in my throat and a dream in my heart, and a feeling that one-two-three-ziss-boom might come true.

Jim seemed like family to me—not that I knew him all that well, but his marriage to one of my closest college friends, Ruth Swanson, and his own effusive warmth brought him automatically close. Ruth, a major in theater and speech, had left Minnesota in 1949 for Los Angeles, the University of Los Angeles, and possibly, Hollywood. She did get some parts in movies, mostly minor, and some roles in television shows. With the passing of time, she devoted her talents more and more to teaching in the speech department at UCLA. During her rounds in the world of show business, she had run into the dark and dramatic Jim Schwartz, a product of Ohio, and active in his brother's public-relations and theatrical agency. He was a graduate of Ohio State in political science, had been four years as an officer in the United States Army, and on coming out had floated West and into his brother's established firm. When he met Ruth in 1949, she urged him to do something he was contemplating anyway, take advantage of the GI bill and study law.

Andreas and I met him first in 1951 when he was a student, and later in 1954 when he was a fledgling lawyer, and intermittently thereafter. As I crawled into bed that night it was comforting to know that Jim was sound asleep on my living room couch and would start his fight for Andreas' freedom in just a few hours.

The following day, while Jim was somewhere in Athens on his rounds, I was standing at the cage for my regular visit with Andreas. He had seen Jim from his perch the night before and was eager to have news. In our long night of talk, Jim had told me the names of people he had seen at Pacem in Terris in Geneva, for he and Brown had attended the conference before coming to Athens, using it as a means to contact people for support for Andreas. I had written the names of these people on a piece of paper to report to Andreas in my visit. Shortly after I arrived, I pulled out the list and started to read: "Ken Galbraith, Raymond Aron, Martin Luther King—"

"Speak in Greek," barked one of the guards.

I turned and looked at him in astonishment. "But these are names," I sputtered.

"I said speak in Greek." There was threat in his voice.

Andreas said from behind the screens, "She is reporting names of foreigners. What you are asking is impossible."

"Either she speaks in Greek or the visit is over." The guard himself was caught. He couldn't reveal his stupidity at not having understood the difference between names and words.

I was unnerved by this sudden outburst, but determined to give Andreas the morale-boosting information. "All right," I said, "Galbraithopoulos, Aronakis, Kingatos . . . "

Andreas smiled. "Marvelous, marvelous," referring to both the names and the technique.

Then I decided to try to get the information about the health plot across to him. This is what I said, the parentheses being what I meant:

"Nellie's son (whose name was Constantinos) was over yesterday to play with our youngest boy (whose name is Andreas). They were having a ball in the backyard, playing cops and robbers, when suddenly our kid (Andreas) got a pain in his side and started to feel dizzy (indication of sickness). He ran up to the porch, where some other kids were, and they pretended to be doctors and checked him. (A set of doctors would examine Andreas to determine what illness he had.) Then Nellie's son (Constantinos) said, 'I'll help you,' and he assisted our boy off the porch and upstairs. (The King was willing to help in this ruse.) After that they played with their airplanes (a flight out of the country). I thought it strange, but awfully kind of Nellie's kid to help ours." (I couldn't quite believe that the King wanted to help Andreas.)

Andreas paused for a second. "Is he all right now?" he asked. I detected an honest concern for little Andreas, for he was always sensitive to problems of their health, and I was afraid that the story was too baffling and complicated for Andreas to read meaning into it.

"I forgot to tell you. It was Hourmouzis who was at the house and told me this story." Hourmouzis was the name we had contrived earlier for the contact to the King.

"And Andrikos," he said, warming up to the story, "do you think it was appendicitis?"

"I was a trifle worried, but I wondered on the other hand if it wasn't a game. You know our boy: he's all theater."

"And he fooled the other kids?"

"Yes. But he won't fool them again unless it continues to seem real, you know, dizzy spells, loss of weight, and other stuff like that." I was trying to indicate a few symptoms that would have to be faked.

"That character," Andreas said, laughing. "He can probably carry it off if he wants to. How are the other kids? George?"

We shifted to general topics. I was sure that I had gotten the idea across, and that Andreas had not rejected it entirely, but would need time—which he had an overabundance of—to think it out. Whether we would pursue this hazardous game could be decided in other visits, and based on more information from my side. I wanted also to discuss it with a Greek I could trust—possibly Menios—to get a Greek reaction to it, although I was quite certain I could predict the reaction ahead of time. The Greeks live and breathe a world of conspiracy, plot, and intrigue—and almost anything goes.

Just as I was getting ready to leave the chicken-wire visiting area, the guard who had been brusque with me came up. I learned later that he was a member of KYP, but I would have guessed it in any case. If one wants a stereotype of a thug, he was it. Six feet tall, he had a big-boned frame, wide hips with a flat fanny where his pants hung in baggy untidiness, and one leg that extended at an angle from his right side as if the bone at the upper end of the thigh had been broken and healed incorrectly. His face was large, with the monkey looks of a Jack Palance, pock-marked skin, and the smashed nose of a boxer. His clothes were unpressed and unclean. His expression was stupid, dark, and contemptuous. If hatred could appear in liquid form, one would see it in the saliva clinging to the corners of his mouth.

"Give me the paper," he commanded.

"Why? Those are my notes. They have nothing to do with you."

He started reaching for my purse. I held on to it tightly, wondering what was my best course of action, knowing that I was powerless, and he could take it by force if necessary. I was unconcerned about the names, but what other notes did I have on the paper? It wasn't the first time I had brought notes to the jail to remind me of certain things to talk to Andreas about in the limited half hour we had, and no one had made an issue of it. All of this was undoubtedly part of the new surveillance placed on me with the arrival of Schwartz and Brown.

"It has some names and my grocery list. How am I going to shop?"

Crooked Leg moved closer to me and rasped, "Give me the note," in a tight-lipped fashion that allowed for no funny business. The smell of garlic and stale sweat emanated from him, and I felt that his weapons for overwhelming me were beyond just the steel grip he now had on my wrist.

His left arm hung down slightly back and away from his body, a position he assumed naturally and automatically as if to be ready for the next step, which in most circumstances would have been a crack across the side of my head. I looked at the other guards standing around. My gaze at one prompted him to gather courage and say, "Let her have it. She don't have to give it."

What he said was true. No rules said I couldn't carry notes into the jail, but just that I couldn't sneak in notes to Andreas. Crooked Leg turned to him and shouted "Papse!" a crude command to "shut up."

"Take it," I said, "and happy reading." It was the only action to take. If I made too much of it, it would give more significance to an innocent piece of paper than was worth it. I thought all of this was out of the hearing of Andreas, who was always kept waiting in his cage until I left the prison building before being led up to his cell, but he told me in our next meeting that he had heard it all, and was furious. But helpless.

From the jail I went directly to the office of Andreas' lawyer and told him what had happened, and asked if there was anything we could do about it. He said, "We can have an ouzo, and you can relax," and he ordered two ouzos from the taverna below which arrived with a slice of fried pepper, an olive with a toothpick sticking from its middle, and a triangle of bread with anchovies on it. I left the food for Menios and drank the ouzo. Menios asked what I had written on the paper, and I told him what I remembered. He called the prison and tried to reach the director, but the director was out to lunch. He assured me that he would try to get it back, although he considered it innocuous, and he chastised me, in a friendly way, for being so nervous over nothing. As he was talking to me, his right leg, crossed over his left, was in constant motion, as if he were pumping a gas pedal of a car, and I thought, "Yes, my dear Menios, don't be so nervous over nothing." The note finally reached Andreas' ASPIDA folder in the prosecuting attorney's office, and Menios was called in for questioning about it. The item that disturbed them the most was the name "King" which I had written to remind me that Jim had talked to Martin Luther King in Geneva. They were sure that this referred to Constantinos and wanted to know what I was saying about the King. Menios shrugged it off as the name of a friend, which he knew it was, and the paper remained along with the other irrelevant and unrelated documents in the ASPIDA file.

All that afternoon I waited for a call from Jim. It was the day he and Pat Brown were planning to see members of the government and the American Embassy. I was terribly anxious to hear the results of these visits. At three o'clock, Jim's call came.

"Hi, honey. I'm exhausted."

"You must be, Jim."

"I won't be able to see you. I've accepted an invitation to go to Crete with Pattakos."

I produced the classic example of "stunned silence."

"Did you hear me?"

"Yes. I heard you. I think that's fine, Jim, just fine. When will I see you?"

"I don't know. I think this thingamajig is a tour and should take two days. I'll call as soon as I get back in. But here's Pat. He wants to make some arrangements for this evening."

We planned to meet at 7 P.M. at the Grande Bretagne cocktail lounge. He suggested I bring my friend Marjorie along, and we'd go for dinner somewhere later. I was delighted, because there were two things I did want: information on the day's events and a visible public appearance with Pat Brown. Since he was acting in the capacity of legal adviser, it was legitimate and proper that I would see him, and difficult for the junta to make an issue of it. I barely knew Brown except as a public figure in California. Andreas had participated on his council of economic advisers and had met him personally. I wanted to kiss him on both cheeks in appreciation for his efforts on my husband's behalf.

I said good-bye to Jim in a flat voice that must have shown my lack of comprehension, told him to take care, and then stood looking at the closed telephone for many minutes before I could take the news to the family so we could try to puzzle it out together. Pattakos, of the three members of the triumvirate who had carried off the coup, had been the most accessible to the press and was thus the best known. He had given the image of a clown, a puritan (it was he who proclaimed the ban on miniskirts and long hair), a soldier, and an ignoramus on international matters. He had said to a Swedish deputy that the deputy would be allowed to see Greece's political prisoners if Sweden would let him see theirs when he visited the country. When the Swede said that Sweden had no political prisoners, he said, "All countries have their political prisoners," and he was serious. He was authoritarian, unpredictable, and rather direct and honest for a Greek. These characteristics, along with his greater accessibility to the press, gave him a more "human" form than either Papadopoulos or Makarezos. Nonetheless, he scared me, as did all the others. He was one person I certainly would not want to be on an island with. I thought of Jim's trip to the island of Crete. Should I have told him not to go?

That evening I dressed up to keep my date with Governor Brown. It was the first time I had ventured out in the evening to downtown Athens—more than just driving in the car, that is—and the first time I had dined out since the coup. No one in our circle felt like any festivities, and there was no spirit for a good time.

When I walked into the Grande Bretagne, I felt I was making an entrance into a Casablanca of the Near East. The air was loaded with the smell of exotic perfume and hair lotion and that special aroma of Greek tobacco. The noise was intense, thick, and suffocating. My body stiffened from tension, the sudden burst of lights, noise, and activity, and the sense that people lived gaily in a world of diamonds and cocktails, unaware or unconcerned about Andreas and the thousands of suffering prisoners and families in all corners of Greece. I walked mechanically through the lobby, passing sinister-looking figures hovering in groups, well-dressed women of all nationalities smoothly tanned from days on the beach, journalists with cameras slung over their shoulders and press cards peeping from their jacket pockets. Near a lounge chair close to the entrance to the bar was Pat Brown, with horn-rimmed glasses, talking to two men, whom he introduced to me as constituents of his from California. They were all very jolly, laughing and loud, whacking each other on the upper arm and calling everybody by his first name—a bit of Americana in a capsule that repelled me, and made me feel homesick, too.

Pat escorted Marjorie and me into the bar, and we ordered whiskey sours. We had been sitting for five minutes, during which time I spotted four different men walking in, taking a long look at our table, and walking out again. Then a man in a dark gray suit took the empty table next to us, pulled out *Le Monde*, and stuck his face in it. I didn't ask whether or not my hunch was right, I just assumed that the man in the dark gray suit was a paid eavesdropper. I glanced at Marjorie, who indicated she felt the same way, and she took the initiative by suggesting we move to a larger table where we would have room to take notes, if necessary. Brown was momentarily taken aback by the image of our taking notes on his conversations with the government, but his moment of hesitation turned into a ready agreement as he too became aware of our neighbor. The waiter was just at that moment bringing our drinks over and we waved him to a table a short distance away. The hands belonging to the nose buried in the pages of *Le Monde* moved slightly downward, but the basic position was kept, and that was the only indication we had that the eavesdropper had understood our move.

Brown told me that while he and Jim were having breakfast together, he was called to the phone and found himself talking to the former counsel of Greece in San Francisco, Mr. Boufides. Boufides said he was now in the Ministry of Foreign Affairs and had been assigned to help them in their activities in Athens. He said he would like to come over and join them and discuss their program with them. Within ten minutes he was there, the Ministry of Foreign Affairs being within a stone's throw of the Grande Bretagne on Vassilis Sophias Street facing Parliament and just beyond the Egyptian Embassy. In order to reach the Grande Bretagne walking, he would have to pass the stalls of fresh flowers, I thought, where the flower merchants, I knew, were fanatic Papandreou supporters. The flower merchants should have thrown one of those man-eating tropical plants in his path. I remembered Boufides from our days in Berkeley, and disliked him intensely. He told them they were scheduled to see Kollias first, then Pattakos. He didn't know whether appointments could be made with other members of the government. Jim told me later that while Pat was upstairs picking up his briefcase, Boufides told him that they were both there on a "bad" mission, that they had been misled, and the less they had to do with helping Andreas Papandreou, the better it was for them. "The only mistake we made," he said, speaking as if he were a member of the inner decision-making body of the junta, which he was not, "was not to have killed him the first night." Boufides had frequently invited us to his elegant consulate home across the bay in San Francisco when Andreas was chairman of the department of economics and a Greek of prestige in the community. Mrs. Boufides was a spoiled, complaining female who talked only about clothes and home furnishings. He was a petulant, dogmatic, self-important representative of the

Greek government and the royal family, or perhaps it was vice versa. I secretly hoped we would meet again someday over martinis. I was wondering how he would look—for a beginning—with two green olives stuffed up his nostrils and the stem of a martini glass just barely visible from his mouth.

Jim and Pat had spent an hour with Kollias. It was an hour of screaming and exhortation, Kollias' face as red as a beet, his little fist pounding the desk to make his points. He argued that Andreas' fate was in the hands of Greek justice, (oh, Lord, I thought), that Andreas would get a fair and open trial. He also said that Andreas had been the head of a secret organization out to overthrow the government and install a dictatorship, that Andreas had announced he would hold Parliament on the lawn of the Parliament building and declare a people's democracy, and that he was a communist. When Jim said they were not interested in Greek internal matters, but simply wanted to have Andreas returned to an academic career, *which was the desire of the Papandreou family*, Kollias shouted that he would be a corrupting influence on the minds of young Americans, or whomever he taught!

They also spent an hour with Pattakos. Pattakos began with some kind remarks, such as calling George Papandreou a beast and all the prisoners dangerous communists. He said that Greece had developed a "filthy climate" and that the army had to cleanse public life. He argued that 95 percent of the people had welcomed and applauded what they had done, having become tired of the old life in Greece. According to Brown, Pattakos took a liking to Jim, who was responding to these comments with directness and correctness, in almost a military style. (Clever Jim. He found the right time to remember his officers' training in the army during the war.) Suddenly Stylianos Pattakos pointed his finger at Jim and shouted, "You want to see the support we get from the people? You want to see how happy they are with us? I leave for Crete this afternoon. Another plane will follow at five o'clock. Can you be on that one?"

Jim was just as taken aback as I was when he telephoned me. He looked at Pat, then back at Pattakos, then to Pat, and finally said, "May I discuss it with my colleague? We had some plans for today, and we must reconsider our program."

To Pat in the corner, he said in a low voice, "What the hell am I supposed to do?"

"I think you ought to go," was Pat's advice. "Your purpose is to have as much contact with him as possible. This is a chance."

"Well, sir," said lawyer Jim, "I will be able to accept your invitation, and thank you. I've always wanted to see your beautiful island of Crete."

At this point in our conversation at the Grande Bretagne, I saw a familiar figure approaching our table. It was Elias Demetracopoulos, a Greek journalist. He greeted us all by name, and Pat motioned to a chair for him to pull up and sit down. I was sure he knew, probably through Pat, that we would be there together. I hadn't seen Elias since before the coup, and I was happy to see him out and free. He was one of Greece's best liberal writers and had been working for the newspaper *Ethnos*, a pro-Andreas paper before April 21. He had important contacts in the United States, and included among his friends people like Governor Brown. His contacts were in fact so good, and his ability to get personal interviews with so many political personalities so remarkable, that it was natural for the suspicious Greek to assume that he was a CIA agent. I pegged him as nobody's agent but his own. He thoroughly enjoyed his journalistic ventures and occasional journalistic coups, particularly when they became a factor in the political life of the country, which they often did. It was Demetracopoulos who leaked out the story of Andreas' office encounter with Joyce of USIS over the cancellation of the Voice of America broadcasts, which had turned out to be a major political event in Greece.

He told us he had just recently come out of hiding. After the coup he had gone underground in anticipation of arrest, and only when it became apparent that no search had been made for him did he expose himself to the light of day and the watchful eye of the colonels' secret police. So far he was unmolested, he said, but he didn't trust the bastards, and he was sorry for me that Andreas was in their hands. "They are murderers!" he whispered to Pat Brown. "Anything you can do to get Andreas out of here will save his life."

I looked at Elias' face and felt sorry for him. Any Greek liberal and lover of freedom was living a nightmare in the Greece of the colonels, counting his days outside of iron bars. I wanted desperately to talk to Elias, since he always had reliable inside information. We made a date at the Hilton bar for the next week, agreeing ahead of time that if he didn't show up I would try again the following week at the same time. Arrangements for seeing people had become complicated, along with every other phase of daily living. No one wanted to use the telephone, and no one knew for sure what his personal situation would be in the future.

We said good-bye to Elias and left the hotel to have dinner elsewhere. I did see him a few times after that at the Hilton bar, as we had arranged, until finally he disappeared, eventually turning up in the United States where he became a *cause célèbre* because of a battle that ensued between Congress and the State Department as to whether he should be allowed entry into the country. It was the State Department that fought him, particularly Dan Brewster on the Greek Desk, who was always an anti-Papandreou, proestablishment force. This raised Elias further in my estimation.

At dinner I did most of the talking, particularly about Andreas. I sensed that Brown's contact with the embassy that afternoon, about which he discreetly told me little, had left some questions in his mind about Andreas, and knowing the hostility that existed within the walls of that rectangular building, it didn't surprise me. I told him that of course I was a biased participant in the affair, but I wanted him to hear my side of the story. I told him I knew that the embassy, as Bernard Nossiter said in one of his letters to a friend, "didn't lose any chance to tell all and sundry what wicked, awful people were the two Papandreous," and I just hoped that after coming all this way to help me he would not be influenced by the atmosphere there. He did not deny that that was the atmosphere. He listened to me patiently and sympathetically, and as the meal progressed, with growing understanding and agreement. He told me that he himself would have to leave, but that Jim was well launched (one might say that his debut had been smashing) and could carry on on his own. He promised me all the help he could give, and would keep in touch through Jim. When we left, I did kiss him on both cheeks. As we came out of the restaurant, two men moved into the shadow of the bushes, and I felt that everything was working out fine.

CHAPTER TWENTY-TWO

Continuing Repression

WHILE many people of influence were working for the freedom of Andreas, others of equal influence were working more generally for the return of democracy to Greece. In Congress, Senators Claiborne Pell, Joseph Clark, Frank Church, Eugene McCarthy, Wayne Morse, and Stephen Young took strong positions against the military dictatorship; and Don Edwards of California and Don Fraser of Minnesota in the House of Representatives urged along with the Senators that no United States aid, economic or military, be given until the colonels were out and Greece had again true parliamentary government. There were a few voices in the State Department, perhaps under the pressure of Congress, who shared, if weakly, this point of view. They could always be shouted down by Dan Brewster on the Greek Desk, the classmate of Andreas' at Athens College and chief bureaucracy spokesman for the disastrous United States policy in Greece from 1963 onward. A stubborn individual, he was caught in the mire of his own mistakes and apparently thought that if he stuck long enough with his initial premises, they would somehow come out all right in the end. He substituted repetition for reason. This is not to suggest that if he had experimented with a different point of view it would have changed much in Greece. The powers that would really determine the fate of Greece—the CIA and the Pentagon—were not talking, but were just waiting for the shock to die down and for the fuss about the need for representative government to fade. This "invisible government," as it has been called, is unresponsive to the demands of the American people and their European friends, undermining democracy throughout the world and in the United States as well.

Unfortunately, these forces got an assist by world events just at a point when their arguments for the maintenance of a military regime were the weakest. The violent response in Europe to the take-over in Greece and the reaction of the intellectuals and progressive forces in the States, with their means for pressure, the threat by Denmark to create problems within the NATO alliance because of the loss of democracy in Greece—all these factors were weakening the junta and causing vacillation in Washington on giving support. Then came the Middle East crisis and the Six Day War between Israel and Egypt and the appearance of the Soviet fleet in the Mediterranean. Americans were evacuated from that area and were given a warm welcome and lush facilities in Athens. The Sixth Fleet found its usual berth in Phaleron ready and snug. It had always been quite clear to the Pentagon that strategic considerations and American interests in that area were far more important than who ruled Greece, and now it was doubly clear—a fact which they didn't hesitate to point out, I am sure, to doubting State Department people or legislators. The argument that in the interests of American security the crushing of a nation is not important is no less cynical than the argument that in the interests of international socialism the crushing of a nation is not important.

I would like to make a parenthesis here in case I sound naïve about the functions of government bodies. I don't really expect or have a vision of Pentagon officials charging out to dismantle their outfit or to start contracting for the breeding of birds rather than the manufacturing of guns. Their mission is the military defense of a nation. But I wonder, where are the countervailing forces to say that these are not the *only* considerations in dealing with other countries. Where are the powers to chop at this octupus which is strangling the peoples of the world? Those powers must be found within the United States.

The colonels, keen to United States military thinking, lost no time in exploiting the Middle East crisis, pointing out to the United States and the world that in a time of need Greece could be counted on completely. At the same time, an editorial appeared in *Eleftheros Kosmos*, the newspaper most aligned with the junta, warning in severe terms that despite pressure from inside and outside Greece, the junta had no intention of leaving "until its job was done." This, it wrote, would take a long time. It also insisted that the traditional parties and leaders would have no further role to play in the country. The junta permitted Constantinos on his name day, May 21, to announce that he had obtained from the governing junta the promise that a constitution would be drafted within six months and then submitted to a referendum—and buried the King's speech on the inside of all but one newspaper.

Jim returned from Crete three kilos lighter and carrying heavy bags under his eyes. He had tagged along with the circus, watching the crowds that turned out—under orders from the military—observing only that they included primarily schoolchildren and old people. The age group twenty to forty was missing. He met the little old Cretan mother of Pattakos, dressed in traditional island black with a black scarf over her head, whom he liked immediately, and whose eyes sparkled and face beamed with pride at her son's newfound prominence. He saw Pattakos and Papadopoulos dance village dances, and in the midst of all this revelry and gaiety, he saw hundreds of secret service men milling around, their suit jackets bulging with concealed artillery. He was depressed by the sight ("Not only depressed, Maggie, *scared!*"), and his only relief was on his unescorted journey from Heraklion to Chania to catch the return plane when he stopped in village stores to make purchases for his family in California and managed to start conversations with the proprietors. They learned from him that he was an American lawyer friend of Andreas Papandreou's, and they surged around to talk, with no hesitation or fear, and expressed their love and faith in Andreas.

On one occasion he had had a chance to talk again to Pattakos and had repeated his request that Andreas be freed and allowed to return to his teaching. He even showed the brigadier general a snapshot (which he carried in his wallet) of Andreas and me with the children. Pattakos assured him that they were looking into the matter, but Jim's dream of bundling us all on a plane—one-two-three-ziss-boom—and getting us out of there seemed about as remote as when he came. Jim was later accused by some of our friends of "consorting with the dictators," but he had not come to topple the dictatorship. He had come on a personal mission out of old friendship.

Pattakos gave him permission to visit Andreas at Averoff for half an hour, and he became Andreas' first nonfamily visitor since his internment in jail. An officer from the Ministry of Interior accompanied him as an "interpreter" which was the acceptable-sounding name for "listener." He reported to an eager audience at home that he found Andreas in good spirits, hopeful, and looking trim, although pale. Jim contributed his bit to the "health plot" by reaching up to Andreas' face and pulling down the bottom lid of his eye ("It's like he's a horse, or something," Nicky commented) and telling him to take care and be sure to watch out, not to forget some of the serious illnesses he had gone through. He told him, "Your health may be essential for old Ski-U-Mah," a reference to the cheer we used to send out to the Minnesota Golden Gopher team from our cheering section in the stands. In this fashion he informed Andreas that health and his release to return to teaching might be tied up. Coming as it did after my story of fantasy about little Andriko and his friend Constantinos, Andreas had no trouble understanding it. He laughed, and merely said, "We'll see, we'll see," and Jim felt that Andreas considered it a farce. The conversation was limited, as mine always had been, by listening ears. Much was said about the past, about Andreas' "beautiful children," as Jim called them, about his own two kids in Los Angeles, and about a swimming pool that was waiting for use by Andreas. I knew for sure that Jim was a tonic for Andreas, speaking as he did with confidence and assurance, and although this was minor as compared to the mission on which he had come, it was something.

After Jim left, I decided to pursue further the health game that had started with the purported conversation with King Constantinos. Andreas might think of it as a bit of low comedy, but this didn't stop me from taking an initial step that would not commit us in any way, but would leave it open as a possibility. This step was to see that a letter from a doctor went on the record expressing concern about Andreas' health. This letter could also be my cue as to what kind of symptoms Andreas would have to show. On June 10 I wrote a letter to Boyd Thomes, M.D., our family doctor and friend in Minneapolis, feeling that I was plunging into a theater of melodrama—that the idea was stupid, unrealistic, and insane, not to mention dangerous—but determined that no stone would go unturned in my effort to remove Andreas from his cage and return him to his home.

On June 19, 1967, Boyd wrote me his reply, through the American Ambassador, and it was perfect. Here are the important passages:

I will send this letter through the American Ambassador, hoping that it will reach you.

All of us Minnesota friends of Andreas are terribly worried about his present circumstances, and we are not able to get much news about how he is actually being treated.

...In 1951 or so, as you also know, he developed a peculiar skin disease called chronic discoid lupus erythematosus.... Usually one would not be very disturbed about this kind of lesion, but subsequent developments make me sufficiently alarmed to at least write you about this problem. I heard from friends that in 1961 Andreas had had a serious and near-fatal illness precipitated by a reaction to some medication, and that this reaction was characterized by a rapid and severe loss of white blood cells, and that he required intensive treatment with cortisone and penicillin.

This bit of medical history changes the picture. About 10% of patients with discoid disease develop a really severe disorder called systemic lupus erythematosus, or SLE, the basic feature of which is an altered immune reactivity with the development of peculiar antibody-like proteins directed against white cells, red cells, or different body tissues. This is a serious disease and may even be fatal.

Acute severe exacerbations may be triggered by taking certain medications, exposure to sun, injuries, operations, and severe emotional stress.

...The symptoms which suggest activity of this disease are many and varied, but usually include fever, malaise, weight loss, poor appetite, and weakness.

...If symptoms even of the general type are occurring, I think the medical situation should be taken seriously. This is a complicated and difficult problem which cannot be handled successfully by casual medical attention. It is one of the diseases that really require supervision by trained specialists, usually to be found only at major medical centers.

A copy of the letter was sent to Ambassador Talbot for his records. The mission accomplished for the moment was that (1) it was on record from a qualified doctor that Andreas had a peculiar and dangerous medical history, (2) the acute form of lupus erythematosus could be triggered by emotional stress, (3) the symptoms were such and such (so I knew what Andreas' "sickness" should look like), and (4) it was difficult to get proper treatment anywhere except outside of Greece.

The symptoms were easy to simulate. Already Andreas had lost weight and it was normal under the circumstances that his appetite would be bad. Fever would be hard to produce, but stomach upsets wouldn't, since I brought the food! The big question was whether Andreas would play the game. And would it work? Apart from whatever role the King might be able to play, it was important that the junta itself believe, either rightly or wrongly, that Andreas in jail was more of a problem to them than out. Thus I watched and listened to anything that might give me a cue to their thinking. An AP item in the *Herald Tribune* in early June led me to believe that the junta was trying to wriggle out of the ASPIDA trial and was searching for a justifiable reason to get Andreas out.

> *Brigadier Pattakos said he was trying to learn whether Mr. Papandreou held United States citizenship as well as Greek citizenship.*
>
> *The inquiry on whether Mr. Papandreou is deportable to the United States was seen as a move by the military regime to get rid of one of its most difficult political problems since taking over Greece on April 21.*
>
> *Andreas Papandreou has rapidly become a cause célèbre among intellectual groups outside of Greece.*

Anschuetz confirmed to me that a junta source (unnamed) had raised the question with the embassy and had asked for a ruling from them. The question was being looked into by the State Department. Andreas had lost his American citizenship when he entered Greek politics. It was lifted from him, that is, by action of the American Embassy, or the State Department through the embassy. He had never officially renounced it. It seemed logical to us at the time that having entered the public life of another country he would lose his citizenship. But recent ruling by the Supreme Court stated that an American citizen who had voted in an Israeli election could not be deprived of his citizenship. On the basis of this decision, questions could be raised about the status of Andreas' American citizenship. The chances that he had retained it seemed unlikely in view of the fact that he had taken an oath of allegiance to the Greek government, administered by the King when he became minister in his father's cabinet. Yet there might be some legal loopholes, and I would need the advice of a lawyer if I wanted to look into it. I remembered that Frank Newman had said he would be glad to return should I need him at any time, and I kept that knowledge tucked handily in a corner of my brain. It was not the citizenship question per se that I was interested in. Andreas would surely declare that he was a Greek citizen. The issue was important as a device for the junta to use to ship him out of the country, and I wasn't feeling choosy about what device that would be, as long as the result was his, and our, freedom, and the opportunity to be active in an anti-dictatorial fight. He had been called many things during his political career; being called an American citizen would not be the worst among them, although many young people in the world might not agree with me.

While I was pursuing all roads that might lead to Andreas' release, my Greek friends were suspicious and slightly hostile toward me, feeling that this parade of American lawyers and talk of citizenship and deportation smelled of a compromise or a deal. I was partly amused and partly irritated. I was amused because of this strange sense of honor one must keep in the face of ruthless dishonor, with the cards completely stacked in the hands of those who held the guns. The jailed man has only his wits to use to outdo his captors. I often wondered why the leadership of the political parties did not send out clandestine orders to their supporters to sign anything in order to gain freedom and the chance to be active in resistance. I was irritated, on the other hand, that they believed that Andreas might compromise his principles in a bargain with the colonels. In fact, his adamancy I knew would be my toughest obstacle in fighting for his freedom. Obviously, however, I had my own internal conflict. I had convinced myself that almost anything was preferable to twenty years in jail, but I felt a tremendous pride in Andreas' devotion to a cause and was angered at doubts about his intentions. I had always admired his unswerving commitment to a set of principles, to values that were humanistic, liberal, and decent, and to his willingness to die for them if need be. I found—for myself—that this was much easier to admire as a hypothetical construct than as a real-life situation. For Andreas, his equanimity in prison, although he displayed signs of tension, was an indication to me that he faced the theoretical and the real with the same attitude. I knew that a compromise was out of the question.

So far I had done nothing inconsistent or compromising to my own values. The health plot was a gimmick, illusory as yet, and I hadn't been faced with the real decision of whether I wanted to use the services of the King, the man who had been charged by Andreas with violating the Constitution and who had stuck him with the ASPIDA charge. The citizenship question was a way out for the junta, and at the moment didn't involve me at all. Accepting the help of friends for Andreas' freedom seemed natural and correct, although an extreme view would be to say that arguing or pleading with the junta meant you recognized its legitimacy. My argument was that I recognized its power, which was apparent, but not its legitimacy. It seemed to me, however, that a part of the ruse to get Andreas sprung from the walls of Averoff would be to support the belief that Andreas wanted to get out of jail just to return to academic life. When I thought this over, it seemed too raw, too abrupt, and too out of character. So when I first mentioned something like this to Anschuetz, and subsequently to Talbot, I clothed it in more fetching garb and told them I thought I understood from what Andreas could tell me (pointing out that open communication was impossible) that he would remove himself from the political life of Greece if this act would speed up the return of democracy to the country. In other words, if he were the obstacle to such a development, he would not hesitate to place the interests of the nation first, and his personal ambitions second. It sounded good, and I could almost see Talbot rubbing his hands and drooling at the prospect of a Greece free of Andreas Papandreou.

It was early June by now and the days had gotten warm. It looked like a long, hot summer ahead. The children would soon be out of school, and I was making plans to send them to a camp at Lagonissi, a seaside area on the road to Sounion, less than an hour from Psyhico. Being that close, they could be picked up by Tito in the morning on Saturdays and brought in for their fifteen-minute visit with their father. George, because he was over twelve, could see his father under the same conditions I did, behind the mesh screen. He stood with me on Saturdays, quiet, responding to his father's questions in monosyllables, seldom initiating a conversation himself, hostility to the environment painted all over his face. He had gotten skinnier and taller, and more brooding. Sophia, Nick, and Andriko were taken into a smaller office after the conclusion of Georgie's and my visit (we were often accompanied by Andreas' mother as well) and allowed to sit with their father, and most important, to kiss and hug him.

Sophia had recently been obliged to sit through a lecture in the large auditorium of her school, Pierce College, on the reasons for the "Revolution" of April 21, 1967, and the merits of same. It had been written by the Ministry of Education and was read by a lucky teacher chosen by the school to deliver it to the students. A similar lecture was given in all the high schools in Greece. She told me she had sobbed quietly all through the speech, and when she came home that day her eyes were still red and her face drawn from the experience. The only alleviating factor had been a teacher who had put her arm around Sophia's shoulders as the pupils filed out, whispering, "Don't worry, Sophoula. Everything will be all right. We all felt like crying."

Nick seemed to be least affected by the new home situation. He explained to me that he had never seen very much of his father that he could remember, and thus didn't notice his absence much. He added that he always felt closer to me, and if anything happened to me maybe he'd feel different. After giving this honest confession, he asked whether there was something wrong with him and was it bad that he didn't feel more affected. His purpose in telling me was apparently to relieve guilt feelings he was having about his ability to lead a normal life and not be terribly distressed by his father's situation. I told him that I wanted him to lead as normal a life as possible, since there was nothing he personally could do about the situation, and that I was sure that was the wish of his father as well.

Andriko was the most puzzled by seeing his father in jail. For him, "bad" guys went to prison, "good" guys stayed out. It was an entirely new concept that he should be proud of his father's being in jail, that his father was in jail for what he believed in, and what he believed in was something fine, civilized, and for the good of the people. One noon he joined me to bring Andreas his food. Walking down the long sidewalk to the prison entrance, his hand clinging to mine, he fastened his eyes on his father standing at the cell window above and suddenly blurted out to me in a poignant voice full of sympathy and compassion, "Oh, my daddy . . ." After giving much thought to this peculiar state of affairs, he ultimately came to a conclusion which he reported to me on another trip we made to the jail together. He said he knew now why it was necessary for his father to be in prison. He had to teach the guards economics. I smiled and told him that undoubtedly his father was doing just that, if I knew his father, and this seemed to resolve the dilemma in his mind for the time being.

My father urged me to take swims in the Aegean, knowing my deep love for the sea. Although naturally slim, I had lost considerable weight quickly; my skin was pallid; and my parents were rightly concerned that I maintain my health and my emotional balance in order to carry the present burdens, and the greater ones I might have to face. Because of my schedule of being at the jail at noon, at 7 P.M., and at 11:30 P.M., I could not take a day off at the sea. Even if I could have arranged with the guards to have someone else deliver the food for a day, I didn't want to deprive Andreas of the little cheer he had in his hideous day—the sight of me, often with one of the children, marching up to the prison door.

But there was a time I could swim, and a favorite time for me—early morning when the water was cool, the sun warm but not like a blast furnace, and when the fish were out for breakfast and easily observable through a mask. We tried it a few times, my dad and I, driving to a small sand and rock beach, generally deserted at 6 A.M., near a village called Mati, on the road that leads to Marathon, and the experiment proved so successful that it soon became a regular program. I recognized that it was the only activity which took me away from thoughts of my personal problems and the problems of the Greek people living under this oppressive dictatorship. There, floating on top of the blue water and gazing at the creatures cavorting below, or diving deep to retrieve a shiny shell from oblivion in the sand, or plowing with long crawl strokes out from the shore to a friendly sandbar, there was peace and forgetfulness and an almost sensuous communion with nature. Here I felt a keen awareness of my body that told me it was something other than a container of nerves and sweat glands. On the way home we would stop at a bakery in the village of Pallini where hot, steaming coarse-textured bread was just being pulled from large stone ovens with long-handled shovels. We purchased a loaf for breakfast, and pulled warm chunks off in the car to munch on.

My father-in-law had been transferred from the hospital to his home and put under house arrest on Wednesday, May 10. The first day that it was announced he had been returned to Kastri, I called Karambelas to see if I could talk to him, but was told that he had no phone in his bedroom. From the tone of Karambelas' voice I understood there were others present, and shortly thereafter the junta removed all telephone communications with the house. I drove up with Tito the following day and found the area barricaded for blocks around and armed policemen and soldiers doing guard duty. His son George was the only person allowed to visit him. His two doctors checked him once a week. All three visitors, Karambelas, and the two maids were thoroughly searched coming in and out of the house to check for possible messages. There was no way of having communication with him without putting someone in danger.

On June 11 in the morning I got a telephone call saying, "Stan here. Let me take you and the kids to dinner tonight. I have my own two kids with me." It was Sheinbaum back in town, and I was pleased, because I had a very special reason to see him.

On the same day in the afternoon, I received another telephone call. This one was not pleasant. It was Kiveli who told me in soft tones that Tito was ill and had been taken to the hospital. This was our code for saying that Tito had been arrested! I felt sick. Two wonderful people were going to suffer for standing by me. I quickly arranged with Antigone what food to prepare for Andreas' supper and told her to have it ready so that I could come back by and take it, then Marjorie and I climbed into the Taunus and drove over to Kiveli's house.

"Marjorie," I said as we were going up to the elevator to Kiveli's apartment, "I feel there's nobody here but us chickens." And that was the sensation we both had. Slowly but surely the men in our entourage were being swept in by the cavernous, hungry mouth of an insatiable dragon, and we were left to fend for ourselves.

Kiveli answered the door, composed but subdued. Intelligent, humane, with a dark sultry beauty, she was incapable of a cruel thought, a catty remark, a snub. She seemed at times not quite of this world; she was too generous and understanding to be real, yet she handled anything she tackled with remarkable capability, courage, and determination. It was she who had taken on the entire Ministry of Interior of Pattakos in trying to get me permits to see Andreas at Pikermi (after my first visit, arranged by Menios), a privilege that I was not given automatically or regularly, but which had to be fought for each time. She had offered to charge in, and many times she waited for hours in the outer office of the minister, waiting to see the officer in charge, or telephoning every fifteen minutes from a kiosk to check whether my permit had been signed and she could come by to pick it up.

"Tell us what happened," I asked.

"We were resting. It was about 3 P.M. The doorbell rang and Tito must have sensed the possibility of an arrest because he told me not to get nervous. He pulled on his clothes, and I put on my housecoat and tagged after him to the door."

"Were they banging hard?" I asked, remembering our own experience.

"No, they rang the doorbell once and had just rung it again when we opened the door. They asked if he was Tito Zographides, and when he said yes they told him he was to come with them."

"Who was it?"

"Two policemen."

"They spoke roughly?"

"Not really. Tito asked to see their identification, and they produced their police cards. Then he said he would get his jacket and put his shoes on, and they stood in the entryway and waited, one with arms stretched across the doorway—like this—not saying anything."

"Did you have a chance to say anything to Tito?"

"I didn't know what to say. What does one say?"

"Yeah," said Marjorie, quietly and bitterly, "what does one say? Good-bye, have a good trip . . . send me a postcard . . .?"

We moved into the living room and sat down. We were silent for a few minutes, each lost in our own thoughts and sensing acutely the absence of Tito.

"What do you plan to do?" I asked.

Kiveli had worked it out. "I thought I would wait a few hours to see if I got a call or a message, or something to indicate where he is. After that I will start calling the police stations, beginning in our district and going on to the central police headquarters. Then if I get no answer by telephone, I'll start going around on foot." She had avoided saying the dread words "security police station." None of us mentioned it, but we were all thinking about it. Bouboulinas Street, the torture chamber. By now many stories had reached our ears. There they beat, kicked, harassed. (The technique most commonly used was beating on the soles of the feet with sandbags, something terribly painful which left no marks. It was called the *falanga*.) There they also stripped women and beat them with wires, and we had heard of cases where they stuffed huge objects up the victim's vagina in order to get her to talk. The fact that the stories got out was not surprising, for the knowledge that such things could happen if you were arrested was an intimidation technique in itself. The junta wanted these things known by Greeks. When knowledge of these practices got out to the rest of the world, the junta denied fervently that any such thing was happening.

We had coffee and talked aimlessly. At 6:15 I left to circle past my house to pick up the food and deliver it to Andreas. I knew Andreas would be startled to see me alone in the car. And I would have to appear unflustered because the slightest indication of grimness would bring a raft of unanswerable questions to Andreas' mind, which could only give him a restless night. His great worry was that something might happen to me, to the children, to the wider family group, and he would be sitting helplessly behind bars, unable to help. Although we communicated little from sidewalk to window, concerned lest this would cause the authorities to move Andreas to an inner cell, there were a few things we could say, and immediately, with a flick of his wrist and a turn of his palm upward, he asked me, "Where is Tito?" I smiled and made the motions of a tiny breast stroke: "He's at the beach" was my answer. It was a bit odd, but not too much so, since Tito loved the sea as I did and had not as yet done any swimming, which Andreas knew from our screen conversations. As soon as I had delivered the food, smiled at "Laughing Boy" a name we had given to one of the more pleasant and grinning guards (and who was ours, according to Andreas), I rushed back to Kiveli's apartment.

When I arrived, Phillip was there, consoling Kiveli, telling her that they had no reason to hold Tito. This was not the best of logic, since one could argue that they had no reason to hold *anybody*, but it was an effort to comfort her. It was then that she said in a strained voice, "But I am afraid they will beat him." This was the true misery. Imprisonment in itself was bad enough, but to feel that your husband, or son, or father, or friend was being tortured like a victim of The Inquisition was too much.

We all pooh-poohed this with loud dissent. Too loud, perhaps, for the sensitive antenna of Kiveli. Like children, we were playing a pretend game. Unlike children, we could not get lost in this make-believe, yet it was essential for our morale.

It was now a bit after seven. Kiveli had called two police stations in my absence and was getting ready to leave on foot. Marjorie said she would accompany her. I wanted to join them, but I had an appointment for dinner with Stan, and it would not have helped Tito for me to appear as someone especially interested in his welfare. Feeling that the longer I stayed the more disturbed I would get at the thought of these two women, forlornly walking

248

the streets from station to station, facing tight-lipped officers and getting negative answers, I decided to be on my way. As I stood up, we heard the sound of a key in the door. It was a warm, friendly metallic sound that filled the room with its implications. It had to be Tito, yet no one said a word until the key had done its work and the door opened up, and Mr. Tito Zographides himself walked in.

Kisses, hugs, tears, joy! What a miserable situation, I thought to myself in the midst of this excitement, that one ends up being grateful for being free, as if this were not a human right and depended on some authority's caprice. Tito was smiling and pleased to be able to present himself to our tense, sober gathering. He told us his story.

"I was taken in the squad car to central police headquarters where I was led to a cell with one chair and told to go in. A young policeman was assigned to stand outside my door. After a few minutes I realized that I had come away with no cigarettes, so I called the fellow at the door. 'Run down to the kiosk and get me a pack of Pallas,' I told him. He looked startled. I shouted at him. 'What the hell is this? I am an officer on active duty. What's happening here is unacceptable!' This truly scared him. Nowadays you say 'officer' and they all jump. He got the cigarettes."

"Bravo," we all chimed in, as if Tito had taken on the Cyclops and performed a Herculean feat.

"I remained there for two hours. Then I was ushered into the office of the chief of police. He asked me questions about my length of service, where I came from, where I had served, etc. I asked him what he wanted me for, and he told me he had been asked to take me to the Ministry of Public Order where I would see Ladas, and as soon as the instructions came through, we would go. In the meantime would I please wait in the upstairs 'room.' I got the distinct impression that when they picked me up they hadn't realized I was an officer on active duty, and were wondering if this was an oversight they might have to pay for."

We had all whistled when he said "Ladas." Ladas was considered the hard nut in the junta and chief rival to Papadopoulos. Little was known about his background. He was, like the others, an unknown name when the coup took place, having no particular record in service nor any special qualities of distinction. What we knew about him we learned after the coup, his manner of talking, his way of dealing with opponents, his extremist stands within the revolutionary council.

"I returned to my guest room and waited for another half an hour or so, when I was called and put into the chief of police's car, accompanied by the chief. I figured I was a real VIP prisoner. Soon I was nudged into Ladas' office, and as I approached his desk he shot the question at me: "What are you doing around the jail with Mrs. Margaret?"

So I had been right. He was paying for standing by me.

"I told him that I was brought up by my uncle, a priest, in Crete, and that I had a Christian philosophy in life—you stand by your friends when they are in trouble. I said that Mrs. Margaret had four children to care for, and three aged relatives, and that all I was doing was assisting her in her tasks. She has to take food to the minister several times a day, I said, and all I was doing was driving her to jail. That's all."

"What do you mean, 'That's all,'" Kiveli asked. "That's all that was said?"

"No, that's all I was doing. He didn't know quite how to respond to this. To argue against Christianity? Then he told me that I was having contact with people around the jail, and he mentioned the fellow in the milk shop. You remember," and he looked at me, "the Cretan from whom you buy pumpkin seeds. I think I've greeted him twice. He also mentioned that I had a conversation near the café on the corner with a fellow named Yannis Andonakos, and he was right. I ran into Yannis one day while waiting for you. He was a fellow student of mine in law school, and I hadn't seen him for years. But our conversation was all about old friends of the past. It had nothing to do with today's situation. I told this to Ladas."

"Wow," said Phillip. "They've been following every move." He said this slowly and thoughtfully. I understood better sometime later why this picture of an all-seeing secret police had meaning to him.

"When I told him that these were acquaintances or friends from the past and unrelated to you or Andreas, he looked at me skeptically. Then he told me to watch my step, and after a long moment, said I was released. I believe he was honestly debating throwing me in jail!"

"Good God," I muttered. "It's now a crime to talk to old friends. Anything else?"

"I can tell you one thing," and he turned to me. "It's not pleasant, but when he said your name he spit it out with a hiss, like the name in his mouth was a sizzling coal."

"If they believe the stupidity that they made up themselves—that I am a Bulgarian communist—what can you expect?" I asked. "Anyway, you're back. That's what really counts." It was time for me to leave and meet Stanley with the children down in Turkolimino, so I kissed Tito and gave him a bear hug that said more than words could and moved toward the door. Phillip sidled over to me and said he would like to accompany me downstairs. Downstairs we stood outside on the sidewalk, waiting for the cab that would bring George and Sophia from home. The sun was falling, having bruised the sky with pink and purple hues. There was a soft breeze, and Phillip helped me pull on a cardigan sweater over my sleeveless cotton dress. Actually, the air was warm; I felt cold from an inner chill.

"I thought you should know", Phillip said, taking advantage of being near me, "tonight is our first act of resistance."

The chill deepened. "Oh, Phillip," I said. "Are you sure you are ready?" Phillip the intellectual, a man of high moral character, unable to tolerate the humiliation of his people, was moving impetuously, emotionally ahead. I didn't know what the act of resistance would be and preferred not to learn. "Do be careful" was all I could think to say, although I knew it was like telling a child to beware of traffic when all his thoughts and efforts were on playing ball.

The cab approached, and Phillip gave my hand a tight squeeze and disappeared down the street. Down in Turkolimino, I reported the news to

Stan who had become part of our resistance effort by having carried out the document to Pacem in Terris Peace Conference. He was pleased and eager for more details, but I told him I had none. What I really wanted to discuss with him was something relevant to Andreas and the ASPIDA case. I had told this to no one, but a few days earlier I had received a visitor in Psyhico who claimed to be acting on behalf of two witnesses in the ASPIDA trial—Andreas Vahliotis and Kyriakos Diakoyannis. He told me that they wanted to recant their testimony, that what they had said in their depositions was untrue and taken under threat of violence.

"Stanley," I said, "I literally gasped, and then I became immediately suspicious."

"Who was he, and why did he come to you?"

"I have his name, although I have no idea who he is, and since I've discussed this with no one, have not learned as yet. He claims to be a friend of Vahliotis and Diakoyannis, but primarily a devoted supporter of Andreas'. As to why he came to me, I can only assume that they want money, although he didn't mention a thing about money. He sounded very sincere and deeply committed to Andreas, and you know, sometimes heroic acts are performed under the most impossible circumstances."

"These guys, they're important in the case?"

"Are you kidding?" I exclaimed. "The only man who had a direct contact with Andreas in the whole ASPIDA case is this Vahliotis. All the rest of the so-called evidence is hearsay. And it is from his false testimony that the prosecuting attorney proclaims they discover the true aims of the conspiracy ASPIDA. It is from his testimony that they attempt to show proof that the organization was put together to oust the King from his throne, take Greece out of NATO, and, in general, turn Greece into a socialist regime. In Greece socialist means communist, so you understand the implications."

Stanley moved his head slowly up and down. "I see, I see," he mumbled.

"The big question is recant to whom? There's no longer a court system here. All justice is handled by the army, either directly or indirectly. If these fellows go traipsing in to whatever court authority exists and say they want to tell the truth about their testimony, they'll end up in cells in Averoff just like Andreas. If they wait until the trial to try to speak, they will be called out of order, muffled, and end up in a cell in Averoff again. Their only court is the so-called court of world opinion. I think that's what they must have in mind. They have a chance to be heroes, help the democratic cause, and—may I be cynical—perhaps they have hopes for some money from supporters of Andreas."

"The thing is tricky. If you involve Andreas' lawyers, they can be accused of bribing state witnesses."

"That's the point. And yet I think I must talk to them. I have to find out for one thing whether this person who saw me is a serious person who can be relied on to speak the truth, or whether he has developed a fantasy about how he can deliver Andreas from the hands of perverted Greek justice. You can't imagine how many fanciful schemes exist these days in the form of plans. The people are so damned frustated and feel so powerless that they

251

have resorted to a Walter Mitty type psychology. And sometimes," I added, "so have I."

Stanley gave me a sympathetic look and patted me on the hand. "There's one thing I can do, Maggie, and I suppose that's why you are talking to me. I can help to reach the 'world court of opinion' through the magazine I represent—*Ramparts.*"

"I knew you would say that. It's too early to do anything yet. I simply don't have enough information, nor do I know how authentic it is. What I want is to work out a way we can be in touch with each other in case this thing develops into anything."

Thereupon we worked out on a piece of paper set between our two plates of seafood a rudimentary code and addresses that could be used, both in Greece and in the States. His two children and mine—all around the same age—were busily engaged at the other end of the table getting to know each other. Their chatter mingled with the sound of the sea, slapping the edge of the concrete block jutting into the water, which made up the floor of our outdoor taverna. I also took Stan's phone number in California for emergency purposes. He advised me to pursue the lead, with care, and when he would be needed, he'd do everything he could to make it a bombshell.

"Stan, you can't imagine what peculiar roads I am traveling down in this god-awful situation." But I didn't tell him I was conspiring with an agent of the King's for Andreas' release. One would have to live longer than Stan had in this Byzantine environment to recognize that the "health plot" made sense and had possibilities. We parted, agreeing to keep in touch.

Two days later, according to my records, I elaborated a scheme in a letter to George Lianis for a letter-writing campaign which I had already described to Leo Hurwicz. This scheme had come to me one restless, sleepless night when I thought I couldn't stand another day of having Andreas couped up in his solitary cell. I was in one of those half-sleeps with my mind working feverishly and repetitively, and everything looked distorted and grotesque. It was then that I saw chubby little men in black uniforms carrying huge sacks of letters on their backs, filing one after the other into the ministries around town, their short legs moving in jerky, fast-stepped silent-movie fashion, and with a cherubic smile, dumping the bag of letters on the minister's desk and saying, "Your letters, Mr. Minister." *And every single letter had to do with Andreas Papandreou.* One by one the letters were opened by the minister, and the name ANDREAS jumped out at him from the text in magnified black letters, changing from fat to thin to wiggly worms on the page. The word ANDREAS filled his eyes, his mouth, his ears, his stomach, until choking, sputtering, gasping, he groped for a black cord dangling from the air in front of his desk, yanked it with all his force, and when secretaries appeared from the wall with oversize pens and stenographic pads, he shouted, "Get him out of my hair! Get him out of here!"

These thousands of letters from all over the world would obtain the release of Andreas, not because the letters asked for his freedom but because they would be an expression of worldwide interest and a warning to the junta that a trial would attract international attention on a large scale. I quote from my letter to Lianis dated June 13:

> I sent a long letter to Leo which you may call and ask him about. I tried to indicate what I consider some important things to do for the next month. I consider this time until July 15th when the voulevma [indictment] comes out critical. It is now that they will decide whether they will release Andy before or after the trial. What is obvious is that they will find ways to kill him off politically for a substantial period of time ... either by imprisonment or by special sections of the Constitution. The fight for democracy will take a long time in Greece. Someday it will triumph. ... I suggested to Leo that letters from prominent and non-prominent people with this request should be solicited from now until July 15th. Let Greece taste what a democratic people can do when they decide on a crusade. Important people to hit outside of Sally [our code name for the King] are Kollias and Papadopoulos. ...

Both Lianis and Hurwicz left for California for the summer on research jobs, Lianis to Los Angeles and Hurwicz to Palo Alto, and I received a letter from Lianis dated June 17 referring to this plan.

> We [Leo and Lianis] exchanged calls and decided (1) to write individual letters of faculty addressed to Sally, and to either Stylianos or the strongman of the group with copies to White House and State Dept. (2) These letters to be ready and mailed around July 3. (3) To involve in this drive as many universities as possible. I conveyed your message to Steve [Rousseas] and asked him to coordinate the same thing in the East, and to another friend in Chicago for the four universities around. Leo was going to contact Wisconsin and a few other midwest universities. ... He told me Steve had objections to the scheme. Although Steve agreed originally, he was convinced by the other boys there that we should not do it. Their reason: any drive to get Mike [Andreas] out of the country from the US will harm his image and also Mike himself should not ask to be free, but should challenge the legality of the court; in short, he should put up a fight there and now!. ... We decided finally to seek the approval of Jim and Pat Brown. ... anyway, both Jim and Pat agreed to the scheme, and I called Leo to confirm it.
>
> Personally, I told Jim I favor Mike's getting out of there. The choice of what he wants or must do afterwards is his. Now he has no choice at all. The question of "image" does not arise in my mind. He has plenty of image and his image will not suffer if he is abroad. He has done more than anybody else for the Greeks. Let them show what they can do themselves. They have been babied too much by Mike and they have not lifted a single finger. I do not want you to think I am abandoning the fight, but simply we should see if they have reached any

253

degree of maturity. What happened there has not happened anywhere else and would not be accepted by any other nation. I am simply asking: why did it happen there and there was so much cowardice? I can give them one year the benefit of the doubt. But beyond that I will have no patience. They should not think that somebody else will do the job for them. No, now I believe it is their move. If they prove they are worthy then they deserve any sacrifice. Otherwise they deserve what they have or what might be coming to them. I would not give a damn. Perhaps I sound pessimistic. No! I am simply angry, very angry.

Two things were clear from this letter. One was that schisms were developing, particularly on the matter of tactics, in the group working outside of Greece against the junta. Some wanted Andreas in jail as a martyr and a symbol of the fight. Others wanted him out, not just for humane reasons, but to give him a possibility to be active in the antidictatorial battle. Needless to say, I fell in the latter category, not just because I was his wife, but because I honestly and objectively could not believe that his being in jail could in any way contribute to the overthrow of the junta.

The letter made clear something else: the frustation of a Greek living outside of his native country at the lack of resistance and reaction within Greece. This was a feeling shared silently by many of us within the country, but better understood. The external resistance against the junta was important, and I felt that I personally had a role there, since I had the contacts, the language, and fairly good means of smuggling out letters and information; but I was also convinced that without internal resistance on a more serious scale than had been thus far shown, there could be no success. The Greeks were lulled by a belief that the fantastic efforts outside their country would accomplish the overthrow of the junta. In fact, sometimes they startled me by saying the junta will "fall," which I pointed out was an expression from parliamentary days when governments could lose a vote of confidence. They were also imbued with the mentality that the problem was not within their ken, that internal Greek matters were ultimately in the hands of a foreign land, the "protector" power, whether it was France, Britain, or recently, the United States. And the final excuse for not taking action was the growing belief that the King would act. No one doubted that he would bring in the old establishment, or the Big Junta, but it was felt that this would be a change that would rid Greece of the tyranny of the colonels and open the way for parliamentary government. This, I think, is an accurate assessment of the mood of the Greeks in the summer of 1967. They were not enthusiastic about the King, but they wanted him to act. Afraid of being condemned to servitude forever, they wanted a change, any change, and this feeling of desperation was shared by all shades of the political spectrum, left to right.

I remembered George Papandreou's remarks to me some months earlier, before the coup. He said that in a democracy there is always a way out. Power can change hands peacefully, through elections—change is possible. In a dictatorship, power can be grabbed easily, painlessly, and perhaps smoothly, but there is no way out, no exit, except by force.

Now we were facing the harsh reality of these words. The Greeks were hopeful that the King, in trying to save the monarchy and in preferring to face a parliament rather than an all-powerful dictator, might provide the way out, that exit so difficult to find.

In the middle of June Andreas started having problems with his stomach, a condition he had had in the past and described by doctors as a preulcer condition, causing great pain and discomfort. An accompaniment was dizzy spells. This was real, not fake. If we had been playing the health plot game, these spells would have come in handy. We were not, however.

There was no question that the days and nights of total isolation in his cell were beginning to take their toll. One day during this month at the visiting cage I found him very tense and using his handkerchief often to wipe sweat off his brow. He said nothing about the spasm of pain he was having, simply muttering, "It's damned hot in here." Suddenly he began to crumble, grabbing hold of the shelf in front of him behind the screens. I turned and shouted to the KYP man who was at my right, "Help him, help him!" He looked at me with contempt, then turned and looked into the cage, and just stood there. I turned to another guard, "Get him water, a chair, *quick!*" This one started to move. I turned to the screens and pounded on them, yelling, "Don't fall, don't fall . . . hold on!" and felt a cruel sense of helplessness as I stood two feet from my husband, unable to do a thing to help.

After what seemed like centuries, a chair and a glass of water were taken into him, and the door to the court opened from the side behind him to give him some air. As the sun streamed in, I got a clear view of him through the screens for the first time, and saw the pallor in his face, the new white hairs at his temple, and the hollows in his cheeks.

As soon as he had a few gulps of water, he looked up at me from his sitting position, then, seeing the worry blazing on my face like a neon sign, stood up and immediately reassured me, blaming it all on his stomach and calling it a spell that occurred once in a while. I knew then that there had been many other times. This was a harrowing enough experience, but I was to have a worse one within a week. I had gone into Athens in the morning on errands, but primarily to pick up messages that were waiting for me at a prearranged place from two of Andreas' key people in northern Greece. It was a nonvisiting day, and Marjorie met me at the jail with the lunch pail. I beckoned her to walk with me to the kiosk on the corner where we bought cigarettes, and I slipped the two messages into her purse. We walked up to the jail doors together, as was customary, and as I moved up to the door I saw her moving toward the bench under the canopy where she usually sat and waited for me. I was in the jail for no more than three minutes. When I walked out, my heart started pounding at the walls of my chest: Marjorie was nowhere in sight.

Andreas was standing at his window high above and must have seen whatever happened, but I had no way of asking him. My eyes shifted

255

automatically to the guardhouse about fifty feet away toward the side of the jail. I knew that people were often picked up on the street accused of loitering around the prison, or making signals to Andreas, and taken to the guardhouse for questioning. Had they finally decided to question Marjorie, and perhaps to search her things? And today of all days? I could see nothing around the guardhouse that suggested something unusual. And I couldn't quite see myself walking over, peering in, and saying, "I say, old boy, do you happen to have Marjorie in here?" I felt my legs carrying me down the pathway away from the jail. About halfway, I turned and gave a valiant smile up to Andreas who at that distance couldn't possibly see the tremble at the corners of my mouth, or the gritted teeth under my lips. Meanwhile, I scanned the area frantically—the prison yards, the sidewalks, the island divider on the boulevard, the shops across the street. Marjorie had never disappeared like this. She was always outside waiting patiently unless we had agreed beforehand on another meeting spot. I looked at my watch, scrupulously kept on time and synchronized with Andreas' watch. It was 1:07. I turned onto the sidewalk of the main boulevard, forgetting to wave up to Andreas at a clearing between two bushes where I always gestured a brief farewell. Calm, calm, courage, I was telling myself. I was picking my way along the sidewalk as if it were littered with garbage. My problem was one of balance as foreboding filled my legs with jelly and the sidewalk thrust itself up to meet my footsteps before they had completed their downward motion. A blue coupe pulled up alongside me. A man leaned over toward the door from the steering wheel and I heard a familiar voice say, "Are you looking for something, Margarita? Can I help you?"

It was Asteri, boyhood friend of Andreas', a doctor who had been active in the Democratic Clubs formed by Andreas, and who knew all the family well. He had come by the house with his wife once after the coup. I was wracked by a wild impulse to scream, "Asteri, take me away, away, away . . ." Instead I directed my rubber legs toward the car, put my hand on the ledge of the open window, and leaned down to say to him, "Asteri, I've lost Marjorie." To my surprise, he told me he had seen her. He said she had gotten into my brother-in-law's car, and the two had driven off down the boulevard.

"But why, how?" I burst out. "It's so strange. It's not like her. She knows how worried I would be to come out and not find her."

"Climb in," said Asteri, by now seeing how distraught and disturbed I was, and realizing also, perhaps, that the suspicious, distrustful eyes of the secret police were watching the whole scene. He pushed the handle of the car down, and the door fell open to offer me the solace of the car's interior and the comfort of a friend nearby.

He put the car into gear, telling me in his best doctor's voice to relax and take it easy, then suggested that we take a run around George's apartment, which was not too far from the jail, and see whether his car was parked outside, in which case Marjorie might be still with him. I didn't like the whole affair. George was the only visitor to George Papandreou, and I had always been extremely careful in my contacts with him not to create problems for the visits, which were virtually the only human contact my father-in-law had.

This blatant driving up in front of Averoff Prison and whisking Marjorie off was an incredible act. I sank back into the seat with a sigh of annoyance and fatigue, my mind a turmoil of bewilderment and confusion, my eyes staring ahead through the windshield as we crawled along the highway crammed with midday traffic.

I glanced at my watch. It showed 1:15. I held it up to my ear to make sure it was functioning. It was a watch George Papandreou had given me on my thirty-sixth birthday. I couldn't hear the gentle ticks in the hum of the car, but I knew it was I who wasn't functioning—not the watch.

"There's his place," Asteri said. "Keep an eye out for his car." We looked on either side of the boulevard, then turned down a narrow side street which led to a small parking area in the rear of the apartment house. There was no sign of George's car. I closed my eyes for a moment and took a deep breath.

"Are you sure, Asteri, that it was Marjorie who got in his car?"

"Positive. A blonde in a green print dress. I was kitty-corner across the street buying cigarettes at the kiosk."

He knew Marjorie, and his certainty relaxed me a bit. I still had visions of a Marjorie on a chair in the guardhouse, or down in the basement of Averoff where newcomers were often kept before being hustled off to assigned quarters, or taken to Security Headquarters for questioning.

"Perhaps we ought to take a run around the prison again," he told me. "She may have returned to try to find you."

The thought of driving back past Averoff intrigued me not at all. I lifted my sunglasses off my eyes and wiped away the perspiration that lay on the bridge of my nose under the nosepiece. With my head down, I leaned my head on the two fingers which were still at my nose and mumbled uncertainly, "I don't know, I don't know." We were around the block now and headed toward the intersection where the car would have to turn on the main boulevard back to the jail. "Look," I finally said. "I don't think it's a good idea either for you or for me to be loitering around the jail too much, or passing by. I just came from there. I have no justifiable reason to be driving by again. Also, I don't think it helps you to be seen with me. Why don't you drop me off here at the corner, take a spin around to see if Marjorie is still there, and if she is, bring her back with you. If she isn't, come by . . ."

". . .and I'll drive you home," he finished. With no more words, I started climbing out of the car which he had pulled to the curbside. I pointed to sidewalk tables in front of a café, and he nodded his head in agreement and was off. I chose a table in the corner toward the front. I glanced at my watch again. It was 1:25. I felt that I was clocking an explosion. It wasn't natural for me to look at my watch so frequently. I felt it was the shock of the unexpected—not seeing Marjorie when I expected to—plus the general level of tension I was living under which caused me to overreact to anything out of the ordinary. But it was more than that. There was something ominous in the air. I wondered when the waiter would come so that I could order an ouzo.

Five minutes passed. Then ten. Asteri should be coming back by now. I tried to gauge how much time it would take to drive by the jail, drive on past the athletic stadium to the break in the island where the car could turn around, pass on the near side of the jail, and come to the café where I was sitting. In spite of the traffic, ten minutes was maximum. In the midst of my calculation, two husky bodies breezed by my table and sank into seats at the table behind me. At the same time, I saw two other figures, risen from the heat waves of the pavement, standing like Siamese twins, talking to each other in quiet tones in front of a kiosk and casting glances my way. Their faces wore black expressions. Black, black, black, I repeated to myself, tapping my ring on the metal table in rhythm to the unspoken words. And at the same time, I said, also to myself, you are surrounded, old girl. Here was KYP again, in all its glory. I studied the ones in front of me in an arrogant, cold way, appraising their bodies, their clothes, their faces, their shoes. Their clothes were ill-fitting, wrinkled, and did nothing to hide the dumpy bodies underneath. Their shoes were pointed—European-style—feminine-looking to me, giving the impression of a ballet dancer's feet on an elephant's body. They made no attempt at subtlety. They were discussing me and didn't care if I knew it. As for the ones behind me, I felt their breath. Where was the waiter? An ouzo would contain that dash of strength I needed now.

As I was lighting a cigarette, displaying the extreme in nonchalance, a character who had been the lone other occupant of the outdoor section of the sidewalk café when I arrived stood up and approached my table.

"You American?" he asked. I felt the four bodies around me tense up.

"Yes," I said, looking at him dumbly.

"I have cozzin in Sikago. You cum mebbe from Sikago?"

Oh, Lord, I thought. Looking for a pickup. I'm too old for a pickup. And the poor bastard. He's walking into the viper's cage—innocently, unaware, and precisely. I looked up into his gnomelike face flushed pink from retsina wine, a rubbery smile trying to give the impression of innocent friendliness.

"No," I said, "I'm not from Chicago," and then I repeated for the umpteenth time the gesture of looking at my watch, this time with the special meaning of impatience and an appointment that was late. My eyes lifted from my watch to the figures at the kiosk. One was telephoning, the other stood with his feet apart facing me directly. We weren't more than eight feet from each other. The watch had told me it was 1:45. Twenty minutes had passed since Asteri left on his mission. Something had gone wrong, terribly wrong. And a second disappearance seemed more than I could handle at the moment. Fading away, without a word, back to his abandoned glass of wine, was somebody's cousin from Chicago. I hoped my coldness had saved him from something even colder—a night or two on the dank floors of the Security Head-quarters (What was it you were saying to Mrs. Margaret?).

The KYP agent at the telephone had reached somebody, talked to him for a minute, and now he appeared to be waiting for a response. He held the phone slightly away from his head and said something to his twin. The twin didn't take his eyes off me. I felt that if at this moment I were to suddenly stand up, guns would be pulled out from behind and in front of me and I would be a well-riddled bundle of summer clothes, blood, and crumpled limbs on the floor of a sidewalk café. But the need to get away from there was overwhelming. The waiter had not come to take my order for the ouzo I was eager to gulp down, and I wondered what divine bit of inspiration had kept him out of this situation. My eyes watched the cars coming from the direction of the jail. Several times I caught a spot of blue and watched with dismay as it appeared—not Asteri's car—and crawled on by.

The voice on the other end of the phone was talking now. The head of the agent went up and down, glanced my way, then the phone went back into its cradle. He reported something to his double. They continued to stand at the kiosk. I decided to make my break. I watched for a moment the white fronds of smoke circling upward from my cigarette, then dropped it on the cement pavement and slowly crunched it out. I took my purse from the table and slowly closed the latch. I did everything in slow motion so as not to make that sudden gesture I thought would trigger off unfortunate consequences. Carefully I uncrossed my legs and rose from my seat. On the other side of the street, just across from where Asteri dropped me off, was another kiosk and behind that, a cab stand. When I reached the kiosk I stopped to buy a bar of chocolate. From that point I could look over and see the area I had just vacated. The two at the table had joined the others and were standing in a huddle, squinting across at me, one with his hand cupped over his eyes to shade them from the sun, as if they were hunters watching a duck which had just gotten out of shotgun range. And it seems that that was actually the case. I learned from Asteri some months later, after he got out of prison, that the call from the kiosk that day was to get orders from Security Headquarters as to whether or not I should be picked up and brought in.

Marjorie was home when I arrived by cab. Her story was simple. Just after I had disappeared into the jail, she had been shouted at by a tall dark figure—my brother-in-law—who had pulled his car up in front of the jail, was halfway down the front sidewalk, and telling her urgently to join him. He seemed agitated. Marjorie knew he was the only one seeing George Papandreou, and she figured it must be something deeply important for him to behave in this fashion. She got into his car, only to find out that he merely wanted to tell her to tell me that his father was in good health, sent his warm regards, and wanted to know how Andreas was. She had insisted that he drive her back immediately, and was dropped off on the other side of the street just in time to see me climb into Asteri's car. Figuring that I had found a friend to drive me home, she returned to Psyhico.

Asteri's story was not so simple. As he drove by the jail after dropping me off, a car pulled alongside him and beckoned him to pull over to the curb. One man climbed in on the driver's side, pushing him over, and took the wheel. The other climbed in on the opposite side and sandwiched him between the two. A short distance farther, they stopped at a kiosk, and after several phone calls, the KYP man to his right returned to the car and told the driver that it had been decided not to pick up Mrs. Margaret.

Asteri was taken and beaten mercilessly. After two days of this, he was given a good meal, wine, and cigarettes. Then he was asked, in nice tones, to tell them about my activities, and to explain why he had certain names in his address book, which, unfortunately for him, were people evidently involved in resistance, some of whom were in the army. When he said he knew nothing about my activities, and that the names were old friends, and with all their cajoling they could get no more out of him, they told him he was to be executed, and the third night he was taken, in the middle of the night, up to an isolated place on the mountain of Dionysus, blindfolded, pushed, and told to start walking. He told me he thought it was the end, and all he could think of at the time was that I must still be sitting at the café table wondering why he hadn't returned. It was a mock execution, a favorite pastime of the sadistic torturers of the security police. Finally he was returned, then taken to a city jail in another part of town where he survived for several months, and one day was released. It took him some months before he could bring himself to come to my house, but he finally did, and told me the story.

It was at times like this that I devoured the encouraging bits and items from here and there and tried to ignore the ugly ones. One such encouraging bit was a piece written by Paul Samuelson, one of America's top economists, who writes a column twice a month for *Newsweek*. It was entitled "The Greek Tragedy."* He pooh-poohed the idea that Greece was a sick economy or had been led to disaster by the Papandreou government, a popular theme with the junta government in Athens, and gave facts to prove it. His last few paragraphs were in defense of Andreas:

> The dictatorship now says it acted in order to avert a Communist takeover. Andreas Papandreou has been charged with "treason," which is defined as conspiratorial action to purge the army of right-wing elements.
>
> For a score of years, American economists have known the younger Papandreou, his numerous books, articles and lectures. Careful reading of them shows no trace of Marxist or totalitarian leanings. The many dispatches of C. L. Sulzberger to the New York Times appear as misleading on Andreas Papandreou as were the disastrously inaccurate appraisals of Fidel Castro by Times reporter Herbert Matthews.
>
> I have before me the text of a February speech, written when Andreas was riding high and with no need to dissemble his true views. They mark him as one who believes in planning by the mixed economy, with allocation of function between public and private enterprise, and regulation of investment by foreigners.
>
> To kill a man for such views would leave few men safe—certainly not de Gaulle, Lester Pearson or Franklin Roosevelt. Our government, and American public opinion, regard the new Greek government as being on trial along with Andreas Papandreou.

The article got him into a hassle with Cyrus Sulzberger, who wrote a letter to the editor, and managed to use even that little space to imply that Andreas was a communist. All Samuelson would have to do, Sulzberger wrote, was to look into the secret files of the Greek security police (the true keepers of the truth, apparently) from before World War II. He neglected to mention the fact that Greece then was also under a dictatorship. Samuelson answered back, and tore him to pieces, an answer that I read in Athens with glee and satisfaction.

*Copyright Newsweek, Inc., May 22, 1967.

Such things were helpful for our morale, but were like flotsam in a churning sea, enough to give momentary assistance, but not enough to save the drowning man. What we were interested in by now were not words, but action. No government had done anything decisive. All were dealing with the new regime, with one excuse or another.

One unpleasant article I could not ignore because it confirmed my belief that the Americans knew about a dictatorial takeover in Greece was a piece by Marquis Childs in May in the Washington *Post*. He described a top-secret meeting in mid-February, 1967, which he said was "like the lament of a Greek chorus for the tragedy to come." He continued:

> *CIA reports had left no doubt that a military coup was in the making with the knowledge if not the sanction of King Constantine. It could hardly have been a secret. Since 1947 the Greek army and the American military aid group in Athens, numbering several hundred, have worked as part of the same team. The team has spent something under 2 billion dollars on the guns, planes, tanks, and ships of the Greek forces.*
>
> *The consensus around the table, after some hand-wringing with agonized appraisals of the consequences, was that no course of action was feasible. As one of the senior civilians present recalls it, Walt Rostow, the President's adviser on national security affairs, closed the meeting with these words: I hope you understand, gentlemen, that what we have concluded here, or rather what have failed to conclude, makes the future course of events in Greece inevitable.*

So, from February, I thought, the Americans could have foreclosed a military takeover. A clear declaration that any attempt to impose totalitarian rule in Greece, by any factor, would mean the immediate withdrawal of all economic and military aid, the severing of diplomatic relations, and the expulsion from NATO, would have halted this development immediately. No individual, not even the King, nor any section of the Greek army, could have proceeded under those declared conditions. Since they had not done it then, I wondered about now, now that the dictatorship had occurred. How was it conceivable that they would take action under more difficult circumstances? What was it in me, I asked myself, that I persisted in holding out hope for a correct action on the part of the United States? How hard dies an illusion!

During the last week of June the representative of the International Red Cross came into town to do an investigation of the situation. My father arranged to pick him up at his hotel and bring him to a friend's home for a talk with me. With Andreas' deterioration in health and my father-in-law's stern house arrest, I felt I must lodge a protest and make it clear that I felt the Red Cross was obliged to intervene.

A wrinkled old man with a whispery voice was ushered into the living room, physically in danger of being blown out the window by a dog's loud bark, and my heart sank when I saw whom I would be dealing with. After explaining my cause for concern, he informed me that he had visited both the Papandreous and found them in good condition. He said their living quarters

261

were quite adequate, and then he went into a long description of some of the prison conditions he had seen in Africa and India, implying, of course, that I should be pleased that Andreas was in a civilized jail and not in some savage stockade. I was flabbergasted. The cup of tea I was drinking remained, along with my arm, in a catatonic pose halfway toward my mouth. (I had told my friend in Greek to offer tea; the old gent would never live through a cup of coffee.) If the criterion for jail conditions was a comparison with what he had seen in India and Africa, I wondered what kind of a report he would submit. Certainly the prisoners in Averoff and on Yaros and Leros should be informed of the hapless condition of their colleagues in foreign jails and urged to send postcards to them saying, "Having wonderful time. Wish you were here."

I started sputtering something like "but this is Europe," then stopped, deciding the conversation was hopeless. Anyway, the whole notion of discussing conditions for jailed political prisoners sounded ludicrous to me. The tragedy was that they were in jail at all. I did ask him one more thing, however. I asked if he would allow me to arrange a meeting for him with a doctor who had treated a torture victim. The doctor had agreed to see the Red Cross representative and describe his patient, if I could arrange it privately. I considered this a major victory because he was risking years in jail if this simple conversation were discovered.

The frail man across from me reached mechanically for his tie and smoothed it down in a way that looked as if he were gathering strength from the inert ribbon of cloth. He looked at me and raised his eyebrows slightly. "Madam, I am here to examine the conditions of the prisoners. That is all."

"Then your answer is no?" I asked, wanting to pin him down. He nodded that it was and reached for his briefcase on the floor next to his chair, indicating that the conversation was taking a turn he didn't like. I let him go and sat for some time wondering what interests he was serving.

Within a day after this visit, the energetic, high-strung secretary of Andreas', Andoni Livanis, was arrested.

And to finish off the month of June, on Friday, the 30th, my dear friend Phillip was clamped into jail.

CHAPTER TWENTY-THREE

ASPIDA Uncovered

JULY'S blast-furnace heat arrived with the dictators still in power and continuing their dirty work of arrests and tortures, accompanied by loud proclamations of a "new Greece" enjoying the total support of the Greek people. Press and radio censorship continued, free speech and the right of assembly remained abolished, political parties were illegal, and the Greek citizen had no legal protection against the dictates of the junta. Andreas sat locked up in his narrow jail cell, my father-in-law remained isolated under house arrest at Kastri, thousands of political prisoners languished in prisons or in exile on rocky, barren islands. A small military Mafia, nicely armed by the American taxpayer, sunk its teeth deeper into the country with each passing day.

On July 13 Frank Newman returned to Athens upon my urging to discuss preparations for the ASPIDA trial. He had agreed to take on the responsibility of organizing the "observer activity," as we called it, to ensure that outside people of prestige would watch and report on the proceedings at the trial. Andreas was getting eager to have the trial take place, wanting above all to have this open forum for a castigation of the dictatorship. No voice had yet been heard from within the country, and he saw this as an opportunity to express the protest of the nation now in bondage. He made several requests through his lawyers that the date be speeded up.

I did not feel this same eagerness. I did not believe that the death penalty was ruled out, despite noises from the junta to press representatives that the maximum sentence he could get was twenty years. Nor can I say that I was jumping with joy at the prospect of a twenty-year prison sentence. Others argued that the junta would have to go through a trial to save face, that Andreas would then serve a year or so in jail, after which he would be given amnesty. None of these hypothetical possibilities gave me comfort. Nor could I see that a trial and then Andreas behind bars would assist very much in resistance to the junta. I was sure that Andreas out and fighting could be much more effective.

Frank made a call to the American Embassy his first day in town and by accident discovered that a man from the junta had returned to the embassy for the second time asking for the answer on Andreas' citizenship, and when told that no answer had come through yet, had asked that a wire be sent to the State Department requesting an immediate answer. Apparently no one thought that I, as the wife of the prisoner, might be interested in this information, and it was learned only by chance. What was critical to me was that it proved that the junta was looking for *a way out*. This meant that Andreas' fate was not sealed, and that international efforts were bearing fruit. It also meant they knew the weakness of their position on the ASPIDA case.

Frank and I agreed on a plan. Since he knew Gene Rostow and Nick Katzenbach in the State Department, he would get in touch with them by phone upon arrival back in Geneva and convince them that it was important not to give a categorical "no" answer to the question of his citizenship. Although they must have understood in the State Department that the junta was looking for a way of getting rid of its biggest political problem, I wanted Frank to emphasize this, knowing that it had also become a headache for the State Department, if not an outright problem. Thus a statement that his status remained in doubt due to recent Supreme Court hearings on the case of the Israeli-American who voted in his native country might be adequate as an explanation for deportation. I didn't want the door shut with a definite answer. I told Frank that they might also mention the fact that the kids and I were American citizens, which somehow made it more logical that we might all be hustled off one night to the United States.

Now there were two plots under way, the "health plot" and the "citizenship plot," to open the iron doors of Averoff. Both of them were kookie and probably straws in the wind, but they added to my feeling of doing something. They also added to my feeling of living in a complicated world of intrigue, plot, and counterplot. And, as many times was the case, I took an action that gave the impression of something happening in the vague hope that it would help bring about the real event: the kids, my mother-in-law, and I got new vaccination certificates, and got our passports in order. I took the children off one single passport and put them on separate ones to add to our maneuverability. The news soon got around town that I was leaving Greece with the children.

Frank tried through the (reluctant) embassy to get an appointment with Pattakos or some other member of the junta. He was told the next day that Pattakos had said he would not discuss "anything in relation to Andreas Papandreou," and he had refused to suggest someone else in the government who might see him. The remark of Pattakos reminded me of my dream of little chubby men in black carrying in letters demanding Andreas Papandreou's release, and I wondered if Mr. Pattakos was beginning to gag on the name. The embassy felt that Frank should not push the point, which was the smoothest way out for them. He tried on his own to get directly to several other ministers, but with no luck.

He decided to write a letter to Pattakos, pointing out that since he had been refused an appointment, he was using this method to ask certain questions. These were the questions his letter contained:

1. Can one learn now of the approximate date of Andreas Papandreou's trial?
2. Will it be possible to arrange for the presence of American

*observers at the trial? (These would include advisers to Mrs.
Papandreou, who you know is an American citizen, as well as
representatives of groups in America who are deeply concerned about
the case.)*

*3. If such observers are permitted to attend, will they also be
permitted to employ interpreters?*

*4. Can one obtain copies now of the rules of procedure that will be
governing?*

*5. Will it be possible to arrange now for obtaining copies of the
indictment and other documents that will be crucial?*

The first paragraph of Pattakos' letter read: "Initially I find myself bound
to admit that it is hard to express the surprise which I experienced when I
read your letter dated July 17, 1967."

Why Pattakos was so astounded was never quite clear. As for the questions,
he stated that Andreas' legal advisers should be able to provide Mr. Newman
with this information. We hadn't really expected answers, but we were pleased
to give an impression of the magnitude of the interest in the case.

During Frank's four-day stay I had time to tell him about the third "plot"
under way, that of breaking the ASPIDA case wide open. Sheinbaum had
been the first to learn of the contact that had been made with two key
witnesses in the trial through the man who arrived unannounced at my house.
Since then I had contacted a lawyer friend of ours, unrelated to the ASPIDA
trial, and got him in touch with the man who had come to see me—a man by
the name of Xifaras—who truly seemed to be acting out of a deep
commitment to justice, a dedication to Andreas, whom he had never met! I
wanted to keep Andreas' lawyer out of it for as long as possible, and this was
what Andreas felt too when I managed to explain the situation to him. All of
us were naturally suspicious, wary, and cautious. It seemed too good to be
true that men considered key witnesses against Andreas would under the
conditions of a dictatorship offer to recant their testimony and describe the
force and pressure under which their depositions were signed.

Andreas' lawyer friend, whose name was Anastasios, felt that the first step
was to get written statements from both Vahliotis and Diakoyannis and hide
them somewhere for use at the trial. After these confessions were signed,
which could hardly please the junta since quite a few of its members, along
with Papadopoulos, had been secret service agents concocting the evidence on
the ASPIDA case before the coup, the two witnesses would not care to stick
around Greece for long. Once they were out it would be my job to contact
legal and journalistic friends to "break the story." This was the plan in its
simplest form, but because it was difficult to believe that these two pigeons,
as we named them, were singing for the love of honor or justice, we were
extremely suspicious of their motives and anticipated a possible trick. We were
primarily concerned that the recantation was meant to embroil Andreas'
lawyers in a charge of dealing with state's witnesses and thus give the
appearance of an attempt to bribe, which would have looked like a desperate
act of our side. For my part, I was also concerned about the timing of the
publicity on the story. If it came out too soon before the final indictment,

the prosecuting attorney's office preparing the indictment could exclude them from the evidence presented (finding some substitutes) and argue that they were in no way considered key witnesses in the case, thus taking the bang out of the explosion, leaving my friends who were working to expose these machinations holding a shriveled balloon.

But we were not at this stage yet, nor could I predict that we would get there. We were in that "underground" stage of contacts, secret meetings, testing of intentions. I took no part in these activities, leaving them to Anastasios, who reported back to me. Apparently Vahliotis wanted the price of an airplane ticket to Paris. Andreas told me under no circumstances should I give any money, and I wondered if that was not too extreme a case of honesty when the ticket might be the price we had to pay for Andreas' freedom. Vahliotis somehow got the resources, and the day after Frank left, Anastasios told me the confessions had been obtained, legally attested to, and the two "birds" were on their way out and would get in touch with Jim Schwartz in California. I was to instruct Jim immediately on what to do.

Jim knew nothing about this new development, and it was my fault that in my discussions with Anastasios I had not picked Frank Newman as the person to see, for he was in Europe and communication could be simplified. It was one of those periods when I had no foreign friends around, nor was I expecting anyone within a few weeks. It was extremely important that the affair be handled with the utmost caution, with legal safeguards, and without publicity until a signal was given from Athens. I was desperate.

After two days had passed and I saw no means of getting a communication out through safe channels, I decided to use the unsafe one—the Athens mail service—sending the letter to a name in Denmark used by Mogens Camre, and indicating the note was to be sent special delivery to Ruthie, our code name for Jim Schwartz. Mogens knew the code name. I had no code worked out with Jim, a ridiculous oversight since we had had the opportunity, so I tried my hand at being oblique and hoped he would get the message. My friends since then have told me I was not a very good codester. In any case, this note got through:

> *Dear Sam,*
>
> *Within the next two weeks someone will call you at home . . .a person who is the key witness in the coming garden show. He is turning defense and wants to spill all. If he does this, it is bomb of the hydrogen variety. He will want moola, but you will tell him it does not exist. However, a big magazine might be induced to buy his petunias, tell him. The important thing here is the publicity and the TV, etc. It must be ballyhooed all over. And you and Patricia must not appear to be connected—for the time being. This is absolutely essential for my protection. Later, for the garden show, you may be called upon to bring in your roses. You probably ask why. I think it is simple. He has gotten all the fertilizer he can get here and he thinks there is a new fertilizer for his flower beds outside. He has left some garden plans with us so his plants are already exposed—there-*

fore, you can milk him plenty. Remember he is a louse and needs to be kicked in the teeth—but right now he looks like, and smells like a gardenia to us. I trust you and Patricia to handle this well. If the setting for the advertisement could be somewhere near the eagle's town [Washington, D. C.]—maybe better. Keep this just to you and my sweet Patricia and I pray to god he arrives.

A week passed with no information on what had happened to the two witnesses, whether they had made contact or not with Schwartz, whether they had left for the States to find him, or whether they were still in Paris, and I waited for a message from the outside world.

The message came in the form of Walter Heller, past chairman of the Council of Economic Advisers under Kennedy and Johnson, and former colleague and friend from the University of Minnesota days. I had been informed that Walt was coming to add his prestige to the pressure for the release of Andreas, and was eagerly awaiting the sight of his six-foot-four frame in the front doorway. An embassy car brought him to the house, the first time since the coup that an official car of an American had approached Guizi Street. He looked cheery and relaxed, hardly aged a bit since the last time I had seen him in California when he attended a conference as John Kennedy's economic adviser, and looking as if he could be a dragon slayer.

He had just come from seeing Kay Bracken at the embassy who had shown him his program for the next day: Pattakos, Makarezos, Totomis, Zolotas, and Kollias—the first three junta members, the last two members of the old Palace and rightist establishment still around.

"No Papadopoulos?" I asked.

"It seems he seldom sees foreigners, and no one who has any interest in Andreas."

"Smart guy," I murmured.

"I know he's considered the real power in the junta, and I asked for an appointment, but the embassy said they couldn't arrange it."

"Or didn't want to," I added.

"I know you are not happy with the embassy here, and we'll talk about that, too, but first I want to tell you that I spent Thursday night in Paris talking to two Greek guys. Here, I have their names...Di-ak-o-yannis and something that starts with an 'X'—Tsifaris?" he asked.

"That's close enough but wow!"

"Yeah, that's what I said when I heard their story."

"Walt, how the hell did you get tangled up with them?"

"Well, I didn't exactly run into them in a bar," he smiled.

I waited.

"When I got to Paris there was a call waiting for me from Sheinbaum in California. He told me these two fellas were staying at such-and-such hotel and were important witnesses in the ASPIDA case, and apparently wanted to spill a story. He asked if I could see them and take some notes before I came down to Athens. He's planning to fly over in a few days to Paris to get formal, legal depositions."

"This Xifaras you mentioned, he's not involved. He's a go-between. He assisted in getting Diakoyannis to agree to tell how he gave false testimony, and if everything works out right I will kiss him for it one day."

"After I talked to them, I understood this. It seems that this Diakoyannis and some other character Vahliotis are key witnesses in the ASPIDA case."

I looked around as he said the name Vahliotis, then jumped up, walked over, and turned up the radio. We were sitting in the corner of the living room, he on the couch and I on an armchair, with a table and lamp in the corner between us. On his lap was a briefcase full of papers and on top of that a folder he had pulled out marked "Andy." It was Sunday noon, bright daylight, and I felt the need to crawl somewhere else, away from the blazing spotlight of the sun, to discuss these things under cover of darkness—and my mind flashed to old, remote roadhouses in Minnesota, a blazing pine fire barely lighting tables in the corners of the rooms. That being impossible, we proceeded in broad daylight.

"You saw Vahliotis, too?" I almost whispered.

"No, it seems he has returned to Athens."

"He has done what?" I shouted and bolted forward in my chair.

"Diakoyannis said he came back down to finish off a few things."

I groaned. "Oh, my God!"

"That's not so good, huh?"

"Look, Walter, of the two guys who somehow have turned round and recanted their testimony against Andreas, Vahliotis is the more important. In fact, Diakoyannis merely backs up some of the stories in Vahliotis' original deposition, but never really had contact with Andreas."

"So Vahliotis is the one you want out of here."

"Not only that, but since he has already signed a declaration recanting his original testimony against Andreas, and that declaration is hidden here in Athens available to us for the trial, it scares the hell out of me that he finds it so easy to come in and out of Greece."

"You mean you wonder what his game is."

"I'm afraid of another frame-up on top of the ASPIDA frame-up—something to discredit Andreas and his lawyers." By this time the two ASPIDA lawyers had been brought in, and were now in charge of the affair.

"Well, I told Kay Bracken about this story. I thought they should know what kind of methods were used to get Andy."

I didn't move. I stared at him for several seconds. The rapid, steady torrent of information we had been exchanging stopped like the abrupt end of a summer storm.

"Oh, Walter," I finally burst out, "you've been in government service too long—or something. You think of the embassy as an *ally*. All along it's been one of our greatest enemies, refusing to understand anything Andreas was doing, and fighting him at every point. They know the dirty methods that have been used; they don't want others to know that they know. Now I *am* afraid."

"I don't think Kay has any desire to make things rougher for you. But I'm sorry. I thought this would help."

"It isn't that any of them have personal animosity toward me, though they may have toward Andreas, but they are all part of a machine and in the end become the cogs that grind out the policy. And the policy is not very favorable toward us, nor toward the Greek people, I am afraid. Well, anyway, it's done . . ."

"Again, I'm sorry." I think he felt that I exaggerated somewhat. "I've got some pretty hot notes here." He reached into his briefcase and pulled out a legal-size yellow pad with hastily scribbled ink notes across many pages. "I tried to take down everything that was said, although I must say that I was pretty confused at times."

"On this particular issue, I have a suggestion, Walt. We should get together with Andreas' lawyer and his partner Lambrinides, who speaks English, and go over this together. They are handling this. Also, I think Menios should know that Vahliotis is back in town. He's not going to like it."

I called Georgie, whom I had seen wandering nervously around in the hallway, as was his habit more and more now, and asked him to run down to the kiosk and put a call through to Menios, after arranging with Walt that we could meet at his room in the Hilton the next day around 11:30 A.M.

"I remember him when you lived in St. Louis Park," Walt said, referring to Georgie. "We came to a cocktail party at your place once, and he was sitting in the corner on a low chair with a table in front of it. He cried when I talked to him. I guess I looked just too big from his vantage point. Then he sat sucking his thumb quietly and watching us at the party with a kind of skeptical, critical look."

"You amaze me, Walt, to remember that." I had forgotten that Georgie was a thumb-sucker, and for a moment I wondered what I could make out of that and his present-day anxieties and psychosomatic problems.

"Let me show you some good things before we get back to more serious discussion," Walt said, reaching into his bulging briefcase and pulling another big folder out.

"And let me suggest that we accompany it with a cup of coffee," I suggested. "Walt, I haven't relaxed for months, and just having you here to help makes me feel like the days when we were fighting to get Stevenson elected, when all was somehow normal—that is, I wasn't living under such a state of fear. Remember the night of election returns at the television set at your house?" That was 1952. "We lost," I said, suddenly deflated.

"This one we'll win, Maggie," Walter grinned, and his voice sounded confident.

What he had to show me was a pile of clippings from all over the States, pieces in the *Congressional Record*, copies of letters to Congressmen, anti-junta bulletins from New York, Canada, Minnesota, California, copies of letters and petitions sent to members of the junta, antidictatorial cartoons, and a few encouraging letters from personal friends. For an hour we pored over these items, relishing every violent attack against the military Mafia and every pro-Andreas piece. When we finished, he announced to me that he had a separate mission apart from his mission to help Andreas, and that was to obey the instructions of his colleagues back in Minneapolis to "give Maggie a good time, something to make her relax and forget her problems for a while." He suggested that he take me to the beach for the afternoon, and then out to dinner in the evening. We drove out to Lagonissi, to a public beach that was sometimes closed off for the private use of Ibn Saud, who was spending about $150,000 per day living expenses in Greece for himself, wives, sons, servants, etc., and who apparently took precedence over the public when he wanted a beach to himself. Today was not a day that the exiled King had requested use of the area. The day was windy, and a hot breeze carried sand and salt spray into our faces as we approached the edge of the water. I made a futile attempt to hold my hair in place in contemplation of a dinner out, and swam with my head stuck up, turtle-wise, from the water, ignoring Walter's challenge to race me to a distant rock. The water, as usual, was a tonic, and it wasn't until we got back to the sand where we sat talking, and I started drawing odd shapes in the sand with my fingers that I realized that tension was returning. We drove back to Athens in time to carry Andreas' dinner to him, disconcerting all the guards when Walt walked up the sidewalk with me and stood grinning and waved at Andreas at his cell window, shouting loudly, "Hi, Andy!" Andreas told me on Monday that it had caused quite a flurry at Averoff. The director, or his Sunday substitute, sent a guard up immediately to ask Andreas who that was, where he came from, what he was doing there, etc. Walter *did* look like a dragon slayer.

The results of Walter's visits with members of government can be summed up best by quoting some passages from his own confidential report written after he left Athens.

> Prime Minister Kollias: *Maggie warned me that Kollias hates Andy, and she was right. When he opened with a bit of humour (which I am told is very uncharacteristic), I countered with a semi-humourous suggestion that I had come to Greece to help him get rid of a problem, namely, Andreas Papandreou. That touched off violent invectives against Americans who were parading to Greece to interfere with its internal problems, that further visitors and letters will only result in a harder attitude towards Andreas, that the matter was in the hands of the courts anyway, and we could not influence them, and besides, Andy is disruptive, conspiratorial, and a treasonous Communist. I told Kollias that eight years of intimate professional and personal association had never yielded the slightest suggestion of Communist thinking or behavior, quite the contrary, he was a real fighter for the very parliamentary democracy and freedom which Kollias was telling me he was aiming at in his caretaker role. (It should be understood that Kollias is the King's—or perhaps the queen mother's—man rather than a formal member of the junta itself.)*
>
> *He took over half an hour to give me chapter and verse of Andy's Communist and conspiratorial activities beginning with his activities and jail sentence in 1938-39, and resumed in 1963 riding the coattails of his father, flouting the judicial process in the ASPIDA trial through parliamentary immunity, and plotting the seizure and overthrow of democratic government in Greece. Obviously, the junta*

line is that Andy was the reason the junta had to take over—and that is why I believe they feel they must try him in order to justify their own actions. . . . He calmed down by the end of our meeting and apologized for his initial explosion—this does not make him a nice man.

Pattakos: *He took pretty much the same hard line against Andy as Kollias had, though with perhaps less personal venom. He also pushed the Communist hard line, indicated that the Papandreou case was in the hands of the courts, that a trial must be held, that anything he might have said about deporting Andy had been overinterpreted—it was after all a matter for the courts to decide, not the government— that the junta had to take over in order to prevent a Communist takeover, end corruption, and bring Greece back to true values. He went on at some length to prove how disruptive and Communistic Andy had been; how he really was guilty in the ASPIDA plot; and how he would be a danger to Greece, wherever in the world he might be. He said some ugly things about people telling him that it would have been better to kill Andreas the first day after the coup for all the trouble he had caused since—government and academic protests, letters, visits (he claimed that Andy had had a number of visits in prison by various intellectuals—which seems a considerable exaggeration), numerous communications from Communist countries on Andy's behalf (but his aide, on request, could produce none of them), and so forth.*
 Then he took up my explicit request to visit Andy in prison, which had been passed along by Kollias. Pattakos went on at some length about how there had been too many visits, there was no point to it, it just served to make Andy think he was more important than he really is (!), and besides, it was directly against Greek law. So the answer, he regretted to say, was "no." But remembering Maggie's briefing on Kollias and Pattakos (which turned out to be very accurate), I appealed to his "Boy Scout mentality." I noted that in the light of our eight years of close association at Minnesota, we had become good friends; that it would be a deep disappointment to leave Greece without being able to do so. Pattakos seemed to soften, quizzed me on what I would talk about, and then he said that if it was just a personal visit, it might be arranged after all, and I should see Totomis at 7:45 A.M. Tuesday. His parting shot was that if I saw Andy on Tuesday, he would desert me on Wednesday. I countered that nothing in my relationship provided any basis for that kind of conclusion.

Makarezos: *The session with him opened with just a brief reference to Andy, and he had obviously been tuned in on the party line that this was a matter for the courts, not the governing junta, and justice had to run its course. Then he and his deputy went on to discuss economic policy.*

Totomis: *Apparently the party line had not been transmitted to him, because he spoke basically good sense. In direct contrast to Kollias, he noted that Andy's 1937-38 "Communist activities" were just the indiscretions of youth and that indeed a young man who didn't protest or belong to some movement to reform the world situation had something wrong with him. Also, he stated flatly that Andreas was not a danger to Greece. He felt that his main sin was that he had been "carried along with the current," had been thrown in with the wrong associates, had made mistakes of ambition and judgment and had pulled his father down with him... On the matter of seeing Andreas, he expressed some puzzlement on why I wanted to see him, and for a time, I thought he was going to veto the whole thing....finally [I got] authorization to see Andy from 10:30 to 11:00 A.M. He was cordial and basically reasonable—and probably has little power in the junta.*

On Monday noon we had our scheduled meeting with Menios and Lambrinides, both looking tanned and relaxed from a Sunday on the beach near Corinth. I met them in the lobby and told them that Walt had notes taken in Paris from Diakoyannis and Xifaras and knew much of the story of how Diakoyannis had perjured himself to satisfy the needs of the Greek KYP and establishment figures. When I told Menios that Vahliotis was back in town, he told me that he had heard that from someone who had seen him near Constitution Square a few days earlier. Once again I had the sensation that Athens was an overgrown village. I thought I was bringing special news of a secret nature, and the word had already reached Menios' ears. He agreed that it wasn't good.

Lambrinides was less concerned about this, and just plain jubilant that Walt had gotten mixed up in the case and had firsthand information about the nature of the frame-up against Andreas.

"We'll call him at the trial!" he leaned over and whispered to me with delight. At that moment Walter appeared through the revolving doors, and we proceeded to his room. Shortly after we started the discussion, there was a knock at the door and a maid and waiter, from their clothes at least, asked if a tray had been left in the room, and pushed their way in to look around. They spent more time looking at us than at the room, then, finding no tray, disappeared. Lambrinides' light blue eyes sought out mine, then moved toward the disappearing figures. He said simply, "Wherever we go, there they are," and winked to show indifference. It was a comfort to be near him. He was a fighter for human rights, it being his special field of legal study, a man who understood Andreas' crusade in Greece and was devoted to him personally as well, and who was important to me in all matters relating to the ASPIDA trial. He had recently been having heart problems—a sign of the times. The tension created by living under the military, essentially a lawless state, for there were no laws to protect the individual from the abuse of power, and the sheer anguish at the plight of the country were enough to try the weak spots in one's organism.

At the end of one hour we were still going over Walt's notes, my eyes

272

popping as I heard for the first time details on the sleazy, filthy manner in which the Greek KYP had concocted evidence against Andreas. It was time for my Monday visit at the jail, and I left in the middle of the story, saying good-bye to three heads intently bent over a low round coffee table, scrutinizing notes on a legal pad.

That was the last time I saw the fine, splendid Lambrinides. He died of a heart attack that afternoon.

With deep, piercing sorrow, I accompanied Walter to the King George dining room for dinner around 10 P.M., not to eat, because I had no appetite, but to hear the details of his visits of the day. He told me frankly that he had been unable to make a dent in his attempt to urge the junta to release Andreas so that he "could return to the academic world," that he felt they would hold the trial, and that he had found much hatred and vicious passion against Andreas. He himself looked white and exhausted, and told me that the experience had been shattering and that trying to reach these minds reminded him of a five-hour session he and his wife once had with key communists in a bloc country. There was no way of finding a common ground for discussion; their minds were one-way streets, closed. With an even heavier feeling, I climbed into bed that night and dreamed fitfully of being sucked into quicksand.

Walter left Tuesday noon. He had seen Andreas and had reported his general conclusions to him. On my next visit to Averoff I found Andreas calm and in amazingly good spirits. I think he was pleased that Walt felt there was going to be a trial. From Menios he had heard—through whatever code they had—of Walter's involvement in the "pigeon" story, and he told me "full speed ahead"—in other words, push for the exposure of the frame-up as fast and as hard as possible.

Thursday night Stanley Sheinbaum popped up for the third time. He was carrying notes from Paris, after a separate and *recorded* session with Diakoyannis and Company (by now a girl was added for translation help), and under the legal eye of Frank Newman, who as former dean of the law school at the University of California gave a serious tone to the meeting. Frank had flown to Paris from Geneva. I asked Stanley whether Jim had gotten my "petunia note," but Stan didn't know. All he knew was that Vahliotis had telephoned Jim long-distance from Paris, Jim had reached Lianis, and Lianis called Sheinbaum. Vahliotis said he wanted to talk to someone. Stanley located Heller in Europe and urged him to have the initial session before arriving in Athens. By the time Heller made the arrangement, Vahliotis had left Paris for Greece, and Heller saw only Diakoyannis. Then Stanley hightailed it in from the West Coast and set up the recorded session with "DK," as he liked to call him, but finding that Vahliotis had returned to Athens, and needing to fill in the gaps by consulting with Menios and me, he hopped down to Athens and walked in my front door, unannounced, as he had done the first time.

At midnight we gathered at a friend's home in Ekali, the small community a half an hour away from Athens, where Andreas and I had lived with the family on our first year in Greece. The highway to Ekali had taken us within a block of the President's house in Kastri and within two blocks of our former home in Ekali. Memories were poignant, and I shut them out. For three hours, along with Menios, who was suffering painfully from the death of Lambrinides, we pieced together the story of the means used, told by one of the two witnesses—Diakoyannis—to frame Andreas. It was only part of the larger fabric of lies and false evidence, but it was a keystone because it was to be the proof of Andreas' intentions to use the phantom military organization ASPIDA to "take Greece out of NATO, dethrone the King, and set up a socialist dictatorship."

About the two witnesses: Vahliotis I had seen twice, once in Paris on our return from Washington in June 1964, when Andreas introduced him to me as a classmate of his from Athens College days, and once, as I described previously, pacing around our backyard one early morning a month or so later, Andreas pacing silently by his side. I did not like the man. The other, Diakoyannis, was a Greek journalist living in Paris for over a decade who published a Greek newspaper called *Patris*. He also served as press attaché of the Greek delegation of OECD (Office of Economic Development). He met Andreas three times briefly, twice in Paris and once in London, but merely to exchange greetings. He wrote at his own initiative an article for a French newspaper praising Andreas. This was the extent of his personal contact with Andreas. He did, however, share a Paris office with Vahliotis and thus was used in the ASPIDA testimony to back up the stories of Vahliotis about telephone conversations with Andreas, meetings, letters, and contacts with representatives.

To follow the machinations of KYP, one must remember the end of the first ASPIDA trial, when, after sentences were pronounced on the unfortunate officers, an announcement was made by the prosecuting attorney's office that an investigation would be undertaken of "other persons, known or unknown, connected with the ASPIDA case." The trial of the officers had been a defeat for those establishment forces hoping to justify the King's action in July 1965, and to prove indirectly Andreas' involvement. All the evidence that could be collected had been collected, and it was nothing. Time was needed to concoct some.

The story that follows contains the main points of the sworn testimony of Diakoyannis given in Paris on the night of July 25, 1967, at the Hilton Hotel, and that of Andreas Vahliotis, given in San Francisco before a notary public on August 24, 1967. Taking Diakoyannis' testimony in Paris was Frank Newman, former dean of the law school at Berkeley, and Stanley Sheinbaum, professor at the Center for the Study of Democratic Institutions at Santa Barbara, California. Also present were Sigmund Mineiko, Andreas' cousin; Xifaras, the Greek who assisted the Papandreou cause and had initially contacted me, and a girl named simply Olga. Taking Vahliotis' testimony was John Merryman, law professor at Stanford University, and Richard Buxbaum, law professor at the University of California.

It is an ugly tale. It shows how the men of Greek KYP conspired to fix evidence, how they used methods of terror, blackmail, and bribery to weave a web around an innocent man, whose major faults were that he had become a popular idol, had a concrete program of reform, and, who, if he came into power, would throw them out of their jobs and try to create a new basis for democracy in Greece.

In June of 1966, two years after his brief summer contacts with Andreas (once in Paris and once in Psyhico), Vahliotis said he was contacted while in Athens by members of the secret service, who had information about secret memorandums he had sent to Andreas Papandreou. (The word "secret" is his word. His letters were suggestions of changes Andreas could make in government posts, a normal kind of letter coming from anyone trying to play the role of "consultant" to Andreas.) This was supposed to be evidence of Andreas' revolutionary designs! He had carbons of these lengthy letters to Andreas, the ones I had seen coming to our home in red and black ink, sentences carefully underlined, in which he developed a scheme proposing the creation of an organization which would control the state machinery, the army, and the police. Vahliotis told Diakoyannis at the time that Andreas had asked him to write up his ideas. The two had discussed some aspects of the proposal; Diakoyannis had read the final drafts of the several letters, corrected them, and mailed them. One letter he claims he himself delivered to a close associate of Andreas' in Athens. There were no letters from Andreas, nor his signature anywhere.

This sounded to me accurate and quite feasible. I remembered George Papandreou giving advice to Andreas once. "When a Greek starts proposing big theories on the problems of Greece, or a critical analysis of what is being done wrong, tell him, no matter how weird his suggestions are, to write them up in a memo and send them to you. Say they are 'very interesting,' and you look forward to reading them. Nine times out of ten, the man will do nothing, because most Greeks dislike working, but enjoy expounding aloud to someone in power." I am sure that this is what Andreas did when he first saw Vahliotis in Paris in 1964. He patted Vahliotis on the back and said, "Fine, fine, send your ideas to me."

The month after being contacted by the secret service—July 1966—Vahliotis came to Paris to see Diakoyannis. He told him, "This story you know about Andreas Papandreou is very important and many people are interested. When he said "story" he was referring to the letters he himself had written, about which Diakoyannis knew. Diakoyannis replied that it might be interesting to many people, but not to him. Vahliotis suggested that he come to Athens for a visit that summer and Diakoyannis replied that he had already made his plans for a holiday there.

Several days after he arrived in Athens he ran into Vahliotis. They chatted together. Vahliotis asked him to meet him the next day at 8:30 at Constitution Square. Diakoyannis went to the appointment, but Vahliotis was not alone. A few steps behind him was a man in a blue suit. There were introductions. The man in the blue suit was introduced as "Colonel so-and-so," a fake name, but the real name was later known, Colonel Takis Apostolopoulos, a KYP officer.

Apostolopoulos told Diakoyannis that all he knew about the relationship between Papandreou and Vahliotis must be told to the Greek government (now under the peculiar apostate-ERE coalition), and according to Diakoyannis, the words were said in a threatening manner. The threat was that if he did not comply, he would never again see Paris, his wife, or his children. He was told that at 9:00 P.M. he must meet with the Prime Minister, Stephanopoulos, which he did.

He was escorted to the Prime Minister's office in the Parliament building by Apostolopoulos. There Stephanopoulos was waiting for him, speaking to him first in his large office, then taking him to a smaller one to continue the conversation. The Prime Minister told Diakoyannis that "someone wants to destroy Greece" (Andreas). He continued, picking up an envelope he had on his desk, that "Andreas Vahliotis has given evidence. He is an excellent person with an excellent record and whose father is a general. You have information about this matter and you must make it known."

Diakoyannis told Frank Newman that he felt the meeting had been arranged by KYP to impress him with the importance of the matter and to intimidate him further into corroborating Vahliotis' story, whatever it was. Stephanopoulos himself called the office of the State Attorney, a man named Papadopoulos (not the dictator Papadopoulos), and made an appointment for Diakoyannis to see him two days later.

When he saw the State Attorney, he told him that he hardly knew Andreas Papandreou and didn't really want to be involved. The answer was, "We don't ask you to testify. We merely want a short memo about what you know."

At this point, according to the taped recording made in Paris, Diakoyannis said, "I made the memo, and it is the same as I said to you, Mr. Newman. I realized that Vahliotis had explained much to KYP and received money from KYP; he, Vahliotis, told me so."

The transcript of the tape recording made in Paris continues as follows:

> Newman: *In the memo was there disclosed contents of the documents from Vahliotis to Papandreou?*
> Diakoyannis: *Yes.*
> Newman: *Only Vahliotis to Papandreou documents, not Papandreou to Vahliotis documents?*
> Diakoyannis: *When Papandreou and Vahliotis were in contact Athens to Paris, Papandreou sent a man "Alec" to come in a plane. Alec changed his plans and his plane and this information came in a wire.*
> Newman: *Could you be sure that these were not from KYP?*
> Diakoyannis: *No, I could not be sure.*
> Newman: *But you never saw anything with Andreas Papandreou's signature?*
> Diakoyannis: *Never [emphatically]. And I cannot even say that the man who did come from Athens was Papandreou's man. But I did see and speak with this Alec.*

This contact with Alec refers to the time Andreas sent a man to learn about the plot to murder his father, which Vahliotis promised to reveal.

> Diakoyannis: *And here begins another story how KYP planned to exterminate Andreas Papandreou. I accepted to follow the second*

*story for personal reasons. I had gone to Paris, Rome, Athens, with
KYP types, but I will not speak of this.*

    Newman: *But if you were in court you would have to speak.*

    Diakoyannis: *I will speak later. This is very revealing. These are
amazing facts for the whole world. If I speak now that would
foreclose Papandreou's trial.*

These enigmatic remarks were never clarified.

In an affadavit made in San Francisco on Thursday, August 24, 1967,
before a notary public, Andreas Vahliotis made a sworn statement telling his
side of the story in the framing of Papandreou. Following are quotes from the
affadavit:

> Q. *Have you been involved in the pending proceedings against
> Andreas Papandreou in Greece?*
>
> A. *Yes, I have been. As a matter of fact, I am considered as a key
> witness to the charges against Andreas Papandreou.*
>
> Q. *What was your first contact with the proceedings against
> Papandreou?*
>
> A. *Well, my first contact was dated about June 1966, in Athens.*
>
> Q. *What was the nature of that contact?*
>
> A. *I was brought in contact by agents of KYP.*
>
> Q. *Will you tell us what the KYP is?*
>
> A. *I would say it is a similar organization as the CIA in this
> country.*
>
> Q. *Will you describe the contact with them?*
>
> A. *Yes. They had information from one of their agents, who was a
> very close friend of mine—and I didn't know he had contacts with
> KYP—and they obliged me to hand them copies of some memoran-
> dums I had sent to Andreas Papandreou.*
>
> Q. *Were these documents, this correspondence and these docu-
> ments you had had with Andreas Papandreou incriminating docu-
> ments?*
>
> A. *No, they were not. Actually, the document in which the KYP
> agents were interested was the last one, dated July 26, 1964, in
> which I was giving some ideas to Andreas Papandreou on how to
> re-establish the strength of the political party he was a member of.*
>
> Q. *The Center Union Party?*
>
> A. *The Center Union Party. And this document was referring to
> replacements of the chiefs of staff of the armed forces of Greece.
> And also the replacement of high officials of the police, plus the
> replacement of certain ambassadors and consuls who were outside
> Greece and who did not agree with the policy of the government of
> Mr. George Papandreou.*
>
> Q. *Was there any suggestion in this correspondence or in these
> documents that these replacements should be done illegally or by
> force?*
>
> A. *No, there was no suggestion that those changes or replacements
> would take place by force or illegally. They were just suggestions and*

they couldn't be illegal suggestions because, after all, we were a democratic country and all replacements were done in a democratic way. And it's only natural that a government has to replace high officials if they don't agree with the policy or like to be involved in politics.

Q. Now, did you make a supplementary statement to the KYP people in addition to giving them the documents?

A. Yes, I did that about ten days later. It should be between the 20th or 22nd or 25th of June 1966. I can't remember exactly. At that time it was Mr. Takis Apostolopoulos, but who was presented to me for the first time under a different name. I didn't know him by name then.

So they asked me to put in writing all my relationship and what I have suggested up to that moment to Andreas Papandreou. In other words, they knew that we had continuous contact from June 30, 1964, starting in Paris, and all the month of July roughly; we were in contact, he in Athens and I in Paris.

So I did write this. There were about 22 typed pages. They took it, read it. And then they asked me to make some changes in it. And those changes were absolutely incriminating against Andreas Papandreou. In other words, I had to put down words and ideas of his to me, which he never said.

Q. In other words, you were asked by KYP to say that Andreas Papandreou had said things to you which in fact he had never said?

A. He had never said. And if I did not agree, they would incriminate me and they will charge me with the same charges as Andreas Papandreou as an accomplice to conspiracy against the state and the regime.

Q. So the KYP threatened you with prosecution?

A. Right.

Q. And other things?

A. Other things. But not the same man. He sent that friend of mine, said besides that they could do other things to myself and to my family which actually will be worse than charging me and imprisoning me.

Q. And it is because of these threats that you made these false statements?

A. Exactly, exactly. They obliged not only me but Mr. Diakoyannis to confirm or verify what I have stated in that document.

Q. Including that part of it that was untrue?

A. Of course. That's the main thing. That document was completely untrue.

Q. Were the documents, including this statement, subsequently presented to the public prosecutor?

A. Right, they were.

Q. And were you then examined?

A. *That was roughly the 15th of August, 1966.*

Q. *And were you then examined by the public prosecutor?*

A. *By the public prosecutor. The first time I was not examined. I was called by the prosecutor, S. Papadopoulos, and he asked me to verify all the evidence he had in the file, in other words, two cables sent to me by Papandreou, a letter which was sent to me by the representative of Papandreou, who came to Paris, and the copies of my memos to Andreas Papandreou.*

Q. *Of which you have already spoken here.*

A. *Yes. That was my first visit to the prosecutor's office. And then 15 days later I was taken—and I say "I was taken"—by the KYP agents to the prosecutor, Mr. Tarassouleas, where I had to verify again documents. I gave a statement there, answered the same questions. And the next step was the magistrate.*

Q. *Excuse me, before you go to the magistrate. The statements you made to the public prosecutor confirmed the truth of the statements you made in the memorandum about Papandreou, which were untrue statements?*

A. *Right.*

Q. *And following your appearance with the prosecutor you came before a magistrate?*

A. *Right.*

Q. *It is a civil magistrate?*

A. *Civil magistrate.*

Q. *What happened in the presence of the magistrate?*

A. *Well, he read me all my statements, Socratides was his name, and he asked me whether I had to add anything. I said no. And then he started asking some questions for his own use. He asked me further questions whether other political personalities were involved in the ASPIDA case. And—well, that was it. I didn't have to add anything else.*

Q. *You said that the evidence was faked and was not true. Specifically what items in the statement you had given to KYP were not true?*

A. *There were two points. Those are put in the last page of the memo. In reviewing the whole whatever happened during the 1st and 26th of July, 1964, I was sure that Andreas Papandreou was a criminal, he was acting against his country; and this I was sure of because he told me that the elimination of his political opponents could not be done in a normal way, a democratic way, but it has to be done by eliminating those people by force, using a scalpel.* And number two was that the Kingdom had nothing to do in Greece any more and the King should be ousted, either by election, or if elections were negative, by force. Those two points actually did*

---

*It is interesting that this figure of speech was one used by Papadopoulos in a press conference shortly after the coup.

indict Andreas Papandreou in charges of conspiring against the regime and the state. *[Emphasis mine.]*

Q. *Had you originally made those two points in your statement?*

A. *In the first statement?*

Q. *In your original statement to KYP.*

A. *No.*

Q. *How did they get into this?*

A. *They read what I had written, and they came with two or three sheets of paper, and crossing certain points. And then they said, "You add that thing here with your own words"—so that it looked like it comes from me—"but we want this to be put here and the other one to be put there." This last page is entirely written by those people.*

Q. *That includes these two points or statements?*

A. *Right. That Andreas Papandreou is a criminal.*

Q. *These KYP people put these statements which are untrue in your mind?*

A. *Yes. They gave them to me in typing and I typed them again.*

Q. *Now, you are making this statement, Mr. Vahliotis. Why are you making this statement?*

A. *Well, Mr. Merryman, I talked with the lawyers of Andreas in Athens, when I gave them that letter denying the charges, and we decided that this thing would greatly help Andreas Papandreou if it could come out publicly and have the free world—when I am talking about the "free world" I mean the western world—to know how Andreas Papandreou was imprisoned and why; and because I know that Andreas Papandreou had never thought in conspiracy against his country. I know that he's an honest man and an honest politician; and because he is honest he had to be eliminated. That is my belief.*

Vahliotis: *I would like to close by reaffirming that whatever I have testified against Andreas Papandreou in the prosecutor's office and the magistrate's office in Athens was the result of pressure and threats against my life and my family's life by agents of KYP, and that everything which is in those depositions are pure lies, everything incriminating Andreas Papandreou is not true.*

By the end of the summer, 1966, approximately one year after the overthrow of the Papandreou government, the foundations were being laid, with the assistance and knowledge of the Prime Minister of the country, Stephanopoulos, to frame Andreas.

In Diakoyannis' recorded testimony to Newman and Sheinbaum in Paris at the Hilton Hotel, he indicates in a hazy fashion that the process of concoction of evidence continued and that he somehow maintained contact with KYP "types," as he calls them, in Athens, Rome, and Paris. This part of the story he never reveals clearly, saying only that "here begins another story of how KYP planned to exterminate Andreas Papandreou." At one point he says, "I apologize for not telling the second part of the story. My wife and children are still in France, and I would be kicked out."

Parts of the story do come out, however. He told Newman, "Here in Paris one day somebody said (he is now a member of the junta) that 'I would give my hands the day Papandreou would be killed.' And here in Paris we discussed . . ."

> Q. *With whom did you discuss?*
> A. *With men of the junta . . . what were the possibilities and what would have been the reactions if they kill Papandreou. They even said that "what reactions . . . When a man like Kennedy was killed this fact was forgotten . . . And you talk about a man like Papandreou." But the head of the group which had come to Paris, a high-ranking officer, he did not like this discussion. He was opposing it.*
> Q. *Approximately when was this?*
> A. *End of November or beginning of December 1966.*
> Q. *Long before the coup?*
> A. *Yes.*

The threat to Andreas' life before the coup had been a real one. In addition to that, the concoction of evidence Diakoyannis talks about during this period of time included several attempts to trap Andreas. From summer, 1966, to December 1966, we were aware of three such attempts. One noon in late summer we were having lunch with George Lianis, who was returning to America after a frustrating year in Greece trying to put together the University of Patras under the Stephanopoulos government. It was a project started under the government of George Papandreou, was Andreas' brainchild as well, and got off to a good start with the acquisition of many acres of land on a Patras mountainside overlooking the city and the sea. Helping in the project was one of Sweden's top economists, Ingvar Svennilson, under the auspices of OECD. The project had rapidly deteriorated under the Stephanopoulos government. Also eating with us was Vassilis Fillias, a Greek social scientist. (Vassili was arrested in the spring of 1968 by the junta for resistance activities and is in Averoff Prison as of this writing.)

The doorbell rang, and within seconds Antigone came into the dining room with a note for Andreas. It read, "I am the lawyer of Bouloukos [the alleged military head of ASPIDA] and have a letter from him for you."

Andreas told Antigone to put him in the living room, and he went to the hall phone and called the head of his political office, Andoni Livanis, telling him something fishy was going on, and asked him to come over immediately. Livanis arrived in fifteen minutes during which time the four of us sat rather tensely eating our food. Andreas told our two guests that he suspected a trap, but wanted Andonis to handle it. In the living room, Livanis looked at the letter. It was many pages, and written in a familiar tone, as if contact were normal between the two. Levanis took a shot in the dark. "This is not the handwriting of Bouloukos," he shouted angrily. The man who called himself a lawyer quavered. "I know," he said, "it's my handwriting. I copied his letter so that he wouldn't get into trouble." Livanis' reaction was quick and decisive. "Get the hell out of here and don't let us see your blasted face again!" What the evil schemers of KYP were concocting is hard to know. The most probable is that they hoped the man would come out with an answer, and they could in that fashion establish the fact that there was contact between Andreas and Bouloukos. It was naïve as a trap, but one shouldn't forget that the operators of KYP, particularly at lower levels, are not so much distinguished for their brains as for their brawn.

Sometime later, a newspaper editor, friend of Andreas', called Andreas to his office. He said that that morning he had received a mysterious phone call from Rome saying that it was urgent that he reach Andreas and tell him to arrange for either himself or a representative to meet someone in Italy to get information important to him for his defense in the ASPIDA trial. Another trap. Diakoyannis' statement that he was with KYP types in Rome during that same period of time reminded me of this story.

The third was a contact with a man who came to our house through an arrangement with a friend. He stated that he was not a follower of Andreas' (an endearing trick to establish that he was being honest), that he held other political beliefs, but that he wanted to see justice done. There was a man on the island of Lemnos, he told him, who knew a lot about the plot against Andreas. Could Andreas send someone *along with his I.D. card for identification* to make a contact there? The I.D. card was necessary, he explained, because the fellow there was taking a great risk to reveal his information, and would have to be sure it would reach only Andreas. It was curious that a stockpile of weapons, charged by the Stephanopoulos government to be "communist" weapons had been recently discovered in a cave on that particular island. The sending of Andreas with his I.D. card to that island to make a contact would have made for ten pages of burning accusation in the ASPIDA indictment. Mr. X, definitely a KYP type, was politely but firmly escorted to the door.

We pick up Diakoyannis again in January 1967, when he got a wire from the Ministry of Coordination firing him from his post as press attaché to OECD. This must have surprised him since he had been cooperative in the plot to frame Andreas. According to his story, he went to Athens shortly thereafter to make some arrangements to get it back then or after elections, since the Paraskevopoulos government was a "temporary one," as he put it. By now, of course, the Stephanopoulos government had fallen, and we were swimming around in the Paraskevopoulos solution.

While in Athens for this purpose, KYP again contacted him. "KYP proposed to me . . . in the month of February . . . a few days after my return to Greece, a person, whose name I can even tell you, who is today among those who govern Greece, proposed to me in the Astoria coffeehouse to cover all my financial needs, and I refused. This man told me that day that a coup was going to take place in Greece . . . within two months at the latest. He did not exactly tell me 'coup d'etat,' but 'in two months, Mr. Diakoyannis, if you are with us and do what we will tell you, you must rest assured that, in two months, I will be in a position to give you all you can imagine.' "

Here in the taped recording Diakoyannis paused, and then repeated to Newman, "I can even tell his name. It is Colonel Tsakas. Evangelos Tsakas. [When I told him no] he told me that 'either by persuasion or force that which you must do, you will do. And for this reason Apostolopoulos has undertaken to carry out that which you must do. And do not think that you will escape!' Then I realized that the telegram which the Minister of Coordination sent and was dismissing me, he did not send on his own initiative but it was a telegram from KYP."

Diakoyannis then explained that he believed the firing from his job was a trap to bring him to Athens. The day following this conversation at the Astoria coffee shop, Diakoyannis says he was escorted by Apostolopoulos and Paleologos, now the Director of the Political Bureau of the Prime Minister, to the office of Socratides, who asked him to repeat what was written in his earlier memo. "Two days later the prosecuting attorney asked for the removal of Andreas Papandreou's parliamentary immunity."

That was the night I sat stunned as the news was brought to us of this precipitate action and had seen big black headlines in my dreams: WANTED FOR HIGH TREASON. Socratides had said that "new and revealing evidence had come out." Diakoyannis and Vahliotis were part of that new and revealing and *false* evidence.

After February, and his last deposition to Socratides before the coup, Diakoyannis told little to Newman and Sheinbaum about his activities. He claimed he lived most of the time at his father's house because he was "broke."

He emerged from this murky period of inactivity, according to him, two days after the coup when he heard on the telephone the familiar voice of KYP man Aspostolopoulos, newly in power as he had predicted when the secret services took over Greece with the help of the Greek army, who said to him, "I have to tell you something pleasant. On the basis of your and Vahliotis' depositions Socratides has decided on preliminary arrest of Papandreou." The word "arrest" was a technicality since Andreas had been brutally arrested the night of the coup and was under heavy guard at Pikermi Hotel. The junta, however, was going through the formalities, trying to give a legal look to their gang activities, and thus Socratides actually did go up to Pikermi and in the presence of Menios Koutsoyergas read the official charges against him and put him "under arrest."

Around the same time, Diakoyannis was given a pass of free access to the Prime Minister's office, the office of Kollias, the puppet of the regime, a pass that he displayed to his interrogators in Paris. It was apparently his reward for collaborating in the ASPIDA frame-up. It bore the word *diarkias,* meaning lasting or permanent pass card. He used this pass as his "in" with the KYP people running the country through the revolutionary council to gain an appointment with Kollias for a *Newsweek* reporter three days after the coup. Next to Kollias, acting as watchdog, was the newly appointed Political

Director to the Prime Minister, none other than Paleologos, his old KYP buddy active in concocting the evidence against Andreas.

Toward the end of the interview in which Diakoyannis was doing the interpreting, Pattakos came in the side door of the Premier's office and stood listening to the conversation. The *Newsweek* reporter had asked to visit Andreas Papandreou, and see "if his head was still on his shoulders." Permission had been granted. Pattakos was to escort him there.

"When he [Pattakos] saw I was interpreting well between the reporter and Kollias, he turns to me and tells me, 'You will come with me.' He did not know me; he had never seen me before. He tells me, 'to help me where I am going. To act as an interpreter.' At that moment the Director of the Political Bureau [Paleologos] jumps up, takes Pattakos by the hand and tells him, 'This is Mr. Diakoyannis. You must not take him where you are going.' And he did not tell him in a beseeching, but in an imperative tone, because he is now a member of the revolutionary council. And then he tells Pattakos that I had been in Paris with him a few months before to gather evidence against Andreas Papandreou. He said, 'Don't take him with you. He is one of the main witnesses we have for the trial against Papandreou, and where you are going nobody must see him.' "

The members of the new Greek government were hoping to keep their scandalous frame-up of Andreas Papandreou under cover. Two of their witnesses turned stool pigeons, however, and fled to tell their story. Bits and pieces of the story remain yet to be told, but one thing became obvious: the unethical thugs of the secret service world who used threats, bribery, deceit, and lies to frame Andreas are the iron-fisted gang rulers of Greece today.

CHAPTER TWENTY-FOUR

A Victory for Our Side

AUGUST was tenser than July. My main problems were George's deepening depression and anxiety, Andreas' announced illness, Andreas' rumored escape from prison, the Vahliotis-Diakoyannis story, and the official, final ASPIDA indictment.

In addition to these, I was still pursuing the citizenship theme, waiting for more official word of what had been decided by the State Department, although Frank had felt quite sure that an idenfinite answer would be given, which was what I wanted.

During the months of June and July, Ambassador Talbot had been in Washington on home leave, briefing the staff there, and being briefed in return. Walter Heller talked to him by phone in the States after his visit with me in Greece prior to Talbot's return and told him of my eagerness to hear a more official version on the citizenship story. According to Walter's report on his trip, and I quote, "I took this up with Talbot, and he promised to talk with Maggie about it after getting back to Athens."

Thus I waited with some interest to see whether at long last I would have a communication from the embassy, initiated by them, to arrange an appointment for me with the ambassador. It would have been at the least courteous. It would have been at the most, a human thing to do. It didn't happen. Before picking up the phone to ask for an appointment myself, I came into possession of a report which started as follows:

> U.S. Ambassador to Greece Phillips Talbot was in town for consultation this week. He agreed to give us his assessment of the Greek situation on the understanding that it was for background only, with no attribution to official sources.

Because this document gives, I think, a fairly accurate picture of Talbot's point of view, and therefore the point of view of the State Department at the time, it would be useful to reprint the report.

> Compared with military takeovers at other times and places, the Greek colonels are running a soft coup regime, Talbot says. This is a relative kind of calculation, of course, but he points out that only about 30-odd political figures aside from left-wingers are under detention or surveillance, only one of them—Andreas Papandreou—is

285

under indictment, and although the hazards for all are obvious, no one is in physical jeopardy or in danger of execution.

At the same time, there are about 3,000 suspected communists or front activists being held in barracks or islands. The official U.S. Government estimate of Communist Party members in Greece is 27,000, out of a total of about 82,000 who back the communist front—EDA. These detainees are being screened by the regime, then instructed to sign a pledge repudiating all future political activity. Those who sign are usually released. Even though almost all of those held are hard core communists whose names have been on Greek security service lists for years.

The regime's decrees are so encompassing that almost any kind of political discussion can be considered a violation, and there are arrests almost every day for security offenses—defamation of the government or the King being leading charges. But Talbot is unable to estimate how many persons have so far been arrested, nor how many have actually been punished for such violations.

Just what this rigid control means to the individual citizen is hard to assess. "From the non-political citizens," says Talbot, "there has been much more acquiescence than we expected. This could be temporary, but it probably also reflects a tremendous relief from the tensions of the pre-election period." The anxiety over what was to come, fear of riots, disruption and chaos is now gone. The innumerable work stoppages, transport interruptions, uncertainties of daily life have largely ended, and "normalcy" has returned. In that way, at least, there has been a relaxation.

In the capital, the evening business at cafés has picked up again, but naturally the bans on assembly have "restricted the social season." Athens is also more quiet than usual because of the Mideast War. Fully a third of Greece's tourists come on package tours to the Mideast, compounding the reduction brought about by the coup itself.

As far as Talbot can tell, there is no underground fighting the regime and "no opposition movement coalescing." No handbills or wall graffiti have appeared to denounce the military government.

The businessmen seem rather pleased. "In fact," says Talbot, "they are getting speedier decisions from the government and the strangling red tape has been reduced. Naturally, the former politicians, intellectuals, liberals, international figures are outraged and ashamed. But before the takeover in April the situation inside Greece was so bad that even those who truly deserve the name 'democrats' were extremely worried about the future." The intellectuals were deeply concerned by the polarization that was taking place—rightwing against leftwing—on the Greek domestic scene. The upshot is at least a temporary feeling among the majority of Greeks that the peace and quiet they now have is better than the upheaval and threat they had before.

Talbot hastens to add that he is merely reporting, not placing a value judgement on the situation. He personally believes the coup was not a good thing, and will not be a good thing for Greece. How much damage it does to the Greek society and economy depends on how long it lasts, he says.

[Copy unclear] . . . is a crowned republic, and its essential organ is parliament about which the provisions of the Constitution are cardinal. It is inconceivable that the parliamentary regime could be abolished. It will not be abolished. Furthermore, provisions will be made for it to operate in Greece in a healthy form, so that it can really become an organ for the nation, not an organ for a party.

On that day it was announced that a 20 man committee had been appointed to draw up the new Constitution within six months. It was the King, we're told, who pushed the cabinet into setting up the six-month deadline—an important ingredient in the effort to make a military step-down look orderly and inevitable.

"The men on the Constitutional Committee," Talbot says, "are distinguished lawyers and scholars, men of integrity and ability. They will not easily be pushed around, so the committee is now a factor in the Greek political equation. Visible steps are in train to replace the colonels. The expectation that this will be done is now seeping down through all levels of the Greek public. The expectation, in fact, might well be an important reason why there has been no organized opposition to the coup regime so far. "But," Talbot warns, "if the colonels break their word and disrupt this process, then there would be a tremendous crisis."

Meanwhile the King is rebuilding his position, he has lost much of his influence with the Army. Of course, he is now touring the bases and inspecting the troops in an effort to get it back. He travels a great deal, talks with the generals, with the ministers, greets the people and his soldiers. "He can't pull strings like the Shah of Iran, but he is gaining influence," Talbot says. "Many of those who criticized the King most harshly before the coup are now solidly behind him. The King is now the strongest force for Constitutionalism in Greece."

More to come.

July 28th, 1967.

In a few words, the report displays mild tolerance of the regime, a belittling of the fact that thousands of citizens had been thrown into jail (they were communists, anyway), and a condemnation of the situation before the coup. He also reports that the "anxiety of what was to come" (a Papandreou victory) is now gone. This was the anxiety not of the majority of the Greeks, but of the Palace, the army, and the American Embassy.

Thus at a stage when the junta was rocky, unsure of itself and not yet entrenched, when American rejection would have been decisive, Talbot expressed a point of view justifying the colonels, reiterating their statements about the chaos of democracy prior to the coup, and breathing life into a struggling monster-infant. The Greeks had been waiting for Talbot's return—the people with desperate hope; the junta with anxiety to see what their fate would be. Only the Americans were capable of stripping them of power. Although there were rumors later of a "scheme" brought back by the ambassador, at the moment one heard an audible sigh of relief on the part of the barbarians in government.

Norbert Anschuetz was transferred from Athens to Washington, and my only sources of information in the United States Embassy were his replacement, whom I did not know personally, and Talbot. In my meeting with Talbot, three weeks after his return, an appointment made by me, he said he knew nothing about any statement on the part of the State Department on Andreas' citizenship. And that was that. He told me the pleasant news, probably true, that American businessmen were interested in investment in Greece under the new situation, that Greece ranked about thirty-two on the list of United States problems, and that it fell in the context, in any case, of a much broader international setting. ("Cold war?" I thought.)

On the morning of August 15, Takis, our Greek reporter friend, arrived to tell me the startling news that Pattakos had announced at a press conference the evening before that Andreas was seriously ill. Because I was seeing Andreas in my weekly visits, I knew his condition well, and knew this was not the case. A tiny mental light, however, flashed through the message to be careful what I said, for this could be the initial step in the "health plot." Of the three army men who led the coup, Pattakos was the most pro-royal and the closest to the King. Since Andreas was obviously not ill, what other explanation could there be for this peculiar announcement? I told Takis that it was true that Andreas had lost weight, that he suffered some pains, that I couldn't be sure of his true condition, since his personal physician had not seen him. Poor Takis was in an awful state. He undoubtedly suspected foul play and smelled a dire scheme to take Andreas' life, and he wanted to make me aware of it without frightening me. So we each talked to the other in a guarded fashion, neither revealing our inner stream of thoughts.

In the London *Times* later that day, I read the story, "Ex-Minister is Ill in Gaol."

> *Brigadier Stylianos Pattakos, the Minister of the Interior, disclosed tonight that Professor Andreas Papandreou, son of the former Greek Prime Minister, is suffering from "an acute case of tuberculosis."*
> *. . . Brigadier Pattakos said tonight that he talked with the professor's physician. "He told me that Andreas is suffering from a severe lung ailment but his condition does not give rise for immediate anxiety. . . . During the meeting Andreas described to me his condition and asked me to speed up his trial. . . ."*

Two days later a new and stranger story reached me, that Andreas had escaped from jail. The story reached far and wide. In Denmark, on the same day, our friend Mogens Camre heard the story and tried frantically to reach

288

someone of influence who could check it. Walter Heller was back in Europe at the time, and was eventually reached by Mogens. Walt tells it as follows:

> *Mogens Camre had a call waiting for me when I arrived in Gothenburg [Sweden] Thursday morning. I called and found him highly agitated about UPI reports that Andy had escaped. He said his telephone calls to the Danish parliamentary group in Athens had been cut off, that Andy might be in great danger, etc., etc. I promised to call Phil Talbot. Late in the day, I reached Phil Talbot, and he told me that there was no escape; that the press had misinterpreted Pattakos on Andy's TB (his reference was to months or years ago, but the press had made it weeks); and he had recently seen Maggie. (Yes, indeed!) (He said our call was on an "open international line and probably being listened to in four countries.") (So shut up, Walter Heller, about Andreas Papandreou.)*

At the same time that all this was happening, another wild event occurred. Averoff, the Foreign Minister under Karamanlis for eight years, respected member of ERE, was sentenced to five years' imprisonment for violating the law of the military regime which stated that no more than five people could gather together in a home without the consent of the local police.

Now the State Department was very upset. A member of ERE? Foreign Minister under Karamanlis? Member of a distinguished Athenian family? And lo and behold and glory be, it came out with its third public statement on the Greek situation since the coup. The first had been a statement by Secretary Rusk on April 28 in which Rusk noted that the United States was waiting for "concrete evidence" that the regime in Greece would return as speedily as possible to democratic government; the second, a statement by McNamara, Secretary of Defense, on May 10, 1967, was made on his return from the NATO Defense Ministers meeting in the same general spirit as Rusk's statement; and the third, on August 17 by a State Department spokesman:

> *Since the present government of Greece took power in April, the United States has expressed hope for the early restoration of civil liberties and concrete steps toward the return of parliamentary government. We therefore regret the sentence imposed yesterday on former Foreign Minister Averoff. We take some encouragement, though, from press reports that the Greek government has recommended that King Constantine pardon Averoff.*

There had been no mad outcry at the thousands of Greek citizens pulled from their beds on that awful night of April 21 and pushed off to island exile or prisons; there had been no strong protest at the loss of all human rights of the Greek nation; there had been no anguish publicly stated at the imprisonment and subsequent house arrest of George Papandreou, true head of the Greek people, or Cannellopoulos, leader of ERE. There had been nothing, nothing said or even whispered, about the arrest and indictment of Andreas Papandreou. There had been nothing about the violent overthrow of a government and the abrogation of the Constitution.

But now, a member of the establishment, a close friend of the United States and potential future political leader, had been harshly treated. A pox on the dictatorship! This was the essence and level of the foreign policy of a great country, the United States!

On the same day as the announcement of the sentence of Averoff, Pattakos went through a vaudeville act for the sake of the foreign press. It seems he had been sternly reprimanded for his unscientific and impulsive remarks on the state of health of Andreas, and he wanted to limit the uproar this had caused. In the presence of reporters, he put in a call to the prison and asked the stunned warden to bring Andreas Papandreou to the telephone.

His first question revealed uncommon intelligence: "Have you escaped?" he asked.

"You want me to answer that?" was Andreas' laconic reply.

"How you feeling?"

"Couldn't be better!"

"Health good?"

"Excellent."

"By the way. Have they brought Averoff there?"

"Who?"

"Averoff. These guys here tell me that he's been sent to your jail."

"I'm not an employee of the jail. I couldn't know. But I'll enjoy the company."

A few more comments followed about the trial, and Pattakos triumphantly hung up. I heard the story from both sides: from Andreas, and from George Anastaplo, lecturer in liberal arts at the University of Chicago, a Greek-American who was present among the reporters at the press conference. Somehow to Pattakos, it was all a big show. And he had proved that Andreas had not escaped and that his health was good.

This about-face on the health story dampened my hopes that it was the face-saving device to get rid of the "Andreas problem." Still, I couldn't be sure, and I dropped another note to Dr. Boyd Thomes urging him to express again his concern over Andreas' jail conditions, and to suggest that he, as Andreas' personal physician, and a group of specialists would be glad to come to Greece to examine the prisoner. Pattakos responded to his letter six weeks later, as follows:

Sir,

I assure you that we have been doing our best to soften your friend's situation, and his health has been under daily medical care and examination.

We are very much concerned about his health because we are sure that if anything happens, you, and all our political opponents, will find the opportunity to accuse us even more.

If you wish to arrange for a team of American physicians or physicians from all over the world, to come to Athens to examine him, such a thing would greatly serve the economy of our Country but not your friend's health. This, because we believe that the Greek

290

physicians are equally capable and sufficient enough to look after this matter.

With friendly regards,

Stylianos Pattakos
Brigadier-General

While Pattakos was enjoying himself on the health-escape-Averoff merry-go-round, and I was trying to assess the significance of it all, I faced a real problem at home. My oldest boy, George, had reached a state of nervous tension that was affecting his ability to function. He ceased having interest in any of his old friends, he spent much time closed up in his room listening to music, playing his guitar, or doing nothing, and as night drew on he became more and more convinced that he had symptoms of a serious disease. For a long time it was lockjaw, until I finally brought a doctor and had George and the other children given an antitetanus shot, which they were about due for in any case. I knew this was treating the symptom and not the cause, but the cause, I feared, was the situation we were in, and this could not be treated. It was savage, cruel, and frustrating. My mother, however, came up with a suggestion that seemed like a solution. She and my father had decided they must return to the States, to their own world, and to the rest of the family. They had already extended their stay in Greece beyond their original plans as a result of the coup and their need to help me. As they watched the months roll by with Andreas still in jail and the prospect that this might be a situation of years, they and I felt they ought to go back. It was a heavy decision on both sides; they hating to leave me with the total responsibility of the family in what to them was a strange and foreign land, and I hating to lose their help and comfort, and also not knowing when we might see each other again. The proposal for George was that he return with them and spend a month in Elmhurst before coming back to start school. It was felt that the change and the atmosphere of freedom would give him a new outlook with which to face the vicissitudes of life in Greece. So that was settled, and George visibly perked up when I told him about the plan. Not, however, as much as I had hoped, for it did not stop his trips to my room in the middle of the night and my long conversations with an anxiety-ridden boy, who understood intellectually his problem, but was unable to handle it emotionally.

With this problem at least semisolved, I turned to the publicity part of the fabulous Vahliotis-Diakoyannis story. Andreas directed me from behind the wire screens, and I executed his orders. A flurry of letters, telegrams, and telephone calls marked this period.

On August 1, 1967, I wrote to Walter Heller:

> *The army is crushed. It's morale broken, and a power struggle between Papadopoulos and the King goes on for control. Last week, for the second week in a row, the King has refused to sign a decree prepared by Papadopoulos for the firing of about 400 more officers. The King considers them "his." Last night Papadopoulos was selected*

by the junta as president of the "Little Council" which is the smaller ministerial council with key government people which makes most of the decisions. Was this the answer to the King's stubbornness? And is our policy of giving moral support to the King working? Or enough? . . .

I asked Walter to make a stink in the States about the interminable and unwarranted delays of Andreas' trial.

I wrote to Steve Rousseas on August 2:

> *I sent you a cryptic letter through the mails trying to get across the idea that a fuss should start up about Mike's [Andreas'] trial. They have held him for over three months now for "investigation," as they put it . . . and have still not come out with a final indictment. The formal charges were supposed to be made on June 15th. Then they discovered that they had a new "witness," a man by the name of Lefakis who had escaped prior to the coup and was hiding in Italy, and seemed to have been flushed out of his hiding place by the smell of money. He was at one time political secretary to Mitsotakis [deputy from Crete who had been the chief defector of Papandreou at the time the King kicked out the prime minister] and claimed to have evidence against the army in the ASPIDA frame-up. He changed his tune in his more recent depositions, but for his agreement to turn State's witness, he was eventually tossed in prison on a charge of trying to plan the assassination of the King, tossed in like a dried, squeezed lemon. His testimony is irrelevant, but his presence was used as an excuse to delay the final report.*
>
> *The next date given was July 18th. Around that time a handwritten report was shown to Mike's lawyer by the head judge, something that would be approximately 50 pages typewritten—and according to Koutsoyergas a series of slanders, lies and fixed pieces of evidence—and would be ready as soon as typed. It doesn't take two weeks to type such a document. Yesterday, when his lawyer went to the Ministry of Justice to inquire, the answer was simply, "It's not ready yet." They can keep this up for weeks on end, as far as I can see, then delay the date of the trial still further yet. I thought a brief editorial in the* Herald Tribune *questioning these tactics and arguing that if the charges are as unsubstantiated by evidence as they were in the first ASPIDA trial, the charges should be dismissed and the prisoner freed. . . .*

And now began the "flight of the pigeons," Vahliotis and Diakoyannis.

On August 12 I received a letter from Mogens:

> *Bob [Lianis] just called me on the phone and asked me to have the following information sent to you by our friend:*
>
> *1. Vahliotis will arrive in Montreal Monday, August 14, 1967.*
>
> *2. Diakoyannis is already there.*

3. Stanley leaves today, August 12, to meet them in Montreal.

4. Frank [Newman] took the deposition of Diakoyannis and Merryman will take the deposition of Vahliotis.

5. Bob and Stanley think that they should not break the story till after the trial. However, they ask you to send a message when exactly to break, i.e. publish, it.

6. Both witnesses have a "second story"—not dealing with Takis [Andreas] but with the general problem—Bob and Stanley want to know whether you think they can break this second story now, if it is very important.

7. The following code names should be used:

a) the junta	*Suzan*
b) the trial	*examination*
c) Menios	*Peter*
d) Vahliotis	*Paul*
e) Diakoyannis	*Tom*
f) Stanley	*Maynard*
g) Deposition	*contract*

On August 12 I wrote back to Mogens:

We have been told that the final report (indictment) will be out this week. This, however, has been the answer we have been getting for many weeks now. In any case, once it is out there must be a trial within two months—according to the law (what law?). Since these things are run at the whim of the junta, we can have no assurance on this. It is important that pressure be built up on this so that it is understood by those involved that this is a case of international interest—and about which no one believes a fair trial can be given. . . .

There is much talk here about a pending change in the situation. Most "armchair prophets" put it at around the end of September. It seems that Talbot came back with some kind of scheme which was to include a first phase transition (non-military, non-political), then a second phase election government, the name Karamanlis playing the predominant role. I believe that this was soundly rejected by Frederika. At the moment everything seems to have ground to a standstill. Few announcements are being made by the government, less prominence is being given to individual ministers, little projection to the King. The anti-communist harangue continues. Attacks on foreign attacks (communist-inspired) continues. And some attempts by newspapers to explain the economic slow-down (world factors—a temporary situation) continue. One can be sure that neither the junta nor the Americans will want the situation to open up too much until certain aims are achieved (a) complete purge of all democratic and liberal elements in the armed forces and in the civil service, (b) Cyprus solved, (c) certainty of a rightist, or conservative-center win in the elections, that is, the political elimination of Andreas, (d) the securing of the throne.

. . . I consider it Step No. 1 to get Takis out. He will not be allowed in any way to be a part of the early phases. He has become a symbol of the fight—but that he will remain, whether in jail or out. And this will not change the intensity of whatever resistance exists. Our fight will be won by the skin of our teeth, by inches—but on such a solid foundation eventually that nothing can overwhelm it. . . .

In the meantime, arrests continue. I have given Steve some bits of information on kinds of things happening of a repressive nature. The secret service is everywhere, and they have modern techniques at their disposal. Tortures go on in the jails. Jail conditions are intolerable. Harassment of the little man exists in every walk of life. Taxes, rules, regulations, phone tapping and cutting, warnings, brief arrests without reason—to terrorize. The villages are worse. . . .

On August 15 I wrote to Walter Heller:

. . . I have two items of this nature I want to talk to you about. One has to do with the trial and your visitors in Paris. [Diakoyannis and Xifaras]. We would like, if there is a trial, to call you as a witness on behalf of Andreas. But we would especially like to use that in a short announcement ahead of time to add to the growing junta opinion that there should not be a trial. In other words, if besides knowing what lousy evidence they have, they also see that top-notch, highly-thought-of Americans will help defend Andreas— they will avoid it at all costs. We don't want a sensational announcement, just a quiet, dignified statement to come from there, such as the following:

> *Several American academicians, among them the well-known Walter Heller, former chairman of the Council of Economic Advisers under John Kennedy and Lyndon Johnson, have agreed to testify on behalf of Andreas Papandreou in the coming ASPIDA trial in Greece. Mr. Papandreou, former colleague of Mr. Heller's, is in Averoff prison in Athens, awaiting trial on charges of conspiracy to commit high treason. Others who will testify are Frank Newman, ex-dean of the Law School at the University of California; Stanley Sheinbaum, professor at the Center for the Study of Democratic Institutions; Stephen Rousseas, economics professor at New York University.*
>
> *It is understood that these academicians will not go just as character witnesses, but as witnesses who will contribute evidence for the defense. Three of the four professors have recently been in Greece.*

Also on August 15 I wrote to Sheinbaum:

. . . about this whole problem of how to handle the pre-publicity on the trial, the particular information we have, Paris, etc. I think that I see it in three stages, and I think we should proceed.

A. The announcement I suggested to Walter on participation in the trial. I wonder if you would take this on as an assignment, get the OK's from Walt, Frank and Steve (although Steve might be excluded on the basis of his articles attacking the junta) and give it out as a special announcement. Perhaps you could improve on my last sentence to give the impression somehow that you all have special knowledge—without, naturally, divulging exactly what at this stage. Whether you can really make it to the trial, if there is a trial—is irrelevant right now. Your willingness to come is the important point.

B. A general article in Ramparts *on the background of the coup. I would like to suggest that in a box at the end you indicate the following: "The second of this series of articles on the Greek situation will discuss the ASPIDA case, the manner in which the attempt was made to frame Andreas Papandreou, and some predictions for the future. . . ." If your first story on the general situation is accurate and seems to show inside knowledge, this tidbit at the end will be particularly shattering for those eager to go ahead with the trial.*

C. The ASPIDA story. Perhaps a TV appearance for Vitos [Vahliotis] at the moment of publication of this article could be arranged, if you think it adds. . . .

On August 18 I wrote to Lianis:

About the same time you receive this, Stan should receive a note with my notion of the way to proceed on giving publicity in advance of the trial. Urge him to proceed as rapidly as possible with A. B and C can follow in quick succession if the information has all been gathered. Their way to handle Vitos, by the way, is to promise him much help (jobs in the States, international positions, etc.) IF he really spills all and gives honest and accurate information—and, also, treat him with some understanding; that is, we all make mistakes in our lives and once in a while, sometimes, there comes the chance to redeem all the bad that has been done, to raise oneself in the eyes of one's compatriots, one's professional colleagues and the world. This is such a time. It will not be forgotten by the friends of Mike—but, of course, they will judge its worth in time, depending on whether he really sincerely tries to give all and retain nothing. The opinion of Mike's lawyer is that he is absolutely in a position to have much information and much evidence. He must, of course, not embellish or exaggerate or fabricate. But must stick to the facts. He should be told to stay out of Greece now until the stories are published (after which he cannot go back). This business of their talking freely in Paris and sailing back into Athens for some days bothers the hell out of me.

Next, and equally important. Sally [the King] is paying a visit to the States (official? unofficial?) and it is assumed that she will see

Heap Big Chief. . . . In any case, could you call Walt . . . and suggest that the President make a pitch for Mike in the discussion? Given that the whole academic community wants two things: the return of Mike and the return of constitutional government, I think the President is obliged to reflect this vast influence group!

And this brings me to the second point under this heading. Is the group going to be unrepresented in the visit of the King? Will there be no demonstrations in Washington, or New York—or wherever he is? There must be. Although it is claimed he has been stripped of all his power, just yesterday when Averoff was given a five year jail sentence, the King stepped in and gave him hari (pardon), and he was released within a few hours. In other words, when he wants to show his power—he does. So is his lack of power a fake, a game? . . . Since the King is also going to EXPO—in fact, that is his first and official stop—the Canadian portion of the committee must be active. . . .

And third, it is an opportunity for some more editorials on the Greek crisis and state of affairs, saying that under no circumstances can the American people condone or accept a totalitarian regime as an ally, and that they are expecting the King to return his country quickly to parliamentary government.

That day, August 18, Frank Newman wrote to Dean Alfange, lawyer, member of the New York Bar, Bar of the Supreme Court of the United States, author, and participant in many humanitarian causes, including the Greek War Relief Association. Newman asked Alfange if he would attend Andreas' trial as an observer. Alfange was to agree, which delighted us all.

On August 19 Sheinbaum wired my father, asking if the ASPIDA frame-up could be exposed in *Ramparts* immediately. I answered Stanley on August 20 by telegram:

"YES JOAN."

But on August 21 Dora Lianis (representing Sheinbaum) telephoned Koutsoyergas in Athens:

Dora: *I am talking on behalf of Mr. Stanley, Mr. Chant's broker. He has bought the shares as per the instructions he received. Recently he requested from Mr. Chant authorization to dispense with the shares. Mr. Chant authorized him by cable to proceed with the selling of the stock. Now Mr. Stanley wants to know the following: Was he understood by Chant that he intends to circulate the shares on the open market? He wants to clarify this point, that is, if he has been authorized by Chant to circulate the stocks in the open market. Can you give me yourself an answer?*

Menios: *Of course a certain number of the shares must be sold.*

Dora: *But how will Mr. Stanley know which shares he can sell? Could you contact Mr. Chant and ask him to clarify this point to Mr. Stanley by cable?*

Menios: *Sure. I will see him today and he will let you know immediately.*

Poor Stanley in California was sweating. He had the two depositions of Vahliotis and Diakoyannis in his hands, and had worked up an article for *Ramparts* on the ASPIDA case. But I had outlined a program which specified that I thought there should be two articles, the first with the general story of the coup, the second with the ASPIDA frame-up. In Stanley's long sessions with the two witnesses, he had come to the conclusion that they had nothing significant to add to what had already been written about the military take-over in Greece, but that the story of real interest was how the Greek KYP had concocted evidence and bribed witnesses to produce a case against Andreas. After he sent his first wire to my father asking if he could publish the ASPIDA story, and received the "Yes Joan" answer from me, he wondered whether I had understood the meaning of the wire, that what he wanted to print was the ASPIDA story, not the general story.

In desperation, Dora Lianis put a call through to Menios to try to clarify this, using a language she felt would not endanger Menios. (He was, however, upset.) When Menios told me about the call, I told him, "Don't worry. By now they've got my cable and it's all straightened out." And Menios forgot to tell me they had already received my answer and that the call came to get clarification on the answer. Then I would have understood that further communication was needed. Andreas had just a few days before given me the go-ahead to have the ASPIDA witness story exposed.

Feeling that the signal had been given, I thought I had nothing more to do than wait for the news while Stanley was stewing in California, wondering why I hadn't given him definite clearance after his phone call to Menios. To make matters worse for Stanley, he received just at that time an excerpt from a letter I had written to Steve Rousseas in the early days of August in which I expressed my grave concern about the recanting of the stories of the witnesses and about the possibility of a trap, and asked what the effect would be on Andreas' fate. There was no date on my excerpt, and Stan naturally assumed it was a very recent letter.

So while Stanley chewed his nails as the date for the *Ramparts* deadline approached, expecting each day some word from me, I turned, oblivious of this problem, to my typewriter, getting out letters whenever I could to people in a position to help. I gave them suggestions, information, my analysis of the situation.

Marjorie and I had now worked out a routine. I typed upstairs in my bedroom with the door open. Marjorie sat in the downstairs hallway with the front door locked. Instructions were given that no one was to open the door except Marjorie. Next to my typewriter I had an iron pot and a big box of kitchen matches. Marjorie could see through the broken glass (which I had left unrepaired as a crude reminder to all who visited me of the night of the coup) who was coming. If she felt for any reason that the visitor was KYP or police, she was to call upstairs in a friendly, unhurried manner, "Mrs. P., you have some guests!" The "Mrs. P." was the cue to burn everything I had written. By the time she retrieved the key from the hallway drawer, fumbled in getting it in the lock, and opened the door, my onionskins would have been black dust.

On August 20 I wrote to Mogens:

There is a growing clash between Papadopoulos and the King. The Averoff case is an example. It is said that the Army is split in loyalties as of now, with Pap holding well the Athens area and the King the Thrace and Macedonia area. It is essential that there be an announced timetable for restoration of the Constitution. There are many people who feel that Pap is maneuvering for THE dictatorial role—with all its meanings. He strengthens himself day by day. . . . And the King? Obviously all kinds of pressure must be exerted for a return to the Parliamentary system, and now. Our fate is that the King may have to become the champion of democratic rule. But he is so inept, and so weak, and makes so many mistakes—that one cannot be sure he will decide on a line and carry it through. . . . My love to your wonderful country and the crusade it is carrying on. . . .

On August 24 I wrote to Walt Heller:

Yesterday Eleftheros Kosmos published an interview taken by an American journalist with Mr. Kollias, the "eminent jurist" as he has been described by some American reports, and in it he was asked "What is ASPIDA?" His answer was, "A communist organization whose leader was Andreas Papandreou." This is the same man who argues that Greek justice is independent and not under the control of the government, and just some days ago he "proved" this by freeing Averoff after the court gave him a five-year sentence. This is also a man for whom obviously law means nothing, for he can decide Andreas' guilt before a trial is held.

I want to express my utter disgust at the Embassy here and at Talbot himself. Yesterday he sent his lackey, Mr. Day, to deliver a letter from Frank Newman with the request that I please not receive letters through the Embassy! The reason was that they might cause trouble with the government! I asked whether the government had complained, and the answer was no—but, you know, for the future, etc. Honestly, Walt, it seems that they not only want to ignore me, but to punish me. They have never helped me! All my requests—that they try to get me a phone back, that they ask the government to stop an attack on me as a Bulgarian communist, that they retrieve my personal papers taken away in the house searches, that they inform me if they hear anything I should know pertaining to the case of Andreas, that they please call Andreas' lawyers and hear an explanation of the case, etc. NOT ONE DAMN THING HAS BEEN DONE! . . .

I thought you would be interested also in a report that reached me through my sources here having to do with a discussion between Talbot and some journalists in Washington. . . . Is it conceivable that this is the way an American representative looks at dictatorship? Doesn't it make sense that we are viewed as imperialists, materialists, ambitious, arrogant—and all those nasty things when we can so shed our basic ideals and give out this kind of statement? . . .

298

Today the King left for Canada. I urge you to do what you can in terms of his visit to the States. It is a rare opportunity—and one that will not likely occur again for a long time. If Johnson were to demand Andreas' release—what could the King do? Say stop meddling in our internal affairs? Good god—we've been meddling in the internal affairs of Greece for the past 20 years. Now, on this issue we should be asked to stop?

The same day, August 24, 1967, I received a report from Sweden on Andreas Papandreou, from Walter Heller: "The *intensity of interest in Andreas Papandreou's case in Scandinavia is difficult to imagine*—it has become an important political issue, is covered in detail in the press, and is the concern of ministers and members of parliament."

On August 24 Frank Newman received a letter from Under Secretary of State Nicholas de B. Katzenbach, assuring him that "we have been in touch with the Papandreou family on a continuing basis and have rendered such assistance as we could. The concern of the United States Government and the interest of various individuals and groups in the United States regarding Andreas Papandreou and other political prisoners in a comparable situation have been made known to the Greek government at the highest level."

On August 26 I read in the Sunday *Times*, London, "Papandreou on Death Charge":

> *After four months of uncertainty, the Greek military regime yesterday decided to press charges of high treason against Andreas Papandreou, one of the most controversial figures in Greek politics before the coup last April and unrelenting critic of King Constantine.*
>
> *The 49-year-old Papandreou, suffering from tuberculosis after four months in prison, was brought before an Athens court, which accepted the Public Prosecutor's indictment and ordered that Papandreou be tried later this year.*
>
> *The news was not published officially in Athens, but released by what was described as reliable sources; and the strong man of the regime, Brigadier Stylianos Pattakos, was quoted as saying that Papandreou had said he would not appeal against the court's verdict.*
>
> *The wording of the charge—high treason—is significant. Friends of Papandreou, particularly in the United States, had been told that the charge would be the lesser one of conspiracy to commit treason, which does not carry the death penalty. Indeed in May it was reported that Papandreou had been formerly charged with conspiracy; and General Spandidakis, the deputy premier, said, "We are not a government of executioners." President Johnson, too, said he would intercede to make certain there would be no summary execution of Papandreou.*
>
> *But with the latest move, there seems to be a real possibility that Papandreou will face a death sentence. . . .*

Things had taken a turn for the worse. We were going to have a trial as Andreas wanted. Now I wondered what had happened on the Vahliotis and

299

Diakoyannis story. I took a chance and found a phone to make a phone call. We had been told that all foreign calls were monitored, so my language was purposely obtuse.

On August 28 from a friend's telephone, I called Stanley Sheinbaum in California:

> Margaret: *Hi, Maynard, did I wake you up?*
> Stan: *Huh? Hello! That you, Maggie?*
> Margaret: *Yes, this is Peggy!* [*Good God, I thought, my name! And Stan told me later he could have bitten his tongue off.*]
> Stan: *Yeah, Peggy. How are things?*
> Margaret: *I'm enjoying my vacation in Greece tremendously. We just got back from a tour of the islands.*
> Stan: *Good girl, you needed the rest.*
> Margaret: *I'm calling about those stocks. I hope you understood to sell them all . . .*
> Stan: *Am I glad you called! I'm about to do so . . .*
> Margaret: *That's great.* All, *you understand.*
> Stan: *Yes, on the public market.*
> Margaret: *Right. When do you think they will bring in dividends?*
> Stan: *In a couple of weeks or so . . .*
> Margaret: *The sooner the better. How are the kids? Your wife?*
> Stan: *Fine, all fine.*
> Margaret: *My love . . . Bye . . .*

Earlier the same day, I had written to Stan:

> *By the time you receive this I hope to have reached you by telephone. We are eager for you to push the story as much as possible. The time is very ripe with the publishing of the indictment —and the presence of the sailing boy in the States. If the magazine cannot hit the stands at the time, or during the time, of the visit, perhaps some advance ballyhoo can be arranged with TV, radio, some news conferences, etc. This means a real slick publicity job with the kind of timing that Melina [Mercouri] pulled at the UN. The indictment repeats all the hearsay evidence (that certain alleged members of the organization overheard that someone else overheard so-and-so saying that Mike was head of ASPIDA) and then ends up by saying that in any case, we have proof of the intention to use legal means to overthrow the regime because of the deposition of Vitos, which really proves what Mike was up to. . . etc. It is an incredible document and would be thrown out after the first reading by any honest public prosecutor. But there is no question that one can peg Vitos as a key witness. As soon as the report is in our hands we will start translating and getting it to you. I will try in any case to get that special part out, although my means of doing this are getting limited with tourist season ending. . . .*

On August 30 I wrote to Walt Heller: "Today the indictment against

Andreas was printed in the Athens *Post*. This is our 16th wedding anniversary. It is a bitter pill." And the same day to Lianis: "I hope by Saturday to get a copy of the report to you—80 pages in all. You must start translating right away—and you must let Stan know any pertinent parts for the purpose of stock plan A—B—C. . . . I think John Buttrick will start a Legal Defense Fund for Andreas. . . . We are rather at the end of our rope in terms of money—and this whole thing will cost very much. . . ."

Later, I learned of a brighter note that day. A letter from Senator Edward W. Brooke had been written to Frank Newman:

> *I visited Greece shortly after the military takeover in April, and was most disturbed at the way in which constitutional government and political freedom were being suppressed. Since my return to this country, I have continued to make my views known on this subject, and continue to work, both publicly and privately, for a restoration of democracy in the land of its birth.*
>
> *Andreas Papandreou spent a great deal of time at Harvard University before taking a position with the University of California, and still has many close friends in Massachusetts. I have been working most closely with them on his behalf, and can assure you I will continue to encourage those in authority in Greece to grant him a fair and speedy trial. . . .*

Then the ASPIDA story broke.

On September 6, 1967, the Washington *Post* headlined: "2 Forced to Frame Papandreou, They Say in Magazine Story":

> *Ramparts magazine yesterday offered the testimony of two Greeks who say they were forced to give perjured testimony against Andreas Papandreou, now in jail on a treason charge.*
>
> *The men, due to appear at a press conference at the Statler-Hilton Hotel today, are Andreas Vahliotis, a lawyer, and Kyriakos Diakoyannis, a journalist.*

On September 7 a headline in the *Times*, London, read: "Greek Exiles Retract Evidence":

> *Two Greeks, described as principal Government witnesses in the forthcoming trial for treason of Dr. Andreas Papandreou, declared here today that they had been forced by the Greek secret police to give perjured testimony. . . .*

These were just two of the many stories appearing on the Vahliotis-Diakoyannis story. In addition, *Ramparts* magazine took a full-page ad in *The New York Times* and a full-page ad in the Washington *Post* with pictures of the two false witnesses, a picture of Andreas, and excerpts from their testimony. The headlines read, "The Greek Junta's secret evidence against Andreas Papandreou has been obtained by *Ramparts* magazine. It is wanton, untrue, perjured, and garnered by blackmail."

Sometime later I received the specially prepared reprints of the article with a picture in color of Andreas on the title page, a gold-embossed picture frame surrounding his photograph. The title was "The Framing of Andreas Papandreou."*

Stanley Sheinbaum wrote the prelude to the witnesses' testimony, and started out this way:

> "I personally got involved in the affairs of Greece when Andreas Papandreou failed to keep a dinner date. Last winter a friend of mine persuaded me to make a tour of Greece. So I wrote Andreas in Athens and suggested we meet when I got there. Fine, come have dinner, he wrote. Fine, except that his letter arrived on April 22, about ten hours after he had been jailed and political life and freedom were stifled in Greece.
>
> Andreas was in prison, his life was in danger, and I joined a committee among an infinity of committees dedicated to bringing freedom to Greece and saving the life of a Keynesian, suddenly alleged to be a communist. . . .
>
> As early as 1964, when Andreas' charismatic leadership became evident, the plot against him was set in motion—as the testimony which follows makes clear. . . .

Mission accomplished! And beautifully! My grin as I visited Andreas at the screens of his repugnant cage almost split the prison in two, and the occupants at Guizi 58 bounced around the house like satisfied cats.

*Ramparts magazine, September, 1967.

CHAPTER TWENTY-FIVE

George Papandreou Released from House Arrest

MY pleasure at our triumph in the ASPIDA affair was spoiled by the news that reached me at the end of August: Virginia had been arrested. I had tried once to see her during this period of time, arranging a rendezvous through an intermediary at a remote beach near Marathon. I told her to take her boy, and I would take one of mine, in separate cars, and we would have a conversation while floating on air mattresses in the Aegean. Even if one of us were followed, let them try to monitor that conversation, I thought! A day prior to the date, she sent me a message that she was ill and would not be able to meet me at the beach. It was an excuse prompted by her concern not to involve me.

I learned the details of her arrest. The security police came in the middle of the night (it's so much more frightening that way), and got both Virginia and her son out of bed. They kept her under guard while they took the child with them to search the house. During the search they kept asking the child questions, such as, "Your mother has many friends. Do they stay here sometimes?" And then, "We know your mother keeps guests at your house from time to time. If you tell us who they are, we won't hurt her, but if you don't ... " The search took an hour and a half, after which they left *with* Virginia and told the child to go back to sleep and to call his aunt in the morning! A frantic Virginia—frantic for her child and the impact of the experience—was driven off to the ominous headquarters of the security police—Bouboulinas Street. She was one of the group charged with protecting Theodorakis, the great Greek composer, and belonging to the Patriotic Front whose members, when arrested, were savagely tortured by the dictatorship. They were perhaps the first group to bring the world's attention to the use of these methods by the junta. Despite what they had gone through, evidenced by their appearance at their trial—broken, beaten, weakened, frightened human beings—several had the courage to describe what they had suffered in the process of being forced to confess.

How many Americans know how it feels to have a dear friend undergoing psychological pressure and physical torture, while you remain helpless in another part of the city? To know that a friend may be lying there without food or water, or being stripped naked and beaten with wires or being spit on, taunted, and abused, or going through a mock execution? How many people living in a free country know what hatred this develops, what a passionate spirit of revenge? It was at these moments that I thought of the mealy-mouthed statements of the State Department in Washington, "hope for early return to democratic government," and the contention of all European governments which had recognized this gang that in this fashion they could influence the colonels to liberalize their regime. What bloody nonsense to think one could compromise with the colonels. How could any kind of just and decent society be built from the foundations of a dictatorship?

During the last ten days of August, while I was involved in the finishing phases of the ASPIDA exposure, another depressing event took place—the trial of Andoni Livanis and Phillip Dimitriades. One noon when I was standing at the cage of Averoff Prison enumerating the items of food in Andreas' lunch basket, the thick iron doors were opened and several men escorted inside. This time it was my turn to gasp and control the tears. It was Andoni, his hands trapped in handcuffs, standing looking at me with his penetrating gaze. He was being brought back to prison from an interrogation session prior to his trial. The strain of his imprisonment showed on his face, and I saw the effort it took for him to maintain his jaunty bearing, to give the impression of dignity under those circumstances. I couldn't run and throw my arms around him, as he had done once to me in those feverish days right after the coup. Impulsively, I threw him a kiss, and with his eyes he accepted it and threw one back. Thirty-four men and women were tried on charges of subversion. Livanis was sentenced to nine years; Phillip was sentenced to seven years. The evidence against them was a fighting resistance tract, said to have been circulated several nights in June. It was the "first act of resistance" reported to me by Phillip the same day Tito got arrested. It was the first and the only one, as the skilled operators of the secret police picked up several young people, and the skilled torturers at Bouboulinas extracted the names of their associates and leaders. The torture Phillip suffered (a smashed nose and broken teeth, a forehead concussion as his head was pounded on the cement wall of the prison, no food and little water for four days, a lit bulb hanging in his eyes for those same four days and nights) was intended to elicit the confession that his activities had been directed by Andreas Papandreou through Margaret Papandreou. This confession he never signed.

The other depressing news was that Theodorakis had been captured. A government spokesman admitted to journalists on August 26 that he had been "apprehended," the euphemistic word for surrounding and trapping a human being. Regardless of their political views, the Greek people had been relishing Mikis' four-month defiance of the junta, a defiance which took ingenuity and skill in terms of hiding, but which also included the circulation of resistance messages and a song of freedom smuggled out to London.

The King left for Canada with Anna Maria on August 24. Speculation was high on the meaning of the second part of his journey which was to the United States. One theory was that he was going to ask for a resumption of full military aid, which would have made him the "errand boy of the junta," as Melina Mercouri so aptly put it. (Melina Mercouri, the Greek star of Jules Dassin's *Never on Sunday*, had become a leading fighter in America against the dictatorship.) Another theory was that the King was going to gain moral support from the administration to raise his prestige within the army for a possible confrontation in the future. Little of the substance of his private sessions with the President and with members of Congress was reported. One statement he made was of great general interest. It was his reply to a Congressman who began a question with the phrase "your government." The King interrupted, "It is not my government." Of more personal interest was the following in the Washington *Post* (September 11, 1967): "As to Andreas Papandreou, the economist-son of a former prime minister, the King gave the impression that he felt the case against him was considerable. Papandreou is due to face a treason trial in November."

So the King had not yet understood, I thought, that the threat against him and the monarchy came from the military clique which took over the government, not from the political personage of Andreas Papandreou.

Just before the King met the President in Washington, my youngest sister Joanne "met" the President in Texas. All of my four sisters, two in Elmhurst, Illinois, one in Los Angeles, and one in Imperial City, Texas, had been doing what they could to help out their "big sister." They had cornered their Congressmen, had carried on petitition-signing drives, and had barraged the State Department with telephone calls. On Sunday, September 3, Joanne and her husband, Al, an officer in the air force went out to the airport where Johnson was leaving from a ranch weekend to return to the White House. As he passed the lines of people waiting to greet him and shake hands with him, she elbowed through a tightly packed crowd and stretched a long arm out into his path to receive a handshake. But she didn't just shake his hand, she hung on. President Johnson stopped in surprise, and she shouted, "Help Andreas Papandreou!" Then she continued, "I'm his wife's sister. Please help him!" Johnson smiled, saying nothing, and having been loosed from her grip, walked forward. After a few steps he stopped, turned around, and shouted back to her, "I'm seeing the King this week . . . " She concluded that this meant he would indeed raise the question with Constantinos.

In my letter to President Johnson, I told him, "Andreas has been charged with a crime he never committed; he is a political prisoner, not a criminal, and he is being persecuted for his ideas, not his acts. There can be no normalcy in Greece if the junta proceeds to a fake trial and a false conviction. It is within the King's powers to give amnesty. It would be a decisive and popular act, and would be the most potent proof of his intentions to lead the nation back to constitutional government, parliament and civil liberties. . . ." A cry in the wilderness, maybe, but I had vowed to leave no stone unturned in the fight for my husband's freedom.

I watched the events in Washington with intense interest, as did all of us in Greece. On September 6 *Ramparts* held the press conference of Diakoyannis and Vahliotis, nicely timed to precede the visit of Constantinos. The two men declared that the ASPIDA case was a sham, a frame-up of Andreas Papandreou. To questions of reporters, they said that the King could overthrow the junta within twenty-four hours if he so decided and charged him with cowardice if he did not proceed to do so. On September 7, the day after the press conference and prior to the King's visit, the United States State and Justice Departments declared they were reviewing the citizenship status of Andreas Papandreou. Robert J. McClosky, State Department spokesman, said the study resulted from a recent Supreme Court decision that United States citizens voting in a foreign election cannot be deprived of their citizenship without their consent. He said that Mr. Papandreou's citizenship was originally withdrawn under provisions of the United States Immigration and Naturalization Act which forbids Americans from voting in foreign elections. As a result of this subsequent ruling by the Supreme Court, he explained, this may not constitute an adequate reason for depriving an American of his citizenship. With this announcement, the authorities in Washington established a doubt that could be used by the junta to kick Andreas out. The timing was good, with the *Ramparts* press conference and the King's visit, and my hopes soared.

On the 11th the King arrived, fresh from facing demonstrations against him at Expo in Montreal, Canada, where large crowds of Greek-Canadians expressed their hostility to a King who had gone along with the junta. In Washington Melina Mercouri led a sizeable group of demonstrators and members of the American Committee for Democracy in Greece to protest against the dictatorship.

No clear result was visible in Greece as a result of these events—for a period of time. The junta continued its dirty work; the King returned and resumed his various official activities. The people clung with hope to his one reported remark, "It is not my government."

The time had come for my parents to return to Elmhurst, Illinois. The *Olympia,* their boat, was leaving at 9 P.M. and we had planned for some days to go together to Averoff to deliver Andreas' evening meal so that they could see him up close through his second-floor window bars and wave good-bye. Georgie was leaving, too, for "three weeks of free air," as he said, his pale face and thin body a stark reminder of what he had been going through. We walked together up the sidewalk, I praying silently that the guards would not turn them back. While I took the food into the jail, the three stood down below, communicating cautiously with facial gestures. As I came out, my father suddenly shouted up in his deep baritone and midwestern twang, "See you at Christmas, Andy!" The guards looked startled and unnerved, but since we had turned to leave, said nothing. We walked away slowly with tears in our eyes. Without being able to see, I knew there were tears in Andreas' eyes, too. That was September 17, 1967.

It was during the week of their departure that the "ship of state" began to rock. First, there was a panicky reaction on the part of the junta to the press conference in Washington with Vahliotis and Diakoyannis. According to the junta press release, these witnesses, who were to give the testimony of the *real* intentions of ASPIDA, about which only confusion existed, were people of no worth, one of whom had a criminal record in Greece. That is, they discredited their own two witnesses! The indictment, of course, had mentioned nothing about their character or past records. In fact, they were presented as serious and heavy witnesses against Andreas. Now, with great alacrity and no shamefacedness, the true conspirators—those ruling Greece—lashed out at their prize witnesses.

Next, they tried to answer questions about the King's statement in Washington. "There is no issue," they said, "between the King and our government."

Then came developments they hadn't counted on. Defiance from the Right. It came first in the form of Eleni Vlahou, the editor of two conservative papers in Athens, *Kathimerini* and *Mesimvrini*. Capable, bright, sharp, an infighter who could hold her own with any Greek male and who, if necessary, could stoop to low levels of journalism to smear and slander, Eleni Vlahou openly declared her defiance of the junta. She had shut down her newspapers the day of the coup, refusing to publish under the censorship rules of the regime. This was a first real clue, at the time, that it was not a King's coup, for Eleni Vlahou was a royalist.

On September 24 an Italian newspaper of Turin, *La Stampa*, published Signor Fattori's special interview with Vlahou. He called her the "only important person still free who has said 'No' to the new regime without hiding, without sheltering abroad, without asking foreign journalists not to mention her name. In this country, struck dumb by fear and conformism, her stubborn and calm voice keeps accusing."

He mentions that the colonel's regime was born officially to fight the communists, according to the old formula of the military coup d'etat. But Mrs. Vlahou's newspapers had always been conservative, anticommunist papers. The fact that the bourgeois press had not collaborated, he wrote, had upset the colonels and wounded their prestige, showing that Greece is not at all firmly united behind the tanks of Brigadier General Pattakos and Colonel Papadopoulos against the proclaimed "communist danger."

To the question "Do you know the colonels?" she answered, "I certainly do. They came to me to persuade me. I have met them here and there many times—the three chiefs, Papadopoulos, Pattakos, Makarezos, and others. Simple people, a bit ignorant. Colonel Papadopoulos is the most intelligent, but his intelligence is that of the secret service man, of the policeman. . . . Altogether mediocre people, rather faded. There is an exception, of course, Brigadier Pattakos. He is mediocre too, but plays the clown."

My dear lady! One doesn't speak about members of the Greek army that way! With an overwhelming amount of self-control, the colonels contained themselves for four days. On the 28th, Eleni was arrested (while giving an interview to a Swedish journalist) and charged with insulting the authorities and disobeying martial law. She was to be tried by military tribunal and faced a maximum sentence of eight years' imprisonment.

It is possible that her arrest was related to another event which added to the thunder from the Right, and the colonels decided she had started a dominolike action which was getting out of hand. On September 27 Panayotis Cannellopoulos, the conservative Prime Minister who was deposed by the military coup, broke his silence and denounced the regime and called for political freedom. Cannellopoulos had been released from house arrest in the early weeks of the dictatorship, but had said nothing publicly. On this day he summoned foreign correspondents to his Athens home, and "with a voice vibrating with emotion," according to a London *Times* report, said the following:

> *Were I to accept that only those who rule my country today are entitled to speak freely, then I would be admitting that freedom of speech is an exclusive privilege of those who possess automatic weapons and tanks. But this I reject. And for this reason I have decided to speak.*
>
> *Today's authoritarian regime must cede its place to free political life, which must, of course, be reformed in the light of lessons from the past and present adventure. If freedom is not quickly re-established, the country will be exposed to dangers which will destroy everything.*
>
> *I consider groundless the claim of those who maintain that, thanks to the April 21 coup, the country was saved from chaos. . . . Certainly democracy is not an easy form of government, but the difficulties are compensated for by the fact that it secures the dignity of the citizen.*

He did not believe that the coup had averted "a great immediate danger," alluding to the colonels' claim that it had thwarted plans for an imminent communist coup.

Mr. Cannellopoulos was again put under house arrest.

On the same day that these rightist protests were silenced by house arrests, Pattakos visited Andreas in his cell at Averoff, bringing with him Mr. Rodinos-Orlandos, the undersecretary of the Ministry of Coordination, the ministry Andreas once headed. When Pattakos introduced Orlandos, Orlandos said to Andreas, "I have admired you very much. I was a student of economics in Germany." Pattakos gave him a quick, stern glance, and Orlandos added rapidly, "I mean I have admired you as an economist. I have read all of your books."

Pattakos asked Orlandos to leave, and then pacing up and down the floor of the tiny cell, said to Andreas, "I don't know what to do with you. If we let you go, the Reds will start shouting in the streets again, 'And-rey-as, And-rey-as.'" And he did a good mimicry of the lilt and rhythm of the chants at political rallies. "If we send you out of the country, the outside world will start flattering you, and it will go to your head, and you will organize against us. I think," he said as if he were musing out loud, "I think . . . well, you're a philosophical man. I think you should stand trial, take your sentence, carry it out in jail . . . you can have your books, your writing . . ."

Andreas interrupted him. "Tell me. You think you can convict me on the evidence you have on the ASPIDA case? As you know, I have been asking for the trial."

"Ah!" Pattakos gave a short snort. "That Bouloukos with his pipe!" And here Pattakos gave an imitation of a man dragging elaborately on his pipe, head tilted upward, arm elbow held high: "That Bouloukos couldn't have organized his own day, let alone a revolution!"

Pattakos rambled on in this fashion for almost twenty minutes. (I was waiting downstairs in the director's outer office for my regular noon visit, wondering why it was being delayed.) Finally, obviously not having settled the question in his own mind, and getting no help from Andreas, he called Orlandos back. Orlandos' surprising question was "What do you think of our economic program?"

Andreas' answer: "Ungodly!"

More specific questions were asked, about development, about investment, about balance of payments.

"You know," Andreas said wryly, "you ask me questions without giving me the facts."

"But the information is all in the newspapers," Orlandos replied.

"The propaganda is in the newspapers" was the answer. "I'm talking about the true figures, the statistics."

Pattakos shifted his weight to his other foot at this remark, but remained silent.

"Well, it could be arranged that you get them" was the astonishing reply.

A bid for help? When I finally got to the visiting screen—after having watched through the bars of the office windows as Pattakos and another figure left in a ministry car which had drawn up to the front door of Averoff—I found a smiling and puzzled Andreas, shaking his head in disbelief. "What the hell!" he told me. "A most peculiar and unclear visit!" He reconstructed the conversation for me as best he could with the listening ears around, although I must say that a new atmosphere of respect existed in those attending shapes standing behind me and Andreas. Andreas had been visited by the Big Boys.

Looking back, this visit can be seen more easily in terms of a ploy, a game being played by Papadopoulos. Up until September, the establishment in Greece had played a waiting game. The King had gone along with the coup. Not many people of the Right doubted the likelihood of a Papandreou victory in the elections. The coup foreclosed this possibility. Only three members of the party of the Right had been arrested the night of the coup: Cannellopoulos, who was considered by many an intruder from the more democratic camp into the ranks of the Right; Papaligouras, the Minister of Defense, who had to be arrested not to upset the plans of the army; and Rallis, Minister of Public Order. In the King's circle, Arnaoutis had been arrested. The bulk of the arrests were of people from the Center and the Left. The army was essentially rightist. The establishment figured that the fighting arm of the Right—the army—had saved the situation for them, that soon the power would be turned over to their civilian leaders, that their business interests would be protected, their privileges preserved, and the country would be saved from a socialist trend. Papadopoulos himself said to the King the morning of the coup, "It is for you, Your Majesty, that we have taken action."

Five months after the coup, when it became more and more apparent that the servants of the establishment were setting themselves up as their own establishment, that they had no intention of handing power over on a silver platter to their masters, the rumblings started. I recall a comment made to me by one man who had contacts with the royal circle. "You should hear," he told me, "the way Papadopoulos speaks to the King! There's no respect! He treats him like an employee!" As it became clear, then, that the monarchy was in danger, that the old political pros of the Right were being shelved, and that establishment figures like Zolotas of the Bank of Greece were being fired, the mood changed, and a reassessment of the situation occurred. Otherwise, how does one explain the passage of five months before the King in Washington finally said, "It is not my government!" and two prominent voices of the Right, Cannellopoulos and Vlahou—free up until then—protested.

Papadopoulos, seeing this movement of the Right, decided, in his cunning way, to scare it and the King into further acquiescence by making contact with their old bugbear and feared political opponent—Andreas. The junta was still in many respects an unknown quantity. It had no coloration, no perceptible political philosophy, and the story had gone around that Papadopoulos' nickname in the army was "Nasser." An early declaration by the Minister of Agriculture on farm policy had sounded like the political platform of the Left. The speech read by the puppet Kollias the night after the coup, which introduced the military clique to the Greek people, had a populist flavor; it said that it represented no political party, no economic oligarchic interests, that they were "people of toil." Still, the King was on his throne; the arch reactionary friend of Frederika, Kollias, was Prime Minister; and as the weeks rolled by, it pursued an economic policy toward foreign investment that was a sellout of the Greek nation. It claimed to be strongly anticommunist, yet was furthering commercial trade with the Soviet Union and the eastern bloc countries. To add to the confusion in the Greek mind was the use of a slogan, "Greece to the Christian Greeks," which was remarkably close to a slogan ("Greece to the Greeks") Andreas' used during the two-year campaign after the fall of George Papandreou. The symbol it chose to represent the "revolution" was the symbol Andreas had used in his publications, and the phrase from the mythological story it represented was the way in which he finished all of his speeches ("Out of the ashes the phoenix shall arise").

The wild thought that Andreas might be the political heir to the coup did occur to some, and the Pattakos-Orlandos visit, written up in its entirety a week later in *The New York Times,* added fuel to this thought.

Just ten days later another event occurred which was a gesture to the Center Union following. It was a Saturday around 4:30 P.M. when my telephone, recently reconnected, rang. (My phone had been disconnected after the Schwartz-Brown visit.) It was Andreas Mothonios, the political secretary of my father-in-law.

"Margaret! They've released the President!"

"That can't be, Andreas. I drove by Kastri this noon and the guards were all around."

"I know. But it's just been told to me by a junta man, and the announcement will come over the radio any minute."

I tried to contain my excitement and joy. "Are you sure, absolutely sure?" There were so many false rumors alive, and I didn't want to build up my expectations only to have them cruelly smashed again.

"Turn on your radio for proof" was his answer.

"Oh, Andreas . . . if it's true . . . "

I hung up and stood staring at the phone. A warmth settled inside of me, a

310

buoyancy, an internal singing. Was it maybe the first step toward Andreas' release? But, apart from that, I realized how much I wanted to see George Papandreou, to talk to him, to hear his views, to be with him. How much I had missed him! All the pain, anguish, and bitterness that I had felt at the precoup personal quarrels between him and Andreas had been washed away like the loose leaves in a gutter in a spring flood. And how was he, I wondered, after all these months of isolation? At seventy-nine, how does a human being tolerate such a fate? I called my son Nick to come down and help me find the newscast. We didn't have to wait long. A program of music was interrupted to make the brief announcement. George Papandreou was released from house arrest.

In half an hour Tito arrived, his usual time, to take me to the prison to deliver food. He hadn't heard the news, and his tired face broke into a wide smile in a mixture of happiness and emotion. Tito had been the Greek male in our entourage, assisted until recently by an American male—my father—and the signs of the responsibility showed heavily. He had lost five kilos on his bony frame, his face was colorless and furrowed. Now he and I had another male to lean on, and a powerful one. We agreed we would drive up to Kastri around 8 P.M. when Kiveli would have arrived at my home from a visit with her mother.

As we approached Kastri, I found myself getting anxious, excited, and tense. The last time I had seen George Papandreou was the Monday evening of the week of the coup, when we had eaten together. I tried to remember that evening, but it had been blurred by subsequent events. I thought we had talked about the kickoff of the campaign in Salonika, candidates for the Center Union party, and odds and ends. I remember an underlying current of worry about coming events, but this we had lived with for many months.

The first proof of a change at Kastri was the changed position of the wooden signs which had blocked the streets leading to the house. They were no longer in the middle of the streets as blockades, but had been pulled up on the curbs so cars could pass. The guards who tended the barriers were nowhere in sight. The house at Kastri had its lights on, and a bright light was ablaze in the second-floor bedroom window where the President slept. At the big iron gates, however, were two guards.

We climbed out of the car, Kiveli, Marjorie, Tito, Sophia (who insisted on coming along to see her grandfather), and myself. We were stopped at the gate. A gruff voice said, "Where do you think you're going?"

"We've come to see the President," Tito replied.

The guard was not intimidated by this authoritative voice, finding courage, no doubt, in the loaded tommy gun he held cockily across his middle.

"He can't have visitors" was the response.

My stomach turned. What was this, a farce? Were we being deceived, deluded? Was this to be some kind of qualified house arrest? After all these expectations, was I not to see that beloved figure—Andreas' father?

"It was announced on the radio," Tito insisted.

"We have been given orders that no one is to be allowed in."

"But this is his daughter-in-law, Mrs. Margaret Papandreou."

I hadn't thought he had noticed me, but he said in a most sarcastic and nasty way, "We know Mrs. Margarita. I said no one was to be allowed in."

Tito was ready to argue more. The thought of entering that house and seeing the President was too compelling to give up easily. Before he had a chance, I piped up. "When will you get new orders?" as if it were a foregone conclusion that the situation would not remain in its present state. The arrogance went out of him. He had hoped in some sadistic fashion to dash our hopes that there was authenticity in the announcement. Obviously he, or his superior officer, disliked the decision of Papadopoulos to release Papandreou.

After a moment of hesitation, he said, "You can come in the morning."

"At nine o'clock?" asked Tito.

"Yeah. After nine."

We had fished out the information. Apparently guards were to remain until nine on Sunday. The junta feared the night, as always. Might there be a demonstration?

That evening driving by the jail at 11:30 P.M., we were feeling delirious and crazily happy. Instead of lighting one cigarette as we passed, the four of us in the car lit candles, holding them below window level, making Tito's car glow like a burning ember in the black of the night. People passing us in cars on the highway seemed puzzled at first, but having heard the radio announcement, they put two and two together and waved at us to show they shared our joy. Andreas knew something excitingly good had happened. The lighting of candles is symbolic in Greece. It is done at midnight the night before Easter and means "Christ has risen!" It has the meaning of rebirth, goodness, joy. Andreas had to wait until morning to learn the news.

From the London *Times* correspondent came an announcement of Papandreou's release (October 8, 1967):

> *The Greek military regime today ended the house arrest of Mr. George Papandreou, the octogenarian former Prime Minister and leader of the Centre Union party.*
>
> *Eight other former deputies were set free on the same Government order. Mr. Totomis, the Minister of Public Order, said that the cases of the remaining 22 non-communist politicians still in custody or in exile were under review.*
>
> *The announcement was made overnight and Mr. Papandreou heard about it from the maid at his country house in Kastri, north of Athens, where he has been for the past five months. . . .*
>
> *Among the first to see him was Mrs. Margaret Papandreou, the wife of his son, Professor Andreas Papandreou, who is in gaol awaiting trial on a charge of high treason.*

The next morning I flew up the marble steps leading to the front door, and although it was just nine o'clock, I found the study already crowded with friends waiting to greet the President. Photographers and television cameramen had been outside, as on many occasions in the past. The house looked the same; many of the old familiar faces were there (and many were not, having been hauled off to jail). I was told by the maid that the President was seeing people in his room and that one of the deputies was upstairs now, but she would tell the President that I had arrived. Wasn't it like him, I thought. His first conversations would be political conversations, for politics was his life, and no amount of punishment or tanks or guns could ever change that.

As I waited in the study, after greeting the people gathered there, I sat quietly listening to the snatches of conversation around the room. Most of these people had been too scared to come to my house, to see how I was getting on, or to find out if I was in financial need. Yet now I was hearing their tales of bravado—how they had seen such and such a minister and told him off, how they had confronted house searches, how they had stood up to the authorities, etc. The conversations were in subdued voices, which belied their descriptions of courage, but slowly everyone was gaining confidence and strength, feeling the comfort and security of this oak-paneled room where so many political discussions had been held with the President. Now he was free. Now things would be all right. I remember thinking that this new sense of freedom was dangerous, but I must admit that I shared it.

"The President is asking for you," Eleni came in and told me. I found him standing at the top of the stairway waiting for me in robe and pajamas. He kissed me and hugged me, then holding my hand with his left in a tight grasp, he shook hands with my "little group," which had followed up behind me—Kiveli, Tito, and Marjorie. Tagging right behind was Sophia, her wide-open brown eyes lovingly fastened on her grandfather's face. He threw his arms around her and kissed her tenderly. Then he put his two big hands around her head and pressed it close to him as if he had been given back a long-lost treasured jewel. He looked thinner and pale. His mouth trembled slightly, and his voice was hoarse with emotion as he said to me, "We have much to talk about, Margarita. This is not the time. Come for dinner tonight." I nodded, unable to speak. As I turned to go back down the stairs, he asked, "Andreas?"

"He's okay," I answered.

That evening I arrived at 8:30. The President was downstairs waiting for me, dressed now, and wearing a tie I had given him years earlier which he considered his "good luck" tie. That was a good sign, I thought. He looked more relaxed, but his face was unsmiling. We hardly knew where to start. We talked about the night of the coup—what had happened to him and what had happened to us. He told me about his stay in the hospital, which had made him feel like a sick man, although he was perfectly well. He told me of the terrible isolation in his home. We raised our wine glasses when we sat down at the table in a sober toast to Andreas' freedom and the freedom of Greece. I was waiting for some word of encouragement, for some sentence of hope. I desperately needed it, and from him. As I started to eat, he asked me in a stern and serious voice, "Do you have the financial means to handle your family for twenty years?"

I froze, and looked at him, amazed. "But, but, what kind of question is that?" I stammered.

"No. I mean it. Do you?"

"I don't understand. What are you trying to tell me? You know I have virtually no financial resources." My appetite was gone, and I felt myself starting to tremble. I examined his face, looking straight into mine, and now I saw real despair and bitterness. I dropped my eyes and dabbled at the food.

"I haven't thought that far ahead. I live by the day. When my resources run out, I will face the problem." I didn't want to ask him the question "Don't you think Andreas will get out?" It was what he meant by his question about finances, but I didn't want to hear that awful "no" in a clear and definitive way.

As I sat picking at my food, he started speaking, telling me that "if this hadn't happened," "if this hadn't been done," if, if, if . . . and in some cases it was "if Andreas . . " It was an expression of the bitterness that had built up in him in five months of extreme loneliness, and instead of a note of optimism which I had hoped for with his release, I heard a dark, pessimistic analysis of the situation, an attempt to assess responsibilities, and a grim picture of the future. At moments I thought he was deliberately trying to hurt me, to punish me for all that had happened in Greece and to him, although this was so unlike him, so unlike his general magnanimity, his intense sensitivity to the feelings of people dear to him.

Tito had told me he would come to Kastri around 11 P.M. to pick me up, but didn't want to come in to disturb the family character of the evening. He said that I should, however, stay as long as I wanted, and not to worry about his waiting. I didn't want to stay later than 11. I was exhausted and desperate. And I was fighting to keep from crying. The pillar I thought I could lean on was not there, at least not that night. The battle for Andreas' freedom had been turned back to me. It was to be my fight, and mine alone.

CHAPTER TWENTY-SIX

The Waiting Game

THE PESSIMISM expressed by my father-in-law the first night of his release was dissipated by human contact, discussion, and debate. It was like watching an undernourished man gain strength and color as good food was fed to him. What helped considerably was my reports that Andreas' morale was fine, and his fighting spirits high. Having his son in jail was a daily poison for him, for no matter what arguments they may have had, the relationship was a close one. It had the complex components of a father-son relationship, complicated by the reality of being in political life together, but he did love Andreas. Once he told me, with a sigh, "He left that beautiful Berkeley campus to enter Averoff Prison . . ." I understood all too well how he felt. It was a thought I often had.

The protests from the Right, the Pattakos-Orlandos visit, the release of George Papandreou from house arrest, all added to the conviction held by the Greeks that the junta was in a state of collapse and that new developments would soon take place to bring about its demise. This conviction was reinforced in my own mind by several separate and recent visits I had had at my home. The visits were contacts from resistance groups. Until now, I had avoided taking part in resistance activities which had as an aim the violent overthrow of the junta. There were many reasons. Foremost was my concern for Andreas and the thought that he might pay with his life for my initiative. At the very least, if I were discovered, they could have put me under arrest or expelled me from the country, either of which would have been a blow to Andreas. As his wife, I was the only person allowed to visit him and who could bring him into contact with the world outside prison walls. Andreas' harsh isolation within the prison, and his need to stay involved with the Greece he loved and was committed to, made this doubly important. In addition was the responsibility of four children.

Yet, the problem was deeper than this and raised a moral question for me, for I am against violence. I have never been able to see that the problems violence resolved did not lead to bigger and larger problems. But as I mulled over these issues, I realized I was thinking about a society where means for reform, for change, existed. The violent overthrow of the Constitution, the discarding of all human freedoms, and the oppressive tyranny set up allowed no democratic way of expression. Even the means for organizing a passive resistance were closed to us, for anyone speaking a word against the junta was immediately jailed. If one said, "Don't buy chickens," and this was considered against an economic policy of the government, imprisonment was the result. There were no openings, no methods for expressing orderly dissent. The bottle was corked. Only force could uncork it.

Even with the growing conviction that force would have to be used, I believed that this kind of resistance, to succeed, would have to be done by unknowns, not by the political activists of the precoup period. The secret police had a bead on all such people, knew their names and watched their movements. As for me, as the wife of Andreas and the person who had communication with him, I was a dangerous, potential "giver of instructions" to the wide circle of Andreas loyalists. Like "Typhoid Mary," I contaminated all who came in contact with me, often with dire consequences as in the case of our friend Asteri.

To add further to my doubts and difficulties, I wasn't convinced that a people's violent resistance was feasible, nor could be successful. Modern weaponry, police techniques, transportation facilities which made mountain areas accessible, ruled out old-fashioned revolutionary methods. City revolution seemed more realistic. But this required tremendous organization and techniques that our democratic camp was not in possession of. We were frustrated further. The people from whom we should be getting support in terms of money and material were in the western world, the world that had already recognized the junta and was supporting it through NATO.

It was only when I had a contact from someone claiming to be working with a resistance group which would collaborate with the King when he attempted a coup, that I got interested, and felt something substantial was in the making, for this would involve the army as well.

Within a few days of each other, two other resistance organizations, nonroyalist, belonging to the Center forces, made contact with me. The contact with me was considered, of course, to be with Andreas. One was largely a Macedonian group, the other from the island of Lesbos. They were serious groups, and their plans well thought out. Democratic resistance coordinated with the King's men could contribute to the success of a royalist coup, and would assure our people of a voice in the postcoup developments. Yet I was hesitant to give information about the two Center resistance organizations to the royalist group. I didn't trust the latter.

My real problem was to whom to talk about these matters. Menios, Andreas' lawyer, had pledged to keep out of any such activities in order to play his primary role of lawyer in the ASPIDA trial. When I brought it up to George Papandreou, he told me, "Stay out of it, Margarita," patted my arm, and dropped the subject as if the issue were closed. I would have to find a way to get this across to Andreas—the only person who could advise me on what to do, and whose advice I respected.

I might have dropped the whole thing, but the right-wing resistance contact man presented to me a bold scheme to rescue Andreas from jail. I was flabbergasted and asked why this had to be part of a coup activity—wasn't Andreas safest in prison until the thing was over? I was not given a direct answer, but was told that several other political personalities would be taken out, too. Whether this meant taken out of house arrest, out of prisons, or rescued from islands was not clear. Nor did he give me the names of the people. Through oblique answers to my direct questions, I understood that they did not want Andreas in the hands of Papadopoulos—not out of any concern for the consequences on his life, but from the conviction that he would be used by Papadopoulos in some fashion against them. Their reasoning was that Andreas' antiroyal stands prior to the coup, his popularity with the people, could rally much of the nation around the Little Junta if it tried to stand up to the King. To block this possibility, the King's forces wanted him with them. The King also needed the political world of Greece for the job that would fall upon him to undo the mess created by the colonels.

But an escape from Averoff? How? I asked. And what people would do it? I was assured that it was not a difficult task, and that it would be studied thoroughly before the day arrived. And the day? The answer was "soon." Again I felt the utter madness of the world I was living in. I sincerely didn't like the scheme, and I told the contact man it held too many dangers, and furthermore, I didn't trust the people who would do the job, and he told me that the break-in team would be made up of people of our trust. I said, okay, let's say they get him out in the prison yard . . . what then? How would they get him away from there? It's been all thought through, he insisted. Helicopter. It was a Walter Mitty daydream, one that all prisoners must dream frequently—a means to be removed suddenly and dramatically from jail, on the wings of a big bird. I myself had often gazed at the flat roof of the prison and tried to estimate how long it would take for a helicopter to land, snatch up a waiting figure (Andreas, of course), and flutter away.

I told him that I needed time to think about all of these matters, and told him also that under no circumstances could this be done without my consent. He said yes, of course, but I felt that he was enchanted with the grand scheme of the operation and considered my consent superfluous. When I asked him what he wanted me to do, he said he would be in touch with me again, and in the meantime to do nothing, say nothing. He gave me a phone number to call in case of urgent need for contact, and told me to ask for Spyro. I was to call from a kiosk and act as if I were arranging a rendezvous of assignation. He would come as soon as possible thereafter to my house.

I felt the need to talk to somebody other than Andreas. I hesitated to involve Tito, partly out of selfishness. He had been my steadfast friend and helper, and if he got jailed I would be entirely on my own. The only person in my immediate circle I could take into confidence was Marjorie. Marjorie gulped when I unfolded the story. "Yeegods!" was her one-word response. Then after a second or two, she moaned "Oh, no!" And the more I thought about it, the more I thought "Oh, no!" too.

In the many months I had been talking to Andreas from behind the screens, we had developed a rudimentary code language. The name for the King had become Hourmouzis inspired by the real name of the original contact man. The name for Andreas was Takis. The next time I saw Andreas I plunged in.

"I saw Hourmouzis the other day. He sends you his greetings. The kids are fine. He's up to his neck in a business deal. He's decided to buy the big hotel."

Andreas understood immediately. "When?" was his question.

"I don't really know, but soon. It's a complicated deal and may take a little time. It seems he wants Takis in on it." I waited for Andreas' reaction.

"That's interesting," he said.

"I told him I didn't know if that was the right thing. Takis would have to be taken by helicopter to the hotel, and, well, it would involve a number of people—and I didn't really know if it was feasible."

Andreas' response surprised me. "It's feasible. That part is feasible. I've often thought about it. I don't believe it would be too difficult."

I wondered if he had understood me completely. "Then you think Takis should join in with Hourmouzis?"

"I don't know to what extent. But he certainly ought to take that flying bird and go look at the site. And, of course, you should look at the hotel plans if you are to give any advice to him. And you ought to discuss it with my father."

"I tried once. But you know him. He doesn't like to discuss business deals. He told me to let Hourmouzis do whatever he wanted to do and to stay out of it."

"I'm not sure he's right. Anyway it's a good tourist investment."

We switched the subject to other matters, not to prolong this particular meaningful conversation. We had established a method of talking about the King's coup. This was already an accomplishment. We also discovered that we were having more luck in throwing in English words as the guards around us took a relaxed attitude now that Andreas was being courted by the junta. Or so they thought. Toward the end of our visit that day Andreas inserted enough English words among the Greek to give me information about telephone connections to the jail, the guardhouse outside, hours of change of guard, time front doors were locked and bolted for the night, etc., which should be known by someone plotting a jail raid. I felt as if mad hornets were circling around my head—when was the last time *you* plotted a jail break?— but Andreas' calm and assured voice cut through the confusion, and I realized this was the real world after all, and I had better deal with it.

In the meantime, news of army "retirements" appeared daily. The purge in the army was continuing. I knew from the inner circles of both the King and Papadopoulos that this was a source of great friction between the two. Each time a list was printed of new retirements, it was pointed out in all newspapers that the King had signed the decree—to give the impression that the two were working as a harmonious team. In view of the fact that most of these officers were considered loyal to the King, this didn't make sense. Was he really signing decrees to kick out his own officers, or were they faked? With what forces, I wondered, would he finally make his coup? What also bothered me was that talk of a King's coup was becoming rather widespread, and thus the element of surprise, critical for success, was removed.

I was of two minds about the King's initiative. On the one hand, he was the only force remaining with power to topple the junta. The people were reaching a stage of willingness to support anything that would fell the colonels. The thinking was "Let's get rid of *them* first, and then we shall see . . ." Many diplomats were of similar mind and gave quiet encouragement to the King. It was generally thought that the British were the strongest prodders behind the King. But the King's power after his coup, if successful, would be supreme. What would this mean for the fate of Greece, for Andreas? Still, he would have to inaugurate a parliamentary regime, I argued. Contacts being made by the King's people with politicians indicated he needed their support, and if they gave their support, he would have to work out with them a solution afterward. Yet, in contacts made by our foreign friends with junta people or government officials, the greatest anti-Andreas passion was expressed by the people who had the closest association with the Palace. Were not the colonels perhaps more remote from the political passions of precoup Greece and less personally vengeful toward Andreas? Papadopoulos, for instance, in the few private discussions which were reported to me had never heaped scorn on Andreas.

With these conflicting thoughts, I saw my father-in-law becoming more expansive, more hopeful, more like his old self. Once he asked me to arrange for Andreas to be at his cell window at a specific time so that he could drive slowly by with his driver as a sign of his love and support. He did this several times, but he found the experience too emotionally upsetting, and from then on he asked me to convey his greetings in my visits.

We spent evenings together, just the two of us, which could almost be described as pleasant, given the fact that underlying every conversation was the remembrance of a man behind prison bars. Many of these discussions were reminiscences of his fifty years of a political career—moments of sorrow, moments of triumph, moments of humor. He spoke about his barefooted boyhood in Kalentzi, his brother Nickolas who was killed fighting the Bulgarians in 1922, and whom he worshiped, and his sister Magdaline, who died at the age of sixteen from a poison dye she was using on a dress. He spoke about his two marriages, and the devilish life he had with his second wife, Kiveli. This he told without hatred or passion. He told me women had been important in his life (a fact well known to the Athens press), and analyzing this, attributed it to the fact that he had never known a mother. His mother died when he was six months old. Whatever it was that attracted him to women, it was certainly equally true that women were attracted to him. At dinner parties it was inevitable that the ladies gathered around him after dinner like metal scrapings to a magnet while the Greek males stood sullenly in various poses of impatience around the edges of the circle.

He spoke mostly about Greece. Sometimes he recited for me from the poetry of Cavafy or Sikelianos. He showed me his correspondence with Kazantzakis. He told me about the great Venizelos, who was his political mentor. He spoke about his exile on the island of Andros during the Metaxas dictatorship. I laughingly told him once that he was giving me a short course in modern Greek history, and I only regretted that I had no tape recorder to get it all.

When we had explored the past together, we would return to the present, and slowly he let me know that he was going to back the King in the King's attempt to overthrow the junta. I assumed that he was having contact through an intermediary.

In Washington, Palamas, Greek Ambassador to the United States, claiming to have been prompted by recent speculation in the American press as to intentions of the Greek government concerning the restoration of the electoral process, made the following statement on October 16:

> *The Greek government has repeatedly and solemnly declared that its mission is to lead the country toward a regime of parliamentary democracy. It is hoped that the application of saner principles in tracing the framework of the new regime will keep it from reverting to the generally recognized as dangerous and self-defeating habits and methods of the past.*
>
> *The present intentions of the National Government are in complete harmony with the above statement of initial policy, in consequence of which, I am happy to say, I am now in a position to announce the official timetable for the return to parliamentarianism, consisting of the following basic phases:*
>
> *1. December 15, 1967: The Constitutional Revision Committee will submit the draft of the new Constitution to the Government.*
>
> *2. The preparation of the final draft to be submitted to the electorate by the Government shall not exceed a period of six months.*
>
> *3. The technical preparation of the constitutional referendum will take approximately two months, subsequent to which the referendum will be held.*
>
> *4. Parliamentary elections will follow according to the appropriate provisions of the new Constitution.*
>
> *I am authorized to state categorically that the Greek Government considers the above timetable as irrevocable.*
>
> *I hope that this announcement will receive adequate attention and consideration from the Press and public opinion of this country. All those who profess an interest in Democracy cannot but find satisfaction and encouragement in the perspectives outlined in this statement.*

On October 17 the State Department commented on the Greek timetable for the return to parliamentary government:

> *The U.S. Government has been consistent in its hope that Greece would return as speedily as possible to constitutional government. We are encouraged that the Greek Government has now set forth a timetable for the resumption of democratic processes and we will be following attentively the various steps in that development.*

The announcement of the timetable for a return to parliamentary government was made first to foreign lands. The poor Greeks, who were primarily concerned, heard about it last, on October 20, four days after Palamas' announcement in Washington. In a letter on the next day I wrote the following to Walter Heller:

320

Yesterday the P.M. announced a kind of time schedule for return to parliamentary procedures. What he pretty much said is that they were announcing the way in which they would legalize and give constitutional form to the present new power structure. They need six months in 1968, he said, to examine the proposals submitted by the constitution committee—with no indication of any public discussion—and two months later will hold a referendum, that is, under the auspices of the military dictatorship. Some time later (no specified date), they will hold elections under the conditions of the new constitution. Some kind of super-body will be set up which will have the authority to screen candidates for parliament, and no communist will be admitted. That means people like you and me will be excluded. . . . Since the American contingent was so caught off guard by the dictatorship here—or so they report it, at least—can they not still be misjudging the situation by not pushing for a faster timetable? That is, do they think they have time? Or do they rather like the dictatorship? This is what is generally thought here.

A. has lost quite a bit of weight since you saw him due to a stomach ailment (diagnosed gastritis) which prevented him from eating much. I have had to order new pants for him twice to keep up with the slimming waistline. He tells me he is proud of his new silhouette, but to me it is symbolic of the strain and tension he is under, and the inhuman treatment.

To George Lianis, also on October 21:

Mike says you must start immediately a campaign of enlightening the American public on the blatant exposure of the aims and designs of this crowd—the fake "legalization" of a fake regime by cover of constitution, referendum and elections. He fears that these false promises may quiet the reactions of our democratic friends—and the words "constitution" and "referendum" lull the public into thinking all is going well. If you could get yourself and others on local radio and TV stations with a question and answer type thing on these recent announcements—this would be good. Also newspaper interviews. . . .

On Monday morning, October 30, I drove into Athens on an errand. After parking the car, I walked to a kiosk to call Mrs. Koutsoyergas.

"Hi. The President would like to have you and Menios for dinner tonight," I said.

There was a long pause. "They took Menios last night" came the answer in a low controlled monotone.

"Oh, no!" I answered. "When? Why? Oh, my God! No, no, don't answer. I'll be by sometime today." I walked away in a daze. Dear, wonderful Menios. The only other person seeing Andreas, and the key to the ASPIDA defense. And what about Andreas? For him Menios was a break in his day, a person to communicate with, even though they were never alone. He was also the only person other than Andreas who knew the dirty details of the frame-up. I walked without knowing where I was walking, my body carrying itself without instructions. Bodies and faces floated by me in a blur. Flocas, Zonars, around the corner past the side entrance of the Grande Bretagne, Syntagma Square, right turn to Ermou Street where the crowds on the pavements increased and I kept bumping into people, back to the square, through the Royal Gardens, past the statue of the discus thrower, over to the Truman statue . . .

"Goddamn the bastards," I was saying again and again, my fingernails slitting my palms. "What next? But why this? For no damned reason! Is it just to break us?" Nearby was another kiosk. My mind a tangle of confusion, I called home and told Marjorie not to bring the lunch to the jail—I was coming home first. I walked back to the parking lot, barely acknowledging the warm greeting of a parking attendant who was a strong Andreas supporter. When I pulled out of the lot and turned my head to the side to check the traffic, I spotted from the corner of my eye a blotch of color on the back seat. Lying there loosely, on top of the morning newspaper, were twelve roses, a token of friendship from the attendant. For a moment I felt tears begin, but I was too anxious to cry, and I drove on, dry-eyed. I walked in the door and reported the news to Marjorie. She had thought something happened by the tone of my voice on the telephone.

Monday was visiting day for me, and I would be the one to break the news to Andreas. This was weighing on me. How does one soften such a blow? Could one make a joke out of it, like one little, two little, three little Indians . . . Impossible. When I finally arrived at the screens, I told it straight. Andreas took it with his usual calm and told me he suspected something of the sort when Menios had not shown up for their regular Monday legal session. Occasionally Menios had come in the afternoon when he was delayed in morning court on another case, and Andreas had been hopeful that that was the explanation. He felt that they had nothing with which to charge Menios and that it was a punitive act more than anything else, but urged me to see Cannellopoulos, the second lawyer on the case, to get whatever information was available. Then he asked me to get the news out to our democratic friends abroad. At the end of a visit, he usually told me "Kisses to the kids" or "Love to the family," but this time he said, "Be careful, darling." He echoed my own feelings, that the net was closing in. A brief note to Walter on the same day expressed my fears:

October 30, 1967

> Walter—they picked up Andy's lawyer last night at 4 a.m.! The situation is going from bad to worse. This is a gang of criminals. All the decent, liberal, intelligent democratic forces are being smashed.
> I may soon be in myself. Please do what you can and help! All my love . . .

I called Cannellopoulos who said he was looking into the matter. There was no need for my coming to his office. The conversation was tense and abrupt. Naturally, I thought. He must be wondering when the knock will come on his door in the middle of the night.

Around 7 P.M. I went to see Mrs. Koutsoyergas. She told me the harrowing details of the arrest. The doorbell had shrilled at 4 A.M. Before Menios had had a chance to put on his bathrobe and slippers, four men had broken down the door and were upstairs. Their shouting and screaming put her two little children into hysteria. In threatening tones they said, "Tell us where the weapons are hidden." Menios answered, "What weapons?" For one hour they tore the house apart, holding Menios and his wife at gunpoint in their bedroom. Finally they left, taking Menios with them. During the day she had received word from one of the lawyers in her husband's office that most likely Menios was at Security Headquarters, but that no direct contact could be made. She was highly nervous and worried. From her home I went to the home of a friend and risked one of my few phone calls abroad. This time it was to Siggie, Andreas' cousin in Paris. I told him the news and asked him to publicize it and to reach our lawyer friends so that they might start a protest.

That night I had dinner in Kastri alone with my father-in-law.

The week went by without any new developments. Mrs. Koutsoyergas was told to bring food to the security offices on Bouboulinas Street and saw Menios from a distance stepping out of a room at the end of a long hallway. We were unable to learn what charges had been brought against him.

On Saturday I had a visitor I had been expecting for a long time, Jack Beck of CBS-TV. A letter from Lianis in the States had informed me that Beck was planning to do a background story on the Greek coup, American involvement, etc., and that he was particularly intrigued with the question of how someone of Andreas' liberal, noncommunist background, with a fine career as an academician in the States, could have been looked upon with such horror by the bureaucrats and policy makers of Washington. (Now there's the $64 question, I thought!) I spent all of Saturday afternoon talking to him and his wife, and Beck took copious notes. I told him I was skeptical about his being able to do anything meaningful in Greece because the junta would not be cooperative. Would he, for example, be able to take shots of Averoff Prison? Of the torture chambers on Bouboulinas Street? Of the detention quarters at Maroussi? Of the mock execution sites at Dionysus? And whatever restrictions they didn't put on him, the Greeks would put on themselves. Who would describe for the CBS television cameras the fear under which the people lived, their hatred for the tyrants who now controlled Greece? But Beck was optimistic. He told me he had an appointment with Totomis, the Minister of Public Order, on Monday morning and expected to line up appointments with government people. I didn't tell him that Totomis was considered the most obvious CIA agent in the cabinet. In any case, he would be around for two weeks, part of the time spent in touring the countryside, and felt he could learn much by keeping his ears open. We agreed to see each other again by the end of next week. I didn't know at the time that I would be seeing him accidentally much sooner.

After he left, I jumped in Tito's car to take Andreas' dinner to the "station master" at the inside cage window of the jail. As I approached the jail I sensed something in the atmosphere. Was it more guards? Was it new faces? Was it more hustle and bustle around the door? After recording the items in my food package, I was informed that the director of the prison wanted to see me. Just at that moment he walked out flanked by two army officers.

"This is she?" I heard one of them ask, pointing at me as if I were a horse, just purchased sight unseen by its new owner.

I stood and waited for them to speak.

The director cleared his throat, and making a stern face to match the stern faces of the officers, he told me that from now on I would have to get special permission to see my husband.

"I have permission," I said, "from Mr. Pattakos."

"You heard him," interrupted an officer. "You no longer have permission."

"But how am I supposed to get special permission. From where?"

"From the Minister of Public Order" was the director's reply.

Now I knew what had changed. All the faces of the guards. Those I had seen outside were strange faces, and now these inside were also strange. Only the director's and the ticket taker's faces were familiar. As I walked down the sidewalk toward the street, I turned to look back at the window where Andreas usually stood. I saw the outline of his body to one side of the window, not in the middle, where he normally stood, several feet back from the bars. His face was in the shadows. It was obvious. There were new developments, somehow tied in with Menios' arrest. My heart sank. So far this week Cannellopoulos, the second lawyer, had not managed to have a visit with Andreas. Were my visits now, too, to be cut off?

I rushed home and found the telephone number of Totomis, the Minister of Public Order. I didn't expect to find him on a Saturday evening at his office, but he was there. Why not, I thought later. Security problems and torture are not reserved for weekdays.

"Mr. Totomis, this is Mrs. Papandreou."

"Yes," in a tight voice, and in English.

"I have been told I must have special permission to see my husband, and I do not understand."

"What do you not understand, madam?" again in a tight and unfriendly voice.

"I have a regular permit from Mr. Pattakos giving me four visits a week."

"Yes. And you will have your visits."

"How?"

"You will have to see me."

"Oh."

"From now on I handle the question of visits."

"All right. Then may I come down now for my permit?"

"No, no. Come Monday morning."

"May I come early then so that I don't lose my regular Monday visit?"

"Come any time after nine o'clock."

At exactly nine o'clock Monday morning I arrived at the building of the Ministry of Public Order. Marjorie had accompanied me for moral support. In the downstairs hallway was a counter tended by the ubiquitous men in uniform. I told them who I was and that I had an appointment with Totomis. One of the men dialed a telephone on the counter, gave the information that

I was downstairs, waited, then, hanging up, told me that the minister had not come in yet. I raised one eyebrow, but said nothing except, "I will wait."

Next to the entryway of the Ministry of Public Order was a small café and outside it the inevitable metal table, with legs like an X and a bumpy, bubbly top. It was the only table and the only two chairs and we took possession of them and settled in, ordering two Turkish coffees, and anticipated—both of us—a lengthy stay. From time to time I checked with the downstairs hallway guard to see if he had any more information about Totomis' arrival, and received always the same answer, "Se ligo," "Soon." From our peeping post we watched the stream of humanity entering that gray building, most of them with faces of worry, seeking help for a loved one. At one point a ministry car pulled up, and a short, bald-headed figure jumped out and with brisk, military stride, disappeared into the building. It was Pattakos. In half an hour he strode out again. By then I was sure Totomis was upstairs playing hide-and-seek with me.

At 11 A.M. I was startled out of my waiting stupor by an unmistakably American voice.

"Margaret! What are you doing here?"

"Oh, hello, Jack, I'm waiting for Totomis."

"I have an appointment with him myself," said Beck.

"They tell me he's not upstairs."

"Well, then, I'll join you in waiting," he answered, nodding a greeting to Marjorie and looking around for another chair.

"No, you don't understand. They tell *me* he's not in. I would be curious to see what they tell *you*."

I walked behind him as he went up to the officer to announce his arrival. Again a phone call. Then, eyeing me sheepishly, the officer said, "You may go upstairs to the minister's office, third floor, Mr. Beck."

"Good luck, Jack," I murmured, and giving a cold look of contempt to the officer, I returned to my waiting post at the table for his descent to verify my belief that Minister Totomis was conducting business in his office. Before he came down, however, I was faced with another problem. This was my regular visiting day, and Andreas would be expecting me to arrive around 12:15. I could not be sure that he had been told my visiting privileges had been removed, but I figured that he was quite aware of the change in personnel and that something was up. If I didn't show up at my regular time, he would be terribly upset. I waited as long as I could for Beck to come back down, then left for the jail where Tito would meet me with the food. I walked sadly toward the massive iron jail doors. Andreas again was standing some distance behind the window, but as I got close to the building he moved nearer and with one facial gesture asked me, "Did you get it?" I shook my head slowly from side to side and tried to think how I could say "tomorrow," but then, was I so sure for tomorrow? After I delivered the food, I walked painfully away from the prison, feeling his eyes on me from that hellhole pulling on me like a magnet to come back and visit with him. Instead I had a rendezvous with Totomis.

I returned to the ministry building and was told that Totomis had not yet arrived. I waited until two o'clock, then left for home. It was all a big game and part of the harassment. I was furious, and determined. At 5 P.M. exactly, when public offices reopened after siesta, I dialed the Ministry of Public Order. I reached a male secretary (officer?) and told him that my appointment with Totomis in the morning had not been kept, and I would like to come down now. After consultation I was told to come at 8:30 P.M.

Mr. Totomis was waiting for me. He was average height, had straight black hair, a flat face, and beady eyes. As I came in, he got up from his desk, walked around it, and extended his hand. I gave him my gloved right hand and let it fall in his clasp. He walked back to his desk and gestured for me to sit down in a leather armchair.

"I missed my regular visit with Andreas today," I told him. "I thought we had an appointment this morning."

"Ah, yes, yes. Sorry. I was involved with business outside the office."

I gave him a look of disbelief.

"Now, how many visits do you have?" he asked, picking up a pen.

"I have four—Monday, Tuesday, Thursday, and Saturday."

"Yes, hmmmmmn. Well, I will call in my secretary and ask him to prepare a new permit for you."

"I would like to understand why I must now get a new permit."

"You know, Mrs. Papandreou, this country has been going through—that is, went through, very difficult times, and we must now watch over everything."

"Does that include arresting Andreas' lawyer?"

"Well, it seems his brother has been involved in some antinational activities."

"I don't know about his brother, but I know about Mr. Koutsoyergas. He is not involved in anything."

"Well, we may not keep him."

"You know, Mr. Totomis, I come from the United States, and in that country no one can be arrested without a warrant, and a lawyer has the right to bring his case through trial, even if he has committed murder."

Here Totomis bristled. "I know your culture, madam. I have lived for some years in the United States. Even there they bring people in for questioning."

"Yes, Mr. Totomis. The word is 'bring,' not 'drag.'"

His face was beginning to perspire, and I feared I had pushed too far. I had heard that he sometimes "dropped in" on the torture activity. Undoubtedly I was dealing with a sick man.

He pushed the button for his secretary, ignoring my last comment. With the air of a steel-company executive giving instructions for a new five-million-dollar investment, he instructed his secretary to write out my permit.

"For Tuesday, Thursday, and Saturday," he said.

"Monday?"

"I'm sorry. That is all that is allowed by law." Pause. "But I'll tell you what I'll do. I'll give you an hour each time instead of the half hour you have had. How's that?"

I was too puzzled by this move to make any judgment. I simply thanked him. It seemed too good. When he told me to come by the next morning to pick up the permit, I thought I spotted the fly in the ointment. Another put-off.

"I'd prefer to wait until it's ready," I said.

"No, no, impossible. Tomorrow morning."

"And will your people down at the door be instructed to let me up?" I asked.

"Yes, yes, of course."

"One more question, Mr. Totomis. When will you hold the ASPIDA trial?"

He looked straight at me, and put on an air of great sincerity.

"Very soon, madam, very soon."

"That's what I had hoped to hear," I told him. As I left, I remembered what he had told Andreas in his cell on one visit he made to Pikermi with Pattakos. Andreas had asked for permission to see me in a room away from the screens. "But your wife is an enemy of the state," he had said. I wondered how he felt having this enemy of the state in his office, breathing the same air?

I arrived at the jail on Tuesday, springing lightly down the long walk, the permit clutched tightly in my hand, and knocked on the peep-window of the jail door. The doorkeeper seemed surprised to see me. He opened the door slightly and asked if I had permission to see my husband.

"Yes, here," I responded smugly. "And for one hour." He asked me to wait outside, and I sat on the bench under the canvas shade, a place where I often watched the comings and goings at the prison. My normal visit had been from 12:30 to 1:00. The Totomis edict gave me from 12:00 to 1:00, thus I had given them an additional surprise by being there at 11:45.

I passed the time by watching the birds that always hopped around the premises pecking at crumbs fallen from big baskets of bread delivered to the prison. One of the sparrows had a snapped leg that had healed jutting out at right angles like a broken toothpick. He hopped around quite nicely on his good leg, picking up bits of bread and flying off when satisfied. At least he's free, I had often thought.

Another frequent visitor of the prison was an old man of seventy in tattered clothes whose function was unclear to me. I saw him getting handouts from time to time from the front door, a tin plate of boiled potatoes with greasy gravy and two big torn pieces of bread. He talked to himself, his toothless mouth moving rapidly and his head answering yes or no as part of the dialogue. Very often he sang a chant as he approached the door: "Long live the King; Long live the Queen; Long live the army; Long live the Greek nation," repeated over and over again. He was considered a crackpot by the prison officials, who occasionally teased him, but he knew how to sing for his supper and turned out to be not as "tetched" as everyone thought. (After the King's attempted coup he dropped the part of his chant that said, "Long live the King; Long live the Queen.")

The antidote to this toothless beggar was another old man, a local drunk, who would go on a toot every so often and plant himself on the island divider in the middle of Leoforas Alexandras in front of Averoff, face the jail, and sing songs of liberty and democracy toward Andreas' window. A tall, lean figure, I remember his swaying body amidst the passing buses and cars, his arms moving as if he were plucking his heart from his chest and throwing it upward toward the serenaded one, his baritone voice hardly audible above the din of the traffic. If an army truck would pass, he would shake his fist at it and shout, "Long live democracy!" Every so often he would disappear for a few weeks, and we were told by the local shopkeepers that he had been booked on drunkenness. He would reappear, paler and subdued, sober for a few days, tipping his hat politely to me as I passed—then his operatic urges, under the prodding of adequate quantities of wine, would be loosed like a torrential storm, and the scarecrow figure would return to his stage. Andreas said he sometimes came at midnight and sang sweet extemporaneous songs of admiration until he was shooed off by the night guard. My father in particular had enjoyed the old man's spunk and spirit, and when he found himself at the same café while waiting for me to finish a visit with Andreas, he would send free bottles of beer to the old man's table. Once in midday traffic I found myself on the same divider with him, waiting for the light to change to cross. He halted his boisterous, tipsy singing, leaned over toward me, and asked in a clear, unslurred tongue, "How is Mr. Andreas?" I told him he was fine. "Kouraiyo!" he told me, meaning "Take heart!" After this aside, he returned to his wailing. I wondered how drunk he really was.

How long would this tragic era in Greek history last, I thought, as I waited for my visit. And how long would I be coming to this jail, watching a sparrow with a crooked leg, and listening to tragicomic liturgies? And waiting, waiting for the heavy doors to open and see Andreas stride out—free?

It was past twelve o'clock. An officer walked out and asked me for my written permit. He took it and disappeared back into the jail. Ten more minutes passed. The doors swung open and the doorkeeper beckoned me in.

"You are wanted in the director's office," he told me.

I stepped into the office to find the director and four young men in uniform. They glared at me.

"Your visit will begin at 12:30 and last till 1:00 P.M.," he informed me.

"No," I argued. "The permit says my visit is from 12:00 to 1:00. I have been given one hour three times a week with my husband," I stated in a pedantic fashion.

The director looked lost, but the eyes of the army were on him. He tried another tack. "The rules of the jail do not permit a one-hour visitation period, only one half-hour."

"I'm not interested in the rules of the jail. I was given one-hour rights by the Minister of Public Order, Mr. Totomis. Are you overruling him?" I knew it was a lost cause, but I had to try. For a moment I wondered if Totomis was in collusion with the jail authorities, giving me something as a gesture of grandiosity, but telling the officials of Averoff to renege. It would have been very much in current style.

"You heard the director," an impatient voice finally piped up. It came from a tall, blond, blue-eyed officer, terribly handsome, and very taken with himself. He was obviously the spokesman for the group.

"I would like then to be allowed to call Mr. Totomis to determine what he meant by this written permit." I cast my eye at the telephone on the director's desk. This created a flurry and some mumbled comments in undertones among the officers.

"It is not only the permit," I continued, "but I was told personally by the minister that I was to have one hour, three times a week." I tried to smile pleasantly as if this were truly an unnecessary fuss about a detail, and it could all be settled very easily by one simple phone call.

The director had given up. The blond Greek (later I learned his name—Vourdakos, from Mani in the Peloponnesus) took over. "You will wait outside," he ordered me.

I was led again to the bench outside the jail walls. This time I glanced up at the window of Andreas' cell and tried to make a sign to indicate that things were going to be all right. I knew he had followed every move—my early arrival, my wait on the bench, the taking of my written permit, the ten-minute delay, my disappearance into the jail—and now, my reappearance on the bench. What theories was he developing about events? And what did they matter anyway? All we wanted was to have that precious visit.

At 12:40 the doors opened again. The officer came to tell me my visit could start. They had checked and there had been some mistake. I was to have only one-half hour. I was sure they had not checked with Totomis. They had checked with the Big Boys. Totomis didn't count that much.

When I arrived at the screens, I found an angry Andreas. "They are trying to harass us," he told me in a loud voice to reach the new pairs of ears surrounding us. "Well, let them try. They can't do it." They did try. They told me first to speak louder. They stopped us every so often to ask if we were discussing family matters, or something else. They argued at one point that I had used an English word ("It's just her accent in Greek," Andreas explained.) They pushed their bodies next to me, almost touching mine, to make me fully aware of their presence. At one o'clock a short officer told us our time was up. Andreas protested saying that we were entitled to half an hour. "Yes" was the answer, "from 12:30 to 1:00." We both argued that I was present at 12:30, but was not permitted in, therefore, they were at fault. After several minutes of this, we won our argument, and then looked at each other blankly, wondering what to do with the short time remaining under the conditions in which we spoke.

Andreas started, "Who loves me at the house?" he asked, grinning.

From the brink of tears, I broke into a grin to match his.

"Nikos loves you," I said.

"Who else?"

"Andrikos loves you. Sophia loves you. George loves you. Your mother loves you."

"Anybody else?"

"Oh, yes, indeed. Antigone loves you. The gardener loves you. Marjorie loves you. And most of all, I love you."

"Is that all? Nobody else?"

I thought hard. "Oh, but of course. Blackie and Gilda love you."

The short, squat Greek interrupted and in a voice filled with suspicion, thinking we were somehow conversing in code, he asked, "Who are those names?"

Andreas and I, almost in unison, said sweetly, "Our dogs."

The man turned red. "Time's up!" he shouted, and I knew from his voice that the two minutes we legitimately had left were not to be bargained for. I blew Andreas a kiss; he blew one back, and I left Andreas in the oppressive atmosphere of Averoff Prison.

That was Tuesday. On Thursday when I arrived I had a new shock. The openings at the ends of the iron railing through which I passed to reach the counter of the cage Andreas stood in were closed up—with barbed wire! Unless I crawled on hands and knees under the rail, I would have to speak to Andreas at a distance of four feet from the screen and with visibility practically zero.

"What's this?" I shouted, pointing to the barbed wires.

"What do you mean, 'What's this?'" said Vourdakos, mocking my question. "The passage has been closed up. That's all."

"What for? For me?"

"Oh, no. For everyone. It's a new prison regulation."

This was a lie, and I knew it. I was unable to protest, because my voice wouldn't have held up. This, of all the things they had done to us, this inhuman reminder that we were all to be treated like animals—caged, penned off, wired up, kept apart by metal barriers—this iron curtain, this symbol of warfare, had just about broken me. I grabbed hold of the iron rail, clenched it tightly, and there in front of Andreas and in the presence of the new boys from the Papadopoulos gang, I wept silently.

"Margaret, Margaret," I heard Andreas say helplessly. "Come on, come on. It's all right. It's nothing." In a way, for him it was nothing, just a part of a series of harassments he had been put through in the last week. Ironsmiths at that very moment were building a cage in the hallway outside his door where he was to take his exercise from now on, like a wild animal pacing back and forth in a zoo. He had had the length of the hallway up until now. A window had been drilled in his cell door as a peephole so that he could be looked at at any moment of day or night. He had been ordered to stay away from the window looking out to the front yard and boulevard, and especially to stay away when I was approaching or leaving. He had been ordered to exchange no words with his guards, not even a "good morning." His room was searched twice, sometimes three times a day.

Shortly I got myself under control. "It's just that I'm tired," I told Andreas. "I'll be all right now."

That evening Jack Beck dropped by. I knew the kind of people he had been talking to when he told me, "You know, it seems this country was in quite a chaotic situation before the coup."

"Yes," I said. "As much as any democracy. Then we should have a dictatorship in the States. Where have you been? To the American Embassy?"

"Yes, I've seen some people there, and I've been talking around."

As I was listening to the policy line of the State Department through his lips—"mild dictatorship, no blood spilled, need to push through some necessary reforms, corruption bad in government prior to April 21," etc.,

330

etc.—the doorbell rang. Antigone interrupted me to tell me Mrs. Koutsoyergas was at the door. I left Jack and met Mrs. Koutsoyergas in the dining room. She was pale and distressed. "Margaret, they've beaten Daskalakis of Patras. They hung him by his feet and lashed him on the back. Menios' lawyer told me. Daskalakis has made depositions against Menios and his brother. He says they were involved in a resistance organization in Patras that has arms caches. The lawyer thinks they want to pin it on Andreas through my husband. Oh, I'm so afraid they are going to torture him!" She started to cry. "Can't we do something?"

Yes, I thought. Kill them all.

"They won't torture him," I said, trying to be convincing. "They don't dare."

"I think Ari has been beaten." (Ari was a close friend of Menios' picked up the same night.) "He passed me in the hallway when I took food to Security Headquarters, and he looks terrible. He didn't say anything to me. He saw me and put his eyes down."

I had a thought. "Just a second. There's someone here I'd like to call in." I didn't tell her he was from CBS-TV, so as not to frighten her, nor to expose her.

I went into the living room and asked Jack Beck if he would like to get a feeling for what was really going on in Greece. He followed me in, and I asked Mrs. Koutsoyergas to repeat her story, which I translated for Beck.

"Please," I said. "You must make these things known."

He shook his head solemnly. He seemed shaken.

On Saturday came the final and ultimate harassment. Georgie and I had finished our visit at the screens. Georgie's tension had returned as soon as he reset foot on Greek soil. The three younger children went in for their usual fifteen-minute visit. I waited on the bench for them. In ten minutes they were out. Sophia was crying uncontrollably. Nick was fighting to keep the tears back, and Andriko looked frightened and lost. I ran to them. "What happened?"

Sophia answered between sobs. "They . . . they didn't let us be with Daddy. They m-made us stand there outside . . ."

"At the screens?" I asked incredulously.

"Yes . . ." and she buried her face in my chest. I remembered my first day and that blurred, shadowy figure behind the screens.

"Sophie cried all the time, and she made me want to cry," said Nick, trying to explain his unmanly behavior. I knew that he didn't want to cry in front of the guards.

"Come on, kids," I said, putting my arms around Sophia and Nick and trying to keep the choke from my voice, "we're going to walk down the pathway as if nothing happened. We won't let them get us down." Brave talk from a mother with her heart aching for her children. "Anyway, I've cried there, too, so it's nothing to worry about." My thoughts were also with Andreas. How horrible to be there with his little girl crying her heart out and be unable to take her in his arms, soothe her, comfort her, tell her all would work out well.

"What did Daddy say?" I asked.

"He kept saying 'Don't cry, Sophoula, don't cry,' but she didn't stop," Nick answered (a trace of annoyance in his voice.)

When we got home, I dialed the phone number of the American Embassy and asked for an appointment with the ambassador. I hadn't had any contact with the embassy since midsummer when Talbot returned from the United States. His secretary said he would see me at 3:30 P.M. With the ambassador when I got there was the chief of the legal section, and I told them both my story. I said that my visiting rights had been reduced to three times a week and on a temporary basis, that I would have to renew my permit again at the end of two weeks. I said that the children by the rules of the prison were permitted to see their father in a separate room and that suddenly they were confronted with the ungodly screens in the adult visiting section. I reminded them that they were American and minors. I asked them to do something about these visitation privileges. Then I told them about Menios, that I knew that some of the people picked up at the same time had been tortured. I said that Menios was not involved in anything, and that I wanted them to protest the arrest of the lawyer who was to handle the ASPIDA case. The ambassador asked whether Andreas had another lawyer, and I answered in the affirmative, adding that Andreas had not seen any lawyer since Menios' arrest, and that, in any case, this was not the key lawyer in the case. No comment was made about my charges of torture.

Talbot took notes and promised to look into the matter. He told me he would be in touch with me. This visit took place on November 11, 1967 (Armistice Day—to make the world safe for democracy). I mention this date for another reason. I was intrigued with a memorandum dated November 7 that later reached my hands. It was addressed to Claiborne Pell, United States Senator from Rhode Island. Apparently our friends in the States had moved quickly when they received the news of the lawyer's arrest, reaching Senator Pell and asking him to make inquiries.

MEMORANDUM

TO: *Senator Pell*
FROM: *Lan Potter*
RE: Mrs. Papandreou

Mr. Daniel Brewster from the Greek desk called late on Monday to respond both to my inquiry to him and to your inquiry to Mr. Battle regarding the matter of legal counsel for Papandreou.

As a result of your inquiry, the Embassy has determined that the attorney, Mr. Koutsoyergas, was arrested last week, along with several other persons, for alleged anti-government activities, but that no specific charges have been placed against him.

The Department points out that they feel that this may not be a serious situation and that Koutsoyergas may not be removed from the scene. Even if he is, they report that Mrs. Papandreou does have another attorney assigned to her whose name is Penalopoulos, and that, in fact, Koutsoyergas was the second ranking of these two attorneys.

Nonetheless, Mr. Brewster is asking the Embassy to check further and to contact Mrs. Papandreou directly to get her viewpoint. I explained to him that I would not be here for the rest of the week and suggested that if he had anything of note to report that he should call you direct in the afternoon.

So Talbot knew about the case, had already made inquiries about it, and had been asked to contact me for my viewpoint. What he had done was to belittle the significance of Koutsoyergas to the State Department, calling him the "second ranking" lawyer and giving incorrectly the name of Cannellopoulos. It was par for the course. As for having the embassy "check further," I wondered how many months I might have waited for him to contact me if I hadn't made that Saturday noon phone call.

On Sunday he called me back to the embassy office and told me that they had contacted the government and that I would not have trouble getting my visiting permit, that he had mentioned the children's seeing their father in a room, but could not guarantee that this privilege would be given, and that he had been told that most likely Koutsoyergas would not be held long. In terms of result, it looked like a big goose egg. On Monday I went myself to the director of the prison and told him that what had happened to the children on Saturday was intolerable, and that I would not allow them again to see their father under such conditions. I reminded him that they were American children, and that I would ask the embassy to interfere (a big boast!). I reminded him also that the rules of the prison allowed for children under twelve to visit in a separate room, and that he had been a stickler for the rules of the prison in regard to the half-hour limit imposed on me.

On Saturday the children returned to their old-style visits, much to the chagrin of the sadistic young guards, and the following week I was given back my four visits on a nonterminal basis. This meant I would not have to trek to the Ministry of Public Order every two weeks and confront Totomis. The last time I had seen Totomis he had been much warmer, and I suspected he was playing a double game, probably in on the King's coup, and he didn't know which way the wind would blow. Menios, however, remained in prison, transferred to Patras. The Americans had spoken, and the puppets had acceded to two thirds of their demands. It remained to be seen what would happen to Menios.

George Papandreou had watched me go through these weeks of special tribulation and did what he could to keep my spirits up. "Things will happen," he would say. "Everything will be all right."

"When?" I ventured.

"Soon, soon" was his answer. Then he would drop into silence, looking as if he were trying to read a crystal ball.

One evening I asked him what would happen to Andreas if the King succeeded.

"I'm not quite sure."

"You mean he may still go to trial?"

"It's possible. But the situation will be different."

I tried to digest that one. It wouldn't go down. "But how can we support something that will not free Andreas?" I was treading on touchy territory. This had been one of my complaints about the Paraskevopoulos solution—it hadn't resolved the ASPIDA issue.

"Margarita, we must get rid of the dictators. They are decided and dangerous people. With them Andreas will rot in jail. It is certain." So the choice was to be between an uncertain rotting in jail and a certain rotting in jail—presuming the prediction was correct.

During the week of November 19 I had a visitor, our friend from Denmark who had been in Athens the night of the coup, Mogens Camre. The last time he had arrived, a coup had occurred within three days. His appearance was almost an omen of things to come. His mission this time was a startling one. He told me the word had gotten around outside of Greece that I was the leader of an armed resistance movement! He said someone had come out of Greece saying he was my representative and asking for arms to supply a resistance group in Greece. He warned me that this would eventually be tied to Andreas and could affect his fate.

"Dammit, Mogens," I said. "I can't help it what people go around saying."

"No, but it has to be stopped somehow."

"It is a sign of the desperation of people. They make up stories. They had counted on the support of the democratic nations of Europe—which they have gotten to some extent—but more than that, they had counted on the ability of these countries to effect a change. And only little Denmark squeaked up in a NATO meeting—and got bashed down."

Mogens winced. "We're still trying."

"I'm sorry, Mogens. I don't mean to belittle your attempts. We live a nightmare and face fantastic obstacles to organize any effective resistance, or even to combat the brainwashing that is going on—but you people are free! You can act, move, make decisions, speak! We are intolerant of you all!" Poor Mogens, who had done as much as anyone to help, was getting the full blast of my frustration, intensified, perhaps, by my concern about the rumors going around.

"Yes, yes. I understand. But this rumor about you has got to stop."

"What can I do?"

"Well, I can try to do something after I leave Greece. I can say I have seen you and you are appalled at the loose talk and false information getting out. How would that be?"

"It's something. I'll see what I can do from my end." But what? Call a press conference and announce that I was not the leader of armed resistance in Greece? There must be something I could do, but whatever it was, it would be a bit silly.

We changed the subject and talked about the situation in general. I told him that the ASPIDA trial was still on ice, but that Theodorakis' trial would start on Wednesday, most likely *without* Theodorakis, but unfortunately, with my good friend Virginia. So far the junta had put on trial only little-known people. They had avoided taking anyone to trial who was known internationally—Vlahou, Theodorakis, Andreas. Now, on the pretense of Theodorakis' sickness, they would keep their star witness out of the limelight. I told

Mogens that this made me feel that they would be equally reluctant to put Andreas on trial and were still trying to find a way out.

We talked about the King. I decided to give him my information about pending action on the part of the King and to express my concern about the peculiar scheme to rescue Andreas from Averoff. I had seen Spyros once more, at which time he had unfolded the tactics of the King's coup, which sounded rather good and well thought out to me, and he told me the next visit he would bring me the names of the people to be selected for the jailbreak for my okay. I had expressed my concern again, but he was amazingly persuasive and fearless. When I didn't hear from him for another week, I twice called the number he had given me, just the day before Mogens arrived, and when I asked for Spyro, the receiver was hung up on me. Something had been fouled up, and I had no way of checking on how the jailbreak plans had advanced, nor controlling in any way their execution.

Mogens asked me the key question: "Are the Americans in on the King's coup?"

"I cannot judge," I answered. "I was told through one source that some of the King's men approached the American Ambassador, and he rebuffed them. But the embassy is not the key. The question is whether the CIA or the military is in on it."

"If the Americans are not behind it, it won't succeed," he stated bluntly.

"And if it doesn't succeed, what about that portion of the scheme that involves Andreas?"

Mogens looked worried. "I don't like it."

"Nor do I."

"Do you think you ought to go and talk to Talbot?"

"My dear Mogens, if I could trust my American compatriots, I would have confided in them long ago. Everyone here believes this is an American-imposed dictatorship and that it was done to foreclose a Papandreou victory and a government in the hands of more progressive forces. How can I be sure that what information I give them will not be used to *protect* the dictatorship? Anyway, I can't imagine that they don't know most of the things I know."

We sat there not saying much. Events were going to unfold over which we had no control and there seemed to be nothing to do but put one's trust in fate. I remembered with chagrin a favorite verse of mine:

It matters not how strait the gate,
How charged with punishment the scroll,
I am the master of my fate;
I am the captain of my soul.

When I quoted this to George Papandreou once, he smiled and pulled my ear. "You are very American, Margarita." Then he added, "Moira, Margarita, moira" (fate).

I asked Mogens if he would like to see George Papandreou. He most definitely did, and I told him I would try to arrange it for ten the next morning, and that it would be better for him to go alone. The next morning he went up to Kastri while I sat home composing a letter to Walter to try to counteract the talk outside of Greece about my role in Greece. I asked him in a separate note to notarize the letter, thinking that I might have to use it in my defense someday. Here is the letter:

> *November 15, 1967*
>
> *Dear Walt,*
>
> *Word has been getting back to me that there are people in the States and in Europe who go around claiming they are representatives of me and Andreas. They claim to be our spokesmen, and to know our every inner thought and desire.*
>
> *I want to make it clear to you, and through you to others, that no one, absolutely no one speaks for us.*
>
> *In this fashion also the rumor has gotten around that I am the leader of an armed resistance in Greece! I want to declare now and forever, that I am not, cannot and care not. It is against all my principles. As I have written to you earlier, and to others, bloodshed must be avoided at all costs. This country cannot go through the tragedy of another civil war. Anyone who claims that that is my desire, or my husband's desire, is an irresponsible liar.*
>
> *Do what you can to stop these ugly rumors.*

The letter was officially stamped by the school of business administration at the University of Minnesota on November 21, 1967.

When Mogens came back from Kastri, he told me that my father-in-law had spent two hours talking with him, and had concluded that a letter to the prime ministers of the Scandinavian countries in which Papandreou developed his point of view on how to throw off the Greek dictatorship was in order. He had given Mogens the main points and asked that the two of us write it up in good English. My father-in-law's English was perfect, but he didn't have complete trust in it and was afraid of a mistake. We worked on it all day and the next. I brought two versions to him on Thursday night when I came for dinner. He chose the shorter of the two, making a few corrections, and we burned the unused one. The next step was to type the letter in three originals, one for Sweden, one for Norway, and one for Denmark. I brought my English portable typewriter the following evening for this purpose. We agreed that after Papandreou signed the letters, I would take them to Mogens at a predetermined place in Athens.

I drove up alone that night, my typewriter a silent companion on the seat next to me. The night was misty and black, and the lamps from the house at Kastri sent out an eerie glow as I approached. I parked the car and slid across the front seat to the other side, scooping up the typewriter as I moved and tucking it under my ample dark winter coat. I told the President that it would have to be assumed by somebody watching me that I had suddenly become pregnant. But light talk was not easy. The President was eager to get started. He had his letterhead stationery on the table, and I opened up the portable. He had kept the copy of the draft from the night before, and he now pulled it out from his inner pocket.

"Read it again, Margarita," he said, "for the last time before you type it."

I sat down in the maroon armchair where I had sat so many times before, laughing and talking, or listening to the political discussion going on between father and son. Now I turned my attention to the document in my hands. George Papandreou sat moodily silent while I read. When I finished, I looked up. He was waiting for a comment.

"Tonight," I said, "I am the typist. Sometime, once in a great while, somebody has to say 'You are the leader' and make no comment, or criticism or praise, but just follow orders. It is your great responsibility, and your judgment."

"Then," he said hoarsely, "will you start typing?"

As I started, he went over and turned on a tape of Greek music, and then, to be sure I was comfortable, poured me a glass of wine. Although I had come at dinnertime, we had decided the night before not to have dinner in order to get the work done. There was bread and cheese on the table, although neither of us touched it. My fingers stumbled over the keys, and I muttered "damn" every so often as I made typographical errors. Once I got up and refilled my wineglass.

My father-in-law sat quietly on the couch. His face still showed the strain of the long isolation, but the fight had not gone out of it. He was doing what he could for the freedom of his countrymen.

When I was in the middle of the second letter, he said, "Make one carbon."

"You want a carbon?" I asked, surprised. Holding a copy of such a letter created problems.

"Yes, just one," he replied. Carbon paper had been laid out on the table with his letterhead stationery, probably by the maid, and I picked up one sheet as I started the third letter. I felt very tender toward George Papandreou that night, and he, I think, toward me. Bitterness was gone, and I saw a man in the twilight of his life struggling for the things he had always fought for—freedom for his people from oppression, their dignity, their right to be heard, a better and richer life. I ripped the last letter from the typewriter and handed the three over to him. He signed each in strong, firm handwriting. I folded them and put them in my handbag.

We both stood up, and he grabbed my hands and for a few seconds we stood silently, looking at each other, the tension of the evening showing clearly on our faces. His look said, "I thank you for what you have done," and my look said, "I love you for fighting." Then he put his two hands on my shoulders, kissed me on both cheeks, and said, "Kali tichi," "Good luck."

Mogens was not in front of the movie house at Ambelokipi when I drove by. My watch was right—11 P.M. I felt a moment of panic. Had something happened to him, and was I now to be picked up with these letters in my possession? It would be jail or house arrest for George Papandreou and similar lovely things for me. As I drove around the block, I pulled the letters from my purse with my right hand and put them on the floor of the front seat next to me. I fished for my cigarette lighter and laid it on the seat. Next I pushed the lock buttons down on all doors. So far I had seen no car tailing me. From Kastri I had turned off the highway at Philothey and wandered through the residential area close to my home to make sure I was alone. If

I'm stopped, I thought, I'll build a fire with the letters on the floor before they can break open the doors.

Twice around. No Mogens. 11:05 P.M. The streets were deserted, and I didn't like the feeling of circling around the same place—a lone car with a lone woman. I decided to drive some distance and return in five minutes. Then started a comedy of errors. As it turned out, Mogens arrived just after 11:05 and not finding me there, decided to stroll a bit and return, not to be seen hanging around the movie theater. When I drove back at 11:10 he was in the vicinity, strolling, but all I could see was an empty theater front. When he came back at 11:15, I had again driven off to make a new circle. At 11:20, finally, we reached Ambelokipi at the Astron Theater at the same time. Mogens climbed in.

"Hey, Mogens! You had me frightened silly."

"But I've been around here since 11:05." Then we discovered our game of hit and miss. "Have you got the letters?"

"There on the floor, on the hump, ready to be burned." Mogens gave a little half-smile and picked them up, putting them in his inside coat pocket. I drove him to a cab stand a block from the American Embassy and dropped him off without looking back. It was just the right amount of time to drive by Averoff for my good-night signal to Andreas. I was pleased when I struck my lighter as I drove by the jail that it was to light a cigarette and not three "subversive" letters to our friends to the north.

My mission was completed. There seemed not much else to do but play the waiting game.

CHAPTER TWENTY-SEVEN

The King's Coup

THE LETTERS to the three Scandinavian prime ministers left Athens Tuesday, November 21, in the hands of a friend of Mogens'. We decided that it was too risky for Mogens himself to carry the letters out, since he had been having frequent contact with me and had had one visit with my father-in-law. We considered him most likely a marked man.

Here is George Papandreou's letter:

> *Your Excellency:*
>
> *As you well know, Greece is in an intolerable situation which must be resolved before we enter a period of greater repression and possible bloodshed.*
>
> *I am using this method of secret diplomacy because all normal political channels are not available to me, nor to my party. I am addressing particularly the prime ministers of Sweden, Denmark and Norway because of the valiant stand of these countries on the side of democracy, a noble service for which, as you understand, we are presently unable to express openly our deep gratitude.*
>
> *I would like to formally re-assert my dedication to the principles of democracy, my commitment to the NATO alliance, which I consider essential to our survival as a Western power, and to the form of the regime of crowned democracy in Greece.*
>
> *It is my belief that a solution lies in a two-stage return to parliamentary government. The initiative must be the King's, for he is the only force today which can move the country in the correct path. If he takes the initiative, he will have my backing 100%, and I speak for the entire party, as well as the majority of the Greek people which we represent.*
>
> *He will need, however, the full backing of the United States and western European powers.*
>
> *In the first stage, he will form a government of nonpolitical people of his choice, all firmly committed to a return of parliamentary government, and which will ready the country for a transition period of political collaboration between the party of ERE and the Center Union in preparation for elections.*
>
> *Under these circumstances we will not raise the question of the legality of the acts of the military government.*

All of this will require the utmost in wisdom, patience and understanding. Political prisoners must be released and liberalization measures taken in a graded fashion. As the leader of the majority of the Greek people, I can guarantee peace during this time.

Hoping that this proposal can be transmitted as early as possible through you to President Johnson and leaders of Western European countries, and that prompt consideration be given to it, since it is my belief that this path must be taken within the next month to avoid the danger of a "new constitution" and to avoid possible conflict and bloodshed, I remain,

Respectfully yours,
[signed] G. Papandreou

If one is to judge this letter, it must be judged in the light of the situation in November 1967. George Papandreou was supporting the only forces he saw which could overthrow the colonels—the King and the western powers. And he was offering them a solution which they in turn could support.

Soon after Mogens left Greece, he wrote a confidential report to key people involved in the Greek cause, dated November 21, 1967. Section E, entitled "The Underground Movement," which read as follows:

It seems that some misunderstandings have developed as to Margaret's involvement in or knowledge about underground activity. I can not understand how this information got out. Margaret was shocked when she heard what fantastic things were told by people coming out of Greece. It is absolutely clear that neither Margaret nor any other person in the Papandreou family or anyone related to it has any connection whatsoever with the underground movement. It is the wish of everybody in the Papandreou family that the junta will fall without bloodshed. Nobody in the family has asked for any kind of help to violent endeavors. I think you all understand how dangerous it would be if they were involved in such work.

Thus in strong, maybe overly protesting language, Mogens tried to stifle the talk about me in circles outside of Greece.

The truth was, of course, that I did know about the underground movement, as did Andreas, and with his advice, I was doing what I could to help. (My letter to Heller was a cover-up.) There was no reason to broadcast this, however; in fact, publicity was the *last* thing wanted by people working to overthrow the dictatorship. It had become impossible not to get involved, simply out of desperation. The tyrants were settling in, moving toward total control of the Greek nation, depriving the Greek of his precious liberty, and with the obvious intent to continue to do so for years to come. More and more Greeks were joining organizations, and not so much on the basis of political coloration, but on the basis of their need to reassert their human dignity, restore their pride, and regain their human rights. It was rewarding and encouraging to meet people from different political worlds in clandestine gatherings, all motivated by one aim—the overthrow of the junta.

We knew the King was contemplating a coup, and we talked about it in these gatherings. We talked about his hesitation and doubted his ability to make a decision. Furthermore, with the passage of time, we felt the chances for success were diminishing. In the judgment of the underground, outside pressure had reached its peak and consisted mainly of harsh words, threats, the formation of committees for the freedom of Greece, etc., but nothing concrete. The European governments were carrying on business as usual, as were those from the eastern bloc. The United States was giving the junta support, either through tolerant little talks to visiting American groups (a friend of mine attending the Greek Heritage Symposium took notes on such a speech given by Kay Bracken of the embassy, and turned them over to me), or through encouraging business investment, or through its military contacts, while making pompous statements about an "early return to parliamentary government." Under these circumstances, the only road left was to mobilize our forces, plan together, and use our wits and our souls in confronting the junta. No means were barred. What disheartened me was the news brought by Mogens, for he proved to me that the Greeks as yet had not learned basic principles of a clandestine operation, and their unquenchable, exuberant need to talk had resulted in the exaggerated information about me.

I had also become convinced that Andreas' fate was tied up with the fate of the dictatorship. Andreas would remain in jail for its duration, which could be a lifetime. If they decided to release him and let him go abroad, he would become the focal point for opposition against them; if they let him out to remain in Greece, they would soon have to arrest him again, for he would not remain silent for long. Continued imprisonment was the only answer for them.

This assessment of the general and personal situation led to my involvement in the underground. More about resistance I cannot say for obvious reasons. My contact and participation in it was exhilarating, for it proved to me what I always believed: that the strength of the human spirit is boundless against all odds. I was certain that the mistakes of inexperience would lessen with time and that one day it would achieve its aims.

The Theodorakis trial was concluded after several days of mock examination of the evidence. A picture of some of the defendants was published in a foreign newspaper, and I saw Virginia's pinched, hollow-eyed visage staring into space among the other like faces in the defendant's box. The most eloquent and passionate statements were made by two men representing different political poles. One was Fillinis, a man who had spent seventeen years in prison charged with being a communist, and who had just been released in 1966; the other was Ioannis Leloudas, a rightist, whose father had been chief adjutant to the King's court in the past. Several had the courage to report the tortures they had undergone, although the judges of the court-martial tried to prevent this testimony. I talked to foreign reporters who sat in on the trial. They all said it was obvious that the group had suffered terribly. When the trial was over the verdicts came in. Fillinis and Leloudas were sentenced to life in prison. My friend Virginia was sentenced to thirteen years.

By the end of November, five mass trials had been held for seditious activities. Hundreds of people were now behind bars in addition to the thousands who had been mauled and dragged off the night of the coup. They all became symbols of the people's protest against the military take-over. The atmosphere of fear and hatred grew.

During the six months of the junta regime, the Cyprus issue had cropped up twice. The people of Greece watched the Cyprus developments with great interest. They remembered that George Papandreou's unwillingness to go along with the Acheson Plan for partition and cantonization of Cyprus was considered the apple of discord between his government and Washington and had contained the seeds of his downfall.

The first junta handling of the Cyprus problem occurred in September when Colonel Papadopoulos, after hasty study of the issues and a secret trip to Cyprus, proposed a summit meeting between the Turkish and Greek governments. I remember hearing the comment of a junta supporter who said with awe and admiration that he (Papadopoulos) "sat for eight hours straight and studied all the material on the problem!" So this student of the Cyprus problem, a dilemma for years and years for diplomats of all countries concerned—England, America, Turkey, Greece, and Cyprus—forged ahead in haste to reach a solution. It further confirmed the suspicions of many Greeks that the Americans needed the dictatorship to impose their plan.

The Greek delegation, consisting of Prime Minister Kollias, Deputy Minister Lieutenant General Spandidakis, and the Prime-Minister-in-Waiting, Colonel George Papadopoulos, along with Foreign Minister Economou-Gouras, were to meet Prime Minister Demirel of Turkey on a border bridge, then travel to Kesan, on the Turkish side, for the first round of talks. The discussion would move the following day to Greek soil at Alexandroupolis. The scheme being discussed, according to leaks in the foreign press, was startingly like the Acheson Plan of 1964: Turkey would accept union of Cyprus with Greece in return for territorial concessions on Cyprus. A Turkish military base (read NATO) would be set up on that portion of the island ceded to Turkey. The problem inherent in this solution remained the same problem George Papandreou faced in 1964—Makarios and the Cypriot people. If Turkey and Greece agreed, the solution would have to be forced on Makarios, and by none other than the Greek army which had many troops on the island to protect it in case of a Turkish attack. Thus Papadopoulos would be put in the ludicrous and tragic situation of having his Greek army fight the Cypriot Greeks in order to give away a portion of their island to Turkey! The conference was a fiasco, and the Greek press, after ballyhooing it as a potential foreign-policy achievement dropped it from its pages with red-faced suddenness.

In November Cyprus came to center stage again and the incidents brought Turkey and Greece perilously close to war. The Turks, encouraged by the compromising mood of the new junta government, and understanding its weaknesses in the diplomatic field after the summit conference in September at the Greek-Turkish border, took aggressive iniatives and sent Turkish fighter and reconnaissance aircraft over the island on November 2 and November 4. With tempers high, outbursts occurred in two Turkish enclaves, that of Ayios

Theodoros and Kophinou, and twenty-odd Turks were killed by the Cypriot National Guard, under the command of General George Grivas.

Grivas was in command of the twelve thousand Greek troops stationed on Cypriot land. An extreme rightist, royalist (and collaborator on the ASPIDA story), one sees him lurking in the background, twirling his long-handled moustache like the villain in a melodrama. He had been the chief of IDEA, the paramilitary group which made up the Big Junta, and he could hardly have been overjoyed at the coup of April 21 by a younger clique of officers (EENA) of the Greek Army.

From all reliable information, the killing of Turkish villagers far exceeded the provocation. Was Grivas trying to create a difficult situation for the weak junta government in Athens, and was this in collaboration with antijunta royalist forces in Greece? With a King's coup in the wings, so to speak, the speculation was high that this was an initial step. The betting on this theory increased when on November 20 Panayotis Pipinelis, a royalist and confidant of Queen Frederika's, was asked to join the government as Foreign Minister, as the Greek rulers found themselves in desperate need of diplomatic talent within their government. It was also true that Pipinelis had always been outspokenly pro-British, hence pro-American, and quite in accord with any partition agreement that might be proposed. But his connections with the Palace made it appear that the royalist forces were to gain the upper hand as a result of these incidents, if they could avoid a war with Turkey, which looked more and more imminent.

Papadopoulos and Company retreated into the scenery as Pipinelis took over the task of appeasing Turkey with the assistance of Cyrus Vance, dispatched from Washington as a special envoy to help avoid a clash between two NATO allies. The final agreement included the dismissal of Grivas, and a promise of withdrawal by the Greek government of all Greek troops on the island. It was a defeat for Greece and for the colonels, who ultimately had to bear the responsibility for control of their commander-in-chief's actions on Cyprus. The stock of the colonels plunged downward, particularly within the army, with the agreement to withdraw troops from Cyprus. The dream of *enosis* and a greater Greece, above all a military man's dream, was dead. The junta's incompetence and inexperience were glaringly obvious. Either that, or it was a willingness to compromise and bow to foreign pressure, equally unacceptable to the army. The stage was set for the King's coup.

While waiting for this event to take place, I tried to assess my efforts over the past six months for the release of Andreas. I had followed two odd trails which led to nothing—the health plot and the citizenship question. I had collaborated in the exposure of the ASPIDA frame-up. I had fostered a letter-writing campaign to harass the junta. I had worked with Frank Newman to set up a committee of observers for the trial. I had smuggled out hundreds of letters on Andreas' situation and on the general situation in Greece in an attempt to keep the fires stoked. I had mailed clippings of events in Greece from the Athens *Post* and Athens *News*, two English newspapers, to committees for democracy in Greece and to key people working against the junta. I had written to the President of the United States. And recently, I had gotten involved in more general resistance activities in Greece, and through my father-in-law, helped in backing the King for a potential coup. Still, Andreas sat in that concrete cage at Averoff Prison.

The idea had been growing in me to try to obtain the services of a well-known American lawyer, one with a top reputation and connections in Washington. The efforts of our friends, in both Europe and America, had been heroic, but they were piecemeal and uncoordinated. What direction I could offer from Athens was given under the most difficult conditions, and response to my suggestions or requests was on a voluntary basis. I thought I needed a professional man who would represent my interests as an American citizen, and indirectly, the interests of my husband. He would be my lobbyist in Washington, and, when necessary, my intermediary in Greece between me and the government, or between me and the embassy. He would also be a consultant at the ASPIDA trial, working with the Greek lawyers—if there were any Greek lawyers for Andreas left out of jail, that is. The Pat Brown-Jim Schwartz team had been an excellent one, but I feared California was too far from Washington. I wanted someone on the scene for daily contacts and a daily harangue. Jim or Pat could be consultants at the trial when the time came, since they had taken the initial steps. Underlying all of this thinking was the hope to stun the junta by introducing a new, powerful name into the ASPIDA affair.

In early November, a lawyer friend* of Frank Newman's, came by the house, and we had a long discussion about this matter. He confirmed my belief that this was the next step to take. This is a portion of the letter from him to Frank in which he outlines his opinion:

> The best interests of the Papandreou family and the cause of justice in this case call for the appointment on a professional basis of a leading American attorney to represent the family and coordinate the work of counsel in the case before the Courts and other helpers in all related aspects of defense.
>
> Again I need not spell out or labor the reasoning behind this recommendation. But to me, it is clear that the valiant and skilled efforts of Greek counsel and friends in Europe and America, with varying degrees of interest and time available, cannot assure the needed preparation and confrontation as the issues now stand. To present, in the various proper forums and media, the belief which you hold so strongly that the government's case is a sham and is being imposed by a grave repression of fair rights of defense will require the intervention of such a leading American lawyer, capable of negotiating at various levels in Greece, elsewhere in Europe and in America.
>
> Mrs. Papandreou said yesterday that efforts and discussions in this direction are now in progress in the States and that she is exchanging letters now about such an appointment. I believe that the sooner

*He has asked to remain anonymous because of his work in the field of human rights in many nations.

such a step is taken the better because (1) the legal, diplomatic, political situation affecting the case may be more malleable than it appears superficially, and (2) lost opportunities may never reappear.

He sent a copy of his letter to the Secretary-General, International Commission of Jurists.

Pursuing this line, I wrote to Walter Heller on November 17:

> *Last week a good friend of F. Newman's came by. We talked at some length about this idea of my hiring a competent Washington lawyer who could represent me and through me, Andreas. He felt, as I have felt for some long time, that this would be an appropriate and perhaps necessary move at this moment. So many of Andy's friends have helped so much that they have paved the way for something like this, I believe—someone who could take this on as a "case," and concentrate on it in a way that is impossible for all of you who are involved in so many things. Naturally, someone who takes it on gets himself a bit involved in Greek affairs. But if he has any savvy on political matters, it wouldn't hurt to have an independent judgment which could go directly to the big boys (in Washington). My chief concern, naturally, is Andreas. . . .*
>
> *Since our talk I have received a letter from Stanley and it seems you have already been giving some serious thought to this and have a name to propose. Let me tell you what I can offer at the moment. Two thousand dollars gathered by my friends for Andy's legal defense for trips to Greece; an equal amount in drachmas for trips back to the States. In other words, $4,000 transportation expenses. I am trying to sell my lot in Berkeley, which should bring in about $12,000—which I throw in the pot, for this purpose. All of his living expenses here in Greece for length of time he stays can be picked up by my friends here. They have already offered this. Undoubtedly he earns very high fees—and I cannot at the moment raise that kind of money. But I suggest this as a starter. Maybe more contributions can be gathered by our friends if they understand the purpose and the need. If he wins the case, Andreas will become a wage earner again—and there is no problem of paying off outstanding obligations.*

While we were struggling in pitiful circumstances—I under conditions of limited freedom—Andreas under conditions of no freedom, to conduct a fight for his freedom and a fight against the military dictatorship, word got back to me of personal feuding going on within the group fighting outside of Greece for the same causes. False information also reached me as one person would take out his personal animosity on another by reporting items to me. The letter would usually begin, "I hate to have to tell you this, Maggie, knowing how difficult your conditions are, but so-and-so has been doing . . ." etc., etc. Not able to ferret out the truth, I would take some of these statements at face value, and explode. I became particularly touchy as I moved into resistance activities. Part of one letter of mine written on Andreas' name day, November 30, shows my attempt to patch up a misunderstanding:

345

I am truly sorry that there seems to have been some big misunderstanding, and somehow I got caught in the middle of it. You must realize, as you indicated, that I am functioning under almost unbearable conditions, that my information is fragmentary at best, that my nerves are indeed on edge, and that one little mistake we may pay for dearly. This particular assignment was the hottest of all, the most delicate, and the most dangerous. I think the fact that I gave it to you shows my faith in you, my confidence and my trust. Perhaps my mistake was to give it verbally to be taken to you—but the nature of it made me feel it was the only way to do it. . . .

I felt that December was the critical month, and it was a point, as events turned out, for a policy change on the part of the United States. The bureaucrats of the Pentagon, however, were quite happy with military men in control in Greece: they spoke the same language, they understood that Greece was part of a broader defense strategy for America, and they knew how to take orders from higher authorities. It was compact, orderly, and neat. And the natives were kept from that messy dancing in the streets, which they used to do as a form of protest before the coup.

During the first weeks of December I occupied myself with family problems and rudimentary plans for a simple Christmas with the children. Andreas and I made the decision during this time to send Georgie outside of Greece for his schooling. His tension had not subsided, and I suspected that it was not only his emotional state causing this, but certain clandestine activities he was engaging in. There were unexplained absences from the home, bus trips, telephone calls at the local kiosk, strange chemicals which appeared at our house and then disappeared. Once when I walked into the garage I found a two-foot-high pressure container of gas used for primitive gas stoves, which he explained was for camping trips he was planning for the summer. Another time I found a bag of large balloons in his desk drawer. At the age of fifteen, he was not interested in balloons to play with. When I confronted him with my suspicions, he was evasive—not like him. It was clear he was involved with a youth resistance group. The three younger children were in fair spirits and quite engrossed in their schoolwork.

My visits to Kastri continued, and underneath every discussion we had were the words "when, when, when?" I wanted something specific to tell Andreas, who would ask me each time, "How does the purchase of the hotel go?" But the President didn't really know an exact date, and I saw that he had doubts, as I did, that the King would actually move.

Reports from within the junta indicated that they were in a state of disarray. Their morale had been shaken by the Cyprus debacle. They were also thrown off-balance by the attacks from the Right, for their thesis had been that there was need to take over because of a communist threat, endangering the nation. They had anticipated that the conservative forces would rally around them; instead, Vlahou and Cannellopoulos had attacked them viciously, and at the end of November Karamanlis, the paragon of conservative, anticommunist, pro-NATO virtue, gave an interview from Paris, saying the colonels must go. This was unnerving for another reason—Karamanlis still had loyal supporters in the army. And finally, the King was an obstacle to their complete power. They knew a showdown was coming, but didn't know how or when, nor what would be the end result. Again, information from within the ruling circle was that Papadopoulos was going to ask for the premiership, thus forcing the King's hand. Unconfirmed reports say he did so on December 12.

The morning of December 13 came—a bleak, drizzly day. It was Wednesday, a nonvisiting day for me at the prison. At 12:30 P.M. Tito picked me up to drive me to jail for the delivery of Andreas' lunch. As we approached the intersection of Diamandidiou and Vassilis Sophias, I spotted an army man directing traffic where a policeman usually stood. He was directing cars with a hurried frenzy, urging drivers to move fast as the streetlight changed.

"Look, Tito. What's that?" I asked.

"Probably some army maneuvers," he answered. Neither of us gave it much more notice. We were accustomed to seeing army people around by now. Two tanks passed us on Leoforas Alexandras, but that too was a familiar sight. At the jail everything seemed normal, and I discarded what I had seen as having any meaning.

At 2:30, while I was eating lunch, my telephone rang. I recognized a friend's voice. He said in a very casual fashion, "Just thought I'd ring you up to tell you it has happened."

"Oh" was my bright response.

"Thought you ought to take care."

"I see. Any advice?" My voice had tightened up and I listened to it as if it belonged to someone else.

"Nothing special."

"Can you tell me where?"

"Up north."

"Thanks. Come see me sometime when you can."

I turned from the phone and shouted to Antigone. "The radio!" and we ran side by side to switch on the knob.

My hopes were high. Up north was the obvious place, for that was where the King had his strength. And it was consistent with the general plan that had been outlined to me. My mood swung from buoyant excitement to worry. Any change held dangers for Andreas, and back in my mind was the knowledge of the jailbreak scheme that I had lost contact with sometime ago.

Athens Radio was playing military music. With a shiver it reminded me of April 21. Within a few minutes the music was interrupted by this short sentence: "The revolution is determined to fulfill its mission and will fulfill it." My heart sank. The junta was in control of the Athens radio station and was challenging the King's coup head on. It was too early, however, to understand anything. All we knew was that something was happening. I called Tito, who had left for home after dropping me off, and Kiveli told me that he was already on his way back. The rest of the afternoon we sat by the radio waiting for news. We heard nothing but the constant repetition of that one sentence: "The revolution is determined to fulfill its mission and will fulfill it."

347

Late in the afternoon a longer announcement was made:

> People of Greece: *A few hours ago a conspiracy against the State and against public order was revealed. Common opportunists, motivated by childish ambitions and ignoring the interests of the Nation, pressured and deceived the King and urged him to turn against the National Revolution, against the peace and quiet of the people, at this especially historical moment in Greek history.*

Tito scotched a suggestion of mine that we drive up to Kastri. He argued that Papandreou's house would be under guard and our approaching it could only get us into trouble. The visit would serve no useful purpose, either to us or to the President.

I waited anxiously for food delivery time at the jail. Now when we drove over, many large tanks were rolling along the highway away from Athens and toward Kamena Vourla, which had a connecting highway to Larissa and northern Greece. From the turret of each tank stood a soldier in battle dress holding his gun in firing position. The Athenians on the streets were going about their business, sometimes stopping to gaze at this sight, as if it were a passing parade. There was something ludicrous about this fighting unit in the midst of late afternoon traffic, rumbling along on iron tires behind buses and cars. I counted twelve tanks on Vassilis Sophias and three on Leoforas Alexandras.

As we drove up in front of Averoff, I automatically looked up at the window where Andreas stood or sat, watching for us to arrive. I gasped. It was shuttered and dark. Within a second of my gasp, I saw through the slats the flash of a lighter. It was Andreas signaling that he was there. As I walked to the jail door to deliver the food, it occurred to me, knowing him, that he would be concerned about the family, about what might happen to us—not to himself. After I listed the food items to the guard inside the door, I told him, "Tell Mr. Andreas that we are all right." It was the first time I had asked him to deliver a message to the prisoner Papandreou, and he nervously looked around to see if anyone had heard. He shook his head almost imperceptibly, and I was given the impression that he would do so. I found out later that he did not.

When we returned home, I met a gathering of old friends and some members of Andreas' close political circle who were still out of jail. Most were jubilant. To them it seemed inconceivable that a confrontation with the King would not result in a royal victory. To all except one, a journalist and shrewd analyst of political events.

"Don't get so excited," he warned the others. "It doesn't look that good to me." He echoed my own feelings. Within the group was a woman friend of mine, looking very worried, and saying nothing. Finally, she drew me aside.

"Where can we talk?" she asked.

"Come," I said, "on the terrace."

Outside she told me the following: "I had a visit this afternoon from the man who had been our informer within the Big Junta. He says Andreas is in danger. The junta is thinking of using him in case things don't go well in the fight with the King."

"Using him?" I asked. "How?"

"Someone close to Papadopoulos told him that they will get the minister on the radio to rally the people against the King."

So the royalist whose name I knew as Spyro had been right in his prediction. This possibility did exist.

"You mean they will force him?"

"Yes."

"Are you sure this is the truth?"

"I haven't seen him since the coup. It is the first time he came to my house, and he came at great risk. If they were to know it, it's the end for him. He said to reach you and tell you to do something."

Andreas with a gun in his back speaking to the Greek people. It was inconceivable.

"He won't do it," I told her. "I know Andreas. He just won't do it. He won't do anything by force."

"He told me to tell Mrs. Papandreou."

We stood there for a few moments silently in the cool evening air which held the promise of more rain. She watched my face and waited for me to say something. I thanked her and told her she had better leave. I asked her please to tell me if she had further information, either to call and I would come to her place, or to return. Then I asked Tito and Marjorie to come out to the terrace. Tito thought it was a wild idea, and not likely. Marjorie was not so sure. Her point of view was that when you are dealing with barbarians, anything was possible. Assuming this might happen, what was I to do?

In the end, I decided to go once again to my only source of power, meager though that was—the American Embassy. Before I left, I made arrangements for the family to sleep away from the house that night, thinking that it would be best not to have extra hostages available in case of some extension of the scheme to use Andreas. Marjorie, George, and I were to go to an apartment we had ready for any emergency, the other members of the family were to be divided among friends' homes, and Antigone was to go with her cousin. To some young supporters of Andreas' who came by about that time and asked what they could do, I told them to patrol the jail throughout the night, and I gave them my phone number to call every hour on the hour during the night to report, or to call me at any other time that they saw an unusual activity at the prison. I still had in the back of my mind the story about the jail rescue scheme. The junta story I would deal with at the embassy.

Once more I walked into the big white pillared building representing one of the most powerful countries in the world. It was approximately 7:30 P.M. Darkness had fallen, and a windy, gusty, sleety rain had begun. Inside, the building lights were on, all over, and people were coming briskly across the lobby to the elevator or going out into waiting cars. After being told by the desk attendant that the ambassador would see me, but that I must wait, I sat on a plastic-covered bench in the lobby. There were men in American uniforms, a handful of Greeks in civilian clothes, but I saw no Greek army uniforms.

After one hour of agonized waiting, a young American of about thirty-five came up to me and told me that it was impossible for Ambassador Talbot to see me, but that he had been assigned to talk to me. He led me to an office on the main floor, closed the door, and waited for me to speak.

"The story I am going to tell you is a strange one," I began in a quiet, tense voice, "but my husband's life may be in danger and I must report this to you. You are the only people who can help." He waited for me to continue.

I told him the Papadopoulos plan, and I told him that it came from a reliable source within the junta. He listened carefully, and when I finished he told me that many peculiar rumors had reached them, although he didn't say whether or not this was among them, and that most had been checked out and found to be false. Then I continued.

"I'm asking just one thing. That the ambassador make it clear and definite that any use of Andreas, or any attempt on his life will bring grave consequences. They must disabuse themselves of the idea that Andreas can be used in any way in any of their sinister plots."

He said he understood, and that he would report immediately to Ambassador Talbot. I felt that I had made it clear that I was not an hysterical wife (which I almost was) and that I had thought carefully about coming to them before I did so. I have no information on the follow-up of this story as far as the embassy was concerned. At the time I was talking, the situation was going well for the junta, and their need for Andreas was diminishing.

From the embassy I went back to the house to pick up Georgie. We took my car, leaving Tito to return to his home where we could be in contact, and wove our way among Athenian streets to lose any car that might be following us. We arrived at an apartment close to the center of Athens to set up an all-night vigil. On the way, to the click-click of the windshield wiper swinging like a pendulum on an old clock, we heard an announcement on the car radio telling of the defeat of the royal coup. That was 9 P.M. I considered it propaganda and was not ready to believe it. We wound past the jail on our way to the apartment. The window was still shuttered closed.

At 11:30 P.M., my usual good-night visit time, I drove by Averoff with Marjorie and George, my hands slippery on the steering wheel, and caught again the flicker of a lighter through the slats. Andreas was there, sitting in the dark, wondering, I was sure, what developments were taking place. The King at last had decided to buy the hotel, but had the purchase been possible?

From midnight until 6 A.M. every hour on the hour I got a phone call from the boys covering Averoff. The report was always the same, that everything was calm, and nothing unusual appeared to be happening. At 3 A.M. Marjorie and George walked on foot to the street above the jail, watched Andreas' window for fifteen minutes, then returned to report that they had seen no lights, nor matches. I hoped he was asleep. At 4:30 A.M. Marjorie and I drove around the jail. I frankly didn't know what action I would have taken if something unusual happened. I simply had the need to be near my husband. In between times we listened to the radio and dozed on chairs or on the couch. About five in the morning I heard an announcement that the King was "running from village to village" in an attempt to escape. What made me believe that there was some truth in this was that the announcer did not say,

"His Majesty, the King," but "Constantinos." Already he had been stripped of his title.

Early in the morning, around 6:30, I left the apartment and went to the home of a foreign journalist friend of mine. He, too, had been up all night monitoring the radio and sending reports by telephone to his newspaper. He told me that a report had come through that Constantinos had arrived in Rome. He was in the process of checking the authenticity of the report.

I was stunned and numb. I couldn't assess the meaning of this unsuccessful coup, for Greece, and particularly for Andreas. On the one hand there was the feeling of relief that the royal family had left Greece. Constantinos' activities as King of the Greeks had been a harmful one. On the other hand, there seemed to be nothing standing in the way of complete power by an army clique which wanted to regulate all phases of the life of every last Greek, a group of men to whom "freedom" and "democracy" were alien and abominable words.

The timetable of the King's attempt to overthrow the junta was roughly like this:

9:00 A.M.	*Orders are prepared by the King for delivery to all Chiefs of Staff and commanders of military formations announcing that he is taking over the government and the armed services.*
9:30 A.M.	*Kollias, the Prime Minister, arrives at Tatoi with his suitcases. Preparations were made for departure. The group includes the King, the Queen, the two children, Queen Mother Frederika, Princess Irene, Kollias, General Dovas, chief of the King's military household, Dr. Koutifaris, the obstetrician, a nurse, two servants, and a dog.*
9:40 A.M.	*Air Marshal Andonakos, Chief of the Air Staff, flies to Larissa to take control of the 28th Tactical Air Force Command and link up with Lt. General Kollias (no relation to the Prime Minister), commander of the army group headquarters.*
10:15 A.M.	*King and party take off from Tatoi aboard a royal aircraft for Kavalla, a town in northern Greece.*
11:00 A.M.	*Lieutenant General Anghelis, Chief of the Army Staff in Athens, receives the King's orders and alerts the junta. Lieutenant General Manetas, Inspector General of the Army, turns up at army headquarters in Athens saying he has orders from the King to take over the General Staff. He is promptly arrested. The King's aircraft lands in Kavalla. The King is met by Major General Zaphiropoulos, division commander. The King is given a popular reception and addresses the crowds. The royal party settles at the Astir hotel. The Queen was said to be seen buying a cot for the baby Crown Prince.*

11:30 A.M.	The King's taped proclamation is broadcast over local Larissa and Kavalla radio stations. Communications between the Athens General Staff and the military in the two cities are cut off.
12 NOON	Troops and tanks surround all airports and air bases in Athens on orders from the Little Junta. The commander of the air base at Elevsis, near Athens, signals the Air Chief of Staff in Larissa that he is surrounded. The message is intercepted by the Athens command and he is told to surrender. He does. The air base at Tanagra, north of Athens, tries to put up resistance, and a few shots are exchanged. One man on either side is injured. Six air force jets attempt to take off from Athens airport and are intercepted. One gets away. The fleet leaves its main anchorages in Salamis and Crete on the King's orders, as Vice-Admiral Dedes, Chief of the Naval Staff, joins the royal rebels.
12:15 P.M.	Papadopoulos sends out armored troop carriers to surround the Athens radio station, while other carriers take up positions at key buildings in Athens. Machine-gun posts are mounted at the Old Palace building, the government headquarters.
2:00 P.M.	Two jets fly low over Athens, while other aircraft drop leaflets with the King's proclamation in Salonika.
2:30 P.M.	Athens Radio gives the first indication of the royal coup through its announcer just before the news program saying the revolution was determined to finish its task.
3:00 P.M.	Brigadier Patilis, Minister for North Greece, takes full control of Salonika, appoints himself commander of III Army Corps. He asks contact at once with the Athens general staff. Lieutenant General Voudouroglou, commander of I Corps in Verria, northern Greece, does not comply.
4:00 P.M.	The King leaves Kavalla by air for Larissa, confers with Air Marshal Andonakos as well as Lieutenant General Kollias. Soon afterward General Kollias and General Voudouroglou are arrested by their own staff officers.
7:00 P.M.	The King flies back to Kavalla. Brigadier Hoerschelmann, commander of 20th Armored Division, loyal to the King, having jailed pro-regime colonels in his division, gets ready to proceed toward Salonika. Junior officers set free the jailed colonels, take over 20th Armored Division and use the tanks to surround III Army Corps headquarters in Komotini, arrest General Perides and Brigadier Vidalis, and set out for Kavalla to intercept the King.

9:00 P.M.	*Athens Radio announces the defeat of the King's coup.*
9:30 P.M.	*The junta appoints Lieutenant General Zoitakis to be regent "in view of the unjustified absence of the King from the performance of his duties," and he nominates a new government under George Papadopoulos. Vice-Admiral Dedes is placed under house arrest and is made to issue orders to the fleet to return to base.*
3:00 A.M.	*Air Marshal Andonakos surrenders.*
3:15 A.M.	*The King and the royal party flee from Kavalla in jeeps and take off from the airport for Rome.*

My journalist friend offered me a cup of coffee as I sat wearily in an armchair. The news had been confirmed that the King was in Rome. We tried to comprehend the situation. My head was heavy, my mouth dry from too many cigarettes and from nervousness, and I wasn't much in the mood for analysis. At seven o'clock I went back to pick up George and Marjorie, and we headed for home. I drove past the jail and saw Andreas' window still shuttered shut.

Thursday was a visiting day for me. I doubted that I would be allowed in the jail. To my surprise I was taken in in the normal fashion and at 12:30 stood at the bar facing Andreas behind the screens.

I tried to sound cheery and unconcerned. "Hi, darling!"

"Hi!" Andreas was watching the expression on my face through the heavy screen barrier.

"What can I say?" I asked. I wasn't sure how much he had been told.

"It was very funny," he commented, meaning funny-strange. He seemed tense, but not overly concerned.

"You read the morning papers?" I ventured.

"Yeah. Oh, well, the hell with it . . ."

Later, at some point, he asked me about Hourmouzis and the hotel purchase. "Maybe he will still buy it," he said tentatively, feeling me out.

"A trifle difficult now. Very expensive." I answered. I felt he wasn't quite sure whether or not to believe the government-controlled press. And he wasn't sure whether or not he really wanted the hotel bought.

"Difficult, huh?"

"Difficult."

In the evening after I delivered his food, I walked to the opposite side of the street and tried to find a means of lingering under the naked bulb of the canvas-topped grocery stand, just to remain a while longer near the jail and near Andreas on a day that had been so puzzling, the personal consequences of which we could not assess. My eye caught a two-foot-high pile of *horta*, wild mountain greens, which are boiled and eaten by the Greeks with olive oil and lemon. They had been freshly sprayed with water, and the leaves were a shiny deep green.

I pointed to the pile. "What beautiful horta," I commented to the vegetable man.

He turned to me with a mischievous grin. Then, leaning toward my ear, he said in a voice of quiet glee, "Those come from one of the villages Constantinos ran through!"

CHAPTER TWENTY-EIGHT

Home for Christmas

WITHIN a few hours after the King started his attempt to overthrow the junta, hundreds of citizens were arrested with the charge that they had conspired with the King. Both George Papandreou and Panayotis Cannellopoulos were put under house arrest.

When the King left with his valises, he forgot to burn his files. This further underlined the amateurish nature of the coup. It also showed, perhaps, how much he was being watched and how handicapped he was to carry out such a venture.

I was told a few days after December 13 that a letter from George Papandreou had been discovered among the King's papers giving support to the King's efforts to topple the junta. That carbon, I thought. It must be the copy I made for him of the three letters to the Scandinavian prime ministers. I began to wonder when the knock would come on my door. We learned also that the King had planned to name Garoufalias, the treacherous Minister of Defense under Papandreou, as Prime Minister. This only added to my relief at the failure of the King's coup.

For the next few days we watched developments with astonishment. Most astonishing had been Archbishop Ieronymos' swearing in of Papadopoulos as Prime Minister on the afternoon of the 13th. Ieronymos for years had been the close spiritual adviser to both Constantinos and Frederika. Then, on the morning of the 14th, junta officers began taking down the pictures of the King and Queen in public offices. Next, the junta announced that Papadopoulos had called Pipinelis (three times the rumors had it), who was in Brussels at a NATO meeting, and that Pipinelis, the loyal servant of the court, had agreed to remain as Foreign Minister in the new government. At the same time, he was reported on his way to see the King in Rome.

The first day after the coup, Papadopoulos had called the King's attempt "insane and illogical." There was reported a great deal of wrath within the revolutionary council over the King's actions. By December 15 there was reason to believe that the junta was making desperate efforts, despite all denials, to persuade the King to return to Greece! The following items are of interest in this respect:

> *1. Papadopoulos ordered all photos of the King and Queen to be restored in government offices and started an inquiry as to who ordered their removal.*

355

2. The synod, or administrative body of the Greek Orthodox Church, issued, with full government approval, instructions to all bishops to continue prayers for the royal family.

3. All rooms in the royal palace in Athens and Tatoi were locked and sealed.

4. Senior officers in the army, and especially in the III Corps, who supported the King, were not to be court-martialed but only liable to loss of rank. Junior officers would be given amnesty.

In a press conference on the same day, the 15th, Papadopoulos made the following statement: "The King left on his own for Rome, and he can return whenever he wants. We swore in a regent simply not to leave that role vacant in the proper functioning of the regime." Pattakos declared that they remained committed to the system of "crowned democracy."

From thinking of declaring a republic on the day of the 13th in that part of Greece they controlled (using Andreas to assist them) to declaring a republic for all of Greece on the 14th after the King's flight to Rome, the junta now did an about-face and declared itself loyal to the system of democracy with monarchy and let it be known that they were negotiating with the King for his return.

There were three intermediaries: Pipinelis, Archbishop Ieronymos, and Air Marshal Potamianos, former aide and close friend of the royal family's. Pipinelis was kept waiting seven hours by the King, who had been informed that Pipinelis intended to stay on with the junta, with or without the King. Pipinelis apparently tried to urge Constantinos to return to Greece under whatever conditions the junta declared. Ieronymos was next. The substance of their conversation was not reported. Potamianos spent six hours with Constantinos in what was considered a last-ditch effort to persuade the King to return.

The junta was concerned about the problem of recognition. All foreign embassies were accredited to the King. The problem of diplomatic recognition, which the junta had so beautifully resolved in its own coup by carrying the King along, was now facing them. Thus they emphasized that the form of the regime had not changed and that the King was officially represented by the new regent, Lieutenant General Zoitakis. The government was desperately in need of respectability. It had been maligned severely by most western European governments since April 21, but could always parade the "saving the country from communism" theme. Now with the King an open, declared foe, this no longer made any sense. This desire for normalcy and respectability for Greece also caused them to drop remarks about the possibility of the release of political prisoners held since April 21. Inside of me a nightingale started to sing, faintly and softly.

This general confusion and uncertainty of the junta officers could be explained by the pressures within their own group and without. Pressures within their group can be epitomized by what happened to Andreas in his jail cell the morning after the King's coup. His window shutters were still drawn when the young army officer Vourdakos arrived to unlock his cell door.

Andreas knew nothing of developments during the night and was forbidden to ask questions. He decided to use the shuttered window as a test.

"May I open my shutters?" he asked.

Vourdakos drew his handsome body up to its full height and took a deep breath. "Yes!" he said dramatically, and then, gesticulating like an actor in an old-time melodrama, he flung his arm toward the window. "Open up your window. The last vestige of parliamentary corruption is out of the country! The King," he paused here to savor the remark, "is in Rome!"

Pressures from outside the junta—the Americans—were in the direction of reconciliation with the King, cautioning the military government not to go too far. A declaration of a republic would have been the obvious next step, and would have had the support of the people who were fatigued with royal initiatives, political sleight of hand between the Palace and politicians, and more basically, royal living in a poor country.

This is what the junior officers wanted: a republic, the King out of Greece forever, and a more equitable distribution of income, if not an outright socialist economy. They found in Andreas' ideology and political platform much of their thinking, strangely enough, and many looked at Papadopoulos as the man of action, the man who would carry out Andreas' program, his reforms. Andreas in a sense was the educator, the tutor; the young officers his pupils. The difference, of course, was that Andreas believed in reform in an open society; the officers wanted to dictate reforms. They also did not understand that Papadopoulos was an agent of a foreign power. Shortly after the King's coup, one officer opened up to Andreas. He was musing on Andreas' fate. "What Papadopoulos, what Andreas!" he said. And then an ancient Greek expression, "A crow doesn't eat out the eye of a crow."

I talked to an embassy man of lower rank two days after the royal coup, and he predicted that Papadopoulos would declare a republic, saying he could make this legal by a plebescite on a republican form of government, and call the plebescite much earlier than the announced date of the constitutional referendum, which was scheduled for September 1968. "He would be crazy not to do it." he remarked dryly. I gathered that this official felt Papadopoulos had the cards on his side, that the Americans would not withdraw their support even under these new conditions because of the importance they gave to Greece strategically. After all, were they to dismantle the American air force base at Hellinikon, which does the servicing of all United States government aircraft between Athens and Pakistan? Were they to stop using Phaleron as a refueling port for the Sixth Fleet? What about the base on Crete, a center of communications for the entire Middle East? The United States needed the territory of Greece as a base and as an arsenal. Papadopoulos, on the other hand, needed United States support because nonrecognition, he feared, would encourage those forces which wanted to pull the rug out from under his personal rule. It was a question of judgment, and his assessment of the situation was that he had to work out a compromise solution which satisfied the Americans and kept the conservative army elements happy. The young radicals he would deal with later. The solution was to be no return of the King, but no change in the form of the regime. The King's job remained open for the future.

As I watched from the sidelines, I became convinced that this was an important moment to renew pressure for the release of Andreas. Whatever scheme the junta worked out should include the release of Andreas. The junta was not going to prosecute officers that had taken action against it, according to their early statements. This made a trial for the ASPIDA affair an absolute travesty of justice. World pressure for the release of Andreas had been very strong, and I thought the State Department might itself find this an appropriate time to bring up the issue.

On December 19 I put a call through to Sheinbaum in Santa Barbara. He informed me that a top-level Washington lawyer by the name of "Charlie" had been found and then backed out. But Charlie recommended another top man, a friend, for replacement, and this man had agreed to take on the case. In my conversation of the 19th, I asked him to get Charlie's friend to make all contacts with people who might be arranging the "marriage" between the junta and the United States—that is, recognition by the United States—to make sure that Andreas was ushered out of the church at the same time.

On December 20 I received further information from within the junta that confirmed my belief that this was the right time. The information had to do with the release of political prisoners. I put a call through in the middle of the night to Santa Barbara, and Stanley clamped a recording device on the telephone. I have a word-for-word tape of that long-distance conversation, my determined attempt to get it across that the time was *now*.

Stanley answered, "Hello."

"Hello."

"Yeah?"

"I'm afraid I'm getting you out of your sleep . . ."

"Oh, that's okay."

"I'm very sorry, but it's the only time I can be absolutely—"

Stan interrupted me, "No, that's fine."

"I'm calling again about the wedding."

"Right."

"And, uh, I was thinking that you mentioned that you have somebody to replace Charlie."

"Right."

"And I was thinking that he should be working very hard in Miami [Washington] at this very moment."

"Right."

"And making sure that the message gets to Phillip [Talbot] in strong language."

"Right."

"I was wondering if there's any chance that he could come and assist in the wedding here in a short period of time. Do you have any idea?"

Stan replied, "Well, I can tell you that the first part of that has been done. He's talked with Phil already."

"Beg pardon?"

"He has talked to Phil already."

"I see. This person, you mean."

"Yes."

"Very good."

"But the second part I can't answer yet."

"Uh-huh."

"But I'll work on it."

"I have the feeling that this is the moment for maximum pressure and we may be able to push up the wedding date." (I meant here the release of Andreas.)

"Right."

"It seems that somehow the conditions and the atmosphere may be just right for that."

"Okay."

"And that's the reason I'm urging so we don't miss the opportunity and it may pass again, you see."

"Right. I need one bit of clarification."

"Yes."

"Ah, it's the sailing boy that you're talking about . . ."

"No, no, I'm talking about the nonsailing boys because I believe that's the way the throw of the dice will go." (The sailing boy was Constantinos, but I was talking about the junta because I believed that it would be recognized by the United States without the King, and the pressure for Andreas' release had to be put on the junta itself. Stanley later told me this part had been unclear to him.)

"Okay, fine."

"And—but in order for that to happen, you see, I think certain conditions should be met. That's why the bargaining position is rather good for the wedding. And this should be one of the conditions somehow." (That Andreas be freed before the junta be recognized by the United States.)

"Okay."

"That's my point. I'm afraid that it may get lost in the shuffle of other things, you see . . . it seems to me that this is absolutely one condition to be demanded."

"Okay. All right. All pressure. Everyone went to work yesterday."

"Wonderful!" Here my voice took on a glad note. "I was thinking also that there should be some coordination with the Vikings and other such places because—"

"The Vikings?" Stanley sounded momentarily puzzled.

"Yeah."

"Okay."

"The people in that general area because they're also trying to decide whether to go ahead with the marriage or not."

"Right."

"And therefore they're also in a position to put some pressure for the correct wedding plans."

"Right. Okay. That's where most of the pressure is coming from."

"Uh-huh. It is, huh?"

"Yeah."

359

"Well, let it come from your area, too. Because that's where it really counts."

"Okay."

"Okay—so you may find out whether it is possible for this other person to come. Of course, I think that the big work is there at the moment."

"Right."

"But in a few days or a week or so it might make some sense to make a trip. And see whether something can be done here as well."

"Right. Okay."

"Sorry to wake you up, but thanks . . ."

"No, that's okay."

"Thanks so much."

"Okay. Merry Christmas."

"Merry Christmas. Bye."

Saturday morning, December 23, my father-in-law's driver came to the house to tell me that the President had been released from house arrest and would await me and the children for lunch. At 12:30 P.M. we had our regular visit at the jail. It was family visiting day, and we took two cars to carry the four children, my mother-in-law, Marjorie, Tito, and myself. As was usual, George, Andreas' mother, and I went in for our visits at the screens first. Monday was Christmas Day, and I had already a deep melancholy at the thought of spending a Christmas with Andreas behind bars. I had been told earlier in the week that because Christmas was a holiday, I would have my normal Monday visit the day before. So I wouldn't even talk to Andreas on Christmas Day.

Our visit got started ten minutes late. Twenty minutes had passed, and it was one o'clock. As we were talking, I heard what sounded like a ferocious roar emanate from the area of the prison court, just beyond the doors of our visiting area. The one o'clock news had been blaring from the loudspeaker in the courtyard and could be heard through the cell windows of the prisoners at Averoff. As the roar continued, it sounded like the response to the game-clinching play of an important sports event, although it frightened me at the beginning.

"What's that?" I said to Andreas.

His thought was the same as mine. "Probably an athletic event" was his answer.

"No, Mom," piped up George, who had been standing silently next to me. "I heard something about 'amnesty.'"

I looked at George. "Say that again," I asked.

"I'm sure. I know. I heard them say 'amnesty.'"

Andreas turned his face to one of the guards next to me. "Tell me . . . what was that about?"

"Nothing, nothing . . . continue with your visit," the guard answered sharply.

"Mommy, Mommy," George now insisted, excited. "The radio said there would be a general amnesty. I'm sure. I'm sure!"

"General amnesty?" asked Andreas in a disbelieving voice. "No, no, don't get excited . . . it's probably not . . ."

Rolling down my cheeks were big, fat, heavy tears that I could almost hear plopping on the cement floor of the prison. I was smiling and shaking my head back and forth, saying quietly, "Oh, my Andreas, oh my Andreas . . . if . . ."

My mother-in-law, very hard of hearing, had been standing next to me watching the conversation, the excitement, my tears. She reached her hand behind me and tugged on Georgie's sleeve and made a Greek gesture which says, "What's up?" with her hand.

"*Am-nes-tia!*" shouted George.

Andreas was vainly attempting to calm us all down, fearful that we might be frightfully disappointed by an order that did not include him. General amnesty for political prisoners could exclude him, since he faced legal charges and was considered a criminal prisoner. At that point the bell-shaped director of the prison came into the hallway, a coy smile playing on his face.

"What's this I hear, what's this I hear?" he said in a singsong voice that teased and taunted in the way relatives do with small children.

"What was the announcement?" Andreas addressed him from behind the cage.

"Hmmmmnnn. Something about general amnesty, something . . ." he replied teasingly, his hands clasped behind his back as if he were hiding there a luscious secret. He walked out the door into the court along with two wardens, and that was all he was prepared to say.

I was convinced by this theatrical appearance that the amnesty did include Andreas. The director's coquettishly friendly attitude was an attempt to be on our side now since the gods had favored us, and tomorrow, well, who knew what role Andreas might play?

I found my voice again, and asked, "Andreas, since they're letting you out, why not now? I want to take you by the hand and walk out of this filthy place *now*."

Andreas smiled wanly. He was in a state of shock, his face whitened by the impact of the news.

When we got out, the three younger children, who were waiting their turn, went inside. I sat down next to Marjorie on the bench, and in a voice drained of emotion, I told her what had happened. While I was talking, Georgie took my car keys and ran to the car to tune in to Athens Radio. Within five minutes he was back, racing down the long wide sidewalk to our bench, his long skinny arms jutting out in all directions, a huge toothy grin on his face.

"Mom, I heard Dad's name. The announcer said that all political prisoners would be released, from Andreas Papandreou down to the last Greek!" His voice cracked from excitement and had a warmth of tone I hadn't heard since before that terrible night of April 21. I was struck by the statement of Papadopoulos: "from Andreas Papandreou down to the last Greek." Did he mean to say it that way, to give such position to Andreas?

The children remained beyond their scheduled time with their father. This was another good sign. The big iron doors opened to spill out sunshine—three faces sparkling and full of joy, excited and happy. They fell over each other to reach me and say, "Daddy's getting out!"

"Did they say when?" I asked.

"The director came to see us and said maybe in a few hours!"

I drew my brood around me, and we walked, like a mother hen with her chicks, fluttering and chirping, down the sidewalk, away from the jail, for what I hoped was the last time. Everyone was talking at once, Marjorie was smiling with tears in her eyes, Tito was bouncing. When we reached our car, we discovered that in his excitement, George had locked the keys inside. Tito took the three boys in his car, and we three ladies and Sophia, hailed a taxi. As soon as we got in, the taxi driver turned to me, smiling, and said, "Merry Christmas, Mrs. Margaret." The word was out, and I had a feeling that the Greek nation was rejoicing with me.

From that point on started the longest waiting period I have experienced in my life. I called the lawyer Cannellopoulos as soon as I arrived home, and he told me that he was in touch with the prison director, and as soon as the papers came for Andreas' release, the director would call him. Cannellopoulos doubted that it would be before evening. With that information, I drove with the children up to the President's house in Kastri, and I found him positively ebullient. He put his big hand on my shoulder and said, "Moira, Margarita, moira." Then he went on to say, "It was the *failure* of the King's coup that made this possible." When we left, I promised to bring Andreas up as soon as I could after his release.

The hours of late afternoon passed slowly, slowly. No call. Other calls came, however, with the excited voices of friends, wondering if Andreas had arrived home yet, promising to come by soon, and then wishing me a merry, merry Christmas, a wish that had a rich and meaningful sound now. They were happy not only for Andreas, but for themselves. All of this seemed to signal a change which would relieve their beastly situation. Just before I left to take Andreas' food to the jail for his evening meal, an act that I now resented, I got a long-distance phone call from my parents. They had heard the news on a morning newscast in Elmhurst, Illinois, while having breakfast. I spoke to my mother first, then to Dad, whose voice broke as he told me how happy they were. "Didn't I tell you we'd see you at Christmas?" he asked, and I remembered his shout up to Andreas when they left for the States in September.

"You're almost a prophet," I told him. "But more than that, you're a wonderful dad . . . and mom."

When I approached the jail, Andreas was standing tall and close to the window, waving at me as I walked toward the doors. I tripped along gaily, swinging my purse, thinking of Little Red Riding Hood going through the woods picking flowers and putting them in the basket. I refused to think of the wolf. It seemed like December had never been so warm and good. I blew kisses to Andreas, then gave a pantomime of looking at my watch to indicate impatience. He responded with the same motion and shrugged his shoulders to indicate he didn't know when he'd get out. No one stopped our conversation; in fact, the guards with the guns turned their backs to me to leave me free.

At 9 P.M. Cannellopoulos called me to say that the release would not take place that night, but the next day. I hadn't expected to spend that night in bed alone. At 11:30 we drove by the jail at least ten times, signaling with lit cigarettes from inside the car, and getting a fast response from behind the bars of Andreas' window. The flames spoke to each other for the first time with hope and excitement. But I was angry that Andreas had to spend one more night on a hard cot inside the degrading walls of a prison.

Sunday morning was sunny and cool. I was the first one up in the house. As I was fixing coffee, Antigone came into the kitchen.

"The minister should be home today," she said. Her voice told me that she had missed him, too.

"He better be!" I replied savagely.

After breakfast the children decided to decorate the house. We pulled out of the storage closet all the Christmas decorations we had initially decided not to use. The house took on a festive air. In one of the bedrooms a poster-making activity began. Most were written in Greek:

"Welcome home, Dad!"

"Democracy will win!"

"Happy New Year!"

"Freedom for all the Greeks!"

One was written in English, "Welcome Home, Hero!" This latter was a huge banner which they hung across the top of the entryway outside the house. Their artwork was photographed and appeared in *Newsweek* magazine the following week.

By noon no news had come of his release, and I went to Averoff with his lunch and to have my visit. One guard came with me and stood far back to indicate he was not interested in listening. The barbed wires had been removed and I was in my old place close up to the screens. I started speaking Greek, out of habit, then switched to English as I understood that the atmosphere had changed utterly and completely. I told Andreas that I couldn't stand the waiting, and he answered, "*You* can't stand it . . .!" and smiled. We talked about his father and the children, but it was perfunctory. Our minds were on the moment when we would be together again, this mesh divider gone, the listening ears absent, when we would have hours before us to talk, to compare notes, to say all the things unsaid for the past eight months, to examine this tragedy that had befallen the Greek nation, and to ask ourselves what we could do to liberate a people.

Lunch at home, and more waiting. Cannellopoulos called around 2:30 saying that the papers were being prepared, but no one could give him a definite time when they would be carried to jail. Marjorie and the rest of the family urged me to rest in the afternoon. As I lay in bed, the absence of Andreas next to me became acute. I got up and fussed around the room, arranging his clothes in the closet, lining up his shoes, fixing his shelf in the bathroom.

At 4:30 Marjorie knocked on the door. "It's the lawyer on the phone," she said.

I raced downstairs.

"Be at the jail by five o'clock. I'll meet you there."

Tito and Kiveli were waiting downstairs. Others had arrived. Some were relatives, some close friends. I wasn't happy to see them. The return of Andreas was a private, family affair, and I wanted to protect that moment for us. The kisses, the tears, the joy—that was our monopoly. But Andreas belonged to more than just the family, and I knew it.

Tito, Kiveli, Marjorie, and I left for Averoff together. The palms of my hands were wet and my mouth dry, but this was a different kind of nervousness than the many other experiences I had had in the past months.

Waiting outside the jail was Cannellopoulos, talking to a tall, distinguished-looking older man. The man was the father of Theodorakis, who was supposed to be released at the same time. Crowds gathered on the other side of Leoforas Alexandras wanting to see Andreas walk out of jail. The guards were edgy about this development and finally two of them went and ordered the crowd to move on.

Two figures surrounded by four police guards approached the entrance of the jail along the sidewalk parallel to the jail from the area of the prison hospital. One was a big, stoop-shouldered shaggy-haired figure whom I recognized as Theodorakis. The other was a shorter, thin, sandy-haired man whose walk looked familiar. I waited for him to get closer. It was Phillip. Without thinking, I charged over to him and threw my arms around his frail body, startling the guards. His face was gray, and he looked sick, but he smiled.

"Ti kaneis, Margarita?" he said in a tired, quiet voice. I backed away as I saw the guards beginning to move toward me. I watched them as they went on by, Phillip's legs looking as if they were unaccustomed to walking. The two men were marched to the front of the prison and the doors closed after them.

At 6 P.M. I was still waiting. Kiveli, Tito, and Marjorie had been told to leave, along with several reporters who had managed to get close to the prison. They returned to the car to wait for Andreas and me there.

I found myself pacing up and down in front of the two big doors of the prison, fixing my eyes on the doors as if with hypnotic glare I could open them and produce the figure of Andreas. Occasionally, I walked away from the wall to look up at his cell. A light was on, but he did not come to the window. At 6:15 an official car drove up. Cannellopoulos whispered to me, "The papers."

"Stavro," I said, pulling him aside, "they aren't going to ask Andreas to sign a loyalty oath, or any declaration that he removes himself from politics, are they?"

"No, no, I don't think so."

"Because then we might as well go back home. Andreas won't sign, and they'll keep him in prison."

He repeated that he didn't consider it likely. It was the one unspoken dread I had had since the announcement of the amnesty, that our bubble of happiness could so easily be broken by a demand of this kind.

Within a few minutes after the arrival of the official car, the lights went out in Andreas' cell and through the downstairs office windows I saw him being brought into the director's office. The bottom ledge of the window was neck height for me, so that I could just barely peer through. Andreas looked very thin, his trousers sagging at the ankles as if he had no hips to keep them up.

He was smoking incessantly. I watched as papers were shuffled and words spoken between the dark-suited official and Tournas, the director of the jail. Andreas was told to leave the inner office, and I watched him walk out to the outer offices where others milled around. I saw him asking some questions and lighting one cigarette after the next. From my position it was as if I were watching a stage play, the stage set split into one large room and one smaller room, action going on in both. My attention was concentrated on the main character. Not once did he glance at the windows, where he might have seen my face watching anxiously in the evening shadows.

At seven o'clock exactly, the doors of the prison opened and a police guard walked out. He came over to me.

"You are to go home, and we will bring Mr. Papandreou to the house."

"What do you mean?" I sputtered. "I have come to take him home . . ." I glanced at Stavros for help, for explanation, but he said nothing.

"You can come in and see him for a few minutes before you leave," he told me.

Again in the jail, I thought. I went in, a churning starting up in my stomach. What strange game was this? Apprehension turned into fear. My feet moved automatically behind his.

Andreas was standing in the outer office. He took me and gave me a tight little kiss on both cheeks. His face was tense and tired looking.

"Why can't I drive you home?" I asked. "I've been waiting forever for this moment."

He turned to the officer. "Can't she accompany me in the police car?" I knew he wanted to make it a demand, but I knew also that the thought of an argument that would delay his walking out of that jail was close to unbearable.

"Impossible," said the officer. He looked at my face and understood that I had a deeper concern, and with a kindness I hadn't experienced in any of my contacts at the jail, he added, "Don't worry. He'll be home within minutes after you arrive."

I kissed Andreas again and with reluctance departed. What did they think we were going to do—drive to Constitution Square and start a demonstration?

The officer had spoken the truth. Within minutes after my return home, the police car pulled up and Andreas climbed out. A police guard was at the house turning cars and people away. About thirty people had made it inside the gates before the guard appeared. The kids ran out first. George had turned on the record player with a favorite tune of Andreas', "Strangers in the Night."

Andreas strode in like a popular political figure moving through the crowds after a successful speech: he shook hands, people touched him, pulled on him, threw their arms around him and kissed him. His face was red from emotion and the attempt to keep himself under control. As he moved through the bodies in what seemed to me a molasseslike pace, his eyes were on mine as I stood waiting for him just inside the door. He reached me and took me in his arms, and this time he really kissed me. There was nothing to say at the moment. I knew Andreas was home.

Aftermath

Aftermath

WE HAVE been in exile now since the beginning of 1968. We left, with the entire family, at 6 A.M. on January 15 from Hellinikon airport on a plane headed for Paris.

A few days after Andreas' amnesty, as he began his long, slow road back to emotional and physical recovery from the eight months of isolation and cruel uncertainty at Averoff, we began to discuss what our next steps should be. For the first week after his release, we all rode a wave of euphoria, believing that Andreas' freedom was symbolic of better days to come for the nation. The President particularly was in a high mood. With his old gusto and sparkle, he discussed politics, Andreas' role in the party (Andreas, he felt, was ready to take over the leadership of the party), formation of committees, and the individual idiosyncrasies of party members that should be taken into consideration. For a week or thereabouts, we lived in this world of unreality. The President spoke as if the dictatorship did not exist.

By the end of the week he and we were talked out. That night, when we came to dinner, his first statement was, "Andreas, you are in danger. Your life cannot be considered safe here." We knew Stage 1, Euphoria, had passed. Now we were to face the difficult realities of life in dictatorial Greece. It was eminently clear to all of us that we could not stay on. There was no way to earn a living because any job would depend on the good graces of the junta. And what was most obvious was that Andreas would soon become the focus of opposition to the dictatorship, would soon speak out condemning it, and, surely, in addition to endangering his contacts, would be quickly reimprisoned. And this time the world protest would be less potent, less active; so with the passing of time he would be a sometimes remembered, but often forgotten, political prisoner somewhere in the Aegean. Outside of Greece he could fight; inside he would be a silenced moral force.

For the junta Andreas Papandreou continued to present a dilemma. Having gone through the bombardment, the attacks, and the pressure for his release, and having finally decided that releasing him might improve the image of the government, they were not too keen on rearresting him. But they knew, just as certainly as we did, that if he stayed in Greece, his rearrest would be inevitable. Out of Greece, though, he was free to talk, to organize, to build up resistance. (Now, more than ever, they must have wondered why they hadn't killed him the first night.) Between the two choices, and with the smug knowledge that they were in power with American Pentagon backing, they were inclined toward his exile, confident they could withstand his barbs and arrows. After all, they were also being recognized by European governments, so how could Andreas rally forces around him strong enough to affect their destiny?

We had to choose between leaving Greece legally or illegally. Within the second week after amnesty, we started planning an illegal escape. At the same time, we decided to *try* to get a passport for Andreas, which would entitle him to leave the country. Andreas' father was certain it would not be given to him. Remembering, however, that Nikiforos Mandiliras had lost his life in an attempt to escape, I was insistent that we attempt the legal method. Tito, as always, handled the preliminaries—application, photos, papers from this and that ministry. We had the impression that the bureaucratic machine was moving faster than normal, and this encouraged us to believe that the higher-ups had wanted him out of the country. When all formalities were finished, Tito was told that Papandreou would be notified when his passport was ready. Then the days started ticking by with no news. We increased our efforts on the escape plan, making two contacts with members of an escape machinery, foreigners who came into Greece. Meantime, Marjorie had flown to the States ostensibly to hand over George to my parents so that he could start school in Elmhurst, but actually to work with Sheinbaum on an alternative escape plan should the first one not be feasible. At this point Andreas and I decided to pay a visit to Talbot at the embassy to see if we couldn't get some of the burrs whirred out of the machinery that had stopped the passport in its forward progress. We decided (a) to be nice to him and thank him for what he had done for us, (b) to practice not gagging when we expressed the sentiments under (a), (c) to show little interest in Greek affairs, except on a high analytical level, and (d) to show inclination toward a return to teaching. I arranged the interview through McClellan of the political section, and on Saturday, January 12, we had a tête-à-tête with the ambassador at noon at his residence—with ouzo—which had the atmosphere of two boxers sparring lightly in the gym while saving their heavy punches for the real fight later. On the following Monday night, Andreas was handed his passport by Pattakos himself and wished "good luck—to you and your family." The thing we had dreaded, a demand for a written renunciation of politics, did not come up. If it had, our only way out of Greece would have had to be the illegal one.

As we walked into Kastri that evening for dinner, our last one with "the old man of politics," George Papandreou, Andreas pulled out the blue passport and plunked it on the table. My father-in-law examined it minutely, shaking his head in disbelief. We sat down in a mood of excitement and deep sadness. The President asked his maid to put champagne on ice and to bring a can of caviar from the basement. But these accoutrements of festivity and celebration could not lighten our mood as the evening slipped away and we faced the final farewell for an indeterminate period of time. We had tickets for a morning plane, and I had begun throwing clothes into suitcases but would have to work through the night to get the family ready. At midnight the President stood up and said, "You had better go now and get yourselves prepared."

"We can stay a bit longer," Andreas protested.

369

"We have said what there is to say" was his reply. That had been politics, what line he thought Andreas should take outside of Greece, and that he, the chairman of the party, was naming him spokesman for the Center Union abroad. "After me," he had added, "you will become the leader. I am positive of that." He had also spoken about the family, and how Andreas had obligations to his children as well and that his duty to his country should not overshadow his responsibilities to his family.

At the door Andreas kissed him good-bye first, then turned with tears in his eyes and started down the steps. The President took both my hands in his and looked me in the face. I wanted to murmur "Kali andamosi," meaning "Till we meet again," but something in his eyes kept me from it. It was a long, deep look, almost hard in its expression of finality.

"Margarita," he said, then stopped. He was struggling now with the emotion that had built up throughout the evening. "Margarita, take care of Andreas. Make him rest for several weeks before he begins his fight. He is not himself yet."

"I will, I will," I whispered, unable to control my quavering voice. I put my arms around his neck and kissed him hard on both cheeks, leaving them wet with tears, then slid my arms slowly away from his shoulders, and without turning back, walked down the stairs saying, "Yasoo, yasoo, my dear President," in a voice that only I could hear.

Two days later in Paris Andreas held his first press conference blasting the junta. From that moment Andreas started a crusade. In February we visited London, Copenhagen, Stockholm, Oslo. Everywhere he saw members of governments, party leaders, youth leaders, the intelligentsia. He held press conferences, gave interviews, spoke on television and radio, wrote articles for magazines, gathered together the Greeks in each country to start an action program. In March he was the guest speaker at the annual ADA dinner in Washington. He spoke to Senators and Congressmen, members of the Department of Defense and the State Department. He spoke to Eugene McCarthy (whose daughter spoke at the ADA dinner on behalf of the cause of democracy in Greece) and spent an hour with Bobby Kennedy in his office on the Hill on the same day Kennedy announced his candidacy for President. He drafted a letter to all presidential candidates pleading for the Greek people, he appeared on "Face the Nation," the "Today" show, and innumerable other television and radio programs in the States. He urged that all military aid be cut off from Greece until democracy was restored. From Washington we traveled throughout the United States: New York, Boston, Chicago (where a huge rally was held in the Chicago Arena along with Melina Mercouri and other celebrities dedicated to the Greek cause), Minneapolis, Los Angeles, San Francisco, Berkeley, Santa Barbara, and Toronto, Canada.

On April 21, 1968, one year after the colonels took over Greece, Andreas spoke to thousands of Greek workers in Bonn, Germany, where emotions were high and anger unrelenting. From there he went to Holland where funds were donated by the people for resistance to the dictatorship. By then he had announced the existence of the Panhellenic Liberation Movement (PAK), the external resistance movement with headquarters in Greece, and, eventually in

Stockholm. In May again a trip to Stockholm and to Copenhagen, then back to Paris to pick up the family for a move to Stockholm. The government in Sweden had made it possible for him to become a visiting professor of economics at the University of Stockholm for one year. By now he was greatly fatigued, and I was worried about his health. A medical examination in Paris in April showed him physically well but emotionally exhausted. The doctor recommended a mountain vacation. Instead, after we were settled in Stockholm, he toured Germany and made a second trip to London. He spoke in Stockholm and Copenhagen to the International Socialist conventions. In September he started his teaching as well.

A few days before the anniversary of the coup, a messenger brought us in Paris a tape made by George Papandreou and smuggled out of Greece, calling on the western world to act now against the resurgence of fascism in Europe, before it was too late. We listened, thrilled, to that message in George Papandreou's voice, slightly less vibrant than in the past—but in past times he was speaking to crowds numbering in the thousands, whereas now he was speaking to a tape recorder in the tense silence of his home in Kastri, performing an act of defiance which would—and did—put him back under house arrest. April 21, 1968, was also Easter Sunday in Greece. We heard the President's message begin:

> *This year, the day of the Lord's Resurrection, coincides with the anniversary of our people's crucifixion. The military coup of the 21st of April has abolished all freedoms . . .*
> *It has abolished the freedom of the press . . .*
> *It has abolished the freedom of speech . . .*
> *It has abolished the freedom of assembly . . .*

And he finished with an appeal to the free world:

> *After World War II we had hoped that fascism had been definitely crushed and that it would not be able to make its appearance again, certainly not in Europe. And yet it did. It is our shame that its first appearance should have taken place in our country, Greece, the cradle of democracy.*
> *However, the fate of the junta will not remain a local affair. Its fate will set a precedent, which will either encourage or disappoint would-be dictators in other countries. . . . International isolation, both political and economic, of the junta will lead to its immediate overthrow. And that is what we appeal for in the name of the enslaved Greek people whom we represent.*
> *By taking such an initiative, the free world will both honor and protect itself. It will become worthy of its name.*

With the leaders of the two major parties under house arrest (Cannellopoulos was also put under arrest about the same time as Papandreou), with new civilian arrests occurring regularly, with continuing purges in the army and civil services, with censored press, radio, no freedom of speech, torture with, in short, martial law, the junta set about holding a referendum on its own

Constitution. It gave continued assurances to the foreign press that Greeks were entirely free to state their opposition to the Constitution. But not one article opposing the Constitution ever appeared in the Greek newspapers. By early September, a month before the referendum (September 29, 1968), Greece was plastered with tens of thousands of *YES* signs, monotonous in their totality. Not one *NO* sign was visible. A touring Colorado professor and his family went through a day of harassment for displaying a homemade OXI (NO) sign on the windshield of their station wagon. The Washington *Post*, September 27, related the incident as follows:

> *Returning to their parked auto after a stroll in Athens yesterday, they [Professor Tennenbaum and Mrs. Tennenbaum and four children] found security police surrounding it. The police took the family to a station house, interrogated the father and Thea for two hours, and then freed them after removing the two signs. Some hours later, at Megara, a historical site a few miles from Athens, the car was stopped by military police, who had apparently heard an "all points alert" about the car earlier.*
>
> *Demanding a further interrogation, the police ordered the Tennenbaums to drive back to Athens under heavy escort.*
>
> *Driving past the U.S. Embassy on the way to military police quarters nearby, Prof. Tennenbaum ducked from behind the lead police car and drove up the Embassy ramp. Mrs. Tennenbaum leaped out and ran into the Embassy Lobby, pursued by a policeman. He placed one hand over her mouth and the other arm around her shoulders and attempted to drag her out. A Marine guard pulled him off.*

The Greeks who attempted similar opposition to the referendum could not turn to the embassy for support. They were given three-year jail sentences. Voting was compulsory and the penalty for not voting was confiscation of the voting passbook—an essential document in Greece for passports, business licences, driver's licences, etc.—and threat of penal action.

In this climate, the Greeks went to the polling booths on September 29. Ninety-two percent of those who voted were reported by the junta to have voted "yes." The figure that was significant, however, in view of the penalties announced, was the number of abstentions. One and a half million, or approximately twenty-five percent of those eligible to vote, refused to participate.

The junta's constitution gave no power at all to the King, increased the authority of the government at the expense of Parliament, and gave the armed forces a major role in the government while at the same time making them virtually autonomous. Its provisions for human rights and civil liberties were worded in a hedged fashion, and in any case, all civic rights and legal protections could be lost by any citizen who "abused" them. They suspended indefinitely those sections of the Constitution pertaining to the establishment of political parties, elections, and parliamentary rule. The rest of the Constitution was to go into effect immediately after the referendum.

Papandreou and Cannellopoulos were released six days prior to the vote, and

Papadopoulos said publicly he hoped "they would do nothing to make him have to put them back again."

A picture of George Papandreou waving from his balcony after release appeared on the front page of the international edition of the *Herald Tribune*. He was smiling, but looked thin and drawn. From Paris where Andreas and I had gone on political business, we sent a telegram:

> *We saw you from your balcony in Kastri. We miss you and we love you.* Andreas, Margaret and the children

By the time of my father-in-law's release and the constitutional referendum, we were in a position to assess the situation outside of Greece. One serious and hopeful piece of work was being done, that of the Council of Human Rights in the European Council. Long and careful investigation, starting with the initial report of Amnesty International prepared by Anthony Marreco, British lawyer, and James Becket, American lawyer, on torture and persecution, was to furnish the base of the case charging Greece with violating Article 3 of the charter of the Consultative Assembly of the European Council, and asking for Greece's expulsion from the organization. The Scandinavian countries led the movement for expulsion. Hearings were to be held in Strasbourg in November with witnesses who had gotten out of Greece attesting to their tortures, and witnesses brought from Greece by the junta declaring that they nor anyone had been mistreated in the hands of the security police. The hearings took a dramatic turn when two of the junta's witnesses escaped from their hotel by contacting members of the Panhellenic Liberation Movement, asked for asylum in Norway, and then appeared at the court, now under protection, to tell their stories of beatings and physical pain inflicted on them.

No major European statesman supported the regime in Greece, labor organizations attacked it, the Swedes continued their tourist boycott, and newspapers wrote increasingly heavy attacks against it. But what was clear beyond doubt was that the American military and its NATO arm supported it fully and wholeheartedly, an attitude embodied in Clark Clifford's statement in May of 1968 when he told the Senate Foreign Relations Committee that "the obligations imposed on us by the NATO alliance are far more important than the kind of government they have in Greece or what we think of it."*

What we saw and knew of the attitude of the United States government in the autumn of 1968 was to appear concisely stated the following spring in an analytical article for the American Security Council's Washington Report (March 10, 1969) written by the newspaperman Anthony Harrigan. It offers those in jail in Greece and in exile, those hapless tortured human beings, who love their piece of craggy, dry, and sun-tipped land in the Mediterranean, and those human beings everywhere who love liberty and freedom a long look at the way Big Brother from across the sea appraises the situation.

*On December 12, 1969, Greece was expelled from the Council of Europe. Technically she withdrew, but that was when Pipinelis, the junta's foreign minister, ascertained that the vote would be for expulsion. Prior to the vote, the United States had exerted tremendous pressure on its European allies not to take this step. European action left the American government nakedly holding up the dictatorship of Greece. In a cheap effort to show its support for the shaken colonel's regime, it gathered up American school children living in Greece and sent them to sing Christmas carols to Dictator Papadopoulos. (Picture, New York *Times*, December 24, 1969)

373

As a practical matter, the U.S. Sixth Fleet in the Mediterranean must have access to the territorial waters and air space of Greece. The Sixth Fleet, in order to carry out its deterrent duties and keep the peace, must be free to thread the maze of Greek islands in the Aegean and the Sea of Crete. U.S. planes must have permission to overfly these islands. The airfield on Crete, with its 9,000 foot runway, provides the planes of the Sixth Fleet with an important safety factor. In addition, the Crete field makes possible vital reconnaissance flights over the Eastern Mediterranean. The security of many NATO countries thus depends on continued use of Greek territories and installations.

That is why there had to be a dictatorship in Greece. It is an important military base, and it has to be run like a base, with military leaders and the people under strict discipline and control, like soldiers in an army. Greeks must be slaves so that others may be free.

Late in October, after our return from France, I picked up the phone at home to hear Andreas' concerned voice from his office. He had just had a call from AP wire services reporting that his father had suddenly been taken to a hospital and was hemorrhaging. We decided to get a phone call through to Greece to someone who could give us the facts. The information was that he had a perforated ulcer, but that the hemorrhaging seemed to have abated, and it didn't look serious. That was Monday, October 28. We were nervous, though, and kept in close touch with the news services in case anything new came up. On Tuesday morning we called the hospital directly and got through to a cousin of Andreas' in the small room adjoining the President's. He sounded worried, but put on that optimistic, cheerful voice that one offers someone else who is helpless to do much more than get reports. Andreas was distressed. Again we called in the afternoon, and again we got through. The President was resting comfortably, but was being fed intravenously. On Wednesday morning an early wire service report said that his condition had worsened.

"I'm going down," I said.

"Not without me" was Andreas' reply.

"You're crazy," I told him. "They have recently indicted you for involvement in the Panagoulis assassination attempt. You think they'd ever let you out of the country once you got in?"

I saw Andreas struggling with this decision. His natural inclination in keeping with his style was to go down—and take the consequences. For a moment I was scared that he would insist.

"What about you?" he finally asked. "So are you in danger."

"I will call the American Embassy and ask them to inform the Greek government that I am coming down. That will give me the protection I need."

Andreas was dubious. In conflict about not going down himself, truly concerned about my being in Greece, and concerned lest his father have no one of the family at his side during a critical illness, he hardly knew what to tell me to do. Zoronikos, a Greek helping him in his Stockholm PAK offices, had come by the house to see what the latest news was, and he supported my point of view.

374

I telephoned the American Embassy in Stockholm and asked for the ambassador. He was out for the morning. Then we decided to call the embassy in Athens and ask for Talbot, or anyone in the political section. Talbot did not come to the phone, but a very friendly voice introduced himself—a new name to me—and said he would immediately get in touch with the government and call me back. I told him I was bringing my son George and my daughter Sophia with me. "Not Andreas?" he asked. When I said no, he relaxed, as if to say that the situation was decidedly easier under those circumstances.

At 6 P.M. we left the house for Ulanda airport, and at 7 P.M. we were in the air headed for Athens. With two stops along the way, our approach to Hellinikon airport was being made at 3 A.M. in the morning. We had slept a bit, fitfully, but were awake long before we reached Greek skyways. As we were descending, I felt the tightness in my stomach return, a feeling I had lived with so long in Greece that it had become a natural accompaniment of daily living. Now it was strange, and freshly painful. I took out my mirror and put some lipstick on my dry lips.

"Are you nervous, Mom?" George asked, next to me.

"George, I never dreamt that I would return to a Greece under the dictatorship. I thought that when we left from that airport below in January, we would only return upon the liberation of Greece. It's a weird feeling."

"Well, anyway, I've got our protection," he smiled slyly. Then he opened up the lapel of his jacket and inside, in clear blue letters on a button clip, were the words "FREE GREECE." Customs, inspection, interrogation—all the words marched through my brain. Then, I thought, the hell with it. Let him wear it.

Hellinikon was virtually deserted as we stepped off the plane. The air was cool and sweet, the hills around the airport were the same, the smells were Greek smells—nothing physically had changed, and the three of us walked toward the passport entrance as if we were returning home. We went through without a bat of the examiner's eyelash.

Our plane had been half an hour early. I looked around for a familiar face, a greeting committee, an embassy official. There was nothing. Just the quiet, depressed heaviness of a totalitarian state. We went to the waiting area of Hellinikon airport and ordered lemonades to give us time to decide on our next move. A young Greek reporter rushed over, a face I remembered from the past.

"I am friend of Andreas," he said in a low voice. "How is the minister?"

I felt the prickles of tension on my skin at this first surreptitious contact, but also a twinge of pleasure that the first Greek to speak to me was on my side.

"He's fine," I said. "Be careful," I added, as if I, a free soul for months now had to tell someone in Greece to be cautious. "Tell me, what news of the President?"

"He was taken into surgery around midnight."

At that moment, looking over his shoulder, I spotted two familiar figures walking into the front entrance. It was Tito and Kiveli. Somehow they had found out I was coming into Athens. Just like them! Tito was hobbling from a recent car accident; Kiveli was heading toward the SAS airline booth for information. George ran and got them. Hugs and kisses out of the way, we moved quickly toward the taxi stand to head for the hospital. At the door I was stopped by one of those grim little security men who introduced himself and told me that two guards would be assigned to me while I was in Athens, "for your protection." Sarcastically I thanked him for the kindness, and the tail started as soon as the cab took off.

The waiting room on the President's floor was full of old, familiar faces, hushed and anxious, and hushed even more now by the presence of two security men who took positions in the corner of the room.

It was a long wait. At 6 A.M. he was wheeled into his room, and I rushed with the children to reach his side. He was just coming out of the anesthetic. I bent down close to his ear.

"It's Margarita. I'm here."

He opened his eyes and tried to focus them on my face. I pulled Georgie over and Sophia. "This is George," I said. "And Sophoula."

"I don't believe it," he mumbled. Then he raised his hand from the bed, searching for mine. I put it under his, and he gave it two pats before falling back into slumber.

George Papandreou died in his sleep the following night. The junta offered a state funeral. Andreas and I refused, as did his other son George. The news was out by morning. In the taxi we took to the small hospital church, the driver, discovering it was Mrs. Margaret in the car, broke down and sobbed heavily.

"They killed him . . . they killed him," he kept repeating.

Later that afternoon I talked to one of the doctors who had been closest to him, who had visited him during his house arrests and attended him during his last illness.

"What did he say about Andreas," I asked. "How did he feel about his activities?"

"He was very proud of Andreas," Evangelos said simply. "He told me, 'My son has the instincts and capabilities of a leader. Someday he will be Prime Minister of Greece. My greatest wish is that I will be here to see that day.' "

I left Greece six days after my arrival. It was the second day of the trial of Panagoulis, the thirty year old army man, former member of the Center Union Youth group, charged with a plot to assassinate Premier Papadopoulos. He stood before the special tribunal and shouted that he had been subjected to "medieval tortures" during his three-month imprisonment. He did not deny the accusation that he had attempted to blow up Papadopoulos in his car in August. He said: "I ask no clemency. For me, the best swan song is the death rattle before the firing squad of tyranny." He added, "This regime will be toppled by violent means, because that is the only way to end it. We have failed, but others will follow."

This was the beginning. The death of George Papandreou served "as a catalyst to mass opposition" according to Maurice Goldbloom, writing for *Commonweal* magazine. He wrote the following:

Papandreou had, at the age of eighty, maintained his intransigent opposition to the junta in spite of repeated periods of house arrest which friends believe significantly hastened his death. More than any other man he symbolized the desire of the Greek people for the return of democracy and freedom, and in death he rallied them to that cause even more eloquently than in life. Some fifty thousand Athenians crowded the cathedral and the square in front of it for his funeral services; at least a quarter million more lined the route of the funeral cortege to the cemetery. In the cathedral itself political leaders of all groups came to pay their respects or if they—like Mikis Theodorakis, who was under house arrest, and the self-exiled Constantine Karamanlis—were absent, they sent wreaths.

Papandreou's old friend and opponent Panayotis Cannellopoulos told the mourners "I bow before George Papandreou in the name of our past conflicts, all of which took place within the arena of democracy." And from the throng in the square and along the route there were cries of "Democracy" and "You will always be our leader." Others shouted "Today is the day we vote NO!" And at the grave some cried out "Papandreou, now you are free!" while several hundred young people took up the shout, "The giant is fallen; he leaves an heir, Andreas! Liberty! Liberty!" Now people knew that they were not alone in their opposition to the junta; there seemed little doubt that far more of them would henceforth be ready to give that opposition an organizational form, in spite of the ever-present danger of imprisonment and torture.*

When I returned to Stockholm, I sat down and wrote an article about my trip to Athens—an experience that left me full of emotion, full of pride for the president and the Greek people, and violently angry at the oppression the colonels had inflicted on a nation with the help of arms paid for by the American people. This is the piece, published in *The Guardian*, November 16, 1968:

Many people say the junta killed George Papandreou. There is no doubt that the harsh conditions of his house arrests since April 21, 1967, contributed to the deterioration of his health, particularly the last arrest which extended from April to September, 1968. He was allowed only occasional contact with his son George; his doctors visited him in the presence of guards; his trusted bodyguard and confidant of twenty years was sent to island exile, and the days were passed in lonely solitude.

For George Papandreou this was the extreme in cruelty, for his life, like that of most political men, was people. Although a man of great wisdom, he was not an intellectual in the sense that books could be his companions. He needed the give and take of personal contacts,

*From *Commonweal* (February 14, 1969). Reprinted by permission of the publisher.

either individually or with crowds, an opportunity to express his ideas, to use powerfully and beautifully, as only he could, the Greek language he loved so well.

For me and for my children, he personified Greece, the Greece which existed before the colonels took over. Warm and generous, hospitable, dynamic, with great strengths and great weaknesses, he was basically a simple man. He grew up in the tiny mountain village of Kalentzi in the Peloponnesus, son of a village priest, and whenever he could he would take us there to enjoy a day with the villagers. He would show us his home, his room, the homes of his relatives, the hills and the trees among which he played, or sneaked off to read ancient Greek history. In one election which he lost he was more disturbed by the fact that two votes in Kalentzi had been cast against him than that he had lost his seat in Parliament.

Papandreou was a pure democrat. He fought fascism on the Right and communism on the Left. He was a romantic, and sentimental, but he had the passion of an evangelist when it came to fighting for his ideals—freedom, democracy, human dignity. It did not surprise any of us who knew him that after his first long and difficult house arrest he smuggled out under the noses of the colonels a taped message to the Greek people and to the world, castigating the dictatorship and urging action on the part of the Western world against the tyrants of Greece.

In the end he gave his life for this cause. But in his death he won a moral victory—the opportunity to explode the myth woven by the colonels that the Greeks have accepted their slavery. Half a million crying, shouting Greeks came to his funeral on November 3 to mourn the loss of a man, and the loss of their freedom, and to protest against their chains.

What I found in Greece the six days I was there was a Fascist atmosphere, and the people under terrible conditions of fear and intimidation. An estimated 10,000 people are in jail, in island concentration camps, or exiled in remote villages. Arrests continue daily. Tortures have not ceased, in spite of the outcry in the Western world. Heavy taxation is combined with a "review" of income and property taxes paid by individuals during the past five years, and retroactive payments are requested arbitrarily as a means of penalizing "wrong" ideas.

Young people whose parents have been in any way connected with the democratic movement in Greece are refused entry into the universities and at the same time refused passports to study outside of Greece so they are denied a professional career and sentenced to menial, unskilled jobs, a form of cultural genocide. Professional men themselves—doctors, lawyers, professors—are denied exit from Greece, even to attend international professional conferences which they need to keep up with modern trends. Young men and women who supported the majority party in Greece, the party of Papandreou, are called in regularly by the security police to sign statements of loyalty to the Government, and rejection of their leaders, and are mistreated and imprisoned until they do. Others who have suffered the barbaric tortures of the security police are forced to sign documents that they were never mishandled and never saw any of their fellow prisoners tortured. These statements will undoubtedly be produced for the Human Rights Commission of the European Council as "proof" that stories of human torture are false.

The army has been purged beyond recognition and a Communist commissar system of control set up. Many well-trained NATO officers have been thrown out. Some are in exile. It is not an army in condition for meeting an external threat, but is well equipped to keep the people under oppression and attempts to keep the Government in power. Apart from the moral arguments against keeping dictatorial Greece in NATO, one wonders how its NATO partners can feel safe about what would happen should mobilization against an external threat become necessary.

I do not know how Greece is going to be liberated. I know that it will. I am merely expressing my deep sadness at what a great nation is going through. That wonderful soul of the Greek people has been torn asunder, although the spirit remains.

The funeral of George Papandreou was political, as his life was political. That is the way he would have wanted it. The voices started with "Pap-and-reou, Pap-and-reou," outside the church while the funeral oration was being read. After the speech of Panayotis Cannellopoulos, leader of the Opposition party—a moving tribute to George Papandreou and democracy—the doors of the church were opened and we filed out into the sunlit day.

At the cemetery Greeks were clubbed when they kneeled and started singing the national anthem, a song of liberty, as George Papandreou's body was lowered into the grave. Thirty-six people were arrested, and with a sense of despair I read in Eleftheros Kosmos of November 6 that they had summarily been given sentences: D. Triambellos, 40-year-old lawyer, four and a half years; E. Valos-opoulos, 25-year-old worker, three and a half years; S. Katsoulas, 33-year-old tapestry maker, three and a half years; K. Voyiatzakis, 34-year-old insurance broker, two and a half years, and so forth. It was said they shouted "Andreas is coming," "Democracy," and "Down with the junta!"

The cry that touched me most was when the crowds shouted, "Sit up, old man, and see us." They wanted him to know that they had not lost their belief in what he had fought for, and that he did not die in vain. Freedom is part of their tradition. George Papandreou died to keep up that tradition.

I would like to describe the developments in the lives of the people who are a part of this book, and will do so in the order in which they enter the story, starting from the day of the coup.

Petros—Finally arrested in June 1968, charge unknown. A report gotten to us in October 1968 said he had been tortured beyond recognition and had become "an old man." I tried to get information about him in November when I was in Athens for my father-in-law's funeral, but no one knew where he was.

Karambelas—Arrested in April 1968, and sent to a remote island near Turkey. He was not permitted to attend George Papandreou's funeral, although a request had been made.

Popi, young secretary of Andreas—Arrested in November 1967, and held for three days incommunicado. Released and lives in Athens.

Angela—Roughly interrogated for four hours in her home in June 1967. House searched. Left Greece in January 1968. Now works for the Panhellenic Liberation Movement.

Marjorie Schachter—Left Greece in January 1968. Now lives in New York City.

Phillip Dimitriades—Amnestied in January 1968, rearrested in April 1968, and sent into exile in northern Greece. Recent news indicates he has been released.

Spyros Angelopoulos, young teacher from Philothey—Arrested in November 1967, tortured, released in March 1968. Rearrested July 1969.

George Mylonas (name not given in text)— Andreas' boyhood friend who stayed at my home first night after coup—Arrested in spring 1968. Exiled to the island of Amorgos. Became known as "The Prisoner of Amorgos" as a result of an article in *The New York Times Magazine*. Escaped and fled to Switzerland in October 1969.

Norbert Anschuetz—Transferred from Athens to Washington, July 1967. Left government service in March 1968, and works for a commercial bank in the Middle East.

Tito—In violent automobile accident one week after we left Greece, January

1968. Broke bones in all his limbs and cracked his hip. Was taken to the hospital near death. After months of care, returned to his home in October 1968.

Kiveli—In Athens with Tito.

Phillips Talbot—Left the ambassadorship just prior to Nixon's inauguration. In Washington, D.C. on assignment from Rockefeller Foundation.

Antigone—Works in the home of Americans. Applied for passport to leave Greece, but was refused.

John Alevras, Andreas' deputy friend and partner at Pikermi—Amnestied at same time of Andreas. Rearrested in August 1968, and sent to island exile.

Mikis Theodorakis—Amnestied in January 1968. Put under house arrest in April 1968, then exiled with his wife and two children to the village of Zatouna, high in the mountains in the Peloponnesus. October 1969, transferred to Oropos prison. Permitted to leave Greece April, 1970.

Virginia Vardoni—Amnestied in January 1968. Lives in Kolonaki with her son.

Andoni Livanis—Amnestied in January 1968. Rearrested in October 1968, and imprisoned in Athens. Later exiled to an island.

Menios Koutsoyergas—Paroled in February 1968. Returned to his legal practice, but is under parole.

Young fellow who brought me first resistance document—Escaped from Greece, November 1967.

Helen Hahnikian, ex-secretary of Andreas—Released summer 1968. Rearrested September 1969 on charges of being responsible for a bomb explosion in the newspaper office *Nea Politea*, a junta publication. Released after a week of interrogation.

Elias Demetracopoulos—Working against junta from Washington, D.C., as a journalist.

Center Union deputies who organized first resistance—Amnestied in January 1968. Almost all are again in prison or exile.

Economist friend who called me to report the King's coup—Escaped from Greece in September 1968. Now working in the United States.

Index

387

public health, 16-7, 175
Public Health Service, U.S., 11, 16-7, 19, 74
Public Order, Ministry of, 249, 309, 323-6, 333

Radio Athens, 222, 347, 352-3, 360-1
Radio Sophia, 215
Rallis, George, 135, 309
Ramparts, 219, 252, 295-7, 300-1, 305-6
referendum, constitutional, 320-1, 357, 371-3
Representatives, House of, 75-6, 239
resistance, 146, 181, 211-4, 219-20, 214-5, 250-1, 254, 259, 281, 294, 304, 315-6, 331, 334, 336, 340-1, 344-6, 368, 370, 377
Resistance, Democratic, 112, 220
Reston, James, 75
Reston, Mrs. James, 75
Reuther, Walter P., 193
Revolution, National. *See* junta
Right, the, 7, 21, 23-4, 26-8, 42, 47, 50, 57, 59, 62, 75, 78, 87, 91-2, 94, 98-9, 101, 105-6, 108, 117, 121, 123, 129-30, 134, 136, 154, 156, 211-2, 214, 286, 293, 307-10, 315-6, 341, 343, 346, 378
right-wing, the. *See* Right, the
Roosevelt, Franklin D., 114, 129, 260
Rousseas, Stephen, 113, 131, 162, 166, 193, 253, 292, 294-5, 297
Rusk, Dean, 74, 86, 192, 289
Rusk, Mrs. Dean, 74

Salonika, 48, 66, 104, 139, 149, 153, 161, 215, 311, 352
Samuelson, Paul, 105, 260
Schachter, Marjorie, 124, 145-52, 158-61, 163, 165-9, 172-3, 175, 188-90, 195-9, 201, 205-6, 208-9, 218-9, 224, 227, 230, 234-5, 247-8, 255-7, 259, 297, 311, 313, 317, 322, 324, 329, 349-50, 353, 358, 361-4, 369, 380
school lunch program, 73-4
Schwartz, Jim, 203, 209, 225-38, 240-1, 253, 266-7, 273, 310, 344
sedition, 341-2
Senate, the, 74-5, 239
service, civil, 293, 371
service, secret, 77, 83, 174, 227, 240, 265, 275, 283, 286, 294, 307
Sheinbaum, Stanley, 218-21, 246, 248, 250-2, 265, 267, 273-4, 283, 293-7, 300-2, 345, 358-60, 369
Simos, J., 110-1
Simos report, 110-1
Sixth Fleet, 59, 147, 239, 357, 374
Skiathos, 36, 39-40

Skyros, 36, 40, 65
Socratides, 109, 124, 126, 139, 184, 233, 251, 266, 274, 279, 283, 292, 299
Spandidakis, Gen., 299, 342
Spetses, 34, 78, 93
Sporades, the, 33, 99
Spyros, 3, 225, 316-7, 335, 349
Square, Constitution, 91, 216, 272, 275, 365
Square, Syntagma, 12, 29, 170, 322
Stanford University, 193, 274
State Department (U.S.), 61, 66, 81, 98, 129-31, 154-5, 163, 172, 237, 239-40, 243, 253, 263-4, 285, 288-9, 304-6, 330, 332-3, 358, 370
Stearns, Monty, 69
Stephanopoulos, Stephanos, 58, 72, 78, 84, 95, 97, 99-100, 106, 108, 114, 117-9, 122, 135, 154, 275, 280-2
Stevenson, Adlai, 19, 76, 86, 269
Stockholm, University of, 105, 373
Stratis, 123, 144
Sulzberger, Cyrus, 31, 92-4, 96, 106, 131, 260
Svennilson, Ingvar, 106, 281
Synod, the, 356
system, electoral, 24-5, 29, 320
system, "kindred party," 24, 27, 29-32, 42, 57
system, parliamentary, 298, 319, 321, 372
system, party, 26, 139
system, "reinforced proportionate," 42
system, simple proportional, 121, 135-37

Takis, 8-9, 11, 149, 288, 317
Talbot, Phillips, 61, 98-9, 113, 131, 143, 145, 148-9, 153, 189-90, 192, 195, 202-3, 209-11, 241-2, 285-9, 293, 298, 332-3, 335, 349-50, 358, 369, 374, 381
Ta Nea, 50, 57
Tatoi, 91, 351, 356
Thant, U, 193
Theodorakis, Mikis, 181-2, 213-4, 220, 303-4, 334, 341, 364, 377, 379
Third Army of Macedonia, 147, 352, 356
Thomes, Dr. Boyd, 241-2, 288, 290
Thornberry, Cedric, 215
Time magazine, 131, 178
Times, London, 50, 215, 288, 299, 301, 307, 312
Times, New York, The, 31, 47, 92-3, 96, 106, 131, 139, 193, 201, 215-6, 260, 301
Times Magazine, New York, 38, 93
"Today" Show, 370
Totomis, Paul, 185, 267, 271-2, 312, 323-9, 333